Michael McCarthy
Jeanne McCarten
David Clark
Rachel Clark

Grammar *for* Business

WITHDRAWN

COVENTRY UNIVERSITY LONDON CAMPUS
East India House,
109-117 Middlesex Street, London, E1 7JF
Tel: 020 7247 3666 | Fax: 020 7375 3048
www.coventry.ac.uk/londoncampus

CAMBRIDGE UNIVERSITY PRESS
Cambridge, New York, Melbourne, Madrid, Cape Town,
Singapore, São Paulo, Delhi, Mexico City

Cambridge University Press
The Edinburgh Building, Cambridge CB2 8RU, UK

www.cambridge.org
Information on this title: www.cambridge.org/9780521727204

First published 2009
5th printing 2013

Printed in Dubai by Oriental Press

A catalogue record for this publication is available from the British Library

ISBN 978-0-521-72720-4 Paperback with answers and audio CD

Thanks and Acknowledgements

The authors wish to thank the many people who have been involved in making this book. First, we would like to thank our editor, Lynn Townsend, who steered us and the book through its long journey from the first drafts to the book you have in front of you. Lynn's views were always helpful, creative and insightful. She was patient when the project suffered the inevitable delays that happen for a variety of reasons and always displayed great good humour. Next, we would like to offer huge thanks to Jessica Errington, our development editor, whose vision as to the ideal shape and content of the units and whose keen eye for detail enabled us to improve our early drafts of the book and to produce this final version. Nora McDonald was also a wonderful editor to work with; she applied her skills and eagle-eyes to the manuscript as it took its final shape. From there on, the production team steered the book through its demanding schedule; Linda Matthews deserves a special thank-you in that respect.

David and Rachel Clark would like to thank their long-suffering friends and colleagues at The London School of English and International House London for their patience, and would particularly like to express their gratitude to Pete Thompson, David Carr, Brenda Lynch and Steve Brent for being so understanding in the face of endless requests for time off; it was much appreciated.

Not least, we thank the publisher, Cambridge University Press, whose publishing teams, in a time when publishers are often reluctant to take risks and push the envelope, were prepared to do something different and to allow us to expand our ideas and grammatical know-how by using the business data in the Cambridge International Corpus to inform the language in this book. We thank Cambridge University Press for giving us the opportunity to publish the book we always had in mind.

The authors and publishers would like to thank the following teachers who commented on the material in its draft form: Katarzyna Staniszewska, Kevin Rutherford, Jeremy Day, Poland; Nick Shaw, Spain; Isobel Drury, Sylvia Renaudon, France; Julian Wheatley, Germany; Martin Goosey, South Korea.

The authors and publishers acknowledge the following sources of copyright material and are grateful for the permissions granted. While every effort has been made, it has not always been possible to identify the sources of all the material used, or to trace all copyright holders. If any omissions are brought to our notice, we will be happy to include the appropriate acknowledgements on reprinting.

For the text on p. 11: © 2009 adidas AG. adidas, the 3-Bars Logo, and the 3-Stripes mark are registered trademarks of the adidas Group.; For the text on p. 12: reprinted with kind permission of www.staranalytics.com; For the text on p. 26: © ING Direct; For the text on p. 53: © Guy Clapperton; For the text on p. 106: © Dane Carlson; For the text on p. 107: reproduced with kind permission of Primark; For the text on p. 132: © Carol Petersen, Director of Dining, University of Northern Iowa; For the text on p. 181: © www.conranandpartners.com; For the text on p. 206: © International Business Leaders Forum 2007, www.iblf.org.

The publisher has used its best endeavours to ensure that the URLs for external websites referred to in this book are correct and active at the time of going to press. However, the publisher has no responsibility for the websites and can make no guarantee that a site will remain live or that the content is or will remain appropriate.

The publishers are grateful to the following for permission to reproduce copyright photographs and material:

l = left, c = centre, r = right, t = top, b = bottom

Adidas Group for p11(l); Alamy/©F1online digitale Bildagentur GmbH for p9, /©Wildscape for p13, /©ImageState for p21, /©Panorama Media for p50, /©Image Source Pink for p81(r), /©geogphotos for p94, /©Radius Images for p95, /©Blend Images for p111(b),/©Radius Images for p182, /©icontec for p185(c) /©Elly Godfroy for p185(r); Corbis/©Lawrence Manning for p89, /©Rune Hellestad for p181(t); Getty Images for p11(r), p190, p198; Google Map data ©2009 Tele Atlas for p154; istockphoto/©Elenathewise for p111(c); Michael McCarthy for P10; Photolibrary/©View Pictures for p65, /©OJO Images for p69; Punchstock/©Blend Images for p17, /©Digital Vision for p18, /©Digital Vision for p30, /©Blend Images for p77, /Stockbyte for p81(l), /©OJO Images for p91; Rex Features/©Per Lindgren for p174; Science Photo Library/©Massimo Brega/Eurelios for p22; Shutterstock/©Zena Seletskaya for p57, /©Tan Kian Khoon for p111(t), /©Alexey Khromushin for p185(l), /©Ian O'Hanlon for p205; Toyota (GB) plc for p181(b), .

Picture research by Hilary Luckcock.

Design by Kamae Design.

Contents

Introduction

Who is this book for?

This book is for intermediate-level students of business English. It teaches the most useful grammar you need to communicate in English, and also gives you lots of practice in the grammar of business communication.

What is 'business grammar'?

To answer this question, we used a large database of written and spoken business English (a 'corpus'). This database contains business texts from newspapers and magazines and a separate database of recordings of spoken business English at meetings, negotiations, presentations and other events in companies from different countries.

The database – or corpus – helps us to find the most common words and grammar structures and to see how business people *really* communicate at work. Many of the examples and practice exercises in the book are edited extracts from the recordings in the database. This symbol – 👁 – means that the information is from the corpus; this is how people really use grammar when they speak or write.

What grammar does the book cover?

- First, we focus on the basics – talking about time, the present, past and future.
- Then we look at modal verbs (*can*, *must*, *may*, *would*, etc.) which help you to be polite or formal or how to ask people to do things, for example.
- Next we go on to look at more complex grammar, such as conditionals and how to report speech.
- Finally, we focus on difficult areas such as prepositions (*at*, *in*, *on*, *with*), articles (*a/an*, *the*) and ways of putting sentences together with conjunctions (*although*, *because*).

How is the book organised?

In each unit, you will see

- a **presentation** page to give you the important information about the grammar of the unit.
- two **practice** pages, where you can do exercises and activities to practise the grammar and relate it your own work situation.
- two **Make it personal** sections with activities you can do beyond the book.
- an **extension** section on speaking or writing; these sections focus on the types of speaking and writing that are common in business, such as organising presentations or writing emails.

After every four units, you will find:

- a **Speaking strategies** unit, which focuses on speaking skills that business people need, such as managing conversations, disagreeing politely or checking information.
- a **test** so that you can review what you learnt in the previous four units.

At the back of the book, you will find:

- an **answer key**, with notes to remind you why these answers are correct.
- the **recording script**, so you can read the conversations and presentations on the CD.
- the **appendices**, with useful information on spelling, irregular verbs, North American English, etc.

How do I use the book?

You can work through the book unit by unit, from Unit 1 to Unit 40. However, if you have a problem with a particular area of grammar, or are interested in a specific point, you can also use any unit or group of units separately.

This book is for self-study students, but teachers and students can also use it in class.

What do I need to use the book?

To use the book, you will need to be able to play and listen to the audio CD which comes with the book. The CD has both listening and speaking activities on it.

We hope you enjoy the book, and we wish you success with business English and success in your business and professional life.

The authors

Michael McCarthy
Jeanne McCarten
David Clark
Rachel Clark

1 Imperative and present simple

Read this information about the search engine Google.

a Which of the verbs in italics give you facts?

b Which verbs tell you to do something?

> Google *provides* interactive maps, images, news and videos and *helps* you find information fast. *Search* by keyword, such as type of business, or *browse* images to find the information you want.

A Forming imperatives

A1 When the subject is *you*, use (*don't* +) infinitive without *to*.

+	**infinitive without *to*** ***Call*** me tomorrow for a chat.
−	***don't* / *do not*** + infinitive without *to* ***Don't be*** late for the meeting. ***Do not forget*** to ask participants for feedback. (*Do not* is generally used in writing)

A2 When the subject is *we*, use *let's* (*not*).

+	***let's*** + infinitive without *to* ***Let's talk*** about their proposal now.
−	***let's not*** + infinitive without *to* ***Let's not do*** it so soon.

B Using imperatives

B1 You usually use the imperative to tell people to do something.

> ***Don't wait*** for customers to contact you. ***Phone*** them.

B2 In spoken English, imperatives can sound very direct so you can add *just* or *please* to soften the message.

> ***Please have*** a seat. ***Just send*** me an email.

> ⚠ Don't use imperatives to waiters, receptionists, shop assistants, etc. if you want to sound polite.

> *Could we see the menu, please?* (**not** ~~Give us the menu.~~)

> ► See Unit 15 (Modals 3).

B3 You can also use imperatives to make offers or invitations.

> ***Come*** and ***see*** the new office when you're in town.

C Forming the present simple

C1

+	I/You/We/They		**work** there.
	He/She/It		**works** there.
−	I/You/We/They		**don't work** there.
	He/She/It		**doesn't / does not work** there.
?	Where **do**	I/you/we/they	**work**?
	Does	he/she/it	**work** there?

C2 The verb *be* is irregular.

+	I		**'m/am** late.
	He/She/It		**'s/is** late.
	You/We/They		**'re/are** late.
−	I		**'m not / am not** late.
	He/She/It		**'s not / isn't / is not** late.
	You/We/They		**'re not / aren't / are not** late.
?	Am	I	late?
	Why **is**	he/she/it	
	Where **are**	you/we/they?	

► See Appendix 1 (Spelling).

D Using the present simple

D1 You use the present simple for things that are generally true and permanent situations.

> *She ****comes**** from Stuttgart.* (**not** ~~She is coming from Stuttgart~~)
> *I ****don't live**** far from the office.*

D2 You use the present simple for actions that happen regularly (e.g. habits and routines). You can use time adverbs (e.g. *always, usually, regularly, often, sometimes, never, every day, twice a week*) with the present simple.

> *He ****always takes**** the underground to work.* (**not** ~~He takes always~~)
> *How ****often do**** you ****check**** the accounts?*

> ► See Unit 30 (Adverbs).

D3 You often use the present simple with state verbs (e.g. *feel, hear, like, see, think, understand*).

> *I ****hear**** you're opening a new office in Madrid.*
> *What ****do**** you ****think****? Is it a good idea to invest in a new logo?*

> ► See Unit 3 (Present simple and continuous).

Practice

◀ A, B   **1**   Read this extract from a charity leaflet supporting Fairtrade. Match each imperative with the rest of the sentence.

1 Don't miss	some wonderful presents for yourself and those you love.
2 Come	lots of games and fun activities.
3 Listen	some great prizes in our raffle to raise funds for Afghan women.
4 Learn	a real difference to many of the world's poorest people.
5 Take part in	how you can improve the lives of farmers in developing countries.
6 Win	to our guest speakers talking about Fairtrade and development issues.
7 Buy	to our first Fairtrade market on 16 July at Cutty Sark Gardens.
8 Make	your chance to support Fairtrade.

◀ A, B   **2**   Complete these sentences using an imperative form of the verbs in the box.

> not call   check   not forget   get   have   ~~leave~~   think   try   walk   not worry

1 ....*Leave*.... the figures on my desk and I'll put them into the spreadsheet for you.

2 .... a look on the computer. His email address should still be on there somewhere.

3 .... there's a health and safety training session tomorrow.

4 We need to contact Owain urgently. .... calling his mobile.

5 .... me between two and five this afternoon. I'll be in a meeting.

6 I need some fresh air after being at the conference all day. .... back to the hotel.

7 .... with Jenny to make sure the invoices are ready.

8 .... – we've got lots of time. The meeting doesn't start until 10.30.

9 We need something to wake us up! .... a coffee.

10 We're all tired. .... about it overnight and make the decision tomorrow.

◀ C   **3**   Complete these FAQs (Frequently Asked Questions) using the verbs in brackets in the present simple.

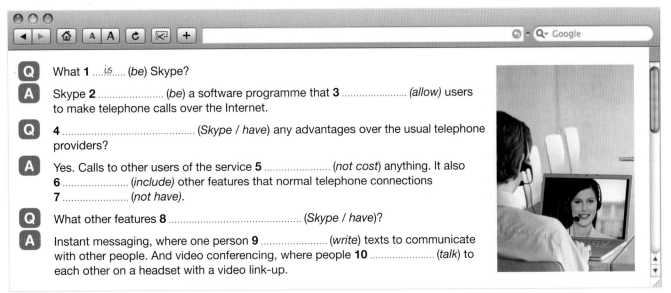

Q What **1** ....*is*.... (be) Skype?

A Skype **2** .... (be) a software programme that **3** .... (allow) users to make telephone calls over the Internet.

Q **4** .... (Skype / have) any advantages over the usual telephone providers?

A Yes. Calls to other users of the service **5** .... (not cost) anything. It also **6** .... (include) other features that normal telephone connections **7** .... (not have).

Q What other features **8** .... (Skype / have)?

A Instant messaging, where one person **9** .... (write) texts to communicate with other people. And video conferencing, where people **10** .... (talk) to each other on a headset with a video link-up.

◀ C, D | **4 a** Colin is answering questions about his job. Write the questions.

1 What / you / do? .... *What do you do?* ....

I'm a graphic designer. I help customers with corporate branding.

2 Who / you / work for? ....

Greentrees Graphics Ltd.

3 Your office / be / near your home? ....

....

Yes, it is. It only takes me 15 minutes to walk to work.

4 How many offices / your company / have? ....

Three. Our main office is in London and the others are in Brighton and Bristol.

5 Where / you / work? ....

I usually work in Bristol but go to the London office once or twice a month.

6 You / like / your job? ....

I love it, especially designing logos and other aspects of corporate identity.

7 How often / you / travel? ....

I don't travel very much these days, maybe two or three times a year.

8 How many days' holiday / you / get? ....

Eighteen, excluding bank holidays.

🔘 **1.1** Listen and check your answers.

b 🔘 **1.1** Listen again and reply to the questions with answers that are true for you.

◀ A–D | **5** Read this extract from some advice on giving presentations. Complete the extract using the verbs in the box in the present simple or imperative.

| be   not forget   help   not like   make   need   start   suggest   not tell   think   try   ~~warm up~~ |

Before your presentation, **1** ....*warm up*.... your brain. Our brain, like our muscles, **2** .... warming up to help it work. Before presentations, I often **3** .... of numbers between one and ten and then **4** .... to remember a professional athlete who wore each number.

A good beginning **5** .... relax the audience, so **6** .... by thanking your audience for coming. Then **7** .... a nice comment about the town or area, but **8** .... careful: audiences **9** .... listening to this for too long.

Many people **10** .... you start with a joke, but **11** .... that humour can be difficult. **12** .... any jokes that could offend people.

Make it personal

1 Write an advertisement for an event your company is having. Use Exercise 1 to help you.

2 Write a short list of FAQs with answers about your company and the products or services it provides. Use Exercise 3 to help you.

1 **Write for business:** Checking your work

Whenever you write in English, it is important to check your writing carefully. This is a useful skill for any piece of writing that you do in English e.g. letters, emails, reports, advertisements and CVs.

Here is a checklist of some common mistakes with the present simple which you should always check for.

- Use -s with *he/she/it*.
  The Economist **sells** over a million copies a week. (**not** ~~sell~~)

- Use *has* with *he/she/it*.
  She **has** ten years' experience in this job. (**not** ~~have~~)

- Don't use statement word order in questions; use *do/does* (except with *be*).
  What **do** the end-of-year results mean for investors? (**not** ~~What mean the end-of-year results?~~)
  Is the new scheme successful? (**not** ~~The new scheme is successful?~~)

- Use *doesn't* with *he/she/it*.
  He **doesn't** know how to log onto the intranet. (**not** ~~don't~~)

- Use *doesn't/don't* when forming the negative.
  Our clients **don't** use our website very often. (**not** ~~no use~~)

- Don't use the present continuous with state verbs.
  The company **has** branches in at least 10 different countries. (**not** ~~is having~~)

- Check the word order when you use adverbs.
  We **always manufacture** excellent-quality items. (**not** ~~manufacture always~~)

► See Unit 30 (Adverbs).

6 **Read this information about Nike and Adidas. If the verbs in italics are correct, tick (✓) them. If they are wrong, correct them.**

Nike, Inc **1** *have* its headquarters in the United States near Beaverton, Oregon. It **2** *is* the world's leading supplier of athletic shoes and sports equipment. The name Nike **3** *come* from Nike, the Greek goddess of victory. Nike **4** *does not market* its products only under its own brand. It also **5** *sometimes uses* names such as Air Jordan and Team Starter. Because Nike **6** *creates* goods for a wide range of sports, **7** *always it has* competition from every sports and sports fashion brand.

Another global leader in the sporting goods industry **8** *are* the Adidas Group. Products from the Adidas Group **9** *are* available in virtually every country in the world. Its head offices **10** *is not* in the US but in Herzogenaurach, Germany.

Adidas' various companies **11** *produces* much more than just sports goods. The company also **12** *operates* design studios and development departments at other locations around the world.

1	has
2	✓
3	
4	
5	
6	
7	
8	
9	
10	
11	
12	

Make it personal

Write a paragraph about your company for its website and then check it carefully for any errors with the present simple, using the checklist above.

If you have a colleague who is also learning English, write a paragraph each and check each other's work.

2 Present continuous

Read this job advertisement.

a Which verb describes a temporary activity?

b Which verb describes a changing situation?

> At Star Analytics we take pride in the high quality of our employees. As a company we are growing, so we are currently looking for excellent individual performers who also want to be part of a dynamic team.

A Forming the present continuous

+	*I*	*'m/am*	
	He/She/It	*'s/is*	
	You/We/They	*'re/are*	
–	*I*	*'m not / am not*	*working today.*
	He/She/It	*'s not / isn't / is not*	
	You/We/They	*'re not / aren't / are not*	
?	*Am*	*I*	
	Where is	*he/she/it*	*working today?*
	Why are	*you/we/they*	

👁 In spoken English *'s not / 're not* + *-ing* are more frequent than *isn't / aren't* + *-ing*. People say *aren't* and *isn't* if it is difficult to pronounce *'re* and *'s* after the word before.

*Prices **aren't** going up this year.* (**not** ~~Prices're not~~)
*This **isn't** selling well.* (**not** ~~This's not~~)

B Using the present continuous

B1 You can use the present continuous to describe actions or situations in progress at the moment of speaking.

*We**'re going** for lunch now – do you want to come or **are** you still **working**?*
*I**'m having** trouble with my phone. Look – the battery**'s not** charging.*

B2 You can use the present continuous to describe actions or situations in progress around the present time, but not necessarily at the moment of speaking.

[conversation at lunch]
A: *What **are** you **working** on?*
B: *I**'m redesigning** the website*

B3 You can use the present continuous to describe temporary actions and situations. These can be single or repeated events.

*The company**'s not having** a very good time at the moment. Sales **aren't going** well.*
*We **are giving away** free samples every day until the end of the month.*

B4 You can use the present continuous to describe changes and trends.

*People **aren't buying** CDs these days – they**'re downloading** music off the Internet.*

C Other uses

C1 You can use the present continuous to describe a longer action in contrast to a shorter one, especially after *while* or *when*.

*I usually close my Internet browser **when I'm working**.*

C2 You can use the present continuous of *be* to describe temporary behaviour.

*Anyone could walk in here and steal the database – or **am** I **being** silly?*

▶ See Unit 3 (B What are state verbs?).

Practice

◄A,
B1–3

1 Complete these conversations using the verbs in the box in the present continuous form.

expect	get	not go	have	leak	
not pay	repair	sit	~~wait~~	not work	

1 A: Is Mr Bohr here yet?
   B: Yes. He ..'s waiting.. for us in reception.

2 A: What's wrong with the phone?
   B: I don't know. It ....

3 Can someone turn the air conditioning off?
   It .... cold in here.

4 Can you answer my phone if it rings while I'm away
   from my desk? I .... a call from my solicitor.

5 A: How are things?
   B: Not good. Sales .... well and customers .... us on time. We .... a really
   hard year.

6 A: This isn't your desk, is it?
   B: No, I .... here today because they .... the ceiling above my desk. It ....

◄A,
B1–3

2 a Write questions using the verbs in the present continuous. Then write answers that are true for you.

1 (you / enjoy) ....Are you enjoying.... your job at the moment? (it / go) .... well?

2 (What projects / you / work) .... on at the moment?

3 (you / hope) .... to get promoted soon?

4 (your colleagues / learn) .... English too?

5 (anyone in your department / look) .... for a new job?

6 (How / your company / do) .... this year?

7 (it / achieve) .... its goals?

8 (What / your company / invest) .... in?

9 (your boss / make) .... any major changes this year?

10 (he or she / run) .... your department well?

b 🔘 2.1 Listen and reply with your prepared answers.

◄B4

3 Read this article about farming. Change the verbs in italics to the present continuous to emphasise that
the article is describing a current trend.

Many farmers **1** *give up* farming because they **2** *find* it dificult to make a living. Every week at least seven dairy farmers **3** *go* out of business because they **4** *have to* sell milk below the cost of production. 'It **5** *costs* us 24 pence a litre to produce, but the supermarkets **6** *pay* us 20,' said a dairy farmer who **7** *plans* to leave farming. 'It **8** *gets* more serious every week and the government **9** *doesn't do* anything to help us,' he added. These days many farmers **10** *concentrate* on finding other sources of income. Some **11** *run* guest houses and others **12** *open* their farms to visitors.

1 ..are giving up..	4	7	10 ....
2	5	8	11 ....
3	6	9	12 ....

2

◄ C **4** **a** Write sentences using one verb in the present continuous and one verb in the present simple.

1 I / never / listen to / music / when / I / work.

I never listen to music when I'm working.

2 When / I / have / lunch with a friend, / I / not talk / about work.

....

3 I / always / switch off / my mobile phone / when / I / talk / to a client.

....

4 When / I / negotiate a deal, / I / never / make / my best offer right at the beginning.

....

5 I / not chat / to my colleagues / when / I / write / a report or something like that.

....

6 When / my team / work / on an important project, / we / often / come / into the office at the weekend.

....

b Change each sentence, if necessary, so that it is true for you.

◄ A–C **5** Read these extracts from an article about corporate environmental responsibility. Complete the extracts using the verbs in the boxes in the present continuous.

a | be   not do   not help   invest   resist

UK businesses **1** .....*are resisting*..... investing in green initiatives, according to a recent survey. A fifth of businesses in London **2** .... enough to protect the environment, it says. Only one-third of companies **3** .... in environmental initiatives, such as buying energy-saving office equipment. Supermarkets especially **4** .... customers make green choices. 'They **5** .... a bit slow to offer green alternatives to plastic bags,' said an environmental watchdog.

b | do   not go   look   make   put   work

'We decided in 1992 to make the organisation greener and **1** we .... (*still*) on it because it is a continuous process, but we feel we **2** .... good progress. We **3** .... a huge amount of money into research and the vast majority of it **4** .... into conventional office technologies, but into new systems. We **5** .... at the idea of the paperless office and we **6** .... (*also*) a lot of research into new systems.'

c | demand   find   introduce   take

Hotels **1** .... a range of green programmes, partly because their business guests **2** .... it, and also because hotels **3** .... that going green saves money. 'The industry **4** .... environmental issues very seriously,' said a spokesman for the Business Travel Association.

Make it personal

Write one or two sentences about each of these questions.

What changes are taking place in your industry or field right now? What issue is everyone talking about? What are people in your office gossiping about? Are any of your colleagues being difficult at the moment? Do you know why?

2 **Business talk:** Present continuous + *always*

You generally use the present simple to talk about habits. However, you can also use the present continuous with *always* to emphasise that a habit is significant or unusual. For example, it may be an annoying or a nice habit.

Clients **are always asking** *us for investment advice*. (a significant habit)

He**'s always falling** *asleep in meetings*. (an annoying, unusual or funny habit)

I'll make the coffee. You**'re always making** *it*. (a nice habit)

6 **a** **Complete the answers to these questions using *always* and the verbs in brackets in the present continuous.**

1 A: Which part of your job do you leave till the last minute?

B: My expenses. I'm always forgetting (*forget*) to do them.

2 A: Do you take on temporary staff in the summer?

B: Yes, we .... (*look for*) people in August.

3 A: Do you think your colleagues enjoy their jobs?

B: I don't think so. They .... (*complain*) about the boss.

4 A: Are you interested in doing an MBA?

B: Very. I .... (*read*) articles about leadership and people management and stuff.

5 A: Is your company concerned about green issues?

B: Yes, they .... (*send*) round emails about recycling and things.

6 A: What are the biggest challenges for human resources managers?

B: Well, employment laws .... (*change*), so that's one thing.

7 A: Do you need any new equipment in your office?

B: Yes, some new photocopiers. The ones we have .... (*break down*).

8 A: Do you think you'll stay in your current job?

B: I don't know. I .... (*think about*) my next career move.

9 A: Is your boss very supportive?

B: Yes, he .... (*say*) things like 'Well done!' or 'That's good.'

10 A: What are your colleagues like? Do you get on with them?

B: Most of them. The woman next to me, though, ... (*borrow*) my stuff, which really annoys me.

b **Write answers to the questions in Exercise 6a that are true for you. Try to use *always* and a present continuous verb.**

Make it personal

Complete these sentences about your own workplace.

1 People at work are always ....

2 Our clients are always ....

3 My worst habit is that I'm always ....

3

Present simple and continuous

Read this extract from a recycling company's brochure and underline the verbs that talk about present time.

a Which verb forms are used?

b Why?

> Imagine a company that makes everything from garbage. Such a company exists, and it is growing rapidly. Its name is TerraCycle.

◀ See Unit 1 (Present simple) and Unit 2 (Present continuous).

A Choosing between the present simple and the present continuous

	You can use the present simple:	You can use the present continuous:
A1	to talk about regular actions, routines and habits. past — present — future *He usually **drives** to work – he **doesn't** often **take** the train. **Do you meet** with her regularly?*	to talk about actions in progress at the moment of speaking or around now. past — present — future *I can't do that mailing – the photocopier **isn't working**. **I'm writing** my report. I'll email it to you soon.*
A2	to give general or generally true information. *How many people **does** your company **employ**? Because of costs, we **don't manufacture** in the UK.*	to talk about trends and changes. *The demand for organic produce **is growing**. **Are** more people **working** from home?*
A3	to talk about permanent situations. past — present — future *Starbucks **run** their operations from their Seattle HQ. The law **gives** all employees maternity rights.*	to talk about temporary situations. past — present — future ***Are** you **doing** Pete's job while he's on holiday? **I'm using** Cathy's office while they**'re redecorating** mine.*

👁 In spoken English the present simple is used much more often than the present continuous.

B What are state verbs?

State verbs are mostly used in simple, not continuous, forms.
*I **have** two mobile phones. (**not** I am having)*
*I **agree**. (**not** I am agree)*

State verbs describe:

- possession (*belong, have* (possess), *own, possess*).
- thoughts (*believe, forget, guess, know, mean, realise, reckon, remember, see* (understand), *suppose, think* (believe), *understand*).
- likes, wants and needs (*dislike, hate, like, love, need, prefer, want, wish*).

- existence and appearance (*appear, be, seem*).
- relationships (*contain, depend, include, involve*).
- senses (*feel, hear, look, see, smell, sound, taste*).
- functions (*admit, agree, apologise, promise, tell*).

👁 In spoken business English, *see* (understand) and *think* are both much more common in the present simple than in the present continuous.

▶ See Business talk for more information about state verbs.

Practice

◄ A **1** Underline the most suitable form of the verbs.

1 The caretaker's *opening / opens* the office at 6:30 every morning.

2 *Are you holding / Do you hold* the office party every year at the same venue?

3 Currently, we're *looking for / look for* a new finance manager.

4 Our MD's *talking / talks* to our New York office at least twice a week.

5 Our manager *isn't making / doesn't make* decisions very quickly.

6 He's very stressed, so he's *trying / tries* to get a part-time contract at the moment.

7 What's *Mark doing / does Mark do* this morning? I need him to help me with something.

8 I'm afraid that the HR Manager *isn't taking / doesn't take* any phone calls this morning.

9 Our company's *changing / changes* its logo for the first time in 20 years.

10 *Is he always coming / Does he always come* to work by car?

◄ A **2** Complete this 'About Us' page from a clothing company's website using the verbs in brackets in the present simple or continuous.

About us

At McConnels we **1** ....sell.... (*sell*) clothing and textiles. We have a good reputation for women's clothes and our new venture, MC's, the women's fashion store, **2** .... (*expand*) steadily. Our customers **3** .... (*rely*) on us for quality fashions at low prices and our Exchange and Refund Policy **4** .... (*let*) them shop with confidence.

Sales through McConnelsdirect.com **5** .... (*grow*) rapidly, at an average of 20% per year. This **6** .... (*make*) us one of the UK's most successful online clothing businesses. We also **7** .... (*produce*) a monthly online magazine for teenagers with articles on fashion, gossip, competitions, and much more!

◄ A, B **3** Complete this interview with a shop display designer using the verbs in brackets in the present simple or continuous.

INTERVIEWER: Amelia Thompson, as Head of Visual Merchandising what **1** ....do you do.... (*you/do*)?

AMELIA: I **2** .... (*manage*) product presentation across Selfridges stores.

INTERVIEWER: What **3** .... (*that/mean*), exactly?

AMELIA: I **4** .... (*try*) to present products in new ways that will attract customers' attention.

INTERVIEWER: So, can you give an example of how you do that?

AMELIA: Well, we have to be creative. For instance, right now we **5** .... (*hold*) a Chinese promotion, so we **6** .... (*display*) a model of Beijing made out of biscuits – just for one month.

INTERVIEWER: How interesting! What other projects **7** .... (*you / work on*) at the moment?

AMELIA: Well, today I **8** .... (*need*) to work out how many pairs of folded jeans **9** .... (*fit*) along a 25-metre wall!

INTERVIEWER: That sounds like a challenge! In general, **10** .... (*you/enjoy*) your job?

AMELIA: Yes. I mean I **11** .... (*not/like*) paperwork , but I can honestly say that I **12** .... (*look forward to*) going to work every day.

◀ A, B **4** Two people are talking informally at a conference reception. If the verbs in italics are correct, tick (✓) them. If they are wrong, correct them.

ALAN: Hi. Alan Hancock, GEM Systems. Do you mind if **1** *I'm joining* you?

SUE: Not at all. I'm Sue Holmes. **2** *I work* for Falconi.

ALAN: **3** *Do you enjoy* the conference, then?

SUE: It's interesting, I suppose. **4** *I'm going* to a lot of conferences, though.
 5 *They all seem* the same after a while.

ALAN: **6** *I agree*! It's OK if your hotel is nice, I think. What **7** *are you thinking* of your hotel?

SUE: I'm quite lucky. **8** *I'm having* a room here. It's very comfortable.

ALAN: Yes, lucky you. **9** *I'm staying* at the Hilton, about twenty minutes away.

SUE: Look, **10** *the waiter comes* over now. Can I get you anything to drink?

ALAN: Why not? A double espresso, please.

1 ....*I join*.......
2 ....✓.......
3 ....
4 ....
5 ....
6 ....
7 ....
8 ....
9 ....
10 ....

◀ A, B **5** Complete this news report on the financial results of two mobile phone companies using the correct form of the verbs in the box.

be	benefit	expect	fall	fall	give	have	~~increase~~	lose	sell

Market share of one of the world's top mobile phone makers, FinTel, **1** ....*is increasing*.... faster than ever before. Meanwhile, its rival, WestCom, **2** .... a second-quarter loss due to poor sales.

US-based WestCom **3** .... market share in several regions, including Europe and Asia. FinTel, which **4** .... more than one in three of all mobile phones sold globally, has taken over much of this market.

'FinTel **5** .... a very strong product mix, and now there **6** .... a good opportunity for FinTel to consolidate its position as market leader,' according to FIM Securities analyst, Jeremy Hilton.

Weak sales in Asia and Europe this quarter **7** .... investors a real headache. 'WestCom's market share **8** .... rapidly and it could continue. As it **9** ...., FinTel **10** .... from the market share that WestCom has lost,' said Danske Markets analyst, Thomas Simonsen.

🔘 **3.1 Listen and check your answers.**

Make it personal

Describe your daily routine at work.

Are there some things you do every day? Are there some temporary projects you are working on? What are the projects?

3 **Business talk:** State verbs

When people discuss rumours – news or information that might or might not be true – they often use these state verbs in the present simple: *appear, believe, guess, hear, know, mean, reckon, say, see, seem, suppose, think, understand*. You can use these verbs when you want to report what someone else thinks, or what someone else told you. They can help you to be more diplomatic and less direct.

I **hear** (*that*) *you're opening an office in Brazil.*
Toby **reckons** (*that*) *the new CEO will be making some big changes in the company.*
It **seems** (*that*) *we've missed our sales targets for the year.*
They **say** (*that*) *Xiao Lin is taking early retirement.*

Some state verbs can be used in both simple and continuous forms, but their meaning is different.

I **think** *we should finish now.* (**my opinion**)
We **'re thinking of/about** *closing our Lima office.* (**intending, planning, considering**)
I **see** *what you mean.* (**understand**)

Sorry, he's busy at the moment. He **'s seeing** *a new supplier.* (**meeting, visiting**)
We **have** *a branch in every European capital.* (**possession**)
We **'re having** *problems with the new computers.* (**experiencing**)

---

6 **Write sentences using the verbs in the present simple or continuous.**

1   I / understand / your company / recruit / staff. / you / expand / the business?

   I understand (that) your company is recruiting staff. Are you expanding the business?

2   They / say / the expansion project / not / go / well.

   ....

3   I / believe / you / have / difficulties with the prototype of your new fuel pump.

   ....

4   Revenue / be / down / so / I / guess / the advertising campaign / need / a rethink.

   ....

5   I / see / you / replace / the CEO. / you / think / of an internal or external candidate?

   ....

7 **Two employees of Peacocks, an office equipment supplier, are talking on the phone. Complete their conversation using the verbs in the box in the present simple or continuous.**

come   complain   guess   ~~know~~   lose   need   reckon   say   seem   not sell   think   visit

MAX: Hi Beth. **1** ....*Do you know*.... (*you*) what the meeting this afternoon is about?

BETH: Maybe it's the poor sales results. It **2** .... that the new scanner **3** .... well.

MAX: Well, one of my colleagues **4** .... that we **5** .... sales to the competition because our prices are too high, so we **6** .... to discuss discounting.

BETH: Yes, and also, apparently customers **7** .... about our problems supplying orders on time.

MAX: Oh dear, that's not very good. It sounds like it's going to be a difficult meeting. By the way, my manager **8** .... that a man from head office in Hong Kong **9** .... us for a few days.

BETH: Yes, that's Mr Lui. He **10** .... here whenever there's trouble. Maybe management **11** .... of making some of us redundant.

MAX: Oh no! Well, I **12** .... we'll find out at the meeting. See you there, Beth. Bye!

Make it personal

Write about your company's latest news or any rumours you know about.

4 Present perfect simple and continuous

Read this extract from a business newspaper article.

a Do the verbs in italics describe the past or the present?

b How do you form them?

> Starling*'s been negotiating* for months to sell the business, which the Johnson family *have run* for generations. Although there*'s been* some interest in the Edinburgh site, potential buyers *haven't put in* any offers for the Glasgow branch.

A Forming the present perfect simple

+	I/You/We/They	**'ve/have**	
	He/She/It	**'s/has**	**worked** hard.
–	I/You/We/They	**haven't / 've not / have not**	
	He/She/It	**hasn't / 's not / has not**	
?	**Have**	I/you/we/they	**worked** hard?
	Where **has**	he/she/it	**worked**?

B Using the present perfect simple

You use the present perfect when something in the past is connected to the present.

B1 You can use the present perfect to talk about something that happened in a time period that is still continuing (e.g. *so far, to date, today*). You can use *for* + a period of time (e.g. *two days*) and *since* + a specific point in the past (e.g. *3 pm, the meeting*) to say how long.

*I've worked here **since January / for a month**.*
***Have** you **seen** Helena at work today?* (it is still today)

B2 You can use the present perfect to talk about something that happened in the past, but you do not know or say exactly when.

I've been here before. (**not** *I've been here yesterday*)
► See Unit 5 (Past simple and continuous) and Unit 6 (Present perfect and the past).

You can use *ever* in questions and *never* in negatives to mean at any time before now.

***Have** you **ever spoken** at a conference?* (ever = at some time)
*No, I've **never done** that.*

B3 You can use the present perfect with *already* in positive statements and questions to talk about something that happened sooner than expected.

*Paul's **already contacted** Mr Wong about the meeting. / Paul's **contacted** Mr Wong about the meeting **already**.*

You can use *yet* in negatives and questions, and *still* in negative statements to talk about things that have not happened but you are expecting to happen.

*They **still haven't replied** to my email.* (I am expecting a reply)
***Have** our ads **resulted** in any orders **yet**?*

B4 You can use the present perfect to talk about something that happened in the past but has a present result.

*My car's **broken** down.* (my car is not working now)
*He's **made** over six million pounds.* (he's very rich now)

B5 You can use the present perfect to talk about a recent past action. You can use *just*.

*He's **just left** me a message. He's on his way in now.*

B6 You can use the present perfect with *this is(n't) the first, etc., time*.

*This is the third time I've **left** M. LeBlanc a message.* (**not** *I leave / I am leaving*)
*This isn't the first time you've **missed** a deadline.*

C Forming the present perfect continuous

+	I/You/We/They	**'ve/have**	
	He/She/It	**'s/has**	**been working** hard.
–	I/You/We/They	**haven't / 've not / have not**	
	He/She/It	**hasn't / 's not / has not**	
?	How long **have**	I/you/we/they	**been working**?
	Has	he/she/it	**been working** hard?

D Using the present perfect continuous

D1 You use the present perfect continuous for longer or repeated actions.

*The economy **has been growing** steadily for several years.*

D2 You use the continuous form when you are interested in the activity more than the result.

*Our product **has been selling** well in Germany.* (the activity – selling – is important here)

*We've **sold** over 100,000 items so far this year.* (the result – the number of items sold – is important)

⚠ **Don't use state verbs in the continuous form.**

*I've **known** him for three years.* (**not** *I've been knowing*)

Practice

◀ A **1** **Complete this extract from an interview using the verbs in brackets in the present perfect simple.**

INTERVIEWER: **1** ....Have you ever held.... (*you / ever / hold*) a position of responsibility?

JEAN: Well, I **2** .... (*never / manage*) a large team of people, but I **3** .... (*run*) two small projects in the local area.

INTERVIEWER: OK, and **4** .... (*your company / ever / send*) you abroad?

JEAN: Yes. I **5** .... (*go*) to France and Spain several times on business. Also, my manager **6** .... (*ask*) me to give a client presentation in Bologna in October. I **7**...................................... (*say*) yes, but I **8** .... (*not plan*) my talk yet.

INTERVIEWER: **9** .... (*you / ever / do*) any training before?

JEAN: My manager **10** .... (*never / ask*) me to, but I'm sure I could!

◀ B3–6 **2** **Complete this conversation using the words in the box.**

first	for	just	just	since	still	~~yet~~	yet

SHAUN: Have you read the article about house prices **1** ....yet....?

BEN: Yes, I've **2** .... read it. Pretty interesting, isn't it?

SHAUN: Yes, especially as I've **3** .... put my house on the market. It's been on the market **4** .... two weeks and I haven't had any interest **5** ....

BEN: Well, this isn't the **6** .... time the papers have promised us that house prices are going to keep going up.

SHAUN: You're right, but I think they've risen by 10% **7** .... January. Although actually I **8** .... haven't decided where I want to move to, so maybe I should take the house off the market and see if prices go up even more.

BEN: Good idea!

◀ B1, C **3** **Complete the second sentences so that they mean the same as the first sentence(s). Use the present perfect continuous and *for* or *since*.**

1 I live in Quebec. I moved there two years ago.

I ....'ve been living.... in Quebec ....for.... for two years.

2 Stone's don't charge for consultations now. They stopped last summer.

They .... for consultations .... last summer.

3 Our CEO is visiting our overseas offices. He started two weeks ago.

He .... our overseas offices .... the last two weeks.

4 Cathy works in the accounts department. You want to know how long. Ask her.

.... in the accounts department .... a long time?

5 Sandy is giving a presentation. He started 45 minutes ago.

He .... a presentation .... 45 minutes.

6 Ian is staying at a noisy hotel, so he isn't sleeping well. He arrived there several days ago.

He .... well .... several days.

7 John is contacting lots of new clients. He met them at the conference.

John .... lots of new clients .... the conference.

8 I'm discussing our profit forecast with the board. We started discussions at nine o'clock.

We .... our profit forecast .... nine o'clock.

4

◀ B, D **4** Tick the most suitable response to each comment.

1 You look exhausted!
    a Yes, I am. I've worked for ages.
    b Yes, I am. I've been working for ages. ✓

2 Are you OK?
    a No, I've lost a very important document.
    b No, I've been losing a very important document.

3 What's the matter with him?
    a His computer's just crashed again.
    b His computer's just been crashing again.

4 How's business?
    a Great, thanks. We've doubled sales in the last six months.
    b Great, thanks. We've been doubling sales in the last six months.

5 Your phone line is always busy.
    a Sorry. I've talked to the marketing department all morning.
    b Sorry, I've been talking to the marketing department all morning.

6 I've got a package for you.
    a Oh, has my order arrived? That's great news.
    b Oh, has my order been arriving? That's great news.

7 Are any more taxis coming?
    a I hope so. I've waited for ages.
    b I hope so. I've been waiting for ages.

8 How is the course going?
    a To be honest, I haven't understood much so far!
    b To be honest, I haven't been understanding much so far!

◀ A–D **5** The CEO of a water company is announcing the acquisition of another company. Complete this extract from her speech using the correct form of the verbs in brackets. Sometimes more than one form is possible.

… and as I'm sure you're all aware, over the past few years Eastern Water **1** ....*has diversified/ has been diversifying*.... (*diversify*) into other areas, including waste management and renewable energy.

In terms of our core business, I'm pleased to announce we **2** .... (*just/complete*) the acquisition of Aqua NE, an American water company that **3** .... (*supply*) the consumers of New England since 1950. Eastern Water and Aqua NE **4** .... (*work*) together closely for three years – we **5** .... (*already/exchange*) executives a few times!

I'm personally very proud of this acquisition, our first step into the US market. Several other British water companies **6** .... (*look*) into the US market, but none of them **7** .... (*ever/take*) it very seriously. With this acquisition, Eastern Water **8** .... (*now/move*) from being a regional-based company to being an international company. It **9** .... (*not/be*) easy, but it **10** .... (*be*) exciting.

The water business **11** .... (*have*) its problems in recent years, but I think we **12** .... (*learn*) a lot from those problems.

🔘 **4.1 Listen and compare your answers.**

Make it personal

Think about a time when you interviewed someone or were interviewed. Write five present perfect simple or continuous questions and answers that were used in the interview. Use Exercise 1 to help you.

4 Write for business: Using the present perfect in the news

Financial and business news stories often start with a headline in the present simple. They often use the present perfect to introduce the key news in the story.

Stock market crashes

The FTSE 100 has suffered huge losses in a disastrous day for investors.

Price of gold hits record high

The price of gold has reached a record price of £600 an ounce.

Sometimes headlines about company performance just use the words *up* or *down* to say what has happened.

Retail profits up

There has been a rise in profits in the retail sector.

New mortgages down

The demand for new home loans has fallen by more than 30%.

6 Complete the opening lines from these newspaper stories using the verbs in brackets in the present perfect.

1 Small businesses get tax help

The Minister of Finance .....*has given*..... small businesses a new tax break. (*give*)

2 Government announces interest rate cut

The government .... a 0.5% reduction in interest rates. (*announce*)

3 TravelJet buys Eagle for £100m

TravelJet .... Eagle airlines for £100m. (*buy*)

4 High street shops suffer 10% sales fall

Sales at high street shops .... by 10%. (*fall*)

5 Micro Tech launch slimmest laptop

Micro Tech .... the world's slimmest laptop computer. (*launch*)

6 Northern Motors axe 2,000 jobs

Northern Motors .... 2,000 jobs at their Oxford factory. (*cut*)

7 Write a suitable first line for these news stories.

1 Central Bank holds interest rates at 5%

The Central Bank has held interest rates at 5%.

2 Microtel share price down

....

3 DVD sales reach a new high

....

4 US and China discuss a new trade agreement

....

5 Insurance costs rise after the bad weather

....

Make it personal

Look at the headlines in some English-language financial newspapers or on websites. Write opening sentences for each headline. Then compare your ideas with the real articles. Were your ideas similar?

Discussing

Read this conversation.

Which words show who agrees or disagrees?

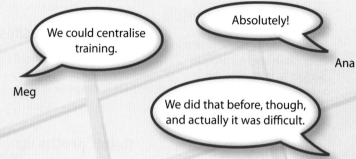

Meg: We could centralise training.

Ana: Absolutely!

Tina: We did that before, though, and actually it was difficult.

A Giving opinions

A1 You can use these expressions to give your opinion:
I think (that), I'd/would say (that), I feel (that), in my opinion, as far as I'm concerned.
Expressions with *would* sound less 'direct'.

__I would say that__ the designer has done a great job. __As far as I'm concerned__, the brochures are excellent.

A2 You can use these expressions to give an opinion about hypothetical situations:
I would have thought, I would think, I would imagine.

Investing in gold should be safe, __I would have thought__.

A3 You can use these expressions to show your attitude to things you say.

When you think …	you can say …
something's obvious	*obviously / of course / clearly*
something's a fact	*in fact / as a matter of fact*
something's bad/good	*unfortunately/fortunately*
this is the main point	*basically/really*
you're giving an honest view	*to be honest*
you're giving a personal view	*personally*

__Obviously__ we need to give priority to external calls, but __to be honest__ we don't always.

👁 People use *as a matter of fact* to give an opinion or a fact that is different from what other people expect.
I'm not against flexitime. __As a matter of fact__, I think it's a good idea.

B Agreeing

B1 You can use these expressions to agree with someone:
(That's) right, (That's) true, Absolutely, Definitely, Exactly, I agree (with you/that).

A: *Customers want 24-hour IT support.*   B: *__Absolutely__.*

B2 You can use these expressions if you want someone to agree with you or see your point of view:
(do) you know/see what I mean? if you know/see what I mean.

We should be looking for partners outside Europe – __you know what I mean?__

C Disagreeing

C1 You can give a different view starting with *Yes/No but, But, However, On the other hand*, or ending with *though*.

A: *We get good service from our cleaning company.*   B: *They're expensive, __though__.*

⚠ *I don't agree (with you)* or *I disagree (with you)* are very strong in English and not very common. People sometimes say *I don't agree with <u>that</u>* to make the disagreement less personal.

C2 You can use *actually* to correct or contradict what someone says or thinks.

A: *This report doesn't include last month's spending.*   B: *Um, it does, __actually__. On page 11.*

C3 You can use these expressions if you partly disagree with someone or think one point is valid:
That's a very good/fair/valid point, but … , You've got a point, but … , I take your point, but …

A: *The phones aren't cheap, but the service plan is good.*   B: *__That's a good point, but__ we can't ignore cost.*

Practice

◄ A–C **1** **a** A manager is talking about annual performance reviews. Change the words in italics to an expression from A3. Sometimes more than one answer is possible.

1 *My main point is* we should change our annual performance reviews. Basically

2 You see, *my personal view is* I'd say that they're not really effective.

3 *My honest view is* the formal interview is a very artificial situation.

4 *The main point is* twelve months is a long time between reviews.

5 *It's a fact* as managers, we should always be looking at staff performance.

6 We should review performance monthly, *speaking honestly*.

7 *It's good that,* staff tell me they'd prefer that too. Some people ask for more feedback.

8 *It's obvious that* it would be better if we supervised staff more closely.

9 *My honest view is* the annual review is embarrassing for staff and managers who have a more informal relationship the rest of the year.

10 And *it's clear that* some people exaggerate their achievements so they get good reviews. And then other people don't like to boast, so *it's not good that* they don't do so well *and this is obvious*.

b ⊙ SS 1.1 Listen and write any other expressions she uses to give her opinions.

1	I think	6	
2		7	
3		8	
4		9	
5		10	

c Decide whether or not to agree with the manager's comments and write a suitable response.

1	Absolutely. / It might be difficult, though.	6	
2		7	
3		8	
4		9	
5		10	

d ⊙ SS 1.1 Listen again and respond with your own prepared comments.

◄ B, C **2** **a** Stefan wants to reduce the amount of travelling that staff do. Edyta doesn't fully agree. Write her responses using words and expressions from B and C.

Stefan says	Edyta thinks
1 We need to cut down on travel costs.	Travel is expensive. It's also useful. Yes, travel's expensive, but it's also useful.
2 We can use video conferencing. It's just as good.	Face-to-face contact is more personal.
3 We don't need to go to the branches to talk.	It makes communication easier.
4 Travel is bad for the environment.	That's true.
5 You waste so much time travelling.	That's partly true. You can work on planes.
6 People see travel as a mini-holiday.	No they don't! It's hard work.

b ⊙ SS 1.2 Listen and practise responding to Stefan with your own views.

Test 1: Units 1–4

1 Complete this text about bank security using the verbs in brackets in the imperative or the present simple.

It **1** ....*feels*.... (*feel*) good to be safe. So, at ING Direct, we **2** .... (*look after*) your money very carefully. However, there **3** .... (*be*) a few security measures that you should use to protect your money. Here **4** .... (*be*) some top tips to protect your account.

- **5** .... (*keep*) your PIN number safe. **6** .... (*not write*) it on your ING Direct card and **7** .... (*not tell*) anyone what it is.

- **8** .... (*make*) sure your memorable date **9** .... (*be*) easy to remember, but not too obvious. For example, the system **10** .... (*not allow*) you to use your own birthday.

- We never **11** .... (*contact*) you by phone or email to ask for your personal security information. If this happens, **12** .... (*call*) us on 0845 603 8888.

2 Underline the correct verb form in each sentence.

1 *Do you do / Are you doing* this test in your office?

2 *Does your manager watch / Is your manager watching* you do this test?

3 *Do you always work / Are you always working* at the same desk?

4 *Do you study / Are you studying* English for an exam?

5 *Do you understand / Are you understanding* financial statements?

6 How often *does your manager review / is your manager reviewing* your performance?

7 *Does your company make / Is your company making* more money this year than last year?

8 *Does your salary go up / Is your salary going up* a lot every year?

9 When you *don't speak / aren't speaking* in a long meeting *do you doodle / are you doodling**?

10 *Do you listen / Are you listening* to music while you study?

> * doodle = to draw pictures or patterns while thinking about something else or when you are bored

3 Two friends are talking about their working conditions. Complete this conversation using the verbs in brackets in the present simple or the present continuous.

GEMMA: **1** ....*Do you share*.... (*you share*) an office?

RASHID: Well, I usually **2** .... (*have*) my own office, but at the moment I **3** .... (*share*) an office with two colleagues because they **4** .... (*redecorate*) mine.

GEMMA: **5** .... (*you like*) sharing?

RASHID: No, actually I **6** .... (*hate*) it. It's impossible to concentrate because my colleagues **7** .... (*always/talk*) about their social lives. And the office **8** .... (*smell*) terrible because one of them **9** .... (*always/eat*) at his desk.

GEMMA: What **10** .... (*he/eat*)?

RASHID: Oh, everything! And the other colleague, who **11** .... (*cycle*) to work every day, **12** .... (*not have*) a shower when he **13** .... (*get*) here. I **14** .... (*not want*) to stay in this office any more!

4 If the sentence is correct, tick (✓) it. If it is wrong, correct it.

1 ~~I am thinking~~ my company is a good place to work.   ......I think......

2 I remember my first day at work.   ......✓......

3 My manager is liking to be at work early, before the rush hour.   ....

4 My line manager has problems with some of the new staff at the moment. ....

5 Our products do not contain any chemicals.   ....

6 I'm agree with you.   ....

7 My partner is seeing some customers at the moment. Can I help?   ....

8 We think of opening a new office in Rome.   ....

9 The new rule about overtime isn't seeming fair to me.   ....

10 Sales are appearing to be lower than expected this quarter.   ....

5 An office worker is talking about their new training manager. Complete these sentences using the verbs in brackets in the present perfect simple or continuous. Then choose the correct word in bold in each sentence.

1 The company (*recruit*) a new training manager **recently/still**.

The company has recruited a new training manager recently...........

2 We (*not have*) a training manager **for/since** a long time.

....

3 We (*ask*) our line managers to get someone to do this **for/since** over a year.

....

4 She (*make*) a lot of changes **already/yet**.

....

5 For example, she (*introduce*) regular training sessions **already/still**.

....

6 I (*go*) to three sessions **this/last** month.

....

7 I (**ever/just** *come*) from a session about spreadsheets.

....

8 I (**ever/never** *understand*) how to use them before.

....

9 I (*learn*) a lot **for/since** the sessions started.

....

10 She (*not give*) us a session on team building **yet/already**.

....

11 She (*promise*) to do that **for/since** she arrived.

....

12 (*you* **ever/never** *go*) to any of her sessions?

....

5 Past simple and continuous

Read this text about the Enron Corporation.

a What do you know about the Enron Corporation? What happened to this company?

b Look at the verbs in italics. Did the concerns about Enron begin before they reported their earnings in July?

In mid July 2001, the Enron Corporation *reported* earnings of $50.1 billion. However, concerns about financial irregularities *were growing*.

A Forming the past simple

+	I/You/He/She/It/We/They	**worked** there.
−		**didn't / did not work** there.
?	Where **did**	I/you/he/she/it/ we/they	**work**?
	Did		**work** there?

👁 Many common verbs are irregular. The most frequent past simple verbs in spoken business English are:
came, could, did, got, had, made, put, said, thought, was/were, went.

► See Appendix 5 (Irregular verbs).

B Using the past simple

B1 You can use the past simple to talk about states or completed actions at a specific time in the past. This time is usually stated or is obvious from the context.

founded Microsoft

Past   1975   Now

Bill Gates **founded** *Microsoft in 1975.*
I **didn't need** *the report for the Board meeting.*

B2 You use the past simple to talk about repeated or habitual actions in the past. This has a similar meaning to *used to*.

stayed at Hilton   stayed at Hilton   stayed at Hilton

Past   Now

Whenever I **went** *to London on business, I* **stayed** *at the Hilton.*

B3 You use two or more past simple verbs in the same sentence to talk about past events that follow one after another.

1 stood up   2 grabbed his bag   3 left the meeting

Past   Now

He **stood up** *angrily,* **grabbed** *his bag and* **left** *the meeting.*
What **did** *you* **do** *when the market* **crashed**?

C Forming the past continuous

+	I/He/She/It	**was**	**working** yesterday.
	You/We/They	**were**	
−	I/He/She/It	**wasn't / was not**	
	You/We/They	**weren't / were not**	
?	**Was**	I/he/she/it	
	Where **were**	you/we/they	**working** yesterday?
	Were	you/we/they	

⚠ Do not use state verbs in the continuous form.

D Using the past continuous

D1 You use the past continuous to talk about a longer action in progress at a specific time in the past.

waiting for bus

Past   8 am   Now

At 8 o'clock this morning, I **was waiting for** *the bus to work.*

D2 You use the past continuous to talk about a temporary action or situation in progress in the past.

I **was working** *overtime a lot before the end-of-year audit.*

D3 You use the past continuous to talk about a background event or longer action that is interrupted by a shorter event or action in the past simple. You often use *when, while* or *as.*

not sitting at her desk

phone rang

Past   Now

She **wasn't sitting** [background event] *at her desk when the phone rang.*
While the speaker **was presenting** *his report, I noticed several mistakes on his slides.*

Practice

◀ A, B **1** A company director is talking about setting up his leather goods business. Complete these sentences using the verbs in the box in the past simple.

be begin buy can not find grow have to introduce ~~open~~ plan reply stay not want

1 We ....*opened*.... the first branch of our business in 1999.

2 We .... to expand too quickly and we .... at that branch for two years.

3 We .... to remain small and exclusive, but when we .... a new line in leather accessories, sales .... very rapidly.

4 So, what .... we do? We .... open another factory.

5 I .... a good factory foreman for months.

6 Then Nick Clee .... to our advertisement and he .... perfect for the job.

7 .... (*you*) one of our briefcases when you first .... working?

◀ C, D **2** Complete this conversation between Rebecca and her manager Martin using the verbs in brackets in the past continuous.

MARTIN: Rebecca, I **1** ....*was trying*.... (*try*) to call you for ages this morning. Why **2** .... (*you / not answer*) your phone?

REBECCA: I'm sorry, Martin, but I **3** .... (*have*) a breakfast meeting with some clients and didn't want to interrupt them.

MARTIN: Oh, yes. Of course. I forgot. But why were you late for our ten o'clock planning meeting?

REBECCA: Again, I'm sorry, but as I **4** .... (*drive*) from the breakfast meeting to the office, I got stuck in traffic. I did try to call in several times but the office number was always engaged and nobody **5** .... (*answer*) at reception.

MARTIN: Hmm. And where were you yesterday afternoon? I **6** .... (*look*) for you everywhere.

REBECCA: Laura and I **7** .... (*prepare*) our presentation for this evening. People **8** .... (*use*) all the meeting rooms in the office, so we decided to go to the venue and work there. We **9** .... (*practise*) for ages. I meant to call you, but I **10** .... (*not feel*) very well by the end and I completely forgot.

◀ A–D **3** Write sentences using one verb in the past simple and one verb in the past continuous.

1 He / write / his report / when / he / spill / coffee on his computer.

He was writing his report when he spilt coffee on his computer.

2 The auditors / arrive / when / he / have / his lunch.

....

3 Share prices / increase / daily until / the market / crash.

....

4 My taxi / arrive / as / I / leave / the office.

....

5 I / tell / her about her new role / while / we / travel / to the conference.

....

6 The Board / announce / the name of the new CEO / while / the staff / celebrate / the opening of the new office.

....

7 He / think / of retiring / when / they / offer / him a promotion.

....

◀ A–D **4** Neil Baker won a television contest to work for the successful British entrepreneur, Peter Salt. Complete this interview with Neil using the verbs in brackets in the correct form.

INTERVIEWER: So, Neil, when you **1** ....*were studying*.... (*study*) at university, **2** .... (*you/ever/think*) you would work for the famous Peter Salt?

NEIL: To be honest, I **3** .... (*enjoy*) my time as a student too much to think about my future!

INTERVIEWER: What **4** .... (*you/do*) when you **5** .... (*apply*) to take part in the show?

NEIL: For my first job I **6** .... (*work*) as an investment banker, but I **7** .... (*want*) more variety in my work, so I **8** .... (*leave*) a year or so before the programme to set up my own business providing IT support to small businesses. Unfortunately it **9** .... (*not/be*) very successful.

INTERVIEWER: You now work for Peter Salt. Tell us about your job.

NEIL: I work in the property section of his business and it's very interesting and challenging. In my first year, I **10** .... (*learn*) a lot from watching Peter at work. When Peter and I **11** .... (*work*) together on our latest project, a plan to build a health spa in the USA, we **12** .... (*negotiate*) a really good price for a great site.

◀ A–D **5** Complete these sentences so that they are true for you.

1 Last year, my company ....*was*.... (*be*) .... (*more/less*) profitable than the year before.

2 When I was a child, I .... (*want*) to be ....

3 I .... (*start*) my first job in .... [year]. I really .... (*like/hate/enjoy*) it.

4 After school, I .... (*live*) in ....

5 While I .... (*study*), I .... (*meet*) ....

6 Yesterday, I .... (*write*) .... [number] emails before lunch.

7 When I .... (*try*) to decide where to work, my friends .... (*help me a lot / not help me much*).

8 When I was a teenager, I .... (*decide to/that*) ....

Make it personal

1 **Write five sentences about your first job or your time at university.**

Where was it? What did you do? What did you like or dislike about it? Why? Who did you meet?

2 **Write three sentences about when your company started.**

Who started it and why? What was happening in the markets at that time? What happened in its first few years?

5 Business talk: Using past tenses to be polite

You can use the past simple or continuous with a present meaning when you want to be less direct or more polite. This is common in shops and restaurants.

*Did you **have** a loyalty card?* (Do you have ...?)
*What **was** the name, please?* (What is your name?)

It is useful when you want to make requests or ask favours.

*I **wanted** to ask your advice about investments.*
*I **was thinking**, maybe we could discuss the offer further.*

Verbs that are often used in this way include *hope*, *think* and *wonder* (*if*). They are often followed by modal verbs *would*, *could* and *might*.

*We **thought** you **might** like to visit the new plant this afternoon.* (Would you like ...?)

*I **was wondering if** I **could** talk to you about the minutes of the next meeting.* (Can I talk ...?)

6 Make these requests less direct using the verbs in brackets in a past tense. Make any other necessary changes.

1 Let's arrange an earlier date for the AGM. (*want*)

 I wanted to arrange an earlier date for the AGM.

2 Tell me about places to stay in Kiev. (*wonder*)

3 Finish the report by lunchtime. (*hope*)

4 I need to talk to you about the standard of your work in your first three months. (*want*)

5 Can you talk me through the figures in the report? (*think*)

7 Make this telephone conversation between a PA and an airline booking agent more polite by changing the verbs in italics into a suitable past form.

PA: I **1** *want* ....wanted.... to book a return flight from London to Paris for two people.

AGENT: When would you like to travel?

PA: We **2** *are hoping* .... to go on Tuesday 21st, but we **3** *are wondering* .... if we **4** *can* .... book different days coming back – the 23rd for one and the 28th for the other.

AGENT: No problem. What time **5** *do you want* .... to travel?

PA: We need to be there for a ten o'clock meeting on Tuesday and we **6** *are thinking* .... we **7** *may* .... leave the returns open. Is that possible?

AGENT: Of course. There's a flight out which would get you there for 9 am.

PA: We **8** *want* .... to go business class. How much would that be?

AGENT: £332 per person each way. How **9** *do you want* .... to pay?

PA: By credit card. Also, I **10** *wonder* .... if you **11** *can* .... add these air miles onto my frequent flyer card?

AGENT: Certainly. I'll book the flights for you now. What **12** *are* .... the names of the people travelling?

🔘 **5.1 Listen and check your answers.**

Make it personal

Think of five occasions when you will talk to your boss or a customer in the next week. Write five polite requests you could use in these situations and then try to use them.

6 Present perfect and the past

Read this extract from a report.

a Which verb in italics refers to a finished event in the past?

b Which verbs refer to something that started in the past and is still continuing now?

c Which verb refers to a past action with a present result?

> Last year we *produced* 627 machines. Over the past two years we *have been spending* a lot of time on improving quality and we *have made* lots of progress. The board *has decided* that now it is time to increase production.

◀ See Unit 4 (Present perfect simple and continuous) and Unit 5 (Past simple and continuous).

A Choosing between the present perfect and the past

	You can use the present perfect:	You can use the past:
A1	to talk about a single or repeated action in an unfinished time period (which is still continuing). **Has** Mr Sanchez **called** this morning? (it is still morning) I'd like to continue the discussions we**'ve been having** this week. (the week has not finished)	to talk about a single or repeated action in a finished (past) time period. Often the time is specified or known. I **went** to Spain on business last week. During the 1990s the company **was trying** to enter the US market.
A2	to talk about a past action or situation that has an effect in the present. The printer **has broken down**. (it isn't working now) John**'s reached** an agreement with Harper's. (they're ready to sign the contract now)	to talk about a past action or situation that does not tell us anything about now. The time is usually stated or is obvious from the context. The printer **broke down** last week. (but it's working now) We **were travelling** around Asia in March.
A3	with these time expressions to show unfinished time: since Monday/2006/ the merger, for ten years/ages, ever, never, so far, the first/second time, before, up till now, recently, yet. He**'s been avoiding** me **since** our last meeting. **Have** you **ever dealt** with Ramcorps?	with these time expressions to show finished time: yesterday, ago, in 2007/January/the summer, at two o'clock, earlier this week, last week/month/year. The project **started** six years **ago**. I **wasn't working** here **last year**.
A4	to ask a general question about past experiences. **Have** you **ever been** to our Paris offices?	to give or ask for more details. A: Oh really? When **did** you **go** there? B: I **went** there last autumn.

B Choosing between the continuous and simple forms

	You can use the continuous form:	You can use the simple form:
B1	to talk about a temporary action or a situation in progress. In January, consumers **weren't spending** much. Consumer confidence **has been falling** since March.	to talk about completed actions or permanent situations. He **worked** in Italy his whole life. (he's dead now) He**'s worked** in Italy all his life. (he still works there)
B2	when you are more interested in the action or process than the result. They **were arguing** about the price. (we don't know if they reached an agreement) UK banks **have been having** an exceptional year.	when you are more interested in the result than the process. Turnover **rose** by 8.5%. Our company **has made** £6m profit this year.
B3	when you want to emphasise how long. I **was waiting** for over an hour. They**'ve been trading** since 1937	when you say how many or how many times. We **took on** 17 new clients last month. I**'ve called** him five times this morning. (**not** I've been calling him five times)

Practice

◀ A **1** Two colleagues are talking about a takeover in India. Underline the correct form of the verbs in italics.

DUNCAN: 1 *Have you heard / Did you hear* how the Mumbai deal's going?

JEAN-MARC: No, I 2 *haven't heard / didn't hear* anything for ages. All I know is that the market 3 *exploded / has exploded* last year and since then we 4 *negotiated / 've been negotiating* to set up a call centre business there.

DUNCAN: That's right. Well, I 5 *'ve been going / went* out there every couple of weeks or so to try to move things along.

JEAN-MARC: Really? So, how 6 *did it go / 's it been going*?

DUNCAN: It's really interesting, and exhausting! But we 7 *made / 've made* a real breakthrough in the discussions last week, and I think we 8 *'ve reached / reached* a preliminary agreement at last. I 9 *only got back / 've only got back* yesterday to brief the CEO.

JEAN-MARC: That's great news. I know how hard it can be setting these deals up.

DUNCAN: That's right. 10 *Didn't you go / Haven't you gone* there earlier this year for some IT project?

JEAN-MARC: Yes, we 11 *opened / 've opened* a small IT outsourcing operation in January. It 12 *was / 's been* pretty hard work at the beginning but it's going really well now.

DUNCAN: Fantastic. Let's hope the Mumbai deal is as successful.

◀ A **2** Match each pair of sentences with the suitable responses.

1 You look absolutely exhausted.   a I had to work late and I forgot to call.

2 Where were you last Friday?   b I've been working late this week.

3 Do you know much about the US market yet?   a We've been doing a lot of research into it.

4 This report on the US market is really comprehensive.   b We did a lot of research into it.

5 I tried to find you at the conference party.   a Sorry, I've been stuck in traffic for the last hour.

6 There you are! I'm so glad to find you at last.   b Sorry, I was stuck in traffic, so I missed it.

7 Why are the prices up in the canteen?   a We haven't been charging enough to cover our costs.

8 Why did we lose money on the deliveries?   b We didn't charge enough for them.

9 Where was Sue during the IT training course?   a What? Hasn't she been attending the sessions?

10 Where's Sue? I never see her in class.   b Why? Didn't she attend any of the sessions?

◀ A3 **3** Complete these sentences using the words in the box.

| ago | at | earlier | ever | for | in | last | never | ~~since~~ | since |

1 Production costs have risen dramatically ....*since*........ last January.

2 Macnab's paid their bill in full every month .... year, but this year they haven't paid anything.

3 Market researchers have been looking at the competition .... several months. They'll be reporting their findings at the next group meeting.

4 Someone from the tax office called you .... today – something about VAT returns.

5 Two weeks .... management were offering us a 3.5% pay rise, but .... ten o'clock this morning they reduced it to 3%.

6 Staff in the factory have been getting £400 extra a week .... that big order came in.

7 We purchased the new scanner .... May last year. We've .... had a problem with it.

8 I need your advice. I'm going to Berlin soon. Have you .... done any business in Germany?

6

◄A, B **4** Write questions using the verbs in the past simple, past continuous, present perfect or present perfect continuous. Sometimes more than one answer is possible.

1 How many companies / you / work for?

How many companies have you worked for?

2 What subject / you / study / at university or college?

3 How many / jobs / you / apply for / when you left university or college?

4 When / you / start / working for this company?

5 your company / expand / since you joined them?

6 you / work / on any interesting projects this year?

7 you / ever / speak / at a conference? If so, what / you / talk about?

8 you / have / a pay rise this year? If so, how much / you / get?

9 How much time / you / spend / abroad in your working life so far?

10 Is this the first time / you / study / another language?

6.1 **Listen and reply with answers that are true for you.**

◄A, B **5** Complete this press release using the correct form of the verbs in the box.

acquire book fly introduce own reach sign ~~start~~ use

In October, JetWays and Pan European **1** ....started..... negotiations over the sale of Globetours Airways. Pan European **2** .... the franchise airline for 12 years.

Today, Pan European is happy to inform customers that we **3** .... (now) an agreement and JetWays **4** .... Globetours. We **5** .... the contracts early this morning. Pan European is therefore no longer selling tickets for Globetours Airways flights.

The takeover will not affect customers who **6** .... to travel before 1st April next year. Anyone travelling on or after that date should visit our website for further information.

Under Pan European, Globetour Airways **7** .... to 38 destinations in southern Europe and North Africa. Although JetWays will continue to run all routes until the end of March, they will not guarantee the future of routes that are not profitable.

Pan European will continue to operate flights out of Gatwick airport. We **8** .... Gatwick for our long-haul leisure routes for more than ten years. In addition, we **9** .... (recently) a number of national routes to and from Gatwick. These will be unaffected by the sale of JetWays.

Make it personal

Choose three of the answers you gave in Exercise 4 and add two more sentences for each. Try to use different verb forms.

For example, *I've worked for three companies. I spent my holidays working for the first one when I was studying at university. I've been thinking about that job a lot recently.*

6 **Business talk:** Using continuous forms to give background information

People often use the continuous form to introduce the topic of conversation by giving the listener some background information. They then use the simple form to make their main point.

I **was thinking** about investing in equities, but I **decided** property is safer.

We **were looking for** the best rate and we **found** someone offering 5.6% over ten years.

I'**ve been thinking** about your offer and I'**ve decided** to accept it.

You can also use the simple form first to highlight the main information and then the continuous form to give some background.

I **left** my job because I **wasn't enjoying** it any more.

I **didn't want** to disturb you while you **were dealing with** Andy yesterday.

We'**ve closed** the plant down because it **hasn't been making** enough money.

6 **Decide which is the main event or action and complete these sentences using a suitable form of the verbs in brackets.**

1 I ....*found out*.... (*find out*) about the restructuring plans while I ...*was talking*... (*talk*) to the Operations Manager.

2 We .... (*consider*) the Canadian market. In the end, though, we .... (*think*) the US might be better as we .... (*not/believe*) Canada would be a big enough market.

3 A: Why .... (*you/decide*) to relocate the office?
   B: Because we .... (*spend*) too much on the rent.

4 A: You .... (*work*) late this week, Denise.
   B: Yes, I .... (*not/get*) home until ten o'clock last night.

5 I .... (*have*) lunch with someone from SatCom yesterday. He .... (*tell*) me all about their latest teleconferencing system.

6 A: What .... (*she/complain*) to you about?
   B: Oh, she's unhappy because she .... (*not/get*) an end-of-year bonus.

7 **Change one of the verbs in each telephone message into an appropriate continuous form to give the listener background information.**

   haven't been waiting

1 Hi Steve? It's Jeremy here. I hope you ~~haven't waited~~ very long for me. I'm stuck in traffic.

2 This is a message for Mr Khan. We checked our records last week and we discovered an unpaid invoice for £250. Please could he call us back on 0835 424265.

3 Yes, hello, um …. This is Paula from Pioneer Furniture. I had some problems with my email system recently, so you probably haven't received my order. Anyway, here it is …

4 Annie? Er, Martin speaking. Listen. I told one of my colleagues about that DVD you showed me, but I forgot the title. Can you remember what it's called?

5 It's Nicky speaking. I've tried to reach you all week, but you haven't replied to any of my messages. Please call me. It's very urgent.

6 Alex Payne here. I wanted to speak to you about something yesterday, but you chaired a meeting. Please call me back as soon as possible. Thanks.

Make it personal

Think of four or five phone calls you might have to make in the next week.

What will you say if the person you want to speak to is out? How will you give the background to your call? What will the main message be?

7 Past perfect simple and continuous

Compare these two sentences.

Which sentence makes it clear that Zetac accepted an offer from Kronos *before* E-Linx made their offer?

a

> At the time that E-Linx made a higher bid for the company, Zetac accepted an offer from Kronos.

b

> At the time that E-Linx made a higher bid for the company, Zetac had accepted an offer from Kronos.

A Forming the past perfect simple

+			'd/had left the office.
–	I/You/He/She/It/We/They		hadn't / had not left the office.
?	Why **had**	I/you/he/she/it/ we/they	left the office?
	Had		

⊙ In informal spoken business English, you can shorten *had* to *'d*, and *had not* to *hadn't*. In formal writing, use the full forms.

*I rang them about the training session but they'**d forgotten** to arrange it.* (spoken)

*By 1991, turnover **had increased** to $950,000 and they made a profit of $170,000.* (written)

B Forming the past perfect continuous

+			'd/had been waiting for ages.
–	I/You/He/She/It/We/They		hadn't / had not been waiting long.
?	How long had	I/you/he/she/ it/we/they	been waiting?
	Had		been waiting long?

C Using the past perfect

C1 You can use the past perfect to describe an event that happened before another past event.

1 James left the office   2 I arrived

```
     1 2
─────────────────────────────────▶
Past                           Now
```

*When I arrived, James **had left** the office.*

C2 You can use the continuous form of the past perfect to emphasise that the first event was in progress or continuing for some time when the second event happened.

```
        I'd been feeling unwell
        ▬▬▬▬▬▬▬▬▬▬▬▬
              I left early
                 ■
─────────────────────────────────▶
Past                           Now
```

*I'**d been feeling** unwell that day, so I **left** the office early.*

C3 You can use time expressions such as *before, after, when, as soon as* and *by the time* with the past perfect.

You can use the past perfect after time expressions with *by*, for events that happened up to or before a certain point in the past.

*By 1999, the company **had** firmly **established** itself in the USA, Canada and Mexico.*

People often use the past perfect with *already*.

*When we arrived, the meeting **had already started**.* (not ~~the meeting already started~~)

People often use the past perfect with *it was the first time*.

*I worked with Tina on the Slovakia project in 2004. **It was the first time** we'**d worked** together.*

C4 ⊙ You can use the past perfect to explain or give reasons for past events. You can also use the past simple.

*I couldn't give the latest figures because our system **had crashed** (or our system crashed) earlier that day.*

*I **had met** (or I met) Dustin Parker before at a sales conference, so I recognised him immediately.*

► See Unit 23 (Reported speech 1) and Unit 24 (Reported speech 2).

Practice

◄ A **1** Complete these sentences using the verbs in the box in the past perfect simple.

ask	decide	~~examine~~	expect	fall	predict	not receive	not sell	speak	suffer

1 The Board ...*had examined*.... three offers for the company but decided that Montech's offer was the best.

2 We .... good news from our Berlin branch as regards sales, but the numbers were disappointing.

3 It seemed their office .... our fax, so they didn't respond to us.

4 The company .... to enter Asia in 2003, and by 2005 it had a big operation in Thailand.

5 I .... (*already*) to our IT manager about the problem with the new server when Peter mentioned it to me.

6 We .... heavy losses during the previous year, so we knew we had to take urgent action.

7 .... (*you*) this downward trend or was it completely unexpected?

8 The figures showed that we .... any units at all in May, so we were very disappointed.

9 I .... (*only*) for a 5% pay rise, so I was very happy when they gave me 10%!

10 Prices .... sharply, but then in 2004 they started rising again.

◄ A–C **2** Complete these sentences using one of the verbs in brackets in the past perfect and one in the past simple.

1 I ...*hadn't heard*... (*not/hear*) about the meeting, so I ....*came*.... (*come*) completely unprepared.

2 Ursula .... (*already/make*) a copy of the bill, but then Vimala .... (*make*) another one!

3 We .... (*close*) the office as we .... (*hear*) there was going to be a transport strike.

4 As we .... (*already/discuss*) the issue once, we .... (*not/want*) to discuss it a second time.

5 Natasha .... (*only/start*) at the company a month before I .... (*arrive*).

6 I .... (*be*) surprised to see the visitors at 9:30 as they .... (*phone*) previously to say they would arrive at 10:00.

7 How .... (*you/know*) about the changes in the schedule? .... (*you/speak*) to her about it before?

8 Transportation costs .... (*rise*) steeply, and therefore we .... (*have to*) put up our prices.

9 Krista .... (*not/leave*) the office yet so I .... (*be*) able to talk to her about the problem.

10 Hilda .... (*say*) it was the first time she .... (*ever/give*) a speech, so she was nervous.

◄ A–C **3** Complete this article. Explain the reason for each event using the past perfect simple or continuous.

Shares rise after merger — **Reasons**

1 Share prices rose on Thursday after the news that
two major banks had announced a merger. — two major banks announced a merger

2 The deal had a dramatic effect as
.... — the banks' shares were falling before the announcement

3 It took a few months to finalise the deal as
.... — the directors were negotiating the terms of the agreement

4 There was some controversy over the merger because
.... — some people said that it would create one of the biggest financial groups in Europe

5 But the markets responded well to the news as
.... — the financial sector was unstable in recent weeks

6 The merger came as no surprise to many as
.... — it was predicted in a popular financial blog

7

◄ A–C **4** Complete this interview using the correct form of the past perfect (simple or continuous). Sometimes both are possible.

HR MANAGER: So, you **1** '*d accumulated* (*accumulate*) ten years' experience in IT when you decided to look for a new position. How long **2** .... (*you/work*) for Dormax at that point?

LEO: About six years. I **3** .... (*think*) of changing jobs for a while but I **4** .... (*not/see*) anything really interesting or challenging enough.

HR MANAGER: Aha. And before Dormax you **5** .... (*work*) for a Swedish company and **6** .... (*live*) in Gothenburg, is that right? Did you learn to speak Swedish?

LEO: Yes. In fact I **7** .... (*study*) the language for about a year in evening classes before I moved there.

HR MANAGER: Right. You said you **8** .... (*not/find*) anything challenging enough before you applied to us, but that you **9** .... (*consider*) making a change. What sort of challenge were you looking for?

LEO: Well, I **10** .... (*do*) more or less the same old thing for six years and I **11** .... (*begin*) to realise that I was missing out on a technological revolution.

HR MANAGER: Could you explain what you mean?

LEO: Well, at that point, web-based applications **12** .... (*just/start*) to take off, but in my company we were still working with static, hardware-based technology, without looking at the new web-based opportunities.

HR MANAGER: And what did you think those opportunities were?

LEO: Well, I think I **13** .... (*already/realise*) that web-based systems could streamline our operations massively. Our branches **14** .... (*miss*) opportunities to network with one another in the most efficient ways, as they were all operating independently and using their own systems. That's the kind of thinking I would like to bring to this post you are offering now.

HR MANAGER: Great.

◄ A–C **5** Complete these podcast extracts using the verbs in brackets in the past simple, past perfect simple or past perfect continuous. Sometimes more than one is possible.

1

In October 2006, Voltra International *was* (*be*) in trouble. The price of raw materials .... (*rise*) steadily, its sales .... (*fall*) and the company's shares .... (*already/drop*) in value by 30%. When the board .... (*introduce*) an emergency budget in January 2007, few people .... (*expect*) that it would transform things so quickly, but in September 2007, the company .... (*report*) a record $15m profit.

2

The biotechnology industry .... (*grow*) out of university laboratories in the 1980s. The first successful gene transfer .... (*take*) place in the early 1970s, and by the end of the decade some pharmaceutical companies .... (*start*) mass-producing some proteins. These later .... (*become*) the first drugs of the biotechnology industry. By the 1980s, scientists .... (*become*) aware of the commercial potential of their work, and many .... (*leave*) the universities to set up their own companies.

3

In 2002, the country's economy .... (*look*) very unstable. It .... (*have*) a budget deficit of 14% of GDP, high inflation and slow growth, and one of the highest unemployment rates in the OECD. By 2005, things .... (*improve*): government measures .... (*cut*) the budget deficit to 7% of GDP, the inflation rate .... (*go*) down to 1.6% and .... (*be*) one of the lowest in the OECD.

🔘 **7.1 Listen and check your answers.**

Make it personal

Think back to your last job interview. Write a short paragraph answering these questions.

Where had you been working/studying before? Had you applied for other jobs too? Had you met any of your new colleagues before? Had you been doing similar work? Had you expected certain things about the job, and were they true?

7 Business talk: Regrets and intentions

If you regret or feel dissatisfied about something in the past, you can use *wish* or *if only* + past perfect.

*I **wish** they **hadn't sent** us so much publicity material – we can't possibly read it all.* (they sent a lot)
*She hates her job. I bet she **wishes** she'd **taken** the job in Hungary instead.* (she didn't take the Hungary job)
***If only** we'd **known** how high the costs would be! We could have looked for another supplier.* (we didn't know)
*We're really struggling at the moment. **If only** the government **hadn't increased** corporation tax.* (the government increased corporation tax)

You can use verbs such as *hope, intend, want, plan* in the past perfect (simple and continuous) to talk about things that you wanted to do but did not do. *Had* is often stressed in these cases.

*We **had hoped** to solve the problem with the servers last week.* (we didn't solve the problem)
*I **had intended** to go to Frankfurt for the Book Fair last year, but I had to cancel at the last minute.*
*The firm **had been planning** to launch the new line in November, but there were delays.*

6 Rewrite these sentences using the correct form of the words in brackets. Make any other necessary changes.

1 I shouldn't have shouted at Tom. (*wish*)

I wish I hadn't shouted at Tom.

2 They should have booked their flights earlier; they would have got a better deal. (*if only*)

....

3 Julio is sorry he didn't take the job in Bucharest. (*wish*)

....

4 It was my intention to meet each new member of staff individually but there wasn't time. (*intend*)

....

5 I should have realised the figures were wrong. I could have corrected them sooner. (*wish*)

....

6 We had a plan to meet up at six o'clock but the traffic was very bad and Henry didn't arrive till 7:30. (*plan*)

....

7 Rosa should have been here when Vladimir arrived; she speaks Russian. (*if only*)

....

8 They were optimistic that property prices would drop so that they could carry out their expansion plans. (*hope*)

....

7 Correct six mistakes in these two emails.

1

Hi Cecilia,

       I'd known
I wish ~~I knew~~ you were in town last Friday! If only you let me know. We could have met and had lunch together, as it was my day off. I planned to have a really relaxing day but my washing machine broke down and flooded the kitchen. It's a very old machine. I just wish I bought a new one.

Don't forget to email me next time you're visiting!

Ben

2

New Message
File   Edit   View   Insert   Format   Tools   Message   Help

Dear Ruben,

Do you remember that awful presentation I gave in Genoa when everything went wrong? Well, last Monday I did a big presentation for the board and it went really well. I expected that it would be a disaster, but actually it was a huge success. I wish you were there to see me.

Olivia

Make it personal

Think of something you had hoped or intended to do in your work last year but were unable to do for some reason. Write sentences about it using *hope/want/intend*, etc. and *wish* and *if only*.

8

Used to and *would*

Read this comment by the founding director of a restaurant chain.

Underline expressions that describe his past business activities.

a Which one describes a state?

b Which ones describe habits?

> Before I became a restaurateur, I was in the music business. I used to go to America regularly and would always come back with lots of ideas: something for a menu, something promotional.

A Forming the past with *used to*

A1 *Used to* has the same form for all subjects and cannot describe the present or the future.

+		**used to work** there.
−	I/You/He/She/It/We/They	**didn't / did not use to work** there.
?	Why **did** I/you/he/she/it/we/they	**use to work** there?
	Did	

> 👁 *Used to* is much more common than *didn't use to*. *Never used to* is three times more common than *didn't use to* in spoken English.

A2 In spoken English you do not always need a verb after *used to* if the verb has already been used earlier in the sentence or conversation.

> A: *Do you work nights?* B: *I **used to**.*
>
> *Our staff don't work as many hours as they **used to**.*

B Using *used to*

B1 You can use *used to* instead of the past simple to describe a past habit or regular activity.

> *When I was a postman, I **used to get up** / **got up** at 5 am every morning.*

You can also use *used to* instead of the past simple to describe past states or situations.

> *This company **used to have** / **had** a factory in France, but we closed it in 2004.*

> ⚠ *Used to* does not describe single events or actions in the past.

> *This company **made** a profit last year.* (**not** *used to make*)

> ⚠ *Used to* does not describe how many times or for how long something happened.

> *Stefan **visited** London twice on business.* (**not** *used to visit*)
>
> *He **ran** the company for 20 years.* (**not** *used to run*)

B2 *Used to* normally indicates that the past habit or state is not true now.

> *I **used to spend** a lot of time travelling for work, but now I'm completely office-based.*

C Would

C1 You can use *would(n't)* like *used to* to refer to past habits or activities if the time or context is clear.

> *When I worked at Stanard's I**'d** always **be** the first into the office.* (context = When I worked at Stanard's)
>
> *In those days she**'d** often **take on** too much work and she **wouldn't delegate** anything.* (context = In those days)

> ⚠ *Would* is not used to describe states in the past. Don't use *would* with state verbs.

> *This garden **used to be** the office car park.* (**not** *would be*)

> ⚠ Questions about past habits or activities with *would* are very unusual in English. Use *used to* or past simple.

> ***Did you use to work** / **Did you work** for Apple?* (**not** *Would you work*)

C2 We can use *would* + adverb of frequency to emphasise how often something happened.

> *Negotiating new contracts **would often involve** weeks of meetings with our suppliers.*

> ⚠ Remember that *would* has many other uses.

> ▶ See Unit 13 (Modals 1) and Unit 18 (Conditionals 2) for other uses of *would*.

Practice

◄ A1 **1** Write questions with *used to*. Then write answers to the questions that are true for you.

1 you / enjoy / school? .... *Did you use to enjoy school* .... ?
.... *Yes, I was really happy there.* ....

2 what things / you / do / in your first job? .... ?
....

3 you / have / a weekend job when you were younger? .... ?
....

4 which companies / you / want / to work for? .... ?
....

5 how / you / keep / in touch before you had a mobile phone? .... ?
....

6 you / work / in London? .... ?
....

◄ A, B **2** Replace the verbs in italics with *used to* where possible or leave them where *used to* is not possible.

1 When I *joined* this company I *worked* [used to work] in the marketing department.

2 With the old computer system we *needed* several days to collect information from all our subsidiaries.

3 When the new manager *took over*, we *got* new job descriptions, which *was* a big improvement.

4 He *didn't enjoy* his old job, so he *decided* to move to Africa. He *got* a place with a charity as a teacher.

5 A: She's a very good presenter, isn't she?

B: Yes, she *was* an actor.

6 A: How *did you keep* in touch with your clients before email?

B: Well, I *made* a lot more phone calls.

7 I don't write as many letters as I *did*.

8 Bill Gates *was* with Microsoft for 33 years before he *left* in 2008.

◄ A–C **3** A manager is describing changes to his company to a new colleague. Complete this conversation using *used to* and the words in brackets. In which gaps could you use *would*?

COLLEAGUE: Have you seen many changes here?

MANAGER: Well, I have worked for Blackheath Engineering for over 15 years, so yes, a lot has changed since I've been here. We **1** ..... *used to be* ..... (*be*) a much smaller company. Now we employ over 360 people. There's a great atmosphere here now. My staff are all really flexible and motivated and very hardworking.

COLLEAGUE: **2** .... (*they / not work*) hard?

MANAGER: No. When I first joined the company, people **3** .... (*not do*) anything that wasn't in their job description. They **4** .... (*go*) home at exactly five o'clock and they **5** .... (*never/get*) to the office before nine. I **6** .... (*always/work*) an eight-hour day. Nowadays I regularly work ten or more hours a day.

COLLEAGUE: What has the best change been?

MANAGER: The new canteen for staff meals has really helped productivity. We **7** .... (*not have*) anywhere to eat lunch on site, so we **8** .... (*have to*) go out for lunch, which took up a lot of time.

COLLEAGUE: Have your customers changed? Are they the same as they **9** .... (*be*)?

MANAGER: One area where we've seen huge changes is in our customer base. We **10** .... (*make*) most of our sales in this country. Nowadays, 60% of our sales are abroad, compared to just 5% fifteen years ago.

COLLEAGUE: How do you feel about the current management?

MANAGER: The CEO changed last year. So far he seems to be getting on OK, although it's still early days. I knew the old CEO very well as we **11** .... (*work*) together years ago. She was great to work with, always very friendly and approachable. Even when she was promoted and got really busy, she **12** .... (*always/make*) time to stop and talk.

◄ A–C **4** **a** Look at this table. Make true sentences by using *used to* or *would* with the verbs in brackets and underlining the correct words in bold.

Company Profile: *Blackheath Engineering*

15 years ago	Now
In London Average salary £14,000 Male/female ratio 9:1 Average time with company: 12 years % of staff with university degree: 38%	20km outside London Average salary £45,000 Male/female ratio 7:1 Average time with company: 10 years % of staff with university degree: 62%

Fifteen years ago …

1 … we ….*used to be*…. (*be*) <u>in</u> / **outside** London.

2 … a typical employee …..................…. (*earn*) about **£14,000** / **£45,000**.

3 … there …..................…. (*be*) **fewer** / **more** women working here.

4 … staff …..................…. (*stay*) with the company **less time** / **longer**.

5 … the **minority** / **majority** of our staff …..................…. (*not have*) a degree.

b Write five sentences about changes to your career or your company.

1 I used to …..….., but I don't any more.

2 The company used to …..............................….., but it stopped in …........................….. .

3 We didn't use to …..….., but now we do.

4 My line manager would always …..................................….., which was helpful.

5 Some of my colleagues used to …....................….., because …........................….. .

◄ A–C **5** Complete this presentation about backing up computers (saving copies of data) using the verbs in brackets in the past simple, or using *used to* or *would*. Sometimes more than one answer is possible.

Originally, only computer experts **1** …*had / used to have*….. (*have*) some sort of tape drive in their home computer and **2** …..................…. (*back up*) their hard drives. Other computer users **3** …..................…. (*not back up*) as they **4** …..................…. (*not know*) how to. And it **5** …..................…. (*not be*) relevant for people using computers at work, as their important data **6** …..................…. (*be*) on an office server. At most, people **7** …..................…. (*occasionally/save*) some of their important files on a floppy disc or CD.

So what has changed and why is it so important to back up your computer now? Firstly, we all **8** …..................…. (*work*) at large desktop computers, but now many people have laptops and the chances of them getting damaged are high. Secondly, hard drives are now much bigger than they **9** …..................…. (*be*), and contain far too much data to store on CDs or DVDs. For example, we **10** …..................…. (*store*) a few favourite photos in albums, but these days we all have thousands of photos stored on our computers. Some of our most important memories are often stored on our hard drive. Thirdly, the number of people using computers, especially children, has risen dramatically in the past decade. Before then, children **11** …..................…. (*never/do*) homework on a computer, they **12** …..................…. (*always/write*) it. Today, the home computer is essential for completing homework, and backing up regularly makes sure this work isn't lost.

Today I want to talk to you about continuous back-up protection systems …

🔘 **8.1 Listen and compare your answers.**

Make it personal

Think of ways that an area of business today is different to the past.

What used to happen that doesn't happen now? What would people do previously that they don't do now?

8 Business talk: *be/get used to*

You can use *be used to* + noun or the *-ing* form of the verb to say that something is familiar to you or that you don't think it is surprising or unusual.

*We**'re used to low interest rates**, so the recent rises were a shock.* (*low interest rates* is the normal situation)
***Are** you **used to setting** the new security system yet?*

Use the negative *not be used to* to say that something is unfamiliar.

*My PA **isn't used to working** with the new software yet.*

You can use *get used to* + noun or the *-ing* form of the verb to describe how something becomes familiar.

*It took me weeks to **get used to wearing** a uniform to work.*

Be/get used to can describe the past, present and future.

*She **was used to commuting** for over two hours a day.*
***Are** consumers **getting used to** online shopping?* (Is it becoming normal for people to shop online?)
*Hot-desking might seem strange at first, but you**'ll** soon **get used to** it.* (*hot-desking* = sitting at a different desk each day)

6 **Underline the correct words in italics.**

1 My clients *are used to* / *get used to* dealing with me. They trust me.

2 After 80 years, the modern consumer *is used to* / *gets used to* the convenience of supermarket shopping.

3 I'm not completely familiar with the culture, but I *'m slowly getting used to* / *'m slowly used to* doing business in China.

4 At first I *wasn't used to* / *didn't get used to* their way of working, but now I am happy to be here.

5 Before the credit crunch, people *weren't used to* / *weren't getting used to* falling property prices.

6 We *were never used to* / *never got used to* her management style – she was too different from our old boss.

7 **a** **Match the questions (1–5) with the answers (a–e). Complete the answers using *used to* or *be/get used to* and the correct form of any words in brackets.**

1 How has your market changed over the past few years?

2 Is it difficult for you to communicate in English at work?

3 What was the most difficult thing to learn when you started your current job?

4 Were you a good employee in your first job?

5 What do you think will be the biggest change to business in the future?

a Yes, it was hard at first, but now I .... (*write*) all my emails in English – I do it every day, and gradually I .... (*speak*) English on the phone. I get more and more calls from the US every month.

b Well, recently we .... high oil prices, but in the future I think we .... (*see*) higher prices for everything.

c We ....*were used to seeing*.... (*see*) sales increase by 20% or more each year. That's certainly changed recently. Now we ....*'re getting used to*.... 2–3% rises.

d It took me ages to .... the internal phone system. I often .... (*put*) callers through to the wrong person.

e No. I .... (*not get up*) early so I often .... (*get*) to work late.

b **Write answers to the questions that are true for you.**

Make it personal

How do you say you *used to* do something in your language? How do you say that you *are used to* something or that you *are getting used to* it? Think of some examples.

Managing conversations

Read this extract from a meeting.

Which words show that the speaker wants to start the main part of the meeting?

> Welcome, everyone. I hope you're all well and keeping busy. OK. Right. So. We've got reports from Derek and Gabriela.

A Starting conversations and meetings

A1 You can start a business conversation with these expressions.

introducing the topic	**I was wondering,** *do we need a new test schedule?* **Oh, can I ask you something?** *Is the IT seminar open to everyone?*
disturbing a busy person	**Could I talk to you for a minute?** **Have you got / Do you have a minute / a moment / a few minutes?**
starting a conversation when the topic is serious	**Could I have a word** (**about** *health and safety*)? **I need to talk to you about / I wanted to have a word with you about** *expenses.*

A2 You can start an informal, social conversation with these expressions.

general questions about people	**How are things? / How's it going? / How are you?**
comments about the weather	**Nice/Lovely/Awful/Horrible weather** (**isn't it**)**!**
questions about people's activities	**Busy day? / Are you busy at the moment?** **What are you doing / up to these days?**

A3 People say *right, so, OK, right then, well, now* (more formal) *let's make a start, let's get started* when they want to start the main part of a meeting or a discussion. They often use more than one expression.

It's good to see so many people here. **So, let's get started.** *Item one …*

B Managing and ending conversations

You can manage and end conversations with these expressions.

changing the topic	**OK, so** *I'll talk to Gina,* **then.** *Are you going to the Berlin conference?* **Right/So/Well/Anyway/Now,** *what about new contracts?*
bringing someone else into the conversation	**What about you / What do you think,** *Paula? Should we eat in the hotel?* **Does anyone else want to comment / say anything?** (in formal meetings)
interrupting the conversation	**Sorry, can I just say something / make a comment / ask a question?** **Can I** (**just**) **stop/interrupt you** (**for a moment**)**?**
going back to an earlier topic	**Anyway, as I/you say / as I was saying / as we/you were saying,** *this is a key project.* **Getting back to** *market research, what about Japan?*
ending the conversation	**Right/So/Well/Anyway, good to talk to you.** *I'll call you tomorrow. Bye.*

C Handling conference calls

You can manage conference calls with these expressions.

managing the line	**So, is everyone here? Can you all / everyone hear me? Are you there,** *Roberta?* **Could you speak up a little,** *Marilyn? The line isn't very good.* **Just stay on / hold the line** *while I try to get Alonso in Valencia.*
managing speakers	**I want to bring** *Josef* **in at this point**. **Does anyone else want to come in** *and comment on this?*
ending the call	*So,* **maybe we can have another call** *next week?* *Well,* **thank you for your time, everyone**. **/ Good to talk to you.** *Bye.*

Practice

◄ A **1** Complete these conversations using the expressions in section A. Sometimes more than one answer is possible.

1 A: ...I need to have a word with you... about a serious problem that has come up in Quality Control.
B: Oh dear! What is it? Come in. Close the door.

2 A: Sorry, Lionel. ....Who should I talk to about room bookings?
B: It's Garry Walker, on, let's see … he's on extension 2653.

3 A: Hi, Louise. ....
B: Oh, you know, when am I *not* busy?

4 A: Hello Derek. ....
B: Yes, of course. Come in. Nothing *too* serious, I hope?

5 A: Bill, ..., what happened to those photos you took at the Helsinki Expo?
B: Oh, they're still on my computer somewhere. I'll find them and send them to you.

6 A: Hello, Kyoko. ....
B: Fine, thanks. And you?

7 A: Hello, Eric. I know you're very busy. ....
B: Well, if it's quick. I have to go to a meeting in five minutes.

◄ A3, B, C **2** Complete this extract from a conference call using suitable expressions from the presentation and the instructions in brackets.

PIETRO: So, **1** ...is everyone here.... (manage the line)? How are you all? **2** .... (manage the line)?

ALL: Yes.

PIETRO: Good. Just **3** .... (manage the line), everyone. I'm going to try to get Felix. **4** .... (manage the line), Felix?

FELIX: Hi everyone.

PIETRO: Felix, we're all here and ready to start. **5** .... (start main business) Penny, you're going to tell us about your visit to Ecuador.

PENNY: Yes. It was very good. I had good discussions with the distributor.

PIETRO: **6** .... (manage the line), Penny? It's not a very good line.

PENNY: Sorry. I'll sit closer. **7** .... (go back to an earlier topic), I met our distributor and we talked about opening up in Guayaquil.

NORBERT: **8** .... (interrupt) ask a question? Can I ask which city that is? I don't know Ecuador.

PENNY: Guayaquil. It's actually the largest city and the main port.

PIETRO: OK, Penny. We look forward to hearing all about that. **9** .... (change topic), **10** .... (manage speakers) Jasmine at this point because she needs to talk to us first about schedules.

JASMINE: Thanks. Well, I hope you all got my email?

ALL: Yes.

◄ A–C **3** a ○ **SS 2.1** Listen to the speakers and answer these questions.

1 Who is going back to an earlier topic?
...Speaker 3...

2 Who is starting a social conversation?
....

3 Who is starting the main part of a discussion?
....

4 Who is ending a conversation?
....

5 Who is bringing someone else into the conversation? ....

6 Who is ending a conference call?
....

b ○ **SS 2.1** Listen again and write the phrases you hear for managing conversations.

Speaker 1 ...Well, anyway, it was good to talk to you. Speaker 4 ....

Speaker 2 .... Speaker 5 ....

Speaker 3 .... Speaker 6 ....

Test 2: Units 5–8

1 Underline the correct form of the verbs.

1 Whenever I _was_ / _was being_ in Paris I always <u>_stayed_</u> / _was staying_ at the Hotel Normandie.

2 The construction work _has started_ / _started_ six months ago.

3 I _did_ / _'ve been doing_ a lot of work with our Korean partners since May.

4 Sorry I _missed_ / _was missing_ your call. I _didn't work_ / _wasn't working_ at my desk when you _rang_ / _were ringing_.

5 _Have you finished_ / _Were you finishing_ with that room yet? You _were_ / _'ve been_ in it all morning.

6 Where _were you going_ / _have you gone_ this morning? You _seemed_ / _have seemed_ in such a hurry.

7 We _were planning_ / _have planned_ to upgrade the IT system this year, but we _decided_ / _were deciding_ it was too expensive.

8 The board yesterday _appointed_ / _were appointing_ Simon Williams to the post of Centre Director.

9 I _wanted_ / _'ve wanted_ to speak to you about my presentation at next week's conference. I _was wondering_ / _'ve wondered_ if you had any suggestions for a case study I could talk about.

10 I _was leaving_ / _left_ the office when the MD _called_ / _was calling_ me into her office for a chat.

11 This morning I _was sitting_ / _'ve been sitting_ on a train in London; now I'm here in Rome. Great!

12 _Did you have_ / _Were you having_ a successful meeting with the buyers? _Have they signed_ / _Have they been signing_ the contract?

2 An HR consultant is describing her best business decision. Complete her story using the verbs in brackets in the past simple or continuous or present perfect. Sometimes more than one answer is possible.

I hope I **1** .....'ve made..... (_make_) a lot of good decisions in my career, but I think I **2** .... (_make_) my best decision about seven or eight years ago.

We **3** .... (_have_) problems recruiting new branch managers. We **4** .... (_look for_) people with both sales and managerial experience but we **5** .... (_not have_) much success, so I **6** .... (_decide_) to introduce my training management programme. We **7** .... (_interview_) our best salespeople and **8** .... (_promote_) the candidates with the qualities we **9** .... (_look for_). The programme **10** .... (_teach_) the candidates the key management skills they **11** .... (_need_) for the branch manager role.

Over the past four years the company **12** .... (_generate_) 30% of new branch managers via the programme. It **13** .... (_be_) great for motivating staff and recently, it **14** .... (_attract_) a lot of attention from training organisations.

3 Complete the second part of the HR consultant's story, describing her worst business decision. Use the verbs in brackets in the past simple or past perfect simple or continuous. Sometimes more than one answer is possible.

I **1** .....worked..... (_work_) for a large international hotels group before I **2** .... (_go_) into HR consulting. My responsibilities **3** .... (_include_) organising company cars for regional training managers. The training department **4** .... (_need_) to cut costs because we **5** .... (_overspend_) our budget for several years. Our training managers **6** .... (_not use_) their cars very frequently, so I **7** .... (_decide_) to start providing them with cheaper second-hand cars, even though we **8** .... (_offer_) them new cars previously.

However, I soon **9** .... (_realise_) that I **10** .... (_make_) a terrible mistake. We **11** .... (_receive_) a lot of complaints from training managers and it **12** .... (_not help_) our image when our regional managers **13** .... (_arrive_) at five star hotels in old cars.

What **14** .... (_I/learn_) from this? Well, within a few weeks I **15** .... (_see_) that we **16** .... (_lose_) so much in terms of trust and respect that it **17** .... (_not be_) worth the money we **18** .... (_save_).

4 Complete this article about how computers have changed business using *used to*, *be used to*, *get used to*, *would* or the past simple. Sometimes more than one answer is possible.

How have computers changed business?

Nowadays, everyone **1** ....*is used to shopping*.... (*shop*) online, but it wasn't always like this. Thanks to the Internet, the business world has changed dramatically in the past few decades. Here are just a few of the ways:

- Storing important data **2** .... (*need*) whole rooms of paper files. Computers have made information easily accessible.

- It **3** .... (*take*) several accountants to do the kinds of calculations that we can now do quickly and easily using standard software.

- Until the late eighties, communication **4** .... (*involve*) either the telephone or writing letters. Email allows businesses to communicate instantly around the world.

- Business people **5** .... (*have*) separate professional and private lives. They **6** .... (*never need*) to be available or contactable out of the office. Wireless Internet and mobile phones now mean we **7** .... (*be*) constantly available – even at home or on the beach.

- Computers have also changed. In the early days of computers, only experts **8** .... (*know*) how to use them. Now everyone **9** .... (*work*) with user-friendly software. In fact, employers these days assume that office workers **10** .... (*use*) a wide range of programmes.

5 Complete this article about newspaper publishing using the time expressions in the box.

ago	already	before	earlier	for	In	last	never	since	When

Bad news for newspapers

'Regional news publishing is a very difficult business at the moment. I've **1** ....*never*.... known a period like it,' said Craig Mitchell, who bought Eastern Courier Newspapers **2** .... year.

Tina Staverton, who bought a Liverpool newspaper just two years **3** .... , agreed, 'It's hard to be positive right now.'

4 '................. we bought the business, we knew that we would have to make hard decisions. But we didn't expect things to be this bad,' said Paul Shah, who has been the owner of *The Southern Herald* **5** .... just six months.

Although all three are successful and experienced businesspeople, they have all had to make savings in their publishing businesses.

6 .... January Ms Staverton said that her company had to cut costs by 10%, and in Bristol **7** .... this month, Mr Shah's management team held crisis meetings with unions.

News publishing has experienced deep recessions **8** .... and has cut costs to survive, but because staff numbers have **9** .... been cut significantly **10** .... 2005, this time the future does not look very bright at all.

9 The future 1 (be going to, present continuous)

Read this extract from a conversation.

Underline the verbs that refer to the future.

> The board meeting's in the diary for next Tuesday, I think. Are you going to be there or not?

> Erm yeah, because I'm not leaving for Norway until Wednesday.

A Using *be going to*

A1 You can use *be going to* to talk about people's plans, intentions and decisions about the future.

I'm going to retrain as a web designer, but I'm not going to tell my boss yet.

Where are you going to advertise the vacancy? Are you going to put an ad in the paper?

⊙ People use *be going to* more in speaking than in writing.

⚠ *Going to* is usually pronounced 'gonna'.

A2 You can use *be going to* to talk about predictions for the future when you have some evidence to believe that something will happen, or when it seems obvious.

Our results are good – we're going to make budget. It's going to be a good year.

Clients are not going to come to us if our fees are too high.

⚠ Don't use modal verbs after *be going to*.

Are they going to be able to raise the capital they need? or *Can they raise …* (**not** *Are they going to can raise*)

We're going to have to spend more money on advertising. or *We must spend …* (**not** *We are going to must spend*)

B Using the present continuous to talk about the future

You can use the present continuous to talk about future arrangements that are already made. It is often used with expressions of time or place.

What are you doing tomorrow? Are you meeting Nigel?

Next Tuesday morning I'm giving a presentation in the conference room at ten o'clock.

C Choosing between *be going to* and the present continuous

C1 There is often little difference in meaning between *be going to* and the present continuous. You can use both to talk about future plans, decisions and arrangements.

What are you going to do / are you doing after work?

C2 You use *be going to*, not the present continuous, to talk about:

- predictions about the future based on evidence.

We've got the plans for the new office. It's going to look great when it's finished. (**not** *it's looking*)

- future intentions.

A: *Helen's got a problem with her PA.*
B: *Again? What's she going to do about it?'*

- future states and situations with state verbs.

It's going to be a tough year. (**not** *It's being*)

◀ See Unit 3 (Present simple and continuous).

C3 You can use the present continuous to show that arrangements are agreed or in place.

I'm getting the 7:20 flight to Brussels tomorrow and Jan's meeting me at the airport.

Practice

◀ A   **1**   Write the questions in this article about writing a business plan using *be going to*.

Writing a business plan

Writing a business plan is the first step in setting up your own business. It is important to get it right to attract investors. Make sure your business plan answers these basic questions:

1   What / you / do / in your business .... *What are you going to do in your business* ....?
2   you / need / to borrow money ....?
3   How much money / you / need ....?
4   Who / buy / your product or service ....?
5   How well / it / sell ....?
6   Where / you / sell / it ....?
7   How much / you / charge / for it ....?
8   Why / customers / buy / your product and not a competitor's ....?
9   How / your competitors / react ....?
10   they / be able to / copy your product easily ....?

◀ A   **2**   Complete this conversation using the correct form of *be going to* and a verb from the box.

> be   not be   not be able to   explain   have to   not lie   not like   say

ANISH: Bad news! The designer's got flu. She
1 *'s going to be* .... off work for a week.

SARA: Oh no. That means that the launch of the new
website **2** .... on schedule.

ANISH: Yeah, we **3** .... meet the deadline.

SARA: No, so we **4** .... tell Peter.
He **5** .... it!

ANISH: I know. Karen and I **6** .... the problem
to him tomorrow. I **7** .... about it. I
8 .... that it's delayed.

◀ B   **3**   Complete this conversation using the verbs in brackets in the present continuous.

WASEEM: Hi Simon. What **1** ...... *are you doing* ......
(*you/do*) today? Are you free?

SIMON: Sorry, I **2** .... (*go*) to a
meeting in five minutes. Then straight after
that I **3** .... (*give*) a talk to
the trainees.

WASEEM: Where **4** .... (*you/do*)
that?

SIMON: Room A. **5** .... (*you/come*)?

WASEEM: Sorry, I can't. Um, what
6 .... (*you/do*) before lunch?

SIMON: Joan **7** .... (*show*) me
the new designs. Then the people from Palgo
8 .... (*come*) for lunch. And
then the new sales rep **9** .... (*take*)
me on some visits.

WASEEM: Oh well, I'll catch you tomorrow morning,
then. What time **10** .... (*you/start*)
tomorrow?

MONDAY 25 APRIL

8.00

9.00

10.00   Department meeting

11.00   Talk to new trainees – Room A

12.00   12.30   Joan (her office) – see new designs

1.00   1.15   Lunch with clients from Palgo

2.00   2.30   customer visits with new rep.

3.00

4.00

5.00

6.00

◄ A–C **4** Complete this conversation between two PAs who are planning a business trip for their managers. Use the verbs in brackets in the present continuous or with *be going to*. Sometimes both are possible.

JUN: Did you look at the weather forecast for next week? Stephan always asks.

EMILY: Yes, I'm afraid **1** it ....*'s going to be*.......... (*be*) cold. But at least **2** it .... (*not rain*).

JUN: What day do they want to travel?

EMILY: **3** They .... (*leave*) on Saturday the 15th.

JUN: And when **4** .... (*they / come back*)?

EMILY: The 19th. The department **5** .... (*move*) office on the 20th, so Chris has to be back for that.

JUN: Do you want me to book them a hotel?

EMILY: That's OK. **6** I .... (*research*) hotels this afternoon.

JUN: OK. Are hotels in Frankfurt expensive, do you know?

EMILY: I've no idea, but I guess **7** I .... (*find out*) this afternoon.

JUN: They've already overspent on their travel budget.

EMILY: I know and **8** I .... (*have to*) tell Chris this afternoon that **9** we .... (*not be able to*) afford a five-star hotel this time.

JUN: So, **10** .... (*you/give*) me a ring with some options before you book?

EMILY: Yeah. It's only a week before the book fair too. **11** We've left it quite late, so it .... (*not be*) easy to find somewhere.

JUN: Well, **12** they .... (*travel*) together, so maybe they can share a room.

◄ A–C **5** **a** If these questions are correct, tick (✓) them. If they are wrong, correct them.

1 Do you think that inflation ~~is rising~~ next year? ....*is going to rise*.......

2 Are house prices going to go down in the next few months? ....✓...............

3 What's going to might happen to interest rates in the coming months? ....

4 Is unemployment rising in the future? ....

5 Is your company having a difficult year next year? ....

6 Is it going to invest in any new areas? ....

7 Do you think you're going to can change jobs next year? ....

8 Are you going to get a pay rise or be promoted, do you think? ....

b Write answers that are true for you.

c 🔘 9.1 Listen to a visitor from another country asking you the questions and reply with your prepared answers.

Make it personal

1 Write about four things you intend to do next week.

2 Write about four things you have arranged to do.

3 Make four predictions about your workplace next year.

9

Business talk: Organising presentations and workshops 1

People often use *be going to* in presentations, workshops and training sessions to organise what they say and to manage the activities. You can use *be going to* to:

- say what the talk or workshop is about.

  *Today I**'m going to talk about** three issues facing the insurance industry.*

- say what you intend to do (or not do).

  *In this second part of the session we**'re going to look at** some case studies.*
  *This slide shows some definitions of marketing; I**'m not going to read** them all out.*

- explain an activity that the participants are going to do.

  *Now I**'m going to ask** you to get into groups of four / pairs.*
  *You**'re going to see** three pictures. Later you**'re going to tell** me the one you remember best.*

- end the session.

  *Now I**'m going to stop** there. Does anyone have any questions or comments?*

You can use a *what*-clause with *be going to* to introduce topics or set up activities.

***What we're going to look at** today is two aspects of advertising.*
***What I'm going to do** now is give you all a handout with questions on it.*

► See Speaking strategies 7

⚠ *be going to* **is one way of managing talks and presentations. You can also use other expressions.**

I'd like to *discuss these slides.*	***Let's*** *have a look at the main issues.*
I want *you **to** get into groups.*	***Can*** *you all find a partner for the next activity?*

► See Unit 10 Business talk (Organising presentations and workshops 2).

---

6 Look at these slides and notes from an HR manager's presentation. Complete his spoken presentation below using phrases with *be going to*.

Effective interviewing	Questioning techniques	Three types of questions • open-ended • self-evaluation • preference	Practice activity 1
Say what I want to talk about	Say what I want to focus on	Say what I want to look at / talk about	· give handout, · ask participants to get into pairs · ask for volunteers

Good morning. Thank you for being on time. OK, so let's get started. **1** ....*What I'm going to talk about*.... today is effective interviewing and interview techniques. In particular **2** .... different questioning techniques, or in other words, different types of questions that you can ask the candidate. **3** .... three types of questions. First, open-ended questions – these are questions that begin 'How ...', 'Why ...', or 'Can you tell me about ...?' Second, **4** .... self-evaluation questions, which ask the candidate to evaluate him- or herself. Then **5** .... preference questions such as 'What do you like or dislike about your current job?'
OK, so now **6** .... is give you all a handout, and in a moment **7** .... you to get into pairs and decide who is going to be the interviewer and who is the candidate. First though, **8** .... for volunteers …

Make it personal

Imagine you have to give a presentation to a new boss about your work. Design three simple slides and write out your introduction, using phrases with *be going to*.

10 The future 2 (*will*, *shall*, the present tense)

Read this press release.

Which verb forms are used to talk about the future?

> The Minister for Enterprise tomorrow *launches* the Youth Enterprise Campaign. It *is providing* a programme of events over the next year aimed at young entrepreneurs, including a speech by teenage businessman Ewan Richards, who *will talk* about his recent £4.2m acquisition of VX Communications.

◀ See Unit 1 (Present Simple), Unit 2 (Present continuous) and Unit 9 (The future 1).

A Forming the future with *will*

+	I/You/He/She/It/We/They**'ll**/**will be** OK.
–	I/You/He/She/It/We/They **will not** / **won't be** OK.
?	**Will** I/you/he/she/it/we/they **be** OK?
	When will I/you/he/she/it/we/they **be** there?

B Using *will* to talk about the future

B1 You can use *will* when you decide to do something as you're speaking.

[Telephone rings] *I'**ll answer** it … Sorry. She's a bit busy. She'**ll call** you **back** later.*

B2 You can use *will* to talk about future facts or events you think of as facts.

*This company **will be** 100 years old in September.*

B3 You can use *will* to make predictions based on personal opinion.

*We probably **won't get** next year's budget ready on time.*

B4 People often use *think* and *expect + will* in statements and *think + will* in questions.

A: *Do you **think** we'**ll reach** our targets?*
B: *Yes, I **expect** we **will**.*

In negative statements, people use *not think/expect + will* rather than *think/expect + won't*.

*I **don't think** he'**ll arrive** before 9:30.* (not ~~I think he won't arrive~~)

C Using *shall* as an alternative to *will*

C1 ⊙ You can use *I/We shall/shan't* as alternatives to *I/We will/won't*, but they are much less common.

*I **shall** be late to the meeting, I'm afraid.* (I will be late)

C2 You can use *shall* in questions with *I/we* to make suggestions or discuss possible plans.

***Shall** I look at your report after lunch?*

▶ See Unit 14 (Modals 2) for other uses of *shall*.

D Using the present simple to talk about the future

D1 You can use the present simple to talk about schedules and timetables.

*The meeting **starts** at 9:30. When **does** your flight **land**?*

D2 You can use the present simple (not *will*) to talk about future time after *when, until, before, after, as soon as* and *once*.

*I'll let you know **as soon as** he **arrives**.* (not ~~when he'll arrive~~)

*When you **leave** this evening, please turn the lights off.* (not ~~When you will leave~~)

E Choosing which future form to use

E1 You can use *will* or *be going to* to make predictions. Use *be going to* for predictions that are based on evidence, and *will* for predictions that are based on personal opinion, or are quite general.

A: *Look at the time. He'**s going to be** late.*
B: *Don't worry! He'**ll be** here.* (this is my opinion)

E2 Do not use *will* to talk about existing plans for the future. Use *be going to* or the present continuous.

*I'**m going to do** / I'**m doing** a presentation in Vancouver next week.* (not ~~I will do~~)

E3 You can use *will* and *be going to* (**not** the present continuous) with state verbs.

*Hopefully our customers **will like** / **are going to like** our new campaign.* (**not** ~~our customers are liking~~)

▶ For more ways of talking about the future, see Unit 11 (Future continuous and future perfect) and Unit 12 (Other ways of talking about the future).

Practice

◄ A–C **1** Three managers are meeting to decide how to celebrate their company's centenary.
Complete their conversation using *'ll*, *won't* or *shall*.

RICHARD: OK, so the company **1** .....'ll....... be 100 years old in March and we need to find a way to celebrate it.

MICHELLE: **2** .... we have some sort of party for all the staff?

THORKILD: I'm not sure. Do you think we **3** .... have the budget for that kind of thing?

RICHARD: Well, we **4** .... get a finalised budget before next month, but I don't think it
5 .... be a problem.

THORKILD: Right. We **6** .... have a party, then. Apart from staff, who **7** .... we invite?
It would be good to get some VIPs or a guest speaker.

MICHELLE: Nice idea, although I hope we **8** .... find it difficult to get someone interesting.

THORKILD: Yeah, good speakers can be hard to find. And what about lunch? **9** .... we use the
visitor's dining room?

RICHARD: OK, but **10** .... we hire some caterers to do a special meal? Now, can we leave the rest of
the details to you, Thorkild?

THORKILD: Sure. I **11** .... prepare a draft plan and we **12** .... meet again next week to
finalise the plans, OK?

◄ A, B2, D **2** Complete this email to staff about the company's centenary celebrations. Use the verbs in brackets with
will or in the present simple. Sometimes both are possible.

> To: All managers
> Subject: Centenary celebration
>
> I've just finalised all the details for the centenary celebration next week, so here is the plan. Each of you
> **1** ...will be.... (*be*) responsible for looking after one of our VIP guests during the day (see attachment for details).
>
> Outline of the day's events:
>
> Gabriela Wulff, the guest speaker, **2** .... (*arrive*) at 11:00. John **3** .... (*meet*) her in the foyer
> and take her to the conference room to prepare for her speech, which **4** .... (*begin*) at 12:00 and
> **5** .... (*end*) at 12:30. Before she **6** .... (*arrive*), please take your VIP to the main meeting
> room.
>
> After Ms Wulff's speech, you **7** .... (*take*) your VIP to the visitors' dining room for lunch, but you
> **8** .... (*not eat*) with them because of the limited space on the VIP table. Staff **9** .... (*eat*)
> together in the canteen.
>
> Lunch **10** .... (*last*) from 13:00 until 14:30.
>
> In the afternoon from 15:00 to 16:00 there **12** .... (*be*) a tour of the company.
>
> Ms Wulff's train **13** .... (*depart*) at 17:00.

◄ A, B2–4, E **3** Complete this blog about the impact of an economic slowdown on small businesses using the verbs in
brackets with *will* or *going to*, or in the present continuous. Sometimes more than one answer is possible.

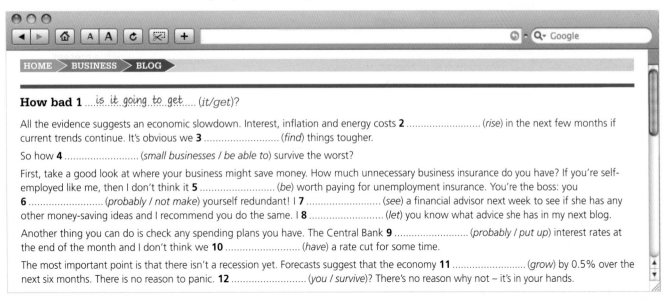

HOME > BUSINESS > BLOG

How bad 1 ...is it going to get.... (*it/get*)?

All the evidence suggests an economic slowdown. Interest, inflation and energy costs **2** .... (*rise*) in the next few months if
current trends continue. It's obvious we **3** .... (*find*) things tougher.

So how **4** .... (*small businesses / be able to*) survive the worst?

First, take a good look at where your business might save money. How much unnecessary business insurance do you have? If you're self-
employed like me, then I don't think it **5** .... (*be*) worth paying for unemployment insurance. You're the boss: you
6 .... (*probably / not make*) yourself redundant! I **7** .... (*see*) a financial advisor next week to see if she has any
other money-saving ideas and I recommend you do the same. I **8** .... (*let*) you know what advice she has in my next blog.

Another thing you can do is check any spending plans you have. The Central Bank **9** .... (*probably / put up*) interest rates at
the end of the month and I don't think we **10** .... (*have*) a rate cut for some time.

The most important point is that there isn't a recession yet. Forecasts suggest that the economy **11** .... (*grow*) by 0.5% over the
next six months. There is no reason to panic. **12** .... (*you / survive*)? There's no reason why not – it's in your hands.

10

◄ A–E **4** Sue is discussing arrangements for a new project with her manager, Terry, before he goes on holiday. Underline the correct words in italics in their conversation. Sometimes both are possible.

TERRY: I just wanted to check everything's OK before the new project **1** <u>starts</u> / *will start* next week. Have you got any last questions for me?

SUE: Only one. I just wanted to confirm where the team **2** *will sit* / *are going to sit*.

TERRY: Well, as you know, the maintenance department **3** *rewire* / *are rewiring* this office from Monday, and they think it **4** *'ll take* / *'s taking* at least two weeks. So why don't you use my personal office while I'm away?

SUE: Oh? But we **5** *'ll need* / *'re needing* enough room for four people. I don't think your office is big enough.

TERRY: Yes, you're right. You **6** *'re having to* / *'ll have to* find somewhere else. Can I leave that with you?

SUE: Of course. Now, regarding the team, as you know, I **7** *'ll meet* / *'m meeting* John Maybury from Marketing and Ian Childers from Logistics tomorrow to confirm their availability.

TERRY: OK. Remember that this project is still confidential. People **8** *will ask* / *are asking* questions sooner or later, but try not to say too much about it. When you **9** *meet* / *'re meeting* John and Ian please remind them, too.

SUE: Don't worry, I **10** *won't forget* / *'m not forgetting*.

TERRY: Is that all, then? I'm afraid my flight **11** *leaves* / *is going to leave* in three hours so I need to rush.

SUE: That's it, yes. I don't expect you **12** *'ll miss* / *'re missing* the office while you're away!

◄ B–E **5 a** Write sentences using the verbs in the correct form. Then match the questions (1–8) with the answers (a–h).

1 What time / your office / open / tomorrow morning?

...What time does your office open...
...tomorrow morning?...

a No, / our sales so far are poor so / we probably / not hit / our targets.

....

2 What / you / do / first / when / you / arrive / at work tomorrow?

....

b No, but / I / make / a presentation to the Board on Tuesday.

....

3 How old / your company / be / this year?

....

c It / open / at 7 o'clock.

...It opens at 7 o'clock....

4 What / you / expect / happen / to your salary next year?

....

d No, / I / expect / I / spend / more time at work than last year.

....

5 you / chair / any meetings this week?

....

e It / be / 42 years old.

....

6 you / think / it / be / a good year for your business?

....

f I / think / it / continue / to rise.

....

7 What / you / think / happen / to unemployment in your country this year?

....

g I / not expect / I / get / a pay rise, unfortunately.

....

8 you / have / more / free time next year?

....

h I / check / my emails.

....

Make it personal

Make three positive and three negative predictions for the next 12 months.

10 **Business talk:** Organising presentations and workshops 2

◄ See Unit 9 for using *be going to* in presentations.

People often use *will* to organise what they say in presentations, workshops and training sessions. You can use *will* to:

- give information about the content.

  *My talk/presentation/session **will focus on** our company's advertising. It **will cover** four main areas.*

- give information about timing.

  *My talk/presentation/session **will take** about half an hour. I **won't take up** too much of your time.*

- structure the session.

  *In the first part, we**'ll look at** our latest advertising campaign. Then, I**'ll show you** / **outline** the results. Finally, I**'ll sum up** before making some recommendations for future advertising strategy.*

- deal with interruptions.

  *I**'ll come** (**on**) to that (point) later / in the next section.*
  *I**'ll go/come back** to that (point) in a second. Is that OK / all right?*

- invite questions.

  *I**'ll be happy/pleased to answer** / I**'ll answer** any questions at the end of my presentation / now.*

6 **Read the speaker's notes for a presentation about her company's online sales strategy. Complete her presentation using *will* and a verb from the box. Sometimes more than one answer is possible.**

answer	cover	deal with	~~focus on~~
look at	outline	show	sum up
make	take		

Online sales strategy (45 mins)
1 why we needed a new website
2 who designed the website
3 technical problems we had
4 online sales so far
5 recommendations for future development of the site
6 questions

My presentation **1** ....will focus on.... our online sales strategy and **2** .... five main areas.
It **3** .... about 45 minutes. In the first part we **4** .... why we needed a website. Secondly,
I **5** .... you who designed the website. Then, I **6** .... some of the technical problems
we had. After that we **7** .... the online sales so far. Finally, I **8** .... and I **9** ....
some recommendations for the future development of the site. I **10** .... any questions at the end of
my presentation.

🔘 **10.1 Listen and check your answers.**

7 **During her presentation the speaker was interrupted several times. Write answers to the questions using an expression with *will*.**

1 DELEGATE: (during section 1) Sorry to interrupt, but did you have any technical problems with the website?

  SPEAKER: ....I'll come back to that point later. Is that OK?..

2 DELEGATE: (during section 4) Can I ask if you have any recommendations for the future?

  SPEAKER: ....

3 DELEGATE: (during section 5) Excuse me, but can you tell me again how you found the designer?

  SPEAKER: ....

4 DELEGATE: (at the end of the presentation) Can I ask a question now?

  SPEAKER: ....

Make it personal

Using *will* and *be going to*, prepare the introduction to a presentation about your company's strategy for the next three years.

11

Future continuous and future perfect

Read this Careers Service advertisement.

a Which actions are in progress during the fair?

b Which action will finish before the end of the fair?

A Forming the future continuous

+	I/You/He/She/It/We/They	*'ll/will be staying* there next week.
–		**won't / will not be staying** there next week.
?	When **will**	**be staying** next week?
	Will	I/you/he/she/it/we/they	**be staying** there next week?

I/we shall/shan't are also possible but much less common than *will*.

◄ See Unit 10 (The future 2).

B Using the future continuous

B1 You use the future continuous to talk about an action in progress at a specific time in the future.

I'll be going through the financial reports this afternoon.

going through reports

```
_____→
Now          This afternoon        Future
```

B2 You can use the future continuous to talk about events that are planned or decided. The meaning is similar to *be going to*.

I'll be meeting the new team later this month. (I'm going to meet)

B3 You can use these time expressions with the future continuous: *all night/week, at 6 pm, for the whole month/year, this time next week, during/in the next month, this week, tomorrow, soon.*

I'll be leaving at 4 pm today.   We*'ll be closing for the whole month* for refurbishments.

C Forming the future perfect

+	I/You/He/She/It/We/They	*'ll/will have finished* by 6 pm.
–		**won't / will not have finished** by 6 pm.
?	When **will**	**have finished?**
	Will	I/you/he/she/it/we/they	**have finished** by 6 pm?

D Using the future perfect

D1 You use the future perfect to talk about an action that you think or predict will happen before a specific point in the future.

I'll have written the report by 2 pm.

finish writing the report

```
_____→
Now              2 pm              Future
```

D2 You can use expressions with *by* to show when you expect the action will be finished (e.g. *by 5 pm, by next week*).

By the end of the year, net profits *will have risen* from £20m to an estimated £50m.

Practice

◄ A, B **1** Complete this conversation between two colleagues using the verbs in brackets in the future continuous.

SIMONE: Are you OK? You're staring into space.

KARL: Sorry, I was just daydreaming about my holiday next week. I can't wait. This time next week I **1** .....'ll be flying.... (fly) to Mexico with my wife.

SIMONE: Wow, that sounds great! Where **2** .... (you/stay)?

KARL: We **3** .... (stay) with some friends near Mexico City for the first week, and then in Cancún for the second.

SIMONE: And do you have any particular plans for your trip?

KARL: Yes, we **4** .... (do) a lot of sightseeing. Our friends **5** .... (take) us to see the Mayan pyramids – Palenque, Chichén Itzá and places like that. I've always wanted to see them.

SIMONE: Yes, me too. Lucky you! And what are your plans for Cancún?

KARL: Well, I **6** .... (try) lots of different water sports, but my wife **7** .... (not join) me. She prefers sunbathing!

SIMONE: Well, I **8** .... (think) about you while I'm stuck here working. I'm so jealous!

🔘 **11.1 Listen and check your answers.**

◄ C, D **2** Complete this conversation using the verbs in the box in the future perfect.

| achieve   announce   ~~appoint~~   choose   have   join   not make   start |

SARA: **1** ....Will you have appointed.... (you) the new manager by the end of the week?

GERARD: Well, the final interviews are this afternoon, so we **2** .... a decision by the end of the day, but I'm sure we **3** .... someone by tomorrow lunchtime. Then if we offer them the post tomorrow afternoon, I expect we **4** .... a reply from them by Wednesday or Thursday. So if they accept quickly, then I hope we **5** .... the appointment by the end of the week.

SARA: I hope they **6** .... working with us before the busy summer period.

GERARD: Don't worry. They'll probably have to work three months' notice maximum in their old company, so they **7** .... us by April at the latest. But remember we mustn't rush this. The most important thing is to find the best person for the job. What **8** .... (we) if we appoint the wrong person?

◄ B, D **3** A manager is talking to his team about the business plan for the next year. If the verbs in italics are correct, tick (✓) them. If they are wrong, correct them.

I'm pleased to announce that we **1** *'ll be making* several key changes over the coming year. The good news is that we **2** *'ll have opened* three new branches this month. We **3** *'ll also have transferred* our head office into new premises by the end of December so that we'll be ready to do business from there from January. As many of you know, by the start of the new financial year the accounts department **4** *will have introduced* a new purchasing system, which we hope will improve efficiency. We **5** *'ll also have taken on* between 50 and 100 new staff during the next four months to help cope with the extra work.

We **6** *'ll have published* more up-to-date guidelines on working practice in the next few weeks and I **7** *'ll be checking* personally that these are clearer and easier to understand than the old version. Despite the extra costs some of these changes will incur, I confidently predict that by the final quarter, the company **8** *will have exceeded* budget for this year. Thank you for all your hard work.

1 ....✓.........

2 ...'ll be opening...

3 ....

4 ....

5 ....

6 ....

7 ....

8 ....

◀ B, D **4** Complete these conversations using the time expressions in the box.

> all night   by lunchtime   by the end of the month   by then
> ~~by this time next week~~   for the whole week   in a few minutes   tomorrow

1 A: The results of the tenders come out in the next four or five days, don't they?

 B: Yes, we'll have heard if we've got the contract ....by this time next week.....

2 A: We're really low on paper and we have to print the new brochures off by lunchtime tomorrow.

 B: Don't worry. The new supplies will have arrived ....

3 A: Do you know when our new computers are being delivered?

 B: Well, I'll be talking to our IT department .... so I'll ask them then.

4 A: The deadline's tomorrow, so I'll be working .... I've no idea if I'll get any sleep.

 B: You poor thing. Well, hopefully you'll get some sleep tomorrow night!

5 A: Hurry up! The meeting will be starting ....

 B: OK, I'm just coming!

6 A: Did you know that Simon has got five interviews in the next two weeks?

 B: Yes. Hopefully he'll have found a new job ....

7 A: I'll have finished reading your report .... Will you be free to discuss it this afternoon?

 B: No, I'm afraid I have a meeting. How about tomorrow morning?

8 A: From the 21st to the 28th you can contact me at the Radisson hotel.

 B: Ah, OK. So you'll be staying there ....

◀ A–D **5** Look at these notes for a presentation about making a company more environmentally friendly. Use the notes to write sentences from the presentation.

1 20 Jan: Meet representatives from the environmental group Go Green

 On 20 January I'll be meeting representatives from the environmental group Go Green.

2 By 30 Jan: Set up a team of employees to lead our green programme

 ....

3 Jan–March: Investigate sourcing raw materials more locally

 ....

4 Feb–June: Look for greener suppliers who provide sustainable products

 ....

5 From now on: Encourage people to print less

 ....

6 By April: Create 20 reserved parking places for car poolers [people who travel together in cars]

 ....

7 By this time next year: Reduce business travel by 40–50%

 ....

8 By 2016: Transfer 30% of our energy to wind power

 ....

Make it personal

Answer these questions.

What will you be doing this time next week? What will you have achieved at work by the end of the year? How many phone calls will you be making tomorrow?

11 Business talk: Using the future continuous to be polite

You can use the future continuous when you want to soften questions about the future and make them more polite.

Direct question	More polite question
When will you come back?	*When **will you be coming** back?*
Do you want me to pay now?	***Will you be wanting** immediate payment?*
How are you going to the airport?	*How **will you be going** to the airport?*
What are you going to do here?	*What **will you be doing** during your time here?*

👁 *Will you be wanting/needing …?* are quite common, especially in the travel or hospitality industries.

***Will you be wanting** someone to collect you from the station?* (person expecting a visitor)
***Will you be needing** any further information about our product?* (sales person to client)

6 Write polite questions using the future continuous. Then match the direct questions (1–10) with the polite questions (a–j).

1 Shall I give you the money today or tomorrow?

2 Do you want to pay cash or by credit card?

3 Will you be here for one night or two?

4 Do you need any equipment, tea and coffee, more chairs, etc. for the talk?

5 Do you want us to telephone you at seven?

6 Do you want to visit the gym?

7 What time will you get here?

8 Do you want us to bring any meals up to you?

9 Are you coming by car or train?

10 What do you expect to do while you are in London?

a you / want / to use the sports facilities?
....

b How / you/ pay?
....

c you / need / anything for your presentation?
....

d you / want / room service?
....

e When / you /arrive?
....

f How / you / travel?
....

g you / need / a wake-up call?
....

h What / do / while you are in London?
....

i How long / you / stay?
....

j When / you / need / payment?
...When will you be needing payment?

Make it personal

Think of situations at work where it would be important to soften questions about the future.
Who would you be most likely to use softened questions to, and why?

12 Other ways of talking about the future

Read this business forecast.

Which expressions refer to the future?

> Manufacturing employment is expected to decline, and the car industry is set to see the biggest decrease. Inflation is likely to rise because of increases in the world oil price.

A *Likely* and *unlikely*

A1 You can use *be/seem* + *likely/unlikely* + *to*-infinitive to say something will probably happen or not happen in the future.

*Economic recovery **is likely to happen** slowly.*
***Is** Anna **likely to visit** us during the coming weeks?*
*Interest rates **seem unlikely to rise** over the coming year.*

> ⊙ Instead of *unlikely*, you can say *not likely*, but this is less common.

*The Extraordinary General Meeting **is not likely to** take place before December.*

A2 You can also say *it is/seems likely/unlikely that … + will.*

***It's likely that** Carlos **will** lose his job at the end of the year.* (Carlos is likely to lose his job)

*It **seems unlikely that** our internet sales **will** increase rapidly.*

> ⊙ *It is/seems likely/unlikely that … is less common than be likely/unlikely to.*

A3 You can use adverbs before *likely/unlikely* to make their meaning stronger or weaker.

weaker ➡ stronger

quite likely	very likely	most likely
rather unlikely	very unlikely	highly/extremely unlikely

*The economy is **very likely** to slow down in the second half of the year.*
*I think it's **highly unlikely** that we'll take on any new projects this year.*

A4 You can compare how probable different things are using *likely/unlikely* with *as … as, more, (the) most, less* and *(the) least.*

*The UK is **as likely** to suffer a recession **as** the US.*
*Are shoppers **more likely** to buy clothes online in the future?*
*The north-east region is **the least likely** to grow economically compared with other regions.*

▶ See Unit 31 (Comparisons 1) and Unit 32 (Comparisons 2).

B Other expressions for talking about the future

You can use the present tense of *be* + *about/due/ supposed/expected/set* + *to* to talk about things that people know or believe will happen in the future.

- *be to* = something will happen in the future (formal, more common in writing)

  *The European Union **is to** introduce new health and safety regulations in the coming year.*

- *be about to* = something will happen very soon. It is not normally used with a time expression (e.g. a date or time)

  *The company **is about to** launch a new range of sports clothing. (**not** is about to launch next week)*

- *be due to* = something is going to happen at a particular time or date

  *Several major companies **are due to** announce half-year dividends next week.*

- *be supposed to* = someone intends to do something or something is intended to happen

  *Sara **is supposed to** arrive from Mexico later this week. Do you know which day?*

- *be expected to* = people believe something will happen

  *Transport costs **are expected to** rise next year.*

- *be set to* = the conditions at present mean that something will probably happen

  *Dubai Airport **is set to** become the world's largest airport.*

C Talking about the future in the past

You can talk about things that were planned in the past but did not happen using *was/were going to* or the expressions in section B with the past tense of *be*.

*Hongyin **was going to / was supposed to / was due to** give a presentation last week but he was off work with a cold.*

Practice

◄ A1 **1** Rewrite the words in italics using (*not*) *likely / unlikely to.* Which sentences are true for you or in your opinion?

1 February *will probably be* a good month for us. ...*is likely to be*....
2 Our company *will, we expect, begin* developing a new website before the end of the year. ....
3 *Will next week be* a busy one? ....
4 I *probably won't be* promoted this year. ....
5 We*'ll probably make* more conference calls later this month. ....
6 *Will anyone need* the projector during the next few days? ....
7 I *probably won't finish* everything I have to do by Friday. ....
8 More countries *will probably enter* the EU over the next ten years. ....
9 Customer needs *are probably not going to change* much over the coming years. ....
10 Electric cars *will probably become* the most popular way to travel in the next ten years. ....

◄ A2 **2** Write predictions based on the information in these diagrams and the words in italics using *likely/unlikely that.* Then write one more prediction for each diagram.

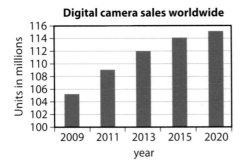

Digital camera sales worldwide

World's biggest Internet users (in millions)			
year	**2000**	**2007**	**2015** (predicted)
USA	124	212	398
China	23	162	450
Japan	47	88	98

1 digital camera sales / continue / grow

.....*It is/seems likely that digital camera*.....
.....*sales will continue to grow.*.....

2 digital camera sales / decline / before 2020

....

3 China / be / the world's biggest Internet user in 2015

....

4 USA / be / the world's biggest Internet user in 2015

....

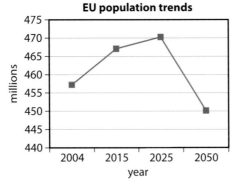

EU population trends

% of UK households with 2 cars

5 the population of the EU / rise / to 470 m by 2025

....
....

6 the population of the EU / continue / to rise after 2025

....

7 more than 25% of households / own / two cars in 2020

....
....

8 car ownership / decline sharply / over the next 20 years

....

12

◀ A3 **3** Write sentences using the correct form of the verbs. Add an adverb (*quite, rather, very, highly, extremely, more, least*) in the gap before *likely* or *unlikely* to show your opinion about the probability.

1 It / be / .... unlikely / that / humans / travel / beyond the solar system in the next ten years.

   It is highly/extremely unlikely that humans will travel beyond the solar system in the next ten years.

2 In the future, people / be / .... likely / have to / work till they are 70 or 75.

   ....

3 It / seem / .... likely / that / organic food production / increase / worldwide.

   ....

4 It / be / .... likely / rain / in London in the next five days.

   ....

5 The English language / seem / .... unlikely / die out / in the next 20 years.

   ....

6 It / be / .... likely / that / internet shopping / continue / to expand rapidly.

   ....

◀ B **4** Underline the most suitable words in italics in these economic predictions.

1 Ro-Steel *is set to* / *is due to* become the world's largest producer of steel by 2020.

2 Eco-tourism *is supposed to* / *is expected to* continue to grow over the coming decade.

3 NX Radio *is about to* / *is expected to* launch a sport-only TV channel. It will start broadcasting this Friday.

4 The government *is to* / *is due to* raise the tax on diesel fuel from midnight, it was announced today.

5 Patora City *is set to* / *is supposed to* have the world's biggest golf course. It will open two years from now.

6 The fashion industry *is expected to* / *is to* grow by 20–25% over the next year, analysts predicted today.

◀ A–C **5** Find and correct three mistakes in each of these emails.

1
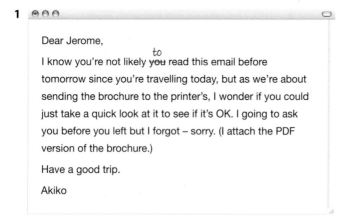

Dear Jerome,
                    to
I know you're not likely ~~you~~ read this email before tomorrow since you're travelling today, but as we're about sending the brochure to the printer's, I wonder if you could just take a quick look at it to see if it's OK. I going to ask you before you left but I forgot – sorry. (I attach the PDF version of the brochure.)

Have a good trip.

Akiko

2
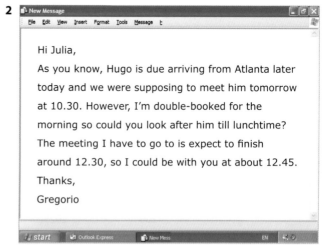

Hi Julia,

As you know, Hugo is due arriving from Atlanta later today and we were supposing to meet him tomorrow at 10.30. However, I'm double-booked for the morning so could you look after him till lunchtime? The meeting I have to go to is expect to finish around 12.30, so I could be with you at about 12.45.

Thanks,

Gregorio

Make it personal

Write a sentence about each of these.

a something you were going to do or were supposed to do recently but didn't

b something that is due to happen at your workplace

c something that is set to change at your workplace

12 Business talk: Future time expressions

Here are some time expressions for talking about the future that are often used in business.

- *going forward* and *looking ahead*

  The company sees excellent opportunities in e-commerce **going forward**. (starting now and continuing into the future)

  Looking ahead, the hotel's advance bookings for the summer are very good. (looking into the future)

  ◉ *Going forward* is especially common in business situations but not in everyday, non-business conversations.

- *In the near/immediate/foreseeable future*

  Intense competition will continue in the electronics market **in the foreseeable future**. (as far into the future as you can imagine or plan for)

  There is no sign of economic recovery **in the near/immediate future**. (soon – *immediate future* usually means sooner than *near future*)

  ◉ *In the near future* is much more common in business contexts than *in the immediate future*.

- *In the short/medium/long/longer term*

  I don't think there'll be any improvement in business **in the short term**. (for a short period of time in the future)

  Autodal International plans to double its production of cars **in the medium term**. (for a medium period of time in the future)

  Space tourism is expected to grow **in the long/longer term**. (over a long period of time)

  ◉ *In the long term* is more common than *in the longer term*.

6 Complete this conversation between two fund managers talking about future growth in their sector. Use expressions from the presentation to mean the same as the words in brackets.

LYDIA: Andreas, what do you think growth is likely to be in your sector this year?

ANDREAS: Well, low interest rates are expected to stimulate consumer confidence by the second half of this year, so we're pretty optimistic **1** *in the medium term* (over a medium period). But **2** .... (for a short period of time) I think we'll continue to see a slight drop in the market, and **3** .... (in the period of time nearest to now) I think we need to continue to be very careful to minimise risk for investors.

LYDIA: And what about the general financial picture **4** .... (as far into the future as you can see)? What's your view?

ANDREAS: Well, after a difficult start to the year, I think that things are likely to improve **5** .... (starting now and continuing into the future). And actually, **6** .... (looking into the future), there is every reason to be optimistic about the general global situation. **7** .... (over a longer period of time) it's harder to predict, but I'm hopeful that the situation will continue to improve.

LYDIA: Well, it's good to hear that you're generally optimistic.

ANDREAS: Yes, I am.

◉ 12.1 Listen and check your answers.

Make it personal

You can search online for texts about the future. For example, search for 'business forecast' and 'going forward' and look at some of the results. Try searching for some of the other expressions presented in this unit.

Emphasising and softening

Read this conversation between two colleagues.

Which words do the speakers use to:
a   emphasise a point?
b   soften what they say?

> It sort of feels a bit strange to have a tidy office.

> I know. I really do think this is the tidiest I've seen your desk.

A Emphasising

People often emphasise what they say to show others how strongly they feel about something.

A1 You can use these words to add emphasis.

extremely/very/really/so + adjective/adverb	*Our boss is **so disorganised**. He's **very often** late.*
really + verb	*I **really hope** we'll do well this year.*
verb + *very much / a lot*	*I'm **enjoying** my new job **very much / a lot**.*
just [stressed] + adjective/adverb/verb/noun	*My new office is **just amazing**. I **just love** it.*
such (a/an) + (adjective) + noun	*My office is **such a** (**terrible**) **mess**.*

A2 You can use *absolutely/completely totally*, especially with adjectives and verbs. *Absolutely* is often used before *no* and *nothing*.

*Sorry, I **completely** forgot.   I've **absolutely no** idea what's wrong with my phone.*

> The most common adjectives used with these words in spoken English are: *absolutely right/fine; completely different/wrong; totally different/wrong.*

A3 In negative sentences and short answers you can use (*not*) *at all*.

A: *Do you mind if I take tomorrow off?*   B: *No, **not at all**. That's **no** problem **at all**.*

A4 You can say *I do* + verb, especially *think, know, like* or *feel*.

*I **do think** we should send out price lists with the new brochures.*

B Softening

People also often soften what they say to sound less direct, less critical or more polite.

B1 You can use these expressions to soften what you say.

I think	*I **think** we need to look at our reporting lines.*
maybe / perhaps / probably	*Perhaps we should cut back on our spending. We **probably** should.*
sort of / kind of + verb/adjective/adverb	*I **sort of** want to leave the arrangements **kind of** flexible for now.*
a (little) bit / a little / slightly + adjective/adverb	*I always feel **a little bit / slightly** uncomfortable when I meet the CEO.*
just [not stressed] + noun/verb/adjective/adverb	*I was **just** calling to say hello. **Just** a second.*

B2 You can also use *not very* or *not really*. *Not really* can be a polite way to say 'no'.

*This program is **not very / not really** easy to use.*
A: *Are you enjoying your new job?*   B: ***Not really**.*

> ⚠ But *really not* emphasises the idea. Compare:

*I **don't really like** our new Account Manager. (softer than I don't like)*
*I **really don't like** our new Account Manager. (stronger than I don't like)*

Practice

◄ A   **1**   **Look at these comments from staff when they were shown round their new modern offices for the first time. Emphasise their comments using the words in brackets.**

        very   so

1   I'm ⁄ impressed – it's ⁄ stylish.   (*very/so*)

2   It's different from what I expected.   (*completely*)

3   I like it.   (*do / a lot*)

4   It'll make a difference, going into work.   (*such*)

5   It's wonderful. It's fabulous.   (*absolutely/just*)

6   I won't miss the old offices.   (*at all*)

7   The furniture looks expensive.   (*extremely*)

8   I'm looking forward to working here.   (*really*)

9   They've planned the space well.   (*really*)

10   I must say thank you to the design team.   (*very much*)

◄ B   **2**   **Two partners are discussing a new advertising leaflet for their business. Soften their criticisms by underlining the most suitable words in italics.**

MIGUEL: It's **1** *so / a bit* disappointing. I **2** *don't really / really don't* like it. Do you?

ELENA: No. **3** *Not at all. / Not really.*

MIGUEL: I **4** *just/really* feel that as publicity it's **5** *not really / really not* projecting the image we want.

ELENA: I know. **6** *I think / I really think* it looks **7** *a bit / so* old-fashioned.

MIGUEL: It's **8** *really / sort of* weird – it **9** *kind of / really* looks like it's from the 1980s.

ELENA: **10** *Perhaps that's / That's totally* deliberate. It's called 'retro'.

MIGUEL: You're **11** *probably / absolutely* right.

ELENA: The marketing message isn't **12** *very clear / clear at all*.

MIGUEL: Yeah. Are the photos **13** *slightly / very much* out of focus?

ELENA: Yes, they are – **14** *a little bit / a lot*.

MIGUEL: We **15** *absolutely / maybe* need to get some alternative designs.

🔘 SS 3.1   **Listen and check your answers.**

◄ A   **3**   **Add expressions to emphasise (↑) or soften (↓) what this office manager says about one of his administrative assistants.**

Have you got a minute? I **1** ….just…. ↓ wanted to talk to you about Hannah. **2** ………………………… ↓ this is nothing to worry about, but I mean she used to be **3** ………………………… ↑ efficient. And lately she's – well, if I'm **4** ………………………… ↑ honest, she's become **5** ………………………… ↓ absent-minded. She's **6** ………………………… ↑ easily distracted, you know. Her mind is not on the job **7** ………………………… ↑. But she's **8** ………………………… ↑ a sensitive person – she **9** ………………………… ↑ gets upset if anyone criticises her. I **10** ………………………… ↑ don't want to take disciplinary action, but I don't know what to do.

🔘 SS 3.2   **Listen and compare your answers.**

Test 3: Units 9–12

1 Complete this advertisement for a new supermarket using *will* or *won't*.

Our new store **1** ....*will*.... offer our customers more products than before. Of course, you **2** .... still be able to buy all your favourite items. And you **3** .... need to worry about higher prices as we **4** .... continue to offer excellent bargains to all our customers.

Please complete our online survey about your shopping habits. This **5** .... help us to offer the products you want. Also on our website there **6** .... often be new products to choose from. Go to the site to see what's on offer.

Visit the new store today. You **7** .... be sorry.

2 Underline the correct words in italics in each sentence.

1 We *expand / 're going to expand* our product range to meet the growing market.

2 Oil stocks are running out, so obviously the price of petrol *is going to rise / rises* steeply.

3 A: My computer's crashed.
B: Don't worry. I'*m going to help / 'll help* you.

4 I'*m meeting / 'll meet* the accountant this afternoon. Do you have anything for him?

5 As soon as Ms Karsova *will arrive / arrives*, please send her in.

6 *I think the meeting won't finish / I don't think the meeting will finish* before 6 pm.

7 *I expect the CEO won't freeze / I don't expect the CEO will freeze* salaries this year.

8 *Will we start / Shall we start*? I think everyone's here now.

9 *Is the company going to make / Does the company make* a profit by the end of this year?

10 How many people *will be / are* at the presentation tomorrow evening?

3 Complete these sentences using the verbs in brackets in the future continuous or future perfect.

1 It is 10 am now. I'm giving a presentation tomorrow between 9 and 12.

This time tomorrow, I'*ll be giving* ..... (*give*) a presentation.

2 It is 12:30 now. I'm giving a presentation tomorrow between 9 and 12.

By this time tomorrow, I .... (*give*) my presentation.

3 My company has moved to a new building. I now work in a new office.

I .... (*not work*) in my old office from now on.

4 We need more staff. We've put an advertisement in *The Economist* from tomorrow.

We .... (*advertise*) for new staff from tomorrow.

5 You took an exam last month. You expect the results next week.

The exam board .... (*not send*) the results yet.

6 I need the report by the end of today. I want to know if it will be ready in time.

.... (*you finish*) it by tonight?

7 Your clients usually stay at the Hilton. You want to know if they will stay at the Hilton again next week.

.... (*you stay*) at the Hilton again?

8 You are getting a new company car. They promised to deliver it this afternoon.

I hope they .... (*deliver*) it by 5:30. I need it this evening.

4 Complete this extract from an airline company's website using the words in the box.

> are due to   are expected to   in the foreseeable future   is extremely unlikely that
> is likely that   is set to   Looking ahead   ~~seems highly likely to~~   were supposed to

Blujet Airways has already won a number of Best Airline awards and it **1** ...seems highly likely... to win many more in the near future. Profits have grown every year and they **2** .... continue to increase.

Our company **3** .... be among the first to run routes using the new 555-seater Airbus super jumbos. The first jumbos **4** .... be ready earlier this year, but they took longer than expected. The good news is that they are now ready and **5** .... be delivered within the next month.

6 ...., we hope that the bigger planes will help us to increase the number of passengers who fly with us. As a result, it **7** .... with these bigger planes we will be able to introduce lower fares. Competitive pricing is critical to the success of this venture, so it **8** .... we will increase the fares **9** ....

5 A CEO is telling her staff about a new conference centre. Underline the correct words in italics in her speech.

As many of you know we **1** *are going to build* / *will build* a new conference centre in King Street. The construction **2** *was supposed to start* / *is due to start* two months ago, but sadly the planning permission was delayed. So I am pleased to announce that we now have the permission and construction **3** *starts* / *isn't expected to start* next week. We **4** *are marking* / *are likely to mark* the occasion with a ceremony on the site. Of course you are all invited.

5 *Looking ahead,* / *It seems likely*, the first phase **6** *doesn't finish* / *is not due to finish* until early in the new year. Once this **7** *happens* / *will happen*, we **8** *are expected to organise* / *will be organising* visits to the site for small groups from each department.

It **9** *was supposed to* / *seems likely that* the final phase **10** *won't be* / *isn't being* complete by the end of the summer, although we don't expect that it **11** *won't be* / *will be* delayed beyond autumn at the latest. By then, we hope that we **12** *are expected to recruit and train* / *will have recruited and trained* a large number of new staff to work in the centre.

As soon as the conference centre **13** *is* / *is going to be* ready, we **14** *are about to invite* / *are going to invite* all the local businesses to an opening party. The new conference centre **15** *is due to host* / *is expected to host* up to 30 conferences a year and I am confident that the venue **16** *will be* / *is supposed to be* a success.

6 Complete the questions in this conversation about a conference using the correct form of the words in brackets.

NATALIE: Hi, David. **1** .Are. you. going. (*you/go*) to the conference tomorrow?

DAVID: Yes, I am. **2** .... (*How many people / you / think / attend*)?

NATALIE: Oh, at least 350, I expect.

DAVID: Wow, that's great. By the way, **3** .... (*what time / the conference / start*)?

NATALIE: At nine, but we'll be there earlier to set up.

DAVID: **4** .... (*I / come along*) then to help you?

NATALIE: That would be great, thanks.

DAVID: No problem. I can help at the end as well, if you want. **5** .... (*What time / we / supposed / leave*) the building?

NATALIE: Around seven, I think.

DAVID: **6** .... (*the presentions / finish*) by then? There are a lot of speakers.

NATALIE: I guess so, but it's a tight schedule.

DAVID: Yes, and I want to have time to meet some of the speakers during the day. **7** .... (*they / sign*) their books during the breaks?

NATALIE: I expect so. It's a good way for them to meet the audience.

DAVID: Great. One last question, **8** .... (*you / likely / need*) any help getting things ready this afternoon?

NATALIE: Thanks, but I think everything's under control.

13 Modals 1 (talking about possibility and ability, asking, offering and giving permission)

Read this sentence about starting a new business.

What do you think *can* means here?

a something is possible but it is not probable

b something is possible and it does actually happen

> When you start a small business, finding answers to the most important questions can mean the difference between success and failure.

A Talking about possibility and ability: *can* and *could*

A1 You use *can* to talk about things which are possible in the present because they do actually happen or are sometimes true.

> You **can** get a train from London to Rome.
> Meetings **can** go on all night if we've got a tight deadline.

A2 You use *can/can't* to talk about people's abilities in the present.

> **Can** you speak Spanish?
> I'm sorry, we **can't** offer free delivery outside the EU.

> ⊙ *Cannot* is possible instead of *can't* but is very formal and emphatic.

A3 You use *could* to talk about things that were sometimes true or people's general abilities in the past.

> My ex-boss was a brilliant salesman; he **could** sell anything!
> Ten years ago you **couldn't** get a flight to Athens for under €200.

> ⚠ Don't use *could* for things people were able to do on one particular occasion.

> The client got angry but I **managed to / was able to** calm her down. (**not** *I could calm*)

B Talking about possibility and ability: *be able to*

B1 You use (*not*) *be able to / be unable to* with other tenses, not *can('t)*.

> In five years' time we'**ll be able to** have high-definition video conferences. (**not** *we will can*)
> **Would you be able to** get here by 9 am?
> I'**ve been unable to** / I **haven't been able to** reach him all morning. He must be in a meeting.

B2 ⊙ You can use *be able/unable to* instead of *can('t)* in more formal situations in the present.

> **Are you able to** join us for dinner tonight?
> We **are not able to / are unable to** give you a guaranteed price at this point in time.

C Asking for something

C1 You use *can/could/may I* to ask someone for something.

> A: **Can/could/may I** have a non-smoking room, please?
> B: Yes, of course (you **can/may**). (**not** *of course you could*)

> ⚠ Don't use *could* in short answers if someone asks for something or asks for permission.

> ⊙ *May* and *could* are more formal than *can*.

C2 You use *can/could/would you* or *would/do you mind + ing* to ask someone to do something.

> A: **Can/Could/Would you** send me a copy of your presentation notes, please?
> B: Yes, of course (I **can/could/would**).

> ⊙ *Could* is more formal than *can*.

> A: **Would/Do you mind giving** me a lift home?
> B: No, not at all. / Sure. / No problem.

> ⊙ *Would you mind + -ing* is more common than *do you mind + -ing*.

▶ See Unit 15 (Modals 3).

D Asking for and giving permission, offering

D1 You use *can/could/may I / do you mind if* + present simple / *would you mind if* + past simple to ask for permission. The positive answer to *do/would you mind if* is *no*, not *yes*.

> A: **Can/could/may I** use your office while you're away?
> B: Yes, you **can/may**. (**not** *Yes, you could.*)

> A: **Do you mind if I come** to your meeting?
> B: **No, of course not**.

> A: **Would you mind if I left** early today?
> B: **No, not at all**.

> ⊙ *Would you mind if* + past tense is less common than *do you mind if* + present tense.

D2 You use *will/can* to offer to do something.

> That's a heavy suitcase. I'**ll/can** carry it for you. (**not** *I carry it*)

Practice

◀ A1 **1** Complete these extracts from a training seminar using the verb in brackets in the present tense or with *can*. Sometimes both are possible.

Good branding of a product **1** ....is...... (be) important because
it **2** ....(create) brand loyalty. If the customer's
experience **3** ....(be) positive, they'll buy more. And
customers **4** ....(be) very loyal to products which they
5 ....(like). If they like a product, this **6** ....(lead)
them to buy other products with the
same brand name.

Your behaviour towards your employees **7** ....(have)
a huge impact on the success of your company. If you
8 ....(have) poor management skills, you are likely
to lose good staff. What's more, bad management
9 ....(result) in low morale, which **10** ....(be)
always disastrous for any business, large or small.

◀ A1–3 **2** Rewrite these sentences using *can('t)*, *could(n't)* or *be able/unable*. Use the full forms *cannot* and *could not* where the situation seems more formal.

1 It's possible to get a direct train from where I live to the station near my office.

  .....*I/You can get a direct train from where I live to the station near my office.*.....................

2 Do you know how to add dates to a spreadsheet? Because I certainly don't know how to do it!

  ....

3 Iris managed to persuade Philip to speak at the sales conference.

  ....

4 I didn't manage to get hold of Flavio yesterday because it was a public holiday in Brazil.

  ....

5 Did they hear what we were saying? It was a terrible line!

  ....

6 Small, local stores found it impossible to compete with the new superstore and were forced to close.

  ....

7 It's normal for the weather to be very hot and humid in New York in August.

  ....

8 The assistant I had at Mantech knew how to speak four languages.

  ....

◀ B–D **3** Choose the correct ending for each question.

1 Do you mind if
2 Are the directors able to
3 Why were they unable to
4 Would you mind
5 Would you mind if

6 May I
7 Could you
8 Have you been able to
9 Can Maria

a observe your team at work? She's just started today.
b get hold of Gina Suarez yet? I really need to talk to her urgently.
c take a look at this later? I'd appreciate your opinion.
d I used your phone? Mine's not working.
e join us for lunch? We would be delighted to have the pleasure of their company.
f I leave early today? It's my son's birthday.
g deliver on time? What was the problem?
h looking after this projector while I'm away?
i sit next to you?

13

◀ A–D **4** Write sentences using *can*, *could*, *be able to* and *may*. Sometimes more than one answer is possible.

1 You see a colleague carrying two large boxes. Offer to carry one of them.

.....I'll carry one of them..........

2 Ask one of your team if it will be possible for them to speak at the sales conference.

....

3 You want to book a business-class flight to Bangkok. Get a price from an airline agent.

....

4 You want a room with a sea view. Ask for one at the hotel check-in.

....

5 Reply giving permission to someone who asks, 'Could I use this desk for an hour or so?'

....

6 Ask a senior manager if it is possible for them to attend your group meeting today.

....

7 Ask someone if it's possible for them to come to your showroom personally.

....

8 Tell someone very politely that it is not possible to offer credit.

....

13.1 **Listen and compare your answers with what the speakers actually say.**

◀ A–D **5** Read this email from a university professor to her MBA students. Rewrite the sentences (1–6) using the words in brackets.

| To: | MBA Students |
| Subject: | Guest seminar |

Dear MBA students,

1 (*can*) I want to ask you all to make sure you are free for a special guest seminar with the President of Quantra International, Mr Jan Rundaf, on 27 October. **2** (*able*) Mr Rundaf is a very busy person but I am delighted to say that we managed to find an evening when he was free. **3** (*we*) It will be possible for us to spend two hours with him to discuss international business trends. **4** (*able*) We have managed to book the Chesham Room, which is a wonderful venue for such an important meeting. **5** (*could*) We hope to start at 7:30, so please all make a special effort to be punctual. **6** (*cannot*) It is not possible for me to say at the moment how many questions Mr Rundaf will take, but do prepare any questions you would like answers to. Please reply to the department office by 15 October.

Best wishes,

Margaret Grossman (Prof.)

1 Can I ask you all to / Can you all make sure you are free for a special guest seminar with the President of Quantra International, Mr Jan Rundaf, on 27 October?

2 ....

3 ....

4 ....

5 ....

6 ....

Make it personal

Think of someone in your company or at your workplace who you often have to be rather formal/polite with. Think of five sentences using *May I …? Do you mind if I …? Would/could you …?* that you could use with that person in an English-speaking context.

13 Write for business: Alternatives to modal verbs

There are other verbs and expressions that can express similar meanings to *can*, and which are often used in formal business writing.

- *enable/allow/permit someone to do something*

  You **can** *organise all your contact information with this software.*
  → *This software* **enables/allows/permits you to organise** *all your contact information.*

- *let someone do something*

  A company **can** *monitor every phone call with this technology.*
  → *This technology* **lets a company monitor** *every phone call.* (**not** ~~lets a company to monitor~~)

- *make it possible (for someone) to do something*

  You **can** *upload large files quickly with broadband.*
  → *Broadband* **makes it possible** (**for you**) **to upload** *large files quickly.* (**not** ~~Broadband makes possible to upload~~)

- *be known to do something*

  Plastic handles **can** *break very easily, so we use high-quality metal ones instead.*
  → *Plastic handles* **are known to break** *very easily, so we use high-quality metal ones instead.*

---

6 Read this webpage for a graphic design company that specialises in designing brochures. Rewrite the words in italics using the correct form of the verbs in brackets.

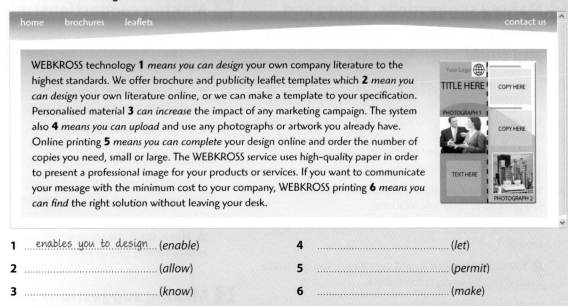

WEBKROSS technology **1** *means you can design* your own company literature to the highest standards. We offer brochure and publicity leaflet templates which **2** *mean you can design* your own literature online, or we can make a template to your specification. Personalised material **3** *can increase* the impact of any marketing campaign. The system also **4** *means you can upload* and use any photographs or artwork you already have. Online printing **5** *means you can complete* your design online and order the number of copies you need, small or large. The WEBKROSS service uses high-quality paper in order to present a professional image for your products or services. If you want to communicate your message with the minimum cost to your company, WEBKROSS printing **6** *means you can find* the right solution without leaving your desk.

1 <u>enables you to design</u> (*enable*)   4 .... (*let*)

2 .... (*allow*)   5 .... (*permit*)

3 .... (*know*)   6 .... (*make*)

7 Correct the mistakes in these sentences.

1 The webcam on our PC at home lets me ~~to~~ see my children when I'm travelling.

2 This database enables us access all our customers' contact details immediately.

3 This type of conveyor belt knows to develop faults after a year or so of operation.

4 The new hardware makes possible to have very good quality video conferences.

5 Our new system allows us tracking orders more efficiently.

6 The server does not permission users to download software upgrades.

Make it personal

Write a sentence about each of the following.

a something that has enabled your company to provide a better product or service

b something that is known to be a regular problem at your workplace and

c an aspect of technology that allows you to do your job more efficiently

14

Modals 2 (making suggestions and giving advice)

Read this advertisement.

a How many suggestions or pieces of advice can you see?

b What structures are used to give advice and suggestions?

Starting a small business? You should talk to our trained advisors. You might want to drop in for a chat sometime. You could give us a call or email us, to set up a meeting.

A Making suggestions, giving and asking for advice: *should, ought to* and *could*

A1 You can use *should (n't)* or *ought (not) to* to make a strong suggestion.

You **should / ought to** *phone and tell him you'll be late.* (this is the best thing to do)
We **shouldn't / ought not to** *have that training session tomorrow. Nobody can come.*

A2 You can also use *you should (n't)* to make informal suggestions or recommendations.

You should *see the Great Wall if you're going to Beijing;* **you shouldn't** *miss it.*

⚠ *You should (n't)* can sound very direct. You can make it less direct by using *I (don't) think.*

I think you should probably *keep your money in euros for now.*
I don't think you should *invest in property at the moment.*

A3 You can make less direct suggestions or give advice using *could*. People also use *could* when they want to suggest one possible action out of several.

A: *Can I help you?*
B: *You* **could** *do the photocopying.* (or you could make some tea)

A: *Where's Henry?*
B: **Could** *you phone him and find out?*

👁 *Should* and *could* are more common for making suggestions than *ought to* in a business context.

A4 You can also use *should I* in questions to ask for advice.

Should I *have the meeting before lunch?*

⚠ Don't generally repeat the second verb in a reply.

A: **Should I** *call our new supplier to find out what's wrong?*
B: *Yes, (I think) you* **should**. (not ~~Yes, you should call.~~)

B Making suggestions: *might*

B1 If you want to make polite suggestions or to say that something is a good idea but not essential you can use *might like/want + to*-infinitive or *might be better off + -ing.*

You **might want/like to attend** *my presentation tomorrow.*
We **might be better off discussing** *this in tomorrow's meeting.*

B2 You can also make suggestions using *might/may as well* when you want to say something is probably the only option, but you do not feel very excited about it.

We **might as well** *stop there as it's getting late.*
The meeting's been cancelled so I **may as well** *finish that report instead.*

⚠ This is spoken language and would not be appropriate in formal written reports.

C Making suggestions and asking for advice: *shall*

C1 You can use *shall we* to make suggestions about what you and other people could do.

So, **shall we** *move on to the next item on the agenda?*

C2 You can also use *shall I* to ask for advice.

What **shall I** *say to our Brazilian agent?* (asking advice)

⚠ Don't use *shall* in a reply.

A: *What* **shall I** *do with the feedback surveys?*
B: *You* **could/should** *present the data at our next team meeting.* (not ~~You shall present~~)

Practice

◄ A1, 3 | **1** Write sentences giving candidates advice about job interviews using these ideas and *could, ought (not) to* and *should (n't)*. Then add two more suggestions of your own.

> At an interview, it's essential to:
>
> * arrive on time
>
> * do some research into the job and the company
>
> It's a good idea to:
>
> * take extra copies of your CV
>
> * avoid discussing salaries before you get an offer
>
> Don't:
>
> * forget to ask questions
>
> * be negative about yourself

1 <u>You should / ought to arrive on time.</u>

2 ....

3 ....

4 ....

5 ....

6 ....

7 ....

8 ....

◄ A, B1, C | **2** Write questions using the words in brackets in the correct order. Then complete the answers using *might, should (n't)* or *could*.

1 A: If I'm feeling nervous in the interview, <u>shall I chew gum to relax</u>? (*chew / gum / I / shall / to relax*)

B: You <u>shouldn't</u> do that. It's impolite.

2 A: I'm going to be late to the interview. ....? (*I / them / phone / shall*)

B: You .... call if possible, so people don't have to wait for you.

3 A: I don't really want this job. ....? (*should / I / what / do*)

B: You .... as well do the interview for practice.

4 A: ....? (*wear / I / a suit and tie / should*)

B: It doesn't matter for this job. You .... wear a suit or you .... dress more informally.

5 A: I want to be ready for the interview. ....? (*practise / questions / answering / should / I*)

B: Of course many people do, but you .... look over-prepared.

◄ A, B **3** Look at this article about negotiation. If the words in italics are correct, tick (✓) them. If they are wrong, replace them with a suitable word or phrase.

Preparing for a negotiation

First and most important, you **1** *could* prepare for a negotiation by thinking in detail about your needs and interests. You **2** *should* also consider the needs and interests of your opponent. Then you **3** *ought to* try to predict all the possible outcomes of the negotiation. If you have time, you **4** *could* research different sources for useful information.

Before you begin you **5** *might as well* prepare a list of the most important negotiating points. You **6** *could* decide how important each point is for you and your opponent, because planning an effective agenda is almost impossible without this information. Then you **7** *might want to* think about other areas for discussion. You **8** *could* look for areas where you want the same outcome; it will save you both a lot of time (and money). You **9** *couldn't* have a fixed idea of your opponent's needs and interests. You **10** *might like to* remain flexible as the negotiation progresses – if you don't, it may be an expensive mistake.

1	~~could~~ should
2	............✓............
3	....
4	....
5	....
6	....
7	....
8	....
9	....
10	....

◄ A, B **4** Complete this talk about laptop security using suitable modal expressions and the verbs in brackets.

Have you marked your computer with your company details? According to the FBI, 97% of unmarked computers are never recovered, so you **1** ....*should mark*.... (mark) your laptop with your company details. Also you **2** .... (buy) a lock or alarm for your laptop.

Unbelievably, almost 40% of laptop thefts occur in the office. A good solution is a laptop docking station, which locks the laptop in place. You **3** .... (use) it whenever you are working in the office. And you **4** .... (install) software that enables your laptop to be tracked by the police, but it is expensive.

You **5** .... (carry) it in a backpack when you're out of the office, not a case with the manufacturer's logo on it. And if you're staying in a hotel, don't assume your room is safe. When you're not in your room, you **6** .... (lock) your laptop in the hotel safe. Remember, you **7** .... (make) it easy for thieves. Finally, make security a habit. You **8** .... (try) to stay in physical contact with your laptop at all times.

◄ A–D **5** Underline the most suitable expressions in italics in these suggestions. Sometimes both are possible.

1 Your manager says: 'Head office are giving each department $1,000 for office improvements.'

You say: '*You might as well ask* / You could ask the staff for their ideas.'

2 A friend at work says: 'Do you know a good restaurant to take some clients to?'

You say: '*You should go* / *You might be better off going* to the Alcazar. It's excellent.'

3 A colleague at work says: 'Could you help me with the slides for my presentation tomorrow?'

You say: '*Shall we do* / *We might as well do* it after lunch.'

4 A new colleague says: 'I've just had my salary and I think there's been a mistake with it.'

You say: '*You should talk* / *You might want to talk* to Mr McNeff, the Accounts Manager.'

5 A junior colleague says: 'I need a couple of days off work to move house.'

You say: '*You ought to talk* / *Could you talk* to your line manager about it?'

6 A supplier says: 'I'd like to renegotiate your payment terms.'

You say: '*Could we arrange* / *We should arrange* a meeting about this.'

Make it personal

Have you got any advice for people who want to do business in your country? Write six sentences using language from this unit.

14 **Business talk:** Other ways of making informal suggestions

People often say *How/What about + -ing/noun* and *Why don't you/we + infinitive without to* to make suggestions in informal contexts.

A: *Where shall we have this presentation?*
B: **What about having** *it in the boardroom?*
C: **How about a meeting room?**
D: *Well,* **why don't we book** *a room in a hotel?*

You can also say *Do you want + to-infinitive.*

Do you want to take *a bit of time to think it over?* (I think you should do this)

You can also use *if I were you, I'd ('d = would)* and *let's* to make suggestions.

If I were you, I'd *go for that promotion.* (you should go for that promotion)
Let's *stop for a coffee.* (shall we stop?)

---

6 **Complete these suggestions with suitable ideas. Sometimes more than one answer is possible.**

1 A: Everyone looks exhausted.
   B: Let's ....*take a five minute break*........................... .

2 A: What's the best way to keep key staff, apart from higher salaries?
   B: Why don't you .... ?

3 A: I'm having problems with my PC – I keep getting error messages.
   B: If I were you, ...

4 A: TV and radio advertising are too expensive for our budget.
   B: How about .... ?

5 A: I can't make Monday's meeting. Any suggestions for a new date?
   B: Do you want .... ?

6 A: Where should we go for the staff party?
   B: How about .... ?

7 **Complete this conversation using expressions for making suggestions and the verbs in brackets. Sometimes more than one answer is possible.**

MANAGER: We want to pay our staff more money without increasing their salaries. Have you got any ideas?

COLLEAGUE: **1** ....*Why not introduce*.... (*introduce*) a bonus scheme?

MANAGER: It'll take too long. I mean, the results aren't out until the new year.

COLLEAGUE: **2** .... (*start*) it in January?

MANAGER: Well, maybe. Anyway, how do you think it should work?

COLLEAGUE: **3** .... (*link*) it to staff performance?

MANAGER: Mmm, I suppose that's the best option. How do you think we should begin?

COLLEAGUE: **4** .... (*talk*) to the staff representatives as soon as possible?

MANAGER: What do you mean by as soon as possible?

COLLEAGUE: **5** .... (*arrange*) a meeting for next week, say Tuesday.

MANAGER: OK, if you think that's manageable. One more thing. Do you think we should announce this yet?

COLLEAGUE: **6** .... (*wait*) until after the first meeting.

MANAGER: I agree. OK, we'll talk about this again tomorrow morning, shall we?

🔘 **14.1 Listen and compare your answers. Then take the role of the colleague and answer the questions.**

Make it personal

What advice would you give to a manager who wanted to motivate staff in your company?

15

Modals 3 (saying what people have to do)

Read this text about how to give a good business presentation.

Underline the different ways the writer tells the reader what to do.

You must make your points clearly and simply; you need to say enough to give all the most important information, but don't give your audience too much information, or they may forget it. You don't need to tell them everything. Remember, everyone in your audience is a busy person, so you have to give them what they feel is relevant.

A Telling people to do things: *must, have (got) to* and *need to*

A1 You can use *must* to tell people to do things.

You **must** call the New York office right away.

⚠ *Must* is very strong and direct, so it can sound impolite or unfriendly. Do not use *must* with more senior colleagues.

A2 *Have (got) to* and *need to* are less direct than *must*, especially *need to*.

👁 In a business context, *you need to* and *you've (got) to* are ten times more frequent than *you must*.

You**'ve got to** / **have to** / **need to** think about your target market.

A3 You can use *have (got) to* and *must* to give orders and instructions.

We **must** / **have (got) to** develop new marketing tools.

Use *have (got) to* (but not *must*) to express an obligation or necessity that is a result of an external situation.

When all the meeting rooms are busy, they **have to** hold their weekly team meeting in a cafe. (**not** ~~they must hold~~)

Use *must* to express an obligation or necessity that the speaker thinks is important.

I **must** remember to cancel my appointment. (**not** ~~I have to remember~~)

B Being polite

B1 In business, people often use *we* instead of *you* when telling someone else to do something. It sounds more friendly and less direct.

We **need to** email this to Erik in Stockholm right away.
We **have to** get it to him by 5 pm.

B2 You can use *can* / *might want to* / *'d better* (the short form of *had better*) to tell people to do things less directly.

You **can** take those spreadsheets away now.
You**'d better** / **might want to** check the exchange rate first .

◄ See Unit 14 (Modals 2).

B3 You can use question forms *can/could/will/would you …?* or *do you want to …?* to tell people to do things. *Could* and *would* are less direct and more polite than *can* and *will*.

Can/**could**/**will**/**would you** let me know when Mr Thompson arrives?
Mark, **do you want to** show us your report?

B4 You can use imperatives to tell people to do things but they can sound impolite in spoken English. Use them mostly in written instructions, rules, signs or notices.

[Tips for job interviews] **Arrive** on time, **dress** smartly, **ask** questions.
[Notice] When you hear the fire alarm, **leave** the building by the nearest fire exit.

direct ──────────► indirect		
must imperatives	have (got) to need to	can might want to 'd better question forms

C Using negative forms

C1 You can use the negative forms *don't need to, don't have to, haven't got to* and *needn't* to tell someone that something is not an obligation or not necessary.

⚠ Don't use *to* after *needn't*.

You **don't need to** / **don't have to** / **haven't got to** / **needn't** do that now; tomorrow will be okay. (**not** ~~You needn't to do~~)

C2 You can use *must not* to tell someone that something is forbidden, urgent or important.

You **must not** make personal calls during work time.
It's 1:45. You **mustn't** be late for your two o'clock appointment!

C3 You can use the negative form of other expressions from section B to tell people not to do things.

You **can't** / **might not want to** leave those papers out on your desk.
You**'d better not** leave the price list where everyone can see it.
Don't arrive before nine o'clock.

Practice

◀ A1–2 **1** How would you tell these people to do these things? Use *must*, *have (got) to* or *need to*. Sometimes more than one answer is possible.

1 Tell a colleague to read Gloria's report first before meeting with her.

You've got to read / need to read Gloria's report before meeting with her.

2 Tell a new customer to fax you their order as soon as possible.

3 Tell a junior colleague that it is important to pay attention to the feedback after her presentation.

4 Tell a friend in your workplace to make sure they get a visa before their trip to Australia.

5 Tell your personal assistant that it is necessary to email an address list to the CEO.

6 Tell a group of colleagues how important it is to check the exchange rate each day.

◀ A3 **2** Complete these sentences using *must* or the correct form of *have (got) to*. Sometimes more than one answer is possible.

1 My flight's at 8 pm, so I ...*have to*... check in at six. I .... remember to book a taxi for five o'clock.

2 She has a child at nursery school, so she usually .... leave the office by 3:30. We really .... try to finish the meeting by 3 pm so that she isn't late. She .... drive right across the city.

3 A: I'm going to the US Embassy this afternoon as I .... renew my entry visa.
   B: Right. You .... remember to take your photographs with you!

4 When you join the company, you .... complete a tax form and give it to HR.

5 We've just opened a new office in York. You .... come and see it!

6 Well, I .... stop now, as I want to make sure that there's plenty of time for questions after the talk.

◀ B **3** A manager is giving instructions to her team. Rewrite the words in italics so that they are less direct and more friendly. Sometimes more than one answer is possible.

We all have some idea of what a bad customer experience is. **1** *Find out* the right customer experience that we want to deliver in our stores. **2** *Think* about this in the existing stores. And **3** *consider* the new stores too, you know, in terms of training. Jean, you told us about the lady who set up the Excel store chain and who also worked at Prima. **4** *Invite* her to talk to us about her own experience. Then **5** *all come up with* some ideas about what the customer experience should be. **6** *Organise* that for the next meeting. In fact, **7** *make* a note of that, please, Chris. Then finally, don't forget, **8** *everyone must attend* the planning meeting tomorrow at three.

1 *You/We need to find out*   **5** ....

2 ....   **6** ....

3 ....   **7** ....

4 ....   **8** ....

🔘 **15.1 Listen and compare your answers.**

◀ **A, B** **4** **Rewrite these sentences using the words in brackets.**

1 Pass me the report, please, Terry. (*can*)

......*Can you pass me the report, Terry?*......

2 Make sure you have the correct email addresses in the database. (*need*)

....

3 Follow up every meeting with a courtesy phone call. Is that clear? (*must*)

....

4 Let me know immediately if Mr Madureira calls. (*could*)

....

5 Cancel your group meeting tomorrow. Something urgent has come up. (*better*)

....

6 Make ten photocopies of this, please. (*would*)

....

◀ **C** **5** **Complete these sentences using *mustn't* or *don't have to*. Say whether the action is not necessary, forbidden or very important.**

1 You ......*mustn't*.... leave your passport behind when you go to the airport. They won't let you check in if you don't have it. *very important*

2 You .... read all those memos from Head Office, only the ones marked 'urgent'.

3 You .... leave the building through any door except the main entrance.

4 You .... go to lunch before the official lunch break. That's a company rule.

5 You .... tell me about every phone call we get. I only need to hear about the important ones.

Make it personal

Write down three things you regularly tell people to do. Then think of two ways to give each instruction in English, one strong way and one less direct way.

Write down three things that are forbidden or not allowed at your workplace, and three things that are not necessary.

You can use *really*, *actually* and *definitely* to make an instruction stronger.

*It's easy to make mistakes, so you **really** have to go through the order in detail.*
*You **definitely** need to contact the agents. You might **actually** want to do that first.*

You can use *just*, *perhaps/maybe* and (*personally,*) *I think* to make an order sound more friendly.

*You can **just** give them a one-off price, **perhaps**.*
(***Personally,***) ***I think*** *we need to send a reminder immediately.*

You can use *please*, especially with imperatives to make instructions sound polite.

Please *copy me in on all the emails.* ***Please*** *don't forget.*

You can give polite instructions using *if*-clauses with *will/would* and *can/could*. *Would* and *could* are more polite than *will* and *can*.

If you'd / you could *come this way, Mr Swan will see you now.* (come this way)
If you can/will *just sign there, please. Thank you.* (sign here)

---

6 Rewrite these instructions using the words in brackets and a suitable modal expression from this unit. Say whether the new version is stronger or more polite. Sometimes more than one answer is possible.

1 Postpone the trip till next month. (*really*)

    You really have to / need to / must postpone the trip till next month. (stronger)

2 Keep an eye on the exchange rate. (*definitely*)

    ....

3 Take on more staff during the busy period. (*personally*)

    ....

4 Try to sort it out today instead of waiting. (*perhaps*)

    ....

5 Don't use the same spreadsheet for both orders. (*actually*)

    ....

6 Finish the meeting by 4 pm. (*really*)

    ....

7 Switch off the lights. (*if*)

    ....

8 Wait another week or so before you call them again. (*just*)

    ....

7 Rewrite these orders using *if* so that they are more polite.

1 Just give me your email address, please. Thanks. I'll email you tomorrow.

    If you'd just give me your email address, please. Thanks. I'll email you tomorrow.

2 Come this way, please.

    ....

3 Just close the door, please, Robert. Thanks. OK, let's begin the meeting.

    ....

4 Get James Hartley on the phone for me, please. I'll return his call.

    ....

Make it personal

Are the ways of telling people to do things in this unit similar or different in your first language? If there are differences, what are they?

Modals 4 (speculating and saying how certain you are)

Read this extract from a business news website.

Which of these statements does the writer think is definitely true?

a The company want a new CEO.

b Jim Brown will be the new CEO.

c The current CEO's job is safe.

d The CEO is under more and more pressure.

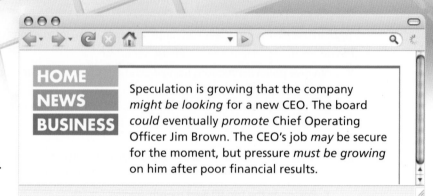

Speculation is growing that the company *might be looking* for a new CEO. The board *could* eventually *promote* Chief Operating Officer Jim Brown. The CEO's job *may* be secure for the moment, but pressure *must be growing* on him after poor financial results.

A Saying how certain you are: *must, have (got) to, can't*

A1 You can use *must* or *have (got) to* to say that you are certain something is true or will definitely happen in the future.

*That **must** be Steve on the phone. (I'm sure it is him because he said he would call now)*

*House prices **have got to** go down – the current level of growth is unsustainable. (I think house prices will go down)*

A2 You can use *can't* to say that you are certain something is not true or will definitely not happen in the future.

*Inflation is 40%? That **can't** be right, it was only 3%. (I'm sure it is a mistake)*

⚠️ Don't use *mustn't*.

*$50 per piece? That **can't** be right. It was only $20 a week ago. (**not** That mustn't be right)*

A3 You can use *will/won't* to say that you think something is definitely going to happen in the future.

*We **will** reach an agreement eventually, I'm sure.*

B Talking about expectations: *should(n't), ought (not) to*

B1 You can use *should(n't)* or *ought (not) to* to say that you expect something is true or will happen in the future.

*Their plane landed at two o'clock, so they **should** get here soon. Paul **shouldn't** be long – he's just gone to get a sandwich. The new part **ought to** be here by Friday. (I think it is probable, but I'm not certain)*

👁️ *Should* and *ought to* have very similar meanings to each other, but *should* is much more common.

B2 You can use *should(n't)* or *ought (not) to* to say that something is not as you expected.

*John **should** be at this meeting. I wonder why he's not here. (I was expecting him)*

*The goods **ought not to** be in the warehouse, still. Our customer was expecting a delivery this morning.*

C Speculating: *may, might, could*

C1 You can use *may/might (not)* or *could* to say something is possibly true or will possibly happen in the future.

A: *Where's John?* B: *He **may/might/could** be at lunch.*

⚠️ Don't use *can* to say something may possibly happen.

*There **might** be a budget meeting next week. (**not** There can be)*

C2 You can use *may/might (not)* or *could* to say that you think something will possibly happen in the future.

*Our turnover **may/might/could** reach $100m next year. The markets **may** be happy to see the dollar go down. (I am not certain about this) The Fed **might/may not** raise interest rates again if we're lucky. (**not** The Fed could not raise)*

C3 You can use *well* to emphasise that you think something is quite likely.

*This new contract **may/could/might well** mean that we need to recruit new staff. (I think this is quite probable)*

👁️ *May* is more formal than *might* and *could*. *May* is more common in business writing than in speaking. *Might* is more common in business speaking than in writing.

Practice

A, B **1** Match the two halves of these sentences and underline the correct words in italics.

1 There seem to be a lot of invoices to deal with. We

2 After all our investment we have an excellent website but it

3 They just called me from the taxi, so they

4 I just saw him getting into the lift, so he

5 According to my research, the new laptops

6 Can you cover for Tony? He

7 We have a good relationship with the bank, so it

8 Why do we only spend $200,000 on training when we

a *should/must* be more profitable than it is.

b *mustn't/ought to* cost a maximum of €900 each.

c <u>*must*</u>/*can't* have over 100 still unpaid.

d *can/should* arrive at any moment.

e *ought to/must* be at the sales meeting but he's off sick.

f *must/shouldn't* easily be able to afford a bigger budget?

g *shouldn't/can't* be in Stuttgart.

h *shouldn't/mustn't* be difficult to arrange a business loan.

A–C **2** Two colleagues are discussing job candidates. Complete their conversation using suitable modal verbs. Sometimes more than one answer is possible.

Claudia Johannes

Age	24
Work experience	2 years (advertising agency)
Management experience	None
Qualifications	Business studies degree
Other	Captain of local athletics team

Tony Mitchell

Age	30
Work experience	10 years (6 with us)
Management experience	2 years (Team Leader + 6 months Assistant Sales Manager)
Qualifications	Diploma in Marketing
Other	Speaks French & German

ANDY: So, Phil, why do you think Tony Mitchell is the best candidate for the role?

PHIL: Well, look at his background. He has a lot of experience, so he **1** ...must / 's got to / should / ought to... know the job better than Claudia.

ANDY: Well, yes, he **2** .... know the job, but Claudia **3** .... know the creative stuff – she's worked in advertising for two years.

PHIL: OK, but don't you think it **4** .... be risky to choose someone so young? She's only 24, so she **5** .... have enough experience yet. She **6** .... not be able to manage an older team.

ANDY: Sure, that **7** .... be a factor, but we have to think long term and Claudia **8** .... be a better long-term prospect. Also she **9** .... be able to lead people – she's captain of the athletics team.

PHIL: Yes, but that's not business! And what about Tony's languages? They **10** .... well be useful if we expand abroad.

ANDY: OK, let's get them both in for a second interview. We can talk to Tony this afternoon.

PHIL: It **11** .... have to be next week. I think he **12** .... be at that sales conference in Manchester at the moment.

◀ A–C **3** Underline the correct verbs in italics in this economic forecast. Sometimes both are possible.

Consumer spending, which has been dynamic so far, **1** <u>could</u> / *must* fall, because of the recent rise in interest rates, although some business leaders predict a further rise.

The government believes inflation **2** *can* / *might* increase to 2.4% due to higher energy prices, but it **3** *may* / *must* fall to around 2% next summer if oil prices then fall as expected.

Employment growth of 1.5% **4** *should* / *might* create up to 3.6 million new jobs in the next 12 months, but this **5** *must* / *should* decelerate to about 1% in the next three to five years as the economy stabilises.

Many businesses are having problems recruiting new staff due to the labour shortages. Some economists believe it is possible that wages **6** *must* / *might* increase as a result.

Some parts of the financial markets have performed poorly in recent months, and this **7** *could* / *must* possibly affect credit conditions more seriously than predicted. The only thing that is certain is that in this economic climate we **8** *can't* / *might* not be sure about anything!

◀ A–C **4** Complete this conversation using phrases with modal verbs that have the same meaning as the words in brackets. Sometimes more than one answer is possible.

SUZIE: This meeting **1** ....*shouldn't / ought not to last long*.. (*I don't expect this meeting is going to last long*). It's a short agenda. Ah, here we are, room 4B. That's funny. The door's locked. It **2** .... (*I expected it to be open*). Robert **3** .... (*I'm certain Robert has the key*). He was using the room yesterday afternoon.

ALEX: Sarah **4** .... (*perhaps Sarah has it*). I thought I saw her with it earlier.

SUZIE: I know she used the room first thing this morning, but she said she'd leave it open. It **5** .... (*possibly it's in my office*).

ALEX: She **6** .... (*it's quite likely she still has it*). Why don't you call her?

SUZIE: … She says it **7** .... (*it is probably in her desk drawer*). I'll go and look. It **8** .... (*I expect it won't take long*) … Found it! Now, shall we make a start?

🔘 **16.1 Listen and check your answers.**

◀ A–C **5** Write answers to the questions using modal verbs.

1 Your colleague isn't at work today, but you saw him with his passport yesterday. Why?

...*He could/might be on a business trip.*...

2 Oil prices have gone up again. What do you think will happen to electricity prices?

....

3 I want to take a taxi from the airport to your office. How much will it cost me?

....

4 And do you know how long the journey will take?

....

5 I'd like to discuss something with you over a coffee. Are you free on Friday morning?

....

6 All my emails to you keep bouncing back. What's the problem?

....

7 Do you know a good hotel near your office for under €100?

....

8 Hello? I'm trying to contact your manager. Do you know what he's doing?

....

Make it personal

Think about the products or services your company offers. Which will be most successful in the next year?

16 Business talk: Responding to other people

In conversation, you can use *must be* + adjective when you respond to news or other information to show that you understand how another person feels about something.

A: *They increased our bonuses this year.*   B: *You **must be delighted**.*

A: *Did you hear about Pete? He left his laptop on a train.*   B: *His boss **must be furious**.*

You can use *that must be* + adjective/noun when you want to refer to the situation.

A: *My boss never listens to any of my ideas.*   B: ***That must be frustrating**.*

A: *I have to make cold calls to clients but I've never had any sales training.*   B: ***That must be a challenge.***

If you think someone is not being serious or has said something ridiculous, you can say *You must be joking!*

A: *The Board are hoping to sell the business for £25 million.*   B: ***You must be joking!***

⚠ **Only use You must be joking! with friends or colleagues you are friendly with. It is not appropriate with managers or people you only have a professional relationship with.**

---

6 Complete these conversations using *must be* and a word from the box.

> furious   joking   ~~nervous~~   pleased   relieved   surprised

1 A: I have to make a presentation to 1,000 people today.

   B: You ......*must be nervous*...... .

   A: Yes, I am. And I thought I'd lost my notes, but I've found them.

   B: You ....

2 A: I'm afraid Mr Singh's going to be late. His car's broken down.

   B: Oh no! He only bought the car a month ago. He ....

   A: Yes, he sounded pretty angry on the phone.

3 A: We closed our first Hong Kong deal last week. It took months of negotiations.

   B: Fantastic! You ....

   A: We are – and exhausted too!

4 A: We've been offered a pay rise of 0.5%.

   B: You .... ! I thought we'd get 3% at least.

5 A: I've just been asked to go to Beijing to negotiate with some new suppliers.

   B: You .... You weren't expecting that, were you?

7 Write suitable answers using *That must be*.

1 A: I travel a lot in my job.

   B: ...*That must be interesting/exciting*......................................

2 A: We've just reached an agreement, after nearly a week of negotiation.

   B: ....

3 A: I didn't get the promotion. They gave the job to an external candidate.

   B: ....

4 A: My computer has crashed. It's the third time this week!

   B: ....

Make it personal

Think of good or bad things that have happened to your colleagues, friends or family recently. How could you show surprise, happiness or sympathy for them?

Simple spoken grammar

Read this conversation between two colleagues

Why do the words in italics make this conversation sound informal and friendly?

Going to the party tonight?

Yeah. *You going?*

Might do. *Depends* what time I leave work.

A Asking questions without *are you*

A1 People often ask short, present continuous questions without *are you* or *are*.

Simple form
How's work? (You) **travelling** *much these days?*

Full form
How's work? **Are you travelling** *much these days?*

A2 People often ask questions without *are you* or *are* when *be* is the main verb, especially before an adjective.

Simple form
Tired*? Do you want to go back to the hotel?*
You *a friend of Carla's?*

Full form
Are you tired*? Do you want to go back to the hotel?*
Are you *a friend of Carla's?*

B Asking questions without *do you* or *have you*

People often ask present simple questions without *do you* and present perfect and *have got* questions without *have you*.

Simple form
Want *some coffee?*
Finished *your report yet?*
Got *a pen?*

Full form
Do you want *some coffee?*
Have you finished *your report yet?*
Have you got *a pen?*

C Using modal verbs without the subjects *I* and *It*

C1 People often say *must*, *can't* and *may/might as well* without *I*.

Simple form
Sorry, **must** *rush! My taxi's here.*
It's six o'clock – **may/might as well** *go home now.*

Full form
Sorry, **I must** *rush! My taxi's here.*
It's six o'clock – **I may/might as well** *go home now.*

C2 People also use modal verbs without *it*, especially in short answers.

Simple form
A: *Is this the right room?*
B: **Must be***. There's only one!*

Full form
A: *Is this the right room?*
B: **It must be***. There's only one!*

D Simple forms of common expressions

People often use simple or shorter forms of some common fixed expressions.

Simple form
I need to call Josh. **Trouble/Problem is***, I can't find his number.*

Full form
I need to call Josh. **The trouble / The problem is***, I can't find his number.*

A: *How long will it take to get there?*
B: **Depends** *on the traffic.*

A: *How long will it take to get there?*
B: **It depends** *on the traffic.*

A: *Is Kristian coming today?*
B: **Don't know. / Think so. / Not sure.**

A: *Is Kristian coming today?*
B: **I don't know. / I think so. / I'm not sure.**

⊙ People only use the simple grammar in this unit in informal conversations and emails, and not in formal contexts.

Practice

◀ A, B **1** Make these questions more informal by crossing out the words that you can leave out.

1 ~~Are you~~ travelling anywhere exciting this year, Jo?

2 Are you in Hannah's team? I hear they're all going to Marrakech next month.

3 Are you going with them?

4 Do you need a personal assistant? I've always wanted to go to Morocco!!

5 Hi Nancy! Are you busy these days? Have you been anywhere interesting?

6 Do you like my new travel bag? Ryan bought it for me.

7 Are you the lucky person who gets all those trips to California?

8 Have you heard the news? Kevin's moving to the North Africa office.

9 Are you ready for lunch? I am!

10 Hi Shirley! Are you hungry? Let's go and get something to eat and dream of exotic trips abroad!

◀ B, C, D **2** Make these emails more formal by adding words which have been left out and using the full grammatical form.

1

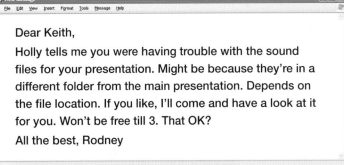

Dear Joanna,

Have you
∧ Got anything you want people to look at before tomorrow's meeting? Must tell you in case you don't know: Richard Wilson's going to be there. Can't be with you myself, though. Really should be, I know – problem is, I'll be in Milan.

Best wishes, Nikoleta

2

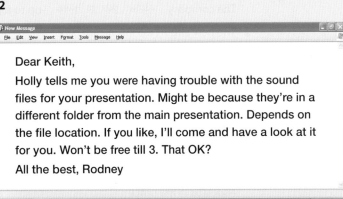

Dear Keith,

Holly tells me you were having trouble with the sound files for your presentation. Might be because they're in a different folder from the main presentation. Depends on the file location. If you like, I'll come and have a look at it for you. Won't be free till 3. That OK?

All the best, Rodney

◀ B, C, D **3** Make this conversation at the start of a meeting more informal. Cross out any of the words in italics that you can leave out.

GRAHAM: **1** ~~*Have you*~~ lost something, Tanya?

TANYA: **2** *I can't find* my agenda. **3** *It must be* on my desk.

GRAHAM: Terry made some extra copies. **4** *Do you want* one?

TANYA: Oh, yes. Thanks.

GRAHAM: Right. Who'll start off? Archie? **5** *Have you got* any technical problems to talk about? What about the databases and the emailing problem?

ARCHIE: Yes, OK, **6** *I might as well just mention* that. **7** *It's something* to do with the Filewiz programme. **8** *The trouble is,* um, **9** *I don't know* what exactly.

GRAHAM: Mm. Maybe it's something to ask Gale in IT to come and look at?

ARCHIE: **10** *It could be,* yeah. **11** *It depends* whether it's a software problem or a server issue. Gale just deals with software, really.

TANYA: Michaela deals with server problems these days, doesn't she?

ARCHIE: Yeah. **12** *I think so.* **13** *I'm not sure,* actually. They're always changing people around in IT.

GRAHAM: Yeah. **14** *It must be* really confusing for you when you don't know who does what!

ARCHIE: Yeah.

🔘 SS 4.1 **Listen and check your answers.**

Test 4: Units 13–16

1 Complete these sentences using each expression in brackets once.

1 Before Eurostar trains started, you ....*couldn't*.... get to Paris in under three hours. Now you .... do it in around two. (*can / couldn't*)

2 I .... easily work 60 hours a week at the moment, but I don't think I'll .... for ever. (*can / be able to*)

3 In a few years' time you'll .... pay by cheque anywhere, although you .... still use them in some countries at the moment. (*can / be unable to*)

4 .... come to my office as soon as possible? And .... bringing those figures with you? (*would you mind / could you*)

5 A: .... I talk to you for a minute?
   B: OK, but I .... only give you a minute. (*may / can*)

2 Complete the second sentence so that it means the same as the first sentence. Rewrite the words in italics using the correct form of the word in brackets.

1 *You can have* up to four weeks' unpaid holiday per year in this company. (*allow*)

The company ....*allows you to have*.... up to four weeks' unpaid holiday per year.

2 The new airport rail link *means people will be able to reach* the city centre in 30 minutes. (*enable*)

The new airport rail link .... the city centre in 30 minutes.

3 *Borrowers can have* a six-month break from payments with our new flexible loan. (*let*)

Our new flexible loan .... a six-month break from payments.

4 International meetings can take place via video conferencing *and so save money on flights*. (*make it possible*)

Holding international meetings via video conferencing .... on flights.

5 Asbestos in the office *can be* extremely dangerous and should be removed by experts. (*be known to*)

Asbestos in the office .... extremely dangerous and should be removed by experts.

3 Underline the correct words in italics.

ZAC: You **1** *should/shall* come to the staff party next month.

ALI: That sounds great! **2** *Should/Shouldn't* I bring a guest, or not?

ZAC: No, you **3** *should/shouldn't*. It's just for employees. Would you be able to help me organise it?

ALI: Of course. What can I do to help?

ZAC: Well, you **4** *could/should* send out the invitations, or help plan the entertainment.

ALI: I **5** *might/should* as well do the invitations. **6** *Ought/Shall* I email them out to the whole company?

ZAC: Yes, and you **7** *could/might* want to put a poster up on the notice board.

4 Underline the most suitable verbs in italics for the contexts.

1 You*'d better / must* tidy your desk. We're expecting visitors.   [colleague to colleague]

2 All visitors *can / must* report to reception upon arrival.   [on a notice board]

3 You *can / have to* give me at least four weeks' notice of your holiday dates.   [manager to member of staff]

4 You *'d better not / don't need to* pay the invoice for 60 days.   [salesperson to client]

5 I *must / might want to* remember to call Ian about that trip to Russia.   [someone thinking]

6 We *need to / must* arrange that conference call with the Rome office.   [member of staff to manager]

5 Complete the second sentence so that it means the same as the first sentence. Use the modal verbs in the box.

> could   have to   must not   need   ~~needn't~~

1 It's not necessary to wear a suit and tie if you work in the IT department.

You ....*needn't*..... wear a suit and tie if you work in the IT department.

2 Company rules say that staff should claim all expenses within one month.

Staff .... claim all expenses within one month.

3 Are you able to look after the French delegation on Friday evening?

.... you look after the French delegation on Friday evening?

4 It's important to tell your colleagues if you will be out of the office.

You .... to tell your colleagues if you will be out of the office.

5 It is forbidden to use the Internet for personal reasons except during lunchtime.

Employees .... use the Internet for personal reasons except during lunchtime.

6 Underline the correct modal verb in italics in each sentence. Sometimes both are possible.

1 A: This report *can't/mustn't* be right – it says we spent £1 million on photocopying last month.
B: You *must/can* be joking … No. you're right. It *should/must* be a mistake.
A: I'd better check the rest of the report. There *might/can* be other mistakes.
B: Well, it *shouldn't/couldn't* take long – there are only six pages.

2 A: I'm afraid transport costs have risen again. We *may/could* well have to look for a new courier.
B: It *might not / can't* be necessary to do that if we can renegotiate our contract with our current provider.
A: They *should/might* want to talk. After all, we're an important customer for them.
B: Yes, I think we *ought to / can* be able to get another 10% cost reduction.

7 Complete this article about energy saving using the words in the box. You can use some more than once.

> able to   can   Change   could   couldn't   Don't   enables   have to
> How about   let's   might want   must   need   needn't   should   shouldn't

Seven steps to saving energy in business

Slowing down climate change? That **1** ....*must*.... take a lot of money and effort, you probably think. Well, no. Some of the simplest things you **2** .... do are in fact the easiest and cheapest.

- Energy-saving light bulbs **3** .... emit 70% less CO_2 than normal ones. **4** .... yours today!

- **5** .... leave electrical appliances turned on all night – you **6** .... save 20% of the running costs.

- You **7** .... get all your electricity from unrenewable sources any more. Some energy suppliers are **8** .... provide you with 100% renewable electricity.

- Good insulation **9** .... keep in 30% of the heat which escapes through the walls.

- You **10** .... to try turning down your heating by just 1°C. This **11** .... cut your CO_2 emissions by over 5%. Do you **12** .... have your office that hot? **13** .... wearing warmer clothes?

- Always ask yourself – do you really **14** .... to fly? You **15** .... go by plane if there is an alternative. Not so long ago you **16** .... rely on trains, but these days, Europe's high-speed rail network **17** .... you to travel quickly and efficiently.

- And finally, **18** .... you live without that new phone or that new laptop? Every time you buy a product you **19** .... take responsibility for the emissions due to its manufacture, packaging and transport. So, from now on, **20** .... only buy stuff we really need.

Conditionals 1 (talking about the present and future)

Read these two extracts from a phone advert.

a Which sentence is offering something?

b Which sentence is giving advice / making a suggestion?

> **1**
> If you don't use your phone much, Pay-As-You-Go is for you.

> **2**
> We'll give you your first month's calls free if you sign up for our package today.

A Forming present conditionals

A1 Conditional sentences usually have two parts: the condition (*if* …) and the result. The result happens (or does not happen) depending on the condition.

A2

if + present tense,	present tense
If you're planning to become self-employed,	*retraining is a good idea.*

You can put either the result or the condition first.

present tense	*if* + present tense
We don't process orders the same day	*if we receive* them after 3 pm.

In writing, a comma is normally used after the *if*-clause if it comes first.

A3 You can also use an imperative or a modal for the result.

Don't get into *an unlicensed taxi if you're travelling alone.*
What **should** *I do if my computer crashes?*

B Using present conditionals

You use these conditionals to talk about present facts and things that normally happen as a result or condition of something else.

If you **want** *to be an accountant, you* **have to** *pass some very difficult exams.*
It's important to take regular breaks if you **work** *at a computer.*

C Forming future conditionals

C1

if + present tense,	*will*
If they **demand** *a lower price,*	*how low* **will** *we go?*

will	*if* + present tense
We **won't accept** *a pay deal*	*if it's less than 5%.*

C2 You can also use modal verbs (*can, could, may, might, should*) with future meaning for the result.

We **might have to** *meet tomorrow instead, if I* **don't** *have time later today.*
If you **order** *it now, we* **could get** *it to you by tomorrow.*

⚠ Don't use *will* in the *if*-clause.

If you **look** *on their website, you'll* **find** *their address.* (**not** *If you will look*)

C3 You can also use an imperative for the result.

If they **arrive** *early,* **take** *them to the canteen.*

D Using future conditionals

You use these conditionals to talk about actions that will or are likely to happen in the future, depending on another action happening.

We'll **be able to** *afford a new car if I* **get** *promoted.* (buying a new car in the future depends on getting promoted)

E Using alternatives to *if*

You can use these alternatives to *if* with conditionals to talk about real present and future.

- *as long as / providing (that) / provided that* = only if
  A sports centre is a low financial risk **as long as / providing (that) / provided that** *you sell memberships.*

  ⊙ *Provided that* is more frequent than *providing (that)*.

- *unless* = except if
  People won't fill in marketing questionnaires **unless** *you offer them a prize.*

- *in case* = to avoid a possible problem later
  I'll keep my mobile with me **in case** *you need to contact me.*

Practice

◄A   **1**   **A manager is training a new phone operator. Complete their conversation using the most suitable present tense or imperative of the verbs in brackets.**

MARGARET: This is the procedure. If two calls **1** ....come in.... (*come in*) at the same time, **2** .... (*pick up*) the internal call first and put the other call on hold. If there **3** .... (*be*) a call waiting, the light **4** .... (*flash*).

SAM: What **5** .... (*I/do*) if there **6** .... (*be*) an external call for someone in the office?

MARGARET: If you **7** .... (*get*) an external call for Joe Johnson, for example, you **8** .... (*have to*) call Joe's extension number. When Joe answers, you usually say who's calling, but if there **9** .... (*be*) other phone calls waiting, **10** .... (*not waste*) time telling him. Just put the call through.

🔘 **17.1 Listen and check your answers.**

◄C1, 3   **2**   **Complete these future conditional sentences using the correct form of the verbs in brackets.**

1 If you ....buy.... five chairs, we....'ll give.... you the sixth one free. (*buy, give*)

2 If you .... the purchase agreement now, you .... a 5% discount on your next purchase. (*sign, get*)

3 We .... make some workers redundant if we .... more orders soon. (*have to, not get*)

4 They .... you for delivery if you .... more than a hundred. (*not charge, order*)

5 You .... better if you .... regular breaks from your computer. (*feel, take*)

6 If I .... my target for this quarter, I .... a large bonus. (*meet, get*)

7 If you .... your staff a pay rise this year, they .... happy. (*not give, not be*)

8 What .... if they .... you the job? (*you/do, offer*)

9 If the meeting .... early, I .... shopping. (*finish, go*)

10 You .... queue for ages if you .... at the airport early tomorrow. (*have to, not arrive*)

◄C, D   **3**   **Read this online tax information for UK businesses. Write sentences using one verb in the present simple and the other with the modal verb in brackets.**

1 If you / not know / how tax will affect your business / you / find out / now. (*should*)

    ..If you don't know how tax will affect your business, you should find out now...................

2 If you / be / self-employed / you / have to / hire an accountant. (*might*)

    ....

3 You / print / this page out to read later / if you / not want / to read all the information online. (*could*)

    ....

4 You / have to / pay taxes on goods / if you / import / them from outside the European Union. (*may*)

    ....

5 If your turnover / reach / a certain level / register / for VAT*. (imperative)

    ....

6 We / need to / see your VAT records / if there / be / any questions about your tax. (*may*)

    ....

7 If you / not have / storage space in your offices for your VAT records / you / arrange / alternative secure storage. (*should*)

    ....

* VAT = value added tax

8 The police / arrest / you / if you / not keep / any records, as this is a legal requirement. (*could*)

....

9 If you / have / an accountant / you / want / to get their advice on keeping VAT records. (*might*)

....

10 If you / need / any help with your taxes / contact / your local Advice Team. (*imperative*)

....

◄ E   **4** **Read this advice on backing up computer files. Underline the correct words in italics.**

1 You may lose important documents *as long as* / <u>*if*</u> your hard drive crashes.

2 You should back up your hard drive regularly *in case* / *unless* your computer crashes.

3 It's worth running a virus scan on your files *in case* / *provided that* some are corrupt.

4 *If* / *Unless* you want to back up important work, save it on an external hard drive.

5 *Provided that* / *Unless* you do a lot of work with video or music files, 80GB should be enough storage space.

6 *If* / *As long as* you don't want to buy an external hard drive, you can rent storage space on the Internet.

7 *As long as* / *In case* you're not backing up very large data files, online storage can be reasonably priced.

8 Backing up is a waste of time *in case* / *unless* you can retrieve your backed-up files easily.

9 With online storage you can retrieve your data or files from any computer *provided that* / *unless* it has an Internet connection.

10 *If* / *Provided that* you have any problems, call us on 0870 432 8765.

◄ A–E   **5** **Finish these sentences so that they are true for your company.**

1 If we get a complaint about our service, *we respond to the customer as soon as possible.*...............

2 Whenever the price of oil goes up, ...

3 Providing the economy remains strong, ...

4 We won't change our corporate branding unless ....

5 As long as customers give us positive feedback, ...

6 We may employ more staff if ....

7 If a rival company opens in our city, ...

8 If our company makes a large profit this year, ...

9 We offer special incentives to staff providing ....

10 Our company will do well this year if ....

Make it personal

Finish these sentences so that they are true for you.

If I get a bonus this year, I ....

If my company moves to a different city, I ....

If I meet my targets for this quarter, I ....

If someone asks me to speak at a conference, I ....

17 Business talk: Negotiating

You can use conditional forms with *if, as long as, on condition that, provided/providing (that)* and *unless* in negotiations. You can use them in reply to offers or suggestions from the other side to make a counter offer of your own. Remember that the verb in these clauses is in the present simple.

A: *Can you deliver to all 50 of our shops?*
B: *Well, we could **if** you **accept** our longer delivery times.*

A: *Are you willing to pay in 60 days?*
B: *Yes, of course, **as long as** you **increase** the discount to 7%.*

A: *We'd like you to start production next week.*
B: *We can pobably do that , **on condition that** you **pay** 10% up front.*

A: *So, you're going to arrange transport, right?*
B: *We'd be happy to, **provided that** / **providing** you **cover** the insurance.*

A: *We'd expect all payments in euros.*
B: *That's fine by me, **unless** the exchange rate **changes** by more than 5%.*

6 Complete this conversation using the most suitable expressions in italics.

SEB: So we'd like you to deliver to all 20 of our stores.

AYEESHA: That shouldn't be a problem, **1** *on condition that* / *unless* you accept delivery in five days after the order, not three.

SEB: Sorry. That's out of the question. Will you accept four days as a compromise?

AYEESHA: I suppose we might be able to, **2** *providing* / *unless* we receive all orders by ten in the morning.

SEB: That's fine by me. And will you deliver at weekends?

AYEESHA: Yes, we'd be happy to do that, **3** *if* / *unless* you're willing to pay extra.

SEB: Well, we might be willing to **4** *provided* / *unless* it's too expensive for us. How much do you have in mind?

AYEESHA: How about 15% extra?

SEB: We could only manage 10%, I'm afraid. If you can accept that, we've got a deal.

AYEESHA: All right, we agree, **5** *as long as* / *unless* you sign a two-year contract.

SEB: Agreed.

AYEESHA: Great. Let's shake on it.

7 Complete these extracts from negotiations using your own ideas.

1 A: Could you work late tonight?
   B: I'd be happy to, if .....*I can come in later tomorrow morning.*.....

2 A: We're looking for an exclusive contract.
   B: There shouldn't be a problem with that, as long as ....

3 A: Would you let me have one day off a week to study for my MBA?
   B: I suppose that would be possible, provided that ....

4 A: Would you consider a lower price for the product?
   B: I might manage that, providing ....

5 A: We'd like you to collect the recycling from the office every week.
   B: No problem, on condition that ....

6 A: Will you give us a longer payment period?
   B: I'm afraid not, unless ....

Make it personal

Think of three changes you want to make to your working life. Plan how to negotiate with your boss to get them. Write down the compromises you are willing to make using conditional forms.

Conditionals 2 (talking about the hypothetical present and past)

Read these comments made by two different managers.

a Which manager is talking about a problem in the past?

b Which is talking about a problem now?

c How do you know?

> If there was just one point of contact, customers would know who to talk to.
>
> Omar

> If we'd given the new assistant better training, she'd probably have stayed longer.
>
> Yasmina

A Forming conditionals about the hypothetical present

if + past tense,	*would* + infinitive
If we **had** a good database,	we **wouldn't waste** so much time.
If we **didn't have** such poor customer service,	we**'d be** much more successful.

You can put either the result or the condition first.

would + infinitive	*if* + past tense
It **would help** our exports	if we **employed** more people in the markets.
Would you **get** there quicker	if you **went** by train?

⚠ Don't use *would* in the *if*-clause.

*If everybody **knew** what was happening, there wouldn't be so many misunderstandings.* (**not** ~~would know~~)

B Using conditionals to refer to the hypothetical present

You can use present hypothetical conditionals when you are thinking about the present situation and imagining how it could be different.

*If I **didn't work** such long hours, I **wouldn't be** so tired all the time.* (but I do work long hours so I am tired all the time)

*If he **spent** more time preparing, his presentations **would be** better.*

C Forming conditionals about the hypothetical past

if + past tense,	*would* + infinitive
If Kevin **had asked** me,	I **would've met** him at the airport.
If we **hadn't checked** our stock levels,	we**'d have run out** of our bestselling range.

You can put either the result or the condition first.

would have + past participle	*if* + past perfect
It **wouldn't have taken** so much time	if they**'d known** who to contact.
Would we **have got** a special deal	if we**'d placed** a bigger order?

👁 The contracted forms *'d* and *would've* are used in informal conversation.

*If we**'d discussed** it more, we **would've decided** it was not worth doing.*

***Would** we **have won** the contract if we**'d offered** a bigger discount?* (we didn't offer a bigger discount so we lost the contract)

D Using conditionals to refer to the hypothetical past

You can use past hypothetical conditionals when you are thinking about a past situation and imagining a different result or outcome.

*I **would've got** a bonus if I**'d hit** my performance targets for the year.* (I didn't hit my targets, so I didn't get a bonus)

Practice

◀ A, B **1** Read these comments from employees who are imagining running their own business. Underline the correct words in italics.

1 If I had my own business, I'*ll take* / '*d take* longer holidays.

2 If I *would work* / *worked* for myself, I'd be in charge of my own life.

3 What *do I do* / *would I do* if I was the boss? I'd pay my employees good salaries.

4 If I was in charge of my own business, I *invested* / '*d invest* in a good website and good advertising.

5 I'd hire the best and brightest people if I *own* / *owned* my own business.

6 I'*ll treat* / '*d treat* my customers well if I ran my own company.

7 If I *was* / *would be* the boss of my own company, I'd introduce an incentive scheme for all staff.

8 Everyone *had to* / *would have to* wear smart suits if I was in charge of my own business.

9 I'd earn more money if I *didn't work* / *wouldn't work* for someone else.

10 I'd have a flexible schedule if I'*m* / *was* self-employed.

◀ A, B **2** Complete the second sentence so that it means the same as the first sentence(s).

1 My colleague travels so much. He misses a lot of important meetings.

If my colleague .....*didn't travel so much, he wouldn't miss*..... so many important meetings.

2 I take taxis all the time. I don't have a company car.

If I .... taxis all the time.

3 You don't spend time building client relationships, so you have poor sales results.

If you .... better sales results.

4 I haven't done a presentations course. I don't speak at many conferences.

If I .... at more conferences.

5 We don't fly business class. It costs so much.

We .... so much.

6 I work in an open-plan office. People interrupt me frequently.

If I .... so often.

7 My boss doesn't have a PA. She's not very efficient.

If my boss .... more efficient.

8 They haven't sent us the final order. We aren't able to close their account.

If they .... their account.

◀ A–D **3** Find and correct five mistakes in these sentences. Tick (✓) the sentences that are correct.

1 If you ~~would want~~ *wanted* to expand into Europe, would you base yourself in Brussels or somewhere else?

2 The job wouldn't have been so bad if there hadn't been so much travelling. ✓

3 If we'd won the Innovation Award, it gave us a lot of free publicity, but unfortunately we didn't win.

4 Our profits for this quarter would be significantly bigger if fuel costs weren't so high.

5 If interest rates would go up, many people would be unable to pay their mortgages.

6 If I moved to Stockholm, I have to sell my house, so I'm going to turn down the Swedish job offer.

7 If investors had more confidence in the CEO, would they be less critical of the company's recent economic results?

8 If they wouldn't have spent so much on the new offices, they wouldn't have had such cashflow problems.

◄ C, D   **4**   **Jeff is talking to his colleague, Cristina, about a recent unsuccessful project in Guatemala. Complete their conversation using the correct form of the verbs in brackets.**

CRISTINA: So why do you think the project was so unsuccessful?

JEFF: Looking back, there were so many mistakes. If we
1 ...<u>'d started</u>.... (*start*) the project in January instead of May,
we 2 .... (*be able to*) launch at the right time for the
buying season.

CRISTINA: OK, but I heard that there were delays in sending out
stock even once the project was established.

JEFF: Well, yes, we had lots of problems organising the packing line.

CRISTINA: I see. 3 .... (*you/get*) more stock out into the
market on time if you 4 .... (*organise*) the packing
line better?

JEFF: Maybe. I think that's something that we should look at in future projects.

CRISTINA: What about the communication problems? 5 .... (*it/help*) if more people
6 .... (*take*) Spanish classes before moving to the Guatemala office?

JEFF: Well, as you know, I studied Spanish for several months before moving. I certainly think it
7 .... (*be*) difficult to communicate with my clients if I 8 .... (*not/know*) any Spanish.

CRISTINA: It's really important to learn from our mistakes this time. If we 9 .... (*learn*) the lessons
from our previous ventures in Latin America, we 10 .... (*not/have*) so many problems establishing
the business in Guatemala.

JEFF: Yes, if we 11 .... (*have*) more support from our other offices, the project probably
12 .... (*succeed*).

  ◉ **18.1 Listen and check your answers.**

◄ A–D   **5**   **Read this extract from a meeting in a pharmaceutical company. Underline the most suitable verb in italics.**

MAX: The problem is that the schedules for manufacturing and delivery are not clear. For instance, if everyone
1 <u>*had stuck*</u> / *has stuck* to the schedules for the Czech order last year, we 2 *wouldn't have had* / *wouldn't have*
so many delays. If we 3 *'d have established* / *'d established* clear schedules right from the start of that order, we
4 *didn't experience* / *wouldn't have experienced* so many problems.

TIM: Right, so I've come up with a model to show how things could be done better next time. Basically, we
have three processes. The first one is the manufacturing process, the second one is the quality control
process and the third one is the distribution and shipping process. So, let's imagine, if we 5 *received* / *'d
received* an order which needed to arrive in Prague by the beginning of June, then the last shipping date
6 *would have to be* / *had to be* 25 May. So, if 25 May 7 *would be* / *was* the shipping deadline, then the deadline
for quality control 8 *would be* / *had been* 23 May, and the deadline for the manufacturing process 9 *was* /
would be 20 May.

MAX: OK. Good.

Make it personal

Complete these sentences to make them true for you.

1 If I owned my own business, …

2 If I decided to learn a new skill, …

3 If I changed my job, ….

4 If I'd chosen a different career, …

5 If I hadn't met (name a person), …

Think of one other thing you would like to change at work, and write a conditional sentence about it.

18 Business talk: More hypothetical conditionals

You can use *if it wasn't/weren't for* … to talk about things that make it possible or impossible for something to happen. *If it weren't for* is slightly more formal.

If it wasn't/weren't for video-conferencing, our business travel costs would be much higher.

If it wasn't/weren't for the high running costs, we'**d offer** more people company cars. (running costs are high, so we do not offer more people company cars)

⊙ In formal situations, and especially in writing, you can use *if* + *were to* to talk about events that are possible, but not very likely to happen. The form *were to* is used for all persons.

If the government **were to** introduce restrictions, we **would have to** reconsider our present situation.

You can use *if it hadn't been for* … to talk about things that made it possible or impossible for something to happen.

If it hadn't been for the many years of losses, the government **wouldn't have privatised** the industry. (there were many years of losses, so the government privatised the industry)

6 Complete these conversations using *if it wasn't / weren't / hadn't been for* and the verbs in the correct tense.

1 A: Without George we wouldn't be able to finish the report today.
   B: Yes, ...*if it wasn't for*... George, we .'d have to......... (*have to*) / carry on tomorrow.

2 A: Luckily, Joanna was there and she persuaded the customer to come back the next day.
   B: Yes, ... Joanna, the customer .... (*not come back*) at all.

3 A: It's a shame that the rain prevented us from showing the prospective buyer all the different outdoor facilities the leisure centre can offer.
   B: Hmm, yes. .... the rain, we .... (*show*) the client everything.

4 A: The insurance premiums are too high to hold an open day for the public.
   B: Yes, ... the high insurance premiums, we .... (*be able to*) invite the public to come and see what we do.

5 A: Without the backup server we would have lost all the files for the Dubai project.
   B: Yes. .... the backup, we .... (*have to*) start all over again.

6 A: Do you agree that we would be more profitable if we didn't have such high costs?
   B: Yes, undoubtedly. .... the high costs, we .... (*make*) a lot more money.

7 James Elroy specialises in financial analysis for the airline industry. Read his notes for a client report. Write sentences for the actual report using *if … were to*.

Possible future scenarios for the airline industry

1 the UK economy might slow down → spending on travel fall
   ...*If the UK economy were to slow down, spending on travel would fall.*...

2 the USA could suffer a recession → possibly mean bankruptcy for a company like Airserve
   ....

3 the EU may raise taxes on carbon emissions → European airports lose business
   ....

4 Skyplan might pull out of the negotiations with Swallow Air → Swallow Air's future be in doubt
   ....

5 more countries could join the EU → open the possibility of new routes
   ....

6 airlines might spend more time finding out what customers actually want → they probably see an increase in revenues
   ....

Make it personal

Think of some things in your job that you would like to happen, but which do not or cannot happen because of something else. Write some sentences using *If it wasn't/weren't for* …..

The passive 1 (forming and using the passive)

Read this extract from a news article.

a Which of these questions *can't* you answer?
   1 What's the news about the factory?
   2 Who told the workers the news?
   3 Who owed the company millions?

b Why didn't the writer include this information?

> After months of speculation, workers were finally told at a meeting on Friday that the factory will close. Staff said the company was owed millions for completed work.

A Forming the passive (*be* + past participle)

Present simple	Our products **are not sold** in there.	Where **are** they **sold**?
Present continuous	The company **'s/is being sold**.	When **'s/is** it **being sold**?
Past simple	The products **were sold** at a loss.	Why **were** they **sold** at a loss?
Past continuous	They **weren't being sold** for a profit.	**Were** they **being sold** too cheaply?
Present perfect	The company **'s/has been sold**.	**Has the company been sold**?
Past perfect	We knew the company **had been sold**.	Why **had** it **been sold**?

👁 People use the passive mostly in writing. The most frequent passive forms are the past simple and present simple. Negative and continuous forms are much less frequent.

B Using active and passive verbs

B1 You can often use an active or a passive verb to describe the same thing, but the focus is different.

Active   *The CEO **bought** the company in 2006.* (the focus is *the CEO*)

Passive   *The company **was bought** by the CEO in 2006.* (the focus is *the company*)

Active sentences tell us who or what does an action. The subject of the sentence is the agent. In the active sentence above, the subject is *the CEO*.

Passive sentences tell us how the action affects the 'receiver' of the action. The subject is the 'receiver'. In the passive sentence above, the subject is *the company*.

B2 You can use the passive when:

- your focus is on the receiver of an action – that is what you are talking or writing about.
  *The order **was invoiced** on 20 May, but it **wasn't dispatched** until 30 May.* (we are interested in what happened to the order)
  *The company **has been renamed**. It**'s** now **called** Healthtec.*

- you don't know the agent or the agent is not important. You can use the passive to describe processes or procedures.
  *All our furniture **is designed** and **manufactured** in Europe.* (the workers' names are not important)

- the agent is obvious or understood.
  *Kitchen staff **are not allowed** to wear jewellery.* (obviously by their employer or the law)

- you don't want to say who or what the agent is.
  *I **was told** the wrong time for the meeting.* (I don't want to say who told me)

B3 You can use *by* to add the agent in a passive sentence.

*Google **was started by** two Stanford graduate students.*

C Verbs with only passive forms

Some verbs only have passive forms (e.g. *to be born*). Other verbs are usually passive (e.g. *to be based (somewhere)*, *to be involved*).

*I **was born** in Hamburg, but I**'m** now **based** in Frankfurt. My company **is involved** in several European projects.*

Practice

1 a Look at this diagram of an electronics company's complaints procedure. Complete the description using the verbs in brackets in the present simple passive.

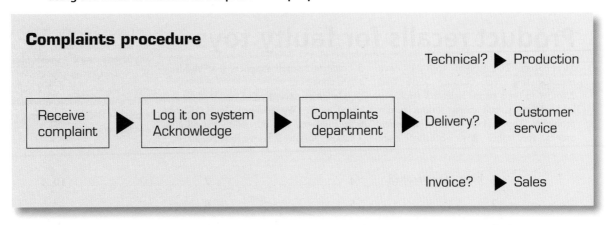

As soon as a complaint **1** ...is received... (*receive*), it **2** .... (*log*) on the system and an acknowledgement **3** .... (*mail*) out to the customer. Complaints **4** .... (*send*) to the Complaints department. Here they **5** .... (*read*) by a supervisor and they **6** .... (*categorise*). Complaints **7** .... (*pass on*) to the relevant department. For example, if the complaint is about a technical fault, it **8** .... (*forward*) to the Production department. If it concerns a delivery, it **9** .... (*answer*) by the Customer Service team. Invoicing problems **10** .... (*sort out*) by Sales. Our company **11** .... (*know*) in the industry for our good customer relations and we try to make sure that complaints **12** .... (*not leave*) unanswered longer than six weeks.

b The Complaints Manager is discussing a complaint with her assistant. Complete her questions using the verbs in brackets in the present perfect or past simple passive.

Manager	Assistant
1 ...Has it been logged... (*it /log*) on the system?	Yes, it has.
2 When .... (*it/receive*)?	We got it on 12 May.
3 How .... (*it/send*)?	It was faxed.
4 .... (*an acknowledgement / mail out*) yet?	No, it hasn't.
5 Where .... (*it/send*) first?	It was sent to Complaints.
6 Which department .... (*it / forward to*) after that?	We don't know – it's lost.
7 .... (*the customers / contact*) at all?	Yes, they have.
8 .... (*they/ask*) to send a copy?	I think they were.

2 Complete these sentences using the verbs in the box in the present continuous or past continuous passive.

ask	audit	bully	criticise	pay	~~promote~~	not replace	sack	upgrade

1 I'm ...being promoted... next year – I'm going to be a director at last.

2 A colleague of mine .... for selling confidential data. She leaves on Friday.

3 Our computers .... after all, but the software .... to the latest version.

4 Some manual workers .... weekly until last year. Now they get a monthly pay cheque.

5 I left my last job because I .... My boss used to shout at me.

6 The accounts .... next week. There'll be a team of five or six people doing it.

7 We .... to work longer hours to finish a contract by the end of next month.

8 The directors of a major bank .... in the press at the moment for receiving large bonuses.

◄ A, B **3** Read this article about problems with manufactured toys. Where necessary, change the active verbs into the passive form of the same tense.

Product recalls for faulty toys

More than 20 million toys **1** *have recalled* this year because toxic lead **2** *found* in their paint. If lead **3** *swallows* by children, it can cause serious health problems. Toy makers **4** *have cancelled* orders for other toys because they **5** *contained* small magnets that children could choke on.

The chief executive of one leading toy brand said, 'We realised our standards **6** *had ignored* and our safety procedures **7** *had not followed*, so we took action.'

Contracts with many toy suppliers **8** *have suspended*. Toy manufacturers say that new inspection procedures **9** *are putting* in place. 'We will now be routinely testing all toys before, during and after painting, and toys with magnets **10** *are* currently *redesigning*,' said a spokesperson for the industry.

1 *have been recalled*   4 ....   7 ....   10 ....
2 ....   5 ....   8 ....
3 ....   6 ....   9 ....

◄ A, B1–2 **4** Underline the correct form of the verbs in italics in this letter to a business advice website.

Last month I **1** *was sacked* / *have sacked* from my job as an accountant. I **2** *had been working* / *had been worked* for the company for a year, and **3** *was doing* / *was done* well. Company policy **4** *states* / *is stated* that we have to use our own email accounts for private communication, so I **5** *applied* / *was applied* online for another job using a webmail account. I **6** *have invited* / *was invited* for an interview and so I **7** *asked* / *was asked* for some time off. Naturally I had to lie about why. The day before the interview, I **8** *told* / *was told* to go to the MD's office. He **9** *was shown* / *showed* me copies of the emails I had sent on my webmail account, and he **10** *was sacked* / *sacked* me there and then for gross misconduct. As I **11** *was escorted* / *escorted* out of the building by another manager, I **12** *was informed* / *informed* that spyware **13** *had installed* / *had been installed* on all computers to monitor activity. We **14** *had not been told* / *had not told* about this and I feel that this is an invasion of privacy.

◄ B3 **5** **a** Look at these security measures taken by an investment bank. Complete the sentences using the passive and *by* so that they mean the same.

- CCTV monitors the entrances to the building.
- Security staff search every employee.
- Receptionists check visitors' identities.
- An outside agency tests members of staff randomly for drugs.
- Antivirus software scans all computer files.
- The IT group backs up the data on each server.
- Fire safety officers test the fire alarm on Fridays.
- Managers train their team members in fire safety procedures.

1 The entrances to the building ..... *are monitored by CCTV* ....
2 Every employee ....
3 Visitors' identities ....
4 Members of staff ....
5 All computer files ....
6 The data on each server ....
7 The fire alarm ....
8 Team members ....

b ⊙ 19.1 Listen to the office services manager briefing a new employee on security. Write down four more security and safety measures mentioned using a passive verb.

Make it personal

Write a short paragraph about a set of procedures in your organisation (e.g. complaints, health and safety, employing new staff).

19 Write for business: Using the passive in business correspondence

The passive is useful in business correspondence when you need to be impersonal or formal.

I **was employed** by the Environment agency to oversee water quality.
I wish to order a HD400 laptop, which **was advertised** in the May issue of Your Laptop.

It is useful if you do not want to name the people who are responsible for something.

Your request for a higher credit limit **has not been approved**.
We are sorry that your shipment **was delayed**.

However, when you want to make clear who did something, then use the active.

I **have instructed** our Accounts Department to send you a cheque for $500.

6 a Rewrite the words in italics so that the email sounds more impersonal.

> ✉ To: | Susannah Binks
> Subject: | Your complaint
>
> Dear Ms Binks,
>
> **1** *Our Order Department has forwarded your email of 2 April to me.* I was sorry to learn of the problems you experienced with our recent service and that **2** *we damaged the goods in your last order during transportation.* I understand that the damage was caused because **3** *we had not packed the goods securely.* **4** *I have investigated the matter* and **5** *we are reviewing our packing procedures.*
>
> I hope you will accept my apology for the way **6** *our Order Department treated you.* I do accept that **7** *Ms Smith did not handle the matter properly.* As a gesture of goodwill **8** *I am crediting the sum of $300 to your account.* I apologise for any inconvenience **9** *this company has caused you.*
>
> Yours sincerely,
>
> Ivan Hough
>
> Customer Relations Manager

1 Your email of 2 April has been forwarded to me.   6 ....

2 ....   7 ....

3 ....   8 ....

4 ....   9 ....

5 ....

b Which two sentences might you want to leave in the active form and why?

7 Make these extracts from a job application letter more formal. Rewrite the verbs in italics using a passive form of the verbs in brackets.

1 I wish to apply for the post of Auditor, which I *saw* in *the Times* on 15 March. (*advertise*)

   I wish to apply for the post of Auditor, which was advertised in the Times on 15 March.

2 As you will see from the enclosed CV, I *studied* at Bristol Grammar School and the University of Manchester, where I *got* a first class honours degree. While at Manchester I *got to be* President of the Debating Society. (*educate, award, elect*)

   ....

3 Since 2005 I *have worked* at Directions plc in the Auditing Department. In April 2007 I *got to be* Senior Auditor. (*employ by, appoint*)

   ....

Make it personal

1 **Find a job on the Internet that you could apply for and write an application letter.**

2 **Write an email to a customer or a colleague apologising for something that went wrong in your department.**

The passive 2 (modal verbs, two-object verbs, *have* and *get*)

A manager is talking about a problem.

Who do you think is responsible for the problem?

a the manager

b Angela

c someone else

> The report won't be finished by Friday. It can't be done. Do you think Angela should be told?

A The passive with modal verbs and *used to*

A1 You form the passive with modal verbs (*can, could, may, might, must, ought to, shall, should, will, would*) with the infinitive *be* + past participle.

	Active	Passive
+	We **can sell** this product. We **ought to sell** this product.	This product **can be sold**. This product **ought to be sold**.
–	We **mightn't/not sell** it.	It **mightn't/not be sold**.
?	**Should** we **sell** it? How **can** we **sell** it?	**Should** it **be sold**? How **can** it **be sold**?

> ⊙ Negative statements and questions with *ought to* are not very common.

You can use the passive with modal verbs when the agent is unimportant, obvious, or when you don't want to say who the agent is. ◀ See Unit 19 (The passive).

*Our products **must be based** on the best market research.*
*These production schedules **might not be sent out** tomorrow.*

A2 You form the passive with *used to* with the infinitive *be* + past participle.

> ⚠ *Used to* always refers to past situations.

◀ See also Unit 8 (*Used to* and *would*).

	Active	Passive
+	We **used to sell** this product.	This product **used to be sold**.
–	We **didn't use to sell** it.	It **didn't use to be sold**.
?	**Did** we **use to sell** it? Where **did** they **use to sell** it?	**Did** it **use to be sold**? Where **did** it **use to be sold**?

B The passive with verbs with two objects

Some verbs take two objects (e.g. *give, lend, offer, promise, sell, send*). Either one of the two objects can be the subject of the passive verb.

Active	Passive
They give **each visitor a gift**.	**Each visitor** is given a gift. **A gift** is given to each visitor.
The firm sold **defective parts** to **120 customers**.	**120 customers** were sold defective parts. **Defective parts** were sold to 120 customers.

> ⊙ The first passive sentence in each pair above, where the person is the subject, is more informal than the second one.

C *Have something done*

When you ask or pay a professional to do something for you, you can use *have* + object + past participle.

*We **had the scanner repaired** when it broke down. (we paid a specialist firm)*
*They're going to **have the office refurbished** in May.*

D Passives with *get* instead of *be*

You can use the passive with *get* instead of *be*, and in the structure *get something done*.

*He **got fined** €100 for parking on a corner. (more formal = He was fined)*
*I **got a suit made** in Bangkok for $400. (more formal = I had a suit made)*

> ⚠ The *get*-passive is quite informal. Don't use it in formal situations.

> ⊙ The *get*-passive is much more common in spoken language than in writing.

Practice

◄ A1

1 Rewrite these sentences using the passive. Use a phrase with *by* for the agent where necessary.

1 You can reach Gina Patel on 02288 33754, or at gpatel@wiscx.com.

...*Gina Patel can be reached on 02288 33754, or at gpatel@wiscx.com.*...

2 The Regional Director will open the new store on 15 May.

....

3 Do you think the bad weather might delay the building works?

....

4 They may not have sent the payment to the right department.

....

5 People must keep the fire exits clear at all times.

....

6 Couldn't we hold the meeting in a bigger room next time?

....

7 We should pay this invoice by Friday.

....

8 We can't avoid some of the technical problems.

....

◄ A

2 Jakob Nussala gives training courses in project management. Complete this interview about his work using a passive form of the words in brackets.

JOURNALIST: What are the main issues you deal with in the training you do?

JAKOB: Well, project management is very complex. It's mostly about asking the right questions. Before a project, you have to ask whether it **1** ...*can be done*... (*can / do*) . Is it likely that everything **2** ....(*will / complete*) within the timescale? What resources **3** ....(*will / need*)? And so on.

JOURNALIST: Yes, and even if people prepare before a project, the follow-up **4** ....(*may not / do*).

JAKOB: Yes, the follow-up **5** ....(*must not / forget*). We train people to ask the questions: How **6** ....(*could / things / improve*) next time? What **7** ....(*ought / change*) in the future? **8** ....(*could / the next project / complete*) more quickly? Which people **9** ....(*should / inform*) of the results? So, you can see, there are a lot of complex issues.

◉ 20.1 Listen and check your answers.

◄ B

3 A company is planning to expand their business into Vietnam. Complete this extract from a meeting using a passive form of the words in italics.

KIERA: Right, so how's the research into the Vietnamese market going?

REX: Well, **1** *someone lent Hilda* ...*Hilda was lent*... a helpful book about doing business in South East Asia. Also, **2** *someone gave her* ....some useful information by a research agency.

KIERA: OK, then make sure **3** *they give that information* ....to everyone involved in this project.

REX: In fact, Hilda said that **4** *people have sent her* ....a lot of literature about business opportunities in Vietnam. And **5** *they've offered her* ....the chance to visit Vietnamese companies when the team goes there next month.

KIERA: That's fantastic. Now, our last Asian campaign was really successful – **6** *they sold 1,000 units* ....to Japanese customers as a result.

ANNA: Yes, **7** *they promised me* ....a promotion after that campaign, but I'm still waiting …!

KIERA: Thank you, Anna. Let's try and keep to the agenda. So we're planning something similar for Vietnam, with a launch at the trade fair in October. **8** *They will send examples of our new product range* ....to our local agent a week before the fair. Now, let's just check that everyone understands their role in the project …

◄ C, D   **4** Read these comments by different speakers and answer the questions.

ULLA: I had my website designed by a local firm.

KIRSTEN: I got contracted to design a website for a new online ticket agency.

GIACOMO: I got my speech written for me by a professional speech-writer.

JOAO: I had written a speech for our sales conference last year.

YUNIS: I had paid twice without realising it.

ELENA: I got paid extra for running the firm's stand at the exhibition.

		answer
1	Who wrote a speech?	Joao
2	Who received money from somebody?	
3	Who asked somebody else to design their website?	
4	Who gave somebody money?	
5	Who paid someone to write a speech for them?	
6	Who designed a website?	

◄ A–D   **5** Complete this text using the words in brackets in a passive form from this unit.

Using the collective brain

How can one scientist **1** *have millions of searches done* (have / do / millions of searches) on millions of computers without doing anything himself? The SETI (Search for Extra-Terrestrial Intelligence) institute has found the answer. They have produced software that is downloaded to millions of computers and then scans the universe in the hope that radio signals **2** .... (will / pick up) from intelligent beings on other planets. The theory is that extra-terrestrial life **3** .... (should / detect) more easily this way instead of **4** .... (get / do / the same searches) by one or two large computers in an observatory.

Well, a similar principle **5** .... (could / apply) more and more in big businesses. The idea is this: large corporations **6** .... (have / make / predictions) about the markets by their employees. This **7** .... (can / do) via the company's computer network. Hundreds of employees then make a prediction about something specific. For example, if 200 out of 250 employees all think a new line will not sell in Europe but **8** .... (could / market) successfully in Asia, this might be more reliable than if the company **9** .... (have / make / the same prediction) by a team of experts. Employees who predict the right answer **10** .... (get / award) prizes or small bonuses.

Make it personal

Read what one freelance graphic designer said about being freelance.

'You don't get paid regularly and you don't get holidays! You agree a price with the client, then they want to have things added for nothing.'

How would you describe your work situation informally? Can you think of things you can say about it using the passive with *have* or *get*?

⊙ Here are some expressions based on modal passives that are very common in written business reports. They are less common in informal speaking.

As might be expected, there is intense competition between manufacturers.
It should be noted that these rules apply only in EU countries.

Exchange rate variations *should be taken into account / considered / included.*
The cost of transporting the goods *should not be forgotten.*
This *can/could/should be seen/regarded as* a major business opportunity.

It could be argued that the over-60s are our most important market these days.
Expanding into South Asia *may/might be described as* the most exciting challenge we face.

As can be seen from Table 4 of this report, sales of soft drinks have increased sharply. (refers to places in a text)
We are making good progress in some new markets, *as will be seen* on page 28.

⚠ Don't add the subject *it* to *as can/will be seen* (not *as it can be seen* / or *as it will be seen*).

6 **Rewrite the words in italics using a suitable passive modal expression.**

1 *You could describe our customer base as* mostly well-off, technically-minded over-50s.

   Our customer base may/might be described as
   ....

2 *It is obvious from the flowchart that* the management structure is very complex.

   ....

3 *We should not forget our environmental responsibilities* when we design new products.

   ....

4 *As you'd guess,* our main competitors usually launch an almost identical product soon after we launch ours.

   ....

5 *We'll see on page 40 of this report that* growth in the airline sector has been slow. However, *we should take notice of the fact that* low-cost airlines have generally done better than large, national carriers.

   ....

6 *We must consider the current slowdown in the housing market* with regard to projected sales for 2012.

   ....

7 *You could say that* this is the wrong time to launch a new facial cosmetic range, but our market research suggests the opposite.

   ....

8 *We can consider 2009 to be* our best year ever.

   ....

Make it personal

Think of:

a something someone did at work recently which could have been done better;

b something important that must get done within the next month;

c something you are going to have done (e.g. something repaired, changed, redesigned, replaced) at your workplace or at home.

Making your meaning clear and avoiding misunderstandings

Read this comment from a manager to his team member, Lucy.

What words does he use so that he doesn't offend Lucy?

> Lucy, I'm sorry. I think there may be a slight misunderstanding. We're not advertising the new position yet.

A Rewording what you say

You can use these expressions if you need to repeat what you say using different words:
I mean, in other words, let me put it this/another way, what I mean is, what I'm saying is, what I'm trying to say is.

⊙ *I mean* and *in other words* are the most frequent.

TV advertising is just a paid form of non-personal communication. **In other words** *you're paying a company to put information about your product into some sort of media.*
We need to be proactive. **What I mean is** *we need to see where the market is going before it happens.*

B Correcting yourself and other people

B1 You can use these expressions if you need to correct yourself:
I don't think that's right, I mean/meant, I should have said, I think I've got that wrong, my mistake, (Oh) sorry, what I really/actually meant was.

⊙ People often use them together. *Sorry* and *I mean* are the most common.

It's room 463. **Sorry, I mean** *436.*
So, it's model B66Q. Oh, **sorry, I think I've got that wrong.** / **My mistake. I should have said** *B66O.*
I said we deliver in 24 hours. **I meant** / **What I actually meant was** *we process the order in 24 hours.*

B2 It can sound rude if you correct someone else, so people often use indirect expressions such as *I think / Are you sure?* and verbs such as *may* and *might* to soften what they say.

You wanted to speak to Henri Velbon? Ah, **I think** *you* **may have been given** *some wrong information. Henri isn't in this office; he's in our Paris branch.*

A: *Angela thinks the new Health and Safety Directive doesn't apply to small firms.*
B: **Really?** / **Are you sure?** / **I think you/she may have got that wrong.** / **I'm not sure that's right.**

C Misunderstanding and getting things clearer

C1 You can use these expressions if you don't understand what someone is trying to tell you or if you want to ask them to make things clearer:
Could you explain that a bit more (for me)? I'm not sure I know what you mean. What does that mean (exactly)? What is that?

People often use them together.

Operational cost pairings? **Could you explain that a bit more for me? I'm not sure I know what you mean.**

⚠ Say *explain something to/for someone.* Don't say *explain someone something.*

Could you **explain the process to/for me** *please?* (not *Could you explain me the process please?*)

C2 People are often polite and indirect about misunderstandings in order to maintain a good relationship. They use 'softening' words such as *maybe, perhaps* and *slight.*

Perhaps I've misunderstood (you)? / **Maybe I've got it wrong?** *Did you say we have to pay the insurance on the goods?*
(I'm afraid) there's been a slight misunderstanding. / **I think we may have misunderstood one another.** *We thought you were going to send your legal representative to us today.*

⚠ Don't say (*I think*) *you're wrong* as you might offend someone.

Practice

◄A **1** Complete this interview with a nurse about performance audits using expressions from A. Sometimes more than one answer is possible.

NURSE: The problem is that we have so many audits but we don't make any connections between them.
1 Let ...me put it another way...., the management do all these audits but they don't look at the whole picture.

RESEARCHER: Can you say more about this? **2** I ...., can you give an example?

NURSE: Well, I wasn't happy about the last audit they did here. **3** What .... there were problems with the last audit process. The nurses weren't prepared for it – **4** I ...., they didn't know it was going to happen, so they couldn't do their jobs properly. So **5** in .... we need to know before the audit people come in.

RESEARCHER: Do senior management realise that? **6** I ...., have they said, 'OK. We'll tell you about it next time'?

NURSE: Not really. And the other thing is the staff can't change some of the things either. So
7 let ....: the audits make recommendations but we don't have the authority to make the necessary changes, and that's the trouble.

◄B **2** Complete this conversation using the information in brackets and expressions from B. Sometimes more than one answer is possible.

DIRK: So, we're suggesting a 15% discount to customers who fly with partner airlines.
1 ...Oh, sorry, I mean 10%.... (corrects himself – 10%)

AHMED: Yes. We trialled that in the high season last year.

DIRK: Actually, **2** .... (corrects Ahmed – low season)

JENNA: Yes, it was January to May, **3** .... (corrects herself – March) It looks like online bookings went up.

AHMED: **4** .... (corrects Jenna – they went down 0.2%)

JENNA: Oh, **5** .... (corrects herself) I'm reading the wrong column here. Yes, online sales were actually down.

DIRK: But I don't think we should rush into an exclusive deal with Flannair.

AHMED: Well, no. That's never been our intention. We know that would be crazy.

DIRK: Yes, sorry, I didn't mean that. **6** .... (explains what he means) we should look at one or two of the new carriers too, such as Streamjet or Air Atlantic.

AHMED: Right. Yes, well, Streamair, **7** .... (corrects himself – Streamjet), are doing well on their Scandinavian routes.

◄C **3** Complete this customer's phone conversation with an insurance clerk using the information in brackets and expressions from C.

CUSTOMER: **1** ...Could you explain the different car insurance policies you offer?...............
(ask for an explanation of the different car insurance policies they offer)

CLERK: Well, there are three basic types. OK? First, there's third-party insurance.

CUSTOMER: **2** .... (ask the clerk to explain what it means)

CLERK: Basically, it means you're insured for damage to other people's cars. Then the second type is third-party, fire and theft.

CUSTOMER: **3** .... (ask her to say more about this)

CLERK: It's the same as the first type, but you're also insured if your car is stolen or if it's damaged in a fire.

CUSTOMER: **4** .... (check if you misunderstood) So, with the second type my car is insured against some things?

CLERK: That's right. And finally, there's fully comprehensive insurance.

CUSTOMER: **5** .... (say you don't understand and then ask her to explain this to you)

CLERK: It means you're insured against damage to your own and other people's cars. It basically covers everything. Why don't you give me your name and phone number and I can arrange for an agent to call you with more details?

CUSTOMER: **6** .... (say there's been a misunderstanding) I'm not ready to buy a policy. I was just interested in the types there are.

🔘 SS 5.1 Listen and compare your answers.

Test 5: Units 17–20

1 Complete this article using the verbs in brackets with *will/may/can* or in the present simple, or an imperative form.

What not to do before you start your own business

Most advice tells you what you should do before you start a business. Here are nine things you *shouldn't* do.

- Don't get a business bank account. Your personal bank account 1 ....will work.... (*work*) perfectly well if someone 2 .... (*want*) to write you a cheque, or if you 3 .... (*need*) to pay for something.

- Don't get a loan. If you 4 .... (*get*) a loan from anyone, you 5 .... (*have to*) pay back much more than you borrow.

- Don't waste money on expensive advertising for your business. If you 6 .... (*spend*) all of your savings on publicity, you 7 .... (*not have*) any money left to pay yourself.

- Don't hire a lawyer. You 8 .... (*not need*) a lawyer unless you 9 .... (*break*) the law, or someone else's lawyer 10 .... (*contact*) you.

- Don't hire anyone. If you 11 .... (*do*) the work yourself, 12 .... (*not waste*) money on paying someone else's salary.

- Don't buy expensive office supplies. If you 13 .... (*need*) a pencil, you 14 .... (*find*) one somewhere in your house!

- Don't buy any equipment – rent it! If it 15 .... (*not be*) something you can rent by the day, there 16 .... (*be*) another local business you can rent it from.

- Don't try to find a partner. What do you need a partner for? If you, the inventor of your product or service, 17 .... (*not sell*) it, no one 18 .... (*be able to*).

- Don't get a business phone number. If someone 19 .... (*want*) to call you, 20 .... (*ask*) them to call your mobile or your home number.

2 a Five children answered the question, 'If you could run your own business, what would it be?' Find and correct one mistake in each answer.

1 If I'd had enough money, I'd open a small hotel ....I had....

2 If I had the choice, I would want to run any business – too much hard work! ....

3 If I had a business, it must be a bus company. Everyone uses the bus! ....

4 If I would choose any business, I'd love to breed dogs or any other sort of animal. People make me crazy!
   ....

5 I volunteered to help anyone in any way that I could. ....

b Five retired employees answered the question, 'If you had run your own business, what would it have been?' Correct one mistake in each answer.

1 If I'd had rich friends, I would sold art because my passion was art. ....

2 If I would be richer when I was younger, I wouldn't have worked at all. I hate working! ....

3 If I'd graduated, I started an international university for students from all over the world. ....

4 If I'd been able to raise the money, I'd had started an air taxi service for executives. ....

5 I don't know, but if I would have started my own company, my staff wouldn't have had to wear suits and ties. ....

3 Underline the correct words in each sentence.

1 If I *'m / were* you, I *'ll speak / 'd speak* to the CEO first.

2 If you *'ll arrive / arrive* late, my PA *will show / shows* you where the meeting is.

3 If we *'d give / gave* a discount, people *would place / placed* bigger orders.

4 If it *wasn't / was* for the rise in fuel prices, we *wouldn't be asking / 'd be asking* for a pay rise.

5 They *'ll offer / offer* the job to Kristina unless Su Young *doesn't contact / contacts* us by 6pm today.

6 We *won't take / 'll take* our stand down before the end of the conference in case delegates *will want / want* to ask us more questions after our presentation.

7 Management *are / aren't* happy to let me take early retirement as long as they *can / can't* find someone to do my job.

8 Small investors *would be / could be* very unlikely to read such information if the company *will / were* to provide it in the audit report.

9 We *would've offered / 'll offer* you the job if you *'ll be able to / 'd been able to* start immediately.

10 If we *won / 'd won* the contract, we *wouldn't have had to / won't have to* made so many people redundant.

4 Complete this article about the clothes retailer, Primark, using the verbs in the box in a suitable passive form.

| award   create   greet   make up   open (x 2)   recruit   sell   use   vote |

In November 2007, Primark **1** ....*was awarded*.... prizes for 'Best New Store' (Primark Oxford Street) and 'Value Retailer of the Year'. Also, Primark **2** ....'Best Value High Street Fashion' by GMTV and ITV viewers.

In the financial year 2006/7, 32 new stores **3** ...., including one in London's Oxford Street in April. In the Oxford Street store, one million items **4** .... in its first ten days of trading.

Since last year, five additional stores **5** .... in Spain.

All of these **6** .... with a great amount of enthusiasm by customers and media. For the new stores, large numbers of staff **7** .... through recruitment programmes to match local circumstances.

Primark mainly sells womenswear, but also 25% of sales **8** .... of menswear and childrenswear.

A strong image **9** .... for the Primark brand – 'Look Good, Pay Less'. Many types of media **10** .... to create an impact upon and target new customers.

5 Complete the sentences using the verbs in italics in a suitable passive form.

1 Health and Safety training sessions ....*must be run*.... by qualified Health and Safety officers. (*must / run*)

2 The item .... carefully to avoid damage in transit. (*should / wrap*)

3 We .... the order yesterday but we haven't received it yet. (*promise*)

4 The maintenance manager .... since it was installed. No wonder it doesn't work! (*not have / the central heating / check*)

5 We've got to .... It's boiling in the office. (*get / the air conditioning / fix*)

6 The water machine .... every two days, but the suppliers haven't been for ages. (*used to / refill*)

7 When ....? I need it in the next hour. (*the report / finish*)

8 How much .... for our old factory? (*might / we / offer*)

21 Questions

A manager who works for an Internet service provider is talking about customer sales.

a Which question can you answer with 'yes' or 'no'?

b Which questions need a longer answer?

> When I meet a new customer I often say, 'Can I ask you a question? If you had no internet access for a day, how much would it cost your business? What would the effects be?'

A Forming questions

A1 Questions usually have a different word order from statements. The subject usually comes after the verb. If there is more than one verb, the subject comes after the first verb.

Statements	Questions
She's the boss.	*Is she the boss?*
Clive is coming.	*Why is Clive coming?*
The meeting was long.	*How long was the meeting?*
You've met Tara.	*Have you met Tara?*
They've been working.	*Where have they been working?*
It's made in China.	*Where is it made?*
The CEO was sacked.	*Why was the CEO sacked?*
We can meet later.	*Can we meet later?*
	When can we meet?

A2 Present simple questions often need *do* or *does*. Past simple questions often need *did*.

Statements	Questions
You need a new laptop.	*What **do** you need?*
	***Do** you need a new laptop?*
He travels a lot.	*How often **does** he travel?*
	***Does** he travel a lot?*
They bought the company.	*When **did** they buy the company?*
	***Did** they buy it recently?*

B Question words as subject and object

A question word can be the subject or object in a question. When the question word is the subject, you do not need *do/does* (present simple) or *did* (past simple).

Question word = subject	Question word = object (The subject is underlined)
***Who** likes the boss?*	***Who** does <u>the boss</u> like?*
***Who** invited him?*	***Who** did <u>he</u> invite?*
***Who** resigned?*	***Who** have <u>they</u> sacked?*
***What**'s going to happen?*	***What** are <u>we</u> going to do?*

Compare:

A: ***Who took Jan*** *to the airport?*
B: *The taxi driver (took Jan to the airport).*

A: ***Who did Jan take*** *to the airport?*
B: *(Jan took) Ursula (to the airport).*

C *What/which/whose* + noun; *how* + adjective/adverb

C1 You can ask questions with *what/which/whose* + noun.

What make *are the computers in your office?*
What kind *of car do you drive?*
Which hotel *does the CEO prefer – the Hyatt or the Sheraton?*
Whose responsibility *is it to do a risk assessment?*

⚠ Use *which* not *what* in questions like these: *Which one(s) …? Which person …?*

Which one *was it?* (**not** ~~*What one*~~)
Which engineer *did you see?* (**not** ~~*What engineer*~~)

C2 You can ask about sizes, amounts and prices with *how* + adjective/adverb/*much/many*.

How big *is your company?*
How far *do you travel to work?* ***How long*** *does it take?*

How much *do you know about computers?*
How many *people work here?*

D Questions with prepositions

Prepositions usually come at the end of questions but before time and place expressions.

*Which company does she work **for**?*
*Who do you report **to** at the moment?*

*Who did you want to speak **to** in Accounts?*
*Which department do you work **in**?*

► See Unit 24 (Reported speech 2) and Speaking strategies 6 (Checking information).

Practice

◄ A **1 a Complete this article about health and safety using *is*, *are*, *do* or *does*.**

The physical safety of your staff is your most important concern. Walk around your building and ask yourself these questions:

Doors

1 ...Are..... the doors locked at night?   2 .... the doors close properly?   3 .... fire exits kept clear?

Furnishings

4 .... every employee have enough light?   5 .... the carpet need replacing?

Fire

6 .... the fire alarm work?   7 .... it tested regularly?   8 .... employees know the fire drill?

General hazards

9 .... there any loose wires on the floor?   10 .... there a first-aid kit available to all staff?

b Complete the second part of the article using *was*, *were*, *did*, *has* or *have*.

If the worst happens and there is an accident, you may have to answer these questions:

1 How ....did....... the accident happen?   6 When .... you told about it?

2 What .... the employee doing at the time?   7 .... this ever happened before?

3 .... he or she know the safety procedures?   8 .... you aware of the hazard?

4 .... the employee badly hurt?   9 What .... you done to reduce the risk?

5 When .... the accident reported?   10 .... you reviewed any safety procedures?

◄ A **2 Read Jane's notes for an interview for an account manager in a construction firm. Write the questions she asks the candidate.**

- what he knows about the company
- why he wants to leave his current job
- strengths & weaknesses?
- applying for other jobs?
- why he wants this job
- happy to travel?
- can work well under pressure?
- how he got on with people in last job
- what he's achieved in his career so far
- how he sees his future career

1   _What do you know about the company?_

2 ....

3 ....

4 ....

5 ....

6 ....

7 ....

8 ....

9 ....

10 ....

◀ B **3** Write two questions for each picture using the correct form of the words in brackets.

1 (who / Cathy / report to)
A: **a** ...Who does Cathy report to...?
B: She reports to the MD, Jun Woong
A: **b** ...Who reports to Cathy...?
B: Matt Black and Jinsook Kim

| Jun Woong MD |
| Cathy Mills HRD |

| Matt Black | Jinsook Kim |

2 (who / Ana / tell)
A: **a** .... to go to the meeting?
B: Katya told her to go.
A: **b** .... to go to the meeting?
B: She told Juan to go.

Hi Juan
Katya wants me to be at the meeting at 10 am.
You need to be there too.
See you there. Ana

3 (who / Beth / email)
A: **a** ....?
B: Kyoko.
A: **b** ....?
B: Yuki did.

From: Yuki
Subject:
Date:
To: Beth

From: Beth
To: Kyoko

4 (who / Sue / want to see)
A: **a** ....?
B: Ms Klein wants to see her.
A: **b** ....?
B: Jo.

Sue, Ms Klein wants to see you. Are you free?

No, I want to go and see Jo now.

◀ C **4** A legal firm has printed its brochures with some mistakes. Write the questions the MD asks the marketing manager using *what*, *which*, *whose*, or *how* and the words in italics.

Marketing manager	MD	
There's a *mistake* on the front cover.	1	What mistake is there?
Well, it's pretty *bad*, I'm afraid.	2	....
Very. It has the wrong *photo* for the CEO.	3	Well, ...
It's a *guy* from the post room.	4	....
I'm not sure. I found something *else* too.	5	....
The text is the wrong *colour*.	6	....
Pink. Anyway, we can do it again *quickly*.	7	....
In two days, but it'll be *expensive*.	8	....
I'll find out. It really wasn't *my fault*.	9	....

◀ A–D **5** Make questions by putting the words in the correct order.

1 for / working / who / you / are / at the moment / ? ...Who are you working for at the moment?...

2 you / are / in / involved / projects / what / ? ....

3 jobs / you / applied / how many / for / have / in the last ten years / ? ....

4 which / have / lunch / you / do / colleagues / with / ? ....

5 ever / colleague / complained / have / about / a / you / ? ....

6 to / you / who / did / complain / ? ....

7 your performance / your salary / does / depend / on / ? ....

Make it personal

21.1 Listen to the questions in Exercise 5 and give answers that are true for you.

21 **Business talk:** Persuading and giving opinions with negative questions

Negative questions have a negative verb. Use them when you want the answer to be 'yes'.

Isn't it a nice day? (the speaker thinks it is a nice day)
Don't you like the new office?
Can't we finish early?

You can use negative questions to persuade someone to do or think something when:

- you suggest an idea and want other people to say 'yes' to it.

  Why don't we / Can't we invite some customers to our conference? (Let's)

- you give your opinion and you want other people to agree with you.

  Isn't it a bit expensive for a basic camera?   **Don't you think** it's expensive?

Notice the meaning of yes and no when you reply to a negative question.

A: **Don't you like** the new office?

B: Yes. (I like it) / No. (I don't like it)

⚠️ **Negative questions about people's actions can have two meanings. Be careful because they can sound rude or critical.**

Didn't you email all the regional offices? (1 I'm sure you said you did – I'm just checking; 2 I think you didn't and you should have done this)

---

6 **a** Three managers are looking at a new logo for their hotel chain and they have different opinions. Write negative questions they could ask to persuade the others of their view. Sometimes more than one answer is possible.

Comfy Inn

Lee: Communications

1 I hope everyone thinks it's successful.

  Don't you think it's successful? / Isn't it successful?

2 It's very memorable. ....

3 Let's use it for the new campaign. ....

Carole: Marketing

4 The colours are a bit bright. ....

5 I think the teddy bear looks a bit silly. ....

6 Let's do some market research on it. ....

Martin: Sales

7 The teddy bear is childish. ....

8 Maybe you can make it a bit less bright. ....

b Look at these comments which Carole and Martin made to Lee about the new logo. What could these comments mean? Why might Lee be upset to hear them? How could you change them so that he wouldn't be upset?

1 Haven't you tested this with customers?   **3** Aren't you going to change it?

2 Didn't we ask for a different colour?   **4** Don't the design people do research?

Make it personal

Look at your company's logo or literature. How might you persuade your colleagues that it needs changing in some way? Write four negative questions to use.

22 Question tags

Read these two conversations.

Which one sounds more natural and friendly? Why?

1

The new receptionist is nice.

Yes. She's not very old.

No. About 22, I think.

2

The new receptionist is nice, isn't she?

Yes. She's not very old, is she?

No. About 22, I think.

A Forming question tags

A1 A question tag is a short verb and a pronoun, added at the end of the statement. A question tag changes a statement into a question.

A2 When the verb in the statement is positive, the verb in the tag is negative. When the verb in the statement is negative, the verb in the tag is positive.

Statement	Question tag
She's very nice.	*She's very nice, **isn't she?***
She's not very old.	*She's not very old, **is she?***

○ Question tags make the conversation more friendly because they invite the other speaker(s) to answer. They are common in conversations and informal emails. They are not used in formal writing.

A3 The form of the question tag depends on the main verb in the sentence.

Subject	Main verb	Tag
It	*wasn't too late,*	*was it?*
We	*buy parts from them,*	*don't we?*
Philip	*bought a new laptop,*	*didn't he?*
You	*aren't leaving,*	*are you?*
They	*were working today,*	*weren't they?*
The invoice	*hasn't arrived yet,*	*has it?*
They	*had missed deadlines before,*	*hadn't they?*

Sentences with modal verbs use the same modal verb in the tag. Sentences with *Let's* use *shall* in the tag.

*Business Class **would** be much more expensive, **wouldn't it?***
*We **can't** compete with large manufacturers, **can we?***
*Let's stop now, **shall we?***

⚠ Sentences with *used to* have *did/didn't* in the tag.

*You **used to** work at Zetac, **didn't you?***

⚠ The question tag for *I'm* or present continuous is *aren't I?*

*I'm late, **aren't I?***
*I'm **taking** you to the airport, **aren't I?***

A4 Notice the difference between *have* and *have got*.

*You **have** my email address, **don't/haven't you?***
*You**'ve got** my email address, **haven't you?*** (not ~~don't you?~~)

○ With the verb *have*, the tag with *do* is much more frequent than the tag with *have*.

B Using question tags

There are two main types of question tags:

- **Type 1: positive verb + negative tag**
  You can use Type 1 when you think the other person will agree by saying 'yes'.

  A: *You **know** Donald, **don't you?*** (I think you know him. I expect you to say 'yes'.)
  B: *Yes, I've known him for years.*

- **Type 2: negative verb + positive tag**
  You can use Type 2 when you think the other person will agree by saying 'no'.

  A: *Text messages **don't** cost much, **do they?*** (I think they don't cost much. I expect you to say 'no'.)
  B: *No, they're very cheap.*

C Intonation

You can use falling intonation ↘ with tags if you are fairly sure of the answer, and rising intonation ↗ if you are not so sure.

🔊 **22.1 Listen and notice the difference.**

Sure	Unsure
*We **met** in Paris, **didn't we?***	*We **met** in Paris, **didn't we?***
*She**'s** not in our group, **is she?***	*She**'s** not in our group, **is she?***

Practice

◄ A 　**1**　**Complete these sentences using the correct form of *do*.**

　　1　You work with Jenny Sharpe, ...*don't*.... you?

　　2　We never reach our sales targets, ... we?

　　3　The warehouse didn't open yesterday, ... it?

　　4　She's not here yet. She always arrives late, ... she?

　　5　We got some interesting news today, ... we?

　　6　Nick doesn't work in the São Paolo office any more, ... he?

　　7　These prices need to go up, ... they?

　　8　Melanie travelled a lot last year, ... she?

　　9　This phone doesn't have an external line, ... it?

　　10　We don't use this old contact list any more, ... we?

◄ A 　**2**　**Add question tags where possible to these conversations to make them sound more natural and friendly. Make changes to the punctuation as necessary.**

　　1　TIM: You don't know each other⁄ ...., *do you?*
　　　　RON: No, we haven't met before⁄ ...., *have we?*
　　　　LISA: No. I'm Lisa. How do you do? ....

　　2　KIM: They delivered the order on time. ....
　　　　LUCA: Yes, but they didn't deliver it for free. ....
　　　　KIM: No, that's true. ....

　　3　ALAN: The meeting lasted a long time. ....
　　　　PILAR: Yes, marketing meetings always last for hours. ....
　　　　ALAN: Yes, and they're so boring. ....
　　　　PILAR: I need a coffee! Let's go to the cafeteria. ....

　　4　RAJIV: We don't have a distributor in Moldova. ....
　　　　NUALA: No, but we've got some contacts there. ....
　　　　RAJIV: Oh yes, Vimala was there last year. I'd forgotten. ....

　　5　ANGIE: The delivery hasn't arrived yet. ....
　　　　BILL: No. It never arrives on time. ....
　　　　ANGIE: No, never. ....

　　6　BLAKE: Michelle isn't working at the Paris office any more. ....
　　　　KIARA: No. She works with Gosia in Warsaw now. ....
　　　　BLAKE: Yes, I think you're right. ....

　　7　NORA: You've got the agenda for the meeting. ....
　　　　ELSA: Yes, and you have the presentation on your laptop. ....
　　　　NORA: Yes. So everything's ready. See you later. ....

　　8　JAN: We weren't advertising much in the Italian press. ....
　　　　ZOË: No, but we had web pages in Italian. ....
　　　　JAN: Yes, I guess the website was enough. ....

◄ A **3** **Complete this discussion about a new online brochure using question tags.**

BRIAN: I've just got the new brochure for the website. We could have a look at it now, **1** ...couldn't we... ?

TONY: Yeah. We should look at it – it's going to be great having it. It's got everything we need, **2** .... ?

BRIAN: Yes, you've got everything in one place now, **3** .... ?

TONY: Great, so I'll be able to visit a client with that now and be completely confident, **4** .... ?

BRIAN: Right. And if we need to make any changes, we can update the brochure as necessary. We might need to change things occasionally, **5** .... ?

TONY: Yes. It used to take ages to make changes to the old paper brochures, **6** .... ? Now, I've got a meeting on Friday with Cattlans. You can't get the final version ready for that, **7** .... ?

BRIAN: Probably. But you'd need it by the end of Thursday, **8** .... ?

TONY: Ah, yes, please. I'll be going straight to their offices on Friday morning.

BRIAN: OK. I should get it ready by Thursday morning, then, **9** .... ? So you can read it before your visit.

TONY: Yes, ideally. Now, I mustn't forget to confirm the meeting with Cattlans, **10** .... ?

◄ B **4** **Write questions using question tags.**

1 Ask a colleague if they are the new IT manager. You expect the answer to be 'yes'.

...You're the new IT manager, aren't you?...

2 Ask a colleague if they need the spreadsheet any more. You expect the answer to be 'no'.

....

3 Ask someone if you should book a room for your meeting. You expect the answer to be 'yes'.

....

4 Ask someone if their firm has a branch in Amsterdam. You expect the answer to be 'yes'.

....

5 Ask a colleague if Linda works on Mondays. You expect the answer to be 'no'.

....

6 Ask someone if they used to work in sales. You expect the answer to be 'yes'.

....

7 Ask someone if the members of the Board seemed interested in further talks. You expect the answer to be 'yes'.

....

8 Ask someone if photo paper can be used with this printer. You expect the answer to be 'no'.

....

◄ C **5** ● **22.2 Listen to the intonation that the speakers use. Decide if they are sure about what they are saying, or not sure.**

1 You're working on the Westin project, aren't you? ....sure...............

2 We're not using this version of the spreadsheet any more, are we? ....

3 Laila's got a new job, hasn't she? ....

4 We could send them our latest report, couldn't we? ....

5 They said they would finish by 4:30, didn't they? ....

Make it personal

Think of situations where you could use question tags in your job e.g. with a colleague, a customer, your boss. Do you think they are suitable for all those situations? Why (not)?

Sometimes, you do not know if the answer to a question will be 'yes' or 'no'. There is a third type of question tag for this situation, which has a positive main verb **and** a positive verb in the tag. You can use this type of question tag when you want to check information. All the other grammar rules are the same as for Type 1 and Type 2 question tags.

- **Type 3 (positive + positive)**
  A: She**'s** the Human Resources Manager, *is she?* (I don't know if she is or not)
  B: No, she's the Financial Controller.

  A: Paul Summers **owns** the company, **does he?** (I don't know if he owns it or not)
  B: Yes, he actually started it in 1997.

These question tags are common in business, when people need to find out or check information. They have rising intonation ⤴.

22.3 Listen to the examples above.

6 **a** **Complete these sentences using Type 3 checking question tags.**

   1 You work with Charles, ...*do you*.... ?

   2 This is your copy of the business plan, ... ?

   3 They sold their shares in Zetac, ... ?

   4 This voice recorder has a USB connection, ... ?

   5 The design team have sent us a drawing, ... ?

   6 We can get a price quote, ... ?

   22.4 Listen and check your answers.

   b **22.4 Listen again and repeat each sentence to practise the intonation.**

7 **Read this conversation about plans for a trade show. Add checking question tags where possible and make changes to the punctuation as necessary.**

   PAUL: Sharon wants some photographs, ...*does she*.... ?

   RITA: Yes, some A4-size photographs.

   PAUL: She's going to use them at the Commercial Vehicle Show.

   RITA: Yeah, we'll have to get them printed by the end of the month.

   PAUL: And we ordered some stickers for the show.

   RITA: Yeah.

   PAUL: It would be nice if we could put a sticker on every invoice we send out before the show to get people interested in visiting our stand.

   RITA: Yeah, I agree.

   PAUL: We can get some more made in time.

   RITA: Yes, they normally do them in 24 hours.

   PAUL: OK. You'll see to that.

   RITA: Yes, I'll do it right away.

Make it personal

Think of four things you are not sure about or really do not know, connected with your workplace or your work situation. It could be where you can find or do something, or how you do something, or who somebody is or what their job is. Write four questions with question tags of different types that you could use to check the information.

Reported speech 1 (statements and instructions)

Read this extract from a report from a British Printing Industries Federation Survey.

What do you think these employers actually said to the researcher?

10.9% of employers said temporary workers were not required to speak and understand English, even for health and safety purposes.

A Reporting things people say

A1 When you talk about or report what someone said, you can use the same words as the original speaker.
*'It's not my fault.' → She said, '**It's not my fault**.'*

A2 You can also use *he/she said* (*that*). The verb the original speaker used often changes to a past form but if you report the original words soon afterwards, you can use the same tense.

*'It**'s** not my fault.' → **She said** (**that**) it **wasn't** her fault.*
*'I**'m leaving** tomorrow.' → **She said** (**that**) she**'s leaving** tomorrow.' (or she **was leaving**)*

A3 You have to add a person after *told*, but not after *said* or *explained*.

*He **told his boss / me / a colleague** (that) he was leaving.*
*He **said / explained** (that) he was leaving. (**not** He said me he was leaving.)*

B Changing the verb form

B1 The verb in the reported statement often 'goes back' a tense, but you do not need to change past simple to past perfect. *Would, should, could, might* and *used to* do not change.

*'I**'m** not **working** on Friday.'*	→	*He said (that) he **wasn't working** on Friday.*
*'I **don't like** conferences.'*	→	*She explained (that) she **didn't like** conferences.*
*'I **flew** first class to Rio.'*	→	*She said (that) she **flew** first class to Rio. (or **had flown**)*
*'I **wasn't feeling** well.'*	→	*He said (that) he **wasn't feeling** well. (or **hadn't been feeling**)*
*'I **haven't seen** Colin.'*	→	*She told me (that) she **hadn't seen** Colin.*
*'I **have been working** all day.'*	→	*He explained (that) he **had been working** all day.*
*'I**'ll** help you with the report.'*	→	*She said (that) she **would** help me with the report.*
*'I **can't** understand it.'*	→	*He told me (that) he **couldn't** understand it.*
*'I **may** be late for the meeting.'*	→	*She said (that) she **might** be late for the meeting.*
*'We **must** be losing money.'*	→	*He said (that) we **had to be** losing money. (or **must be**)*

*'I **would / should / could / might / used to** cycle to work.' → He said (that) he **would / should / could / might / used to** cycle to work.*

B2 Use the same tense changes with *know, think, realise, believe.*

*Hi! I **didn't know/think/realise** you **worked** here.*

C Changing time expressions

You often need to change time expressions in reported statements and instructions.

*yesterday → **the day before / the previous day***   *today → **that day***
*last week → **the week before / the previous week***   *this morning → **that morning***
*tomorrow → **the next day / the following day***   *next week → **the following week***

*'You have to sign the contract by **this evening**.' → He told us we had to sign the contract by **that evening**.*

D Reporting instructions and requests

If you report what someone tells someone else to do, use *ask/tell* + someone + *to*-infinitive.

*'Sue, could you call the IT Manager?' → Sue's boss **asked/told her to call** the IT Manager.*

Practice

◄ A, B **1** **a** Read the results from a survey on outsourcing. Report each sentence using *said*. Change the verbs to a past form.

1 66% of respondents are disappointed with the results of outsourcing their contracts.

66% said that they were disappointed with the results of outsourcing their contracts.

2 49% have seen only part of the benefit they expected from outsourcing.

....

3 39% will renew their outsourcing contract with their existing supplier.

....

4 15% plan to bring the service back in-house.

....

5 78% are satisfied with the service provided by their main outsourcing supplier.

....

b Read the results from a survey of the printing industry. Report the sentences using the verbs in brackets. Change the verbs to a past form.

		Employers agreed	Employees agreed
1	Employees are regularly briefed on the company's performance.	71.2%	37.6%
2	Employees are involved in decisions and can influence them.	83%	21.9%
3	Employers work in close partnership with the union.	31.6%	18.8%
4	Employers have taken steps to improve the working environment.	87.5%	30.9%
5	The management need to do move to improve the working environment.	54.3%	84.7%

1 *71.2% of employers and 37.6% of employees agreed that employees were regularly briefed on the*

company's performance. .... *(agreed)*

2 .... *(thought)*

3 .... *(believed)*

4 .... *(said)*

5 .... *(stated)*

► You can read the original survey reports on page 222.

◄ B **2** **Four colleagues are meeting to choose a corporate gift for a client. Report their meeting, changing the verb forms where possible.**

TIM: Choosing the right gift is difficult. I've been looking at the catalogues and I haven't found anything. We could give the client a clock.

KLARA: We used to give people clocks years ago. But they're bad luck in some cultures. I might do some research on that.

YURI: We should give something fun, like an electronic sudoku. I'll look online.

FATMA: We must be careful because we can't have things like wine coolers or penknives. And as Klara said, if we choose the wrong gift, we may run into cultural problems.

Tim said that choosing the right gift
was difficult. He said that he ...

....

....

....

....

....

....

....

....

....

◄B, D **3** You showed some potential clients around your office yesterday. Read what some people said during their visit.

1 Can you pick us up at our hotel?

2 We didn't sleep well.

3 I'll order some coffee.

4 Don't worry about it.

5 Will you show our visitors round the building?

6 Don't leave your valuables in the meeting room.

7 Please don't smoke.

8 Can you speak a little slower?

9 We've met before.

10 We're definitely going to place an order.

Tell a colleague about the visit, using reported speech with *said*, *asked* or *told*.

1 I live near their hotel, so they ...*asked me to pick them up*... .

2 There are some noisy building works in the hotel and they ....

3 None of them had had breakfast, so I ....

4 One guy spilled coffee over my suit. He was embarrassed but I ....

5 They all wanted to see the offices, so my boss ....

6 We're always worried about security, so I ....

7 One woman got out a packet of cigarettes, so I ....

8 I was speaking a bit too fast and one of the guys ....

9 I recognised one of the group and I ....

10 They were impressed with our service and they ....

◄B **4** Complete these conversation extracts using the correct form of the verbs in italics.

1 A: My wife works in Accounts.   B: I didn't realise you ...*were*... (*be*) married.

2 A: I love all the travel I do in my job.   B: Oh, I thought you .... (*not enjoy*) it.

3 A: My job isn't going very well.   B: Hm. I knew something .... (*be*) wrong.

4 A: You can fax the order.   B: I thought you .... (*not use*) faxes any more.

5 A: Can you come to the meeting?   B: I didn't know there .... (*be*) a meeting.

6 A: Jon hasn't qualified yet.   B: But I thought he .... (*do*) all his exams.

◄A–D **5** Lynn left her assistant, Ray, a voice mail about a customer order which he didn't receive. Later she emailed her boss to explain the situation. Complete her email using the correct verbs or time expressions.

Hi Ray, it's Lynn. Can you do me a favour? Seatons rang with an urgent order this morning. Can you check that we have stock available to send them this afternoon? There was enough stock in the warehouse yesterday, but I don't know what we have in stock today – my computer wasn't working before lunch. The order has to be with them by tomorrow or they'll cancel. I'm away the rest of the week, but I'll try and call you this evening. Thanks.

I left my assistant, Ray, a voice mail on 9 May. I told him that Seatons **1** ...*had rung*... with an order **2** .... and I asked him **3** .... that we **4** .... stock to send them **5** .... I didn't know the stock levels. I knew that there **6** .... enough stock in the warehouse **7** ...., but I didn't know what we **8** .... in stock **9** .... because my computer **10** .... earlier. I explained that the order **11** .... to be with Seatons by **12** .... or they **13** .... I said I **14** .... away the rest of the week but that I **15** .... and call him **16** .... Unfortunately I didn't have time to call him and check.

Make it personal

Find a survey from your own industry or company and write a short report in English. Or report five things people said at work last week. Use five different reporting verbs.

23 Business talk: Talking about news

In informal conversations and emails, you can use reporting verbs like *ask*, *say* and *tell* in the past continuous to report things you have heard. You can use the past continuous to:

- talk about news or something you have only recently heard about.

  *Lee **was telling me about** his new boss last night.*
  *Someone **was telling me that** you can't bring children into the office now.*

- focus on the topic of conversation instead of the words the original speaker used.

  *Sara **was saying that** the food in the canteen has been a lot better lately.*
  *Peter **was asking me about** the new rep. How's he getting on?*

⚠ **Don't use the past continuous in this way in formal writing.**

---

6 Complete these conversations using the past continuous of *ask*, *say* or *tell*.

1 A: I was just down in HR and Pam ….*was telling*…. me about the new training programme. She ……………………………… that all members of staff are now entitled to five days' training a year.

   B: Oh, it's funny you should mention that, because someone in Production ……………………………… me about that the other day. I didn't know what to tell them as it was the first I'd heard about it.

   A: Yeah, well as I ……………………………… Pam – it's long overdue.

2 A: My bank manager ……………………………… that the branch is very involved with the local community. She ……………………………… it's so important these days.

   B: Well, you remember I ……………………………… you about that event I went to on social responsibility? All the speakers ……………………………… it's high on the agenda in all the big companies these days.

3 A: How much are we paying for buildings insurance?

   B: A lot! We're thinking about changing our insurer next year. Leslie ……………………………… it's a good idea to shop around and get several quotes. He ……………………………… we could probably get it much cheaper than we're paying now.

   A: That's exactly what I ……………………………… him last week but he wouldn't listen to me then!

4 A: John ……………………………… me about the GHI exhibition. He wanted to know if we were going this year.

   B: I don't know. Someone ……………………………… me how expensive it was to exhibit there last year with the number of people attending.

   🔘 **23.1 Listen and check your answers.**

Make it personal

Write an informal email to a close colleague about four pieces of news that you have heard at work recently using past continuous reporting verbs.

Reported speech 2 (questions)

Read this sentence, which reports two questions.

What were the original questions?

> We asked Mr Walsh if he would become a board member and what his schedule was for the coming year.

A Reporting questions

A1 The word order in a reported question is the same as a statement: 1 subject 2 verb.

'How much is the car?' → *He asked how much **the car was**.* (**not** *how much was the car*)

⚠ Don't use *do/did* in reported questions.

*She asked what he **wanted**.* (**not** *what did he want*)

⚠ Don't put a question mark at the end of reported questions.
(**not** *He asked me who my boss was?*)

◀ See Unit 23 (Reported speech 1) for rules on tense changes in reported speech.

A2 When you report *wh-* questions, you can use *ask (someone) / want to know* + question word (e.g. *who, what, how much*).

'Where is the meeting?' → *He **asked where** the meeting was.* (**not** *where was the meeting*)
'When can I start?' → *He **wanted to know when** he could start.*

A3 When you talk about or report *yes/no* questions, you can use *ask (someone) / want to know* + *if/whether*.

'Is the shop open yet?' → *She **wanted to know if** the shop was open yet.*
'Do you speak any other languages?' → *He **asked whether** she spoke any other languages.*

A4 With *ask* you can put the person asked after the verb.

*He asked **me** who my boss was.* (**not** *He asked to me*)

⚠ Don't put the person after *want to know*.
(**not** *He wanted to know me who my boss was.*)

B Asking polite questions

You can use the reported question structure when you want to ask or request something politely. We often use *Do you know …? Can/Could you tell me …? Could I just ask you …? I wonder …* in polite questions.

Direct question	More polite question
What time is it?	***Do you know** what time it is?*
How much is it?	***Can/could you tell me** how much it is?*
Is there a restaurant near here?	***Could I just ask you** if there's a restaurant near here?*

⚠ Don't use a question mark after *I wonder if* + reported question structure.

*I **wonder if** you could open the window.* (**not** *I wonder if you could open the window?*)

C Saying that you are sure/unsure about something

You can use the reported question structure with *be (not) certain, be (not)sure, have no/an idea, (not) know* and *wonder*.

*We**'re not sure** what we should do.*
*I **have an idea** why they didn't buy our products.*
*I **was wondering** who the new manager was.*

Practice

◀ A1–2 **1** Some HR staff are telling each other about inappropriate questions that job candidates have asked them in interviews. Complete the reported questions.

1 'How many personal phone calls can I make a day?'

One candidate asked me *how many personal phone calls he could make a day.*

2 'How many days a year can I take off sick?'

Someone asked me ....

3 'When will I get a pay rise?'

One candidate wanted to know ....

4 'How much do you earn?'

One candidate asked me ....

5 'Why did you keep me waiting before the interview?'

Someone asked me ....

6 'Who is the worst candidate you've interviewed today?'

One interviewee wanted to know ....

7 'Which five-star hotels will I stay in when I travel on business?'

Someone asked me ....

8 'Where can I get the best lunches near to the office?'

Someone asked me ....

◀ A3 **2** During a meeting with a supermarket's Customer Relations department local people asked questions about a new food store. Complete the reported questions in the supermarket's report from this meeting.

1 Are you going to source your food products locally?

2 Are all your products organic?

3 Do you do home deliveries?

4 Can I order my shopping online?

5 'Are you open on Sundays?'

6 Do you offer free reusable bags instead of plastic bags?

7 Is there disabled access?

8 Do you sell your own branded products?

9 Will someone help with packing?

10 Are you going to ask for our comments again in a few months?

1 Customers asked *if/whether we are/were going to source our food products locally.*

2 They wanted to know ....

3 They asked ....

4 They asked ....

5 They wanted to know ....

6 They wanted to know ....

7 They asked ....

8 They asked ....

9 They wanted to know ....

10 They asked ....

◀ A3–4 **3 a** ◉ **24.1 Listen to the questions and report what they ask.**

1 *He asked (me) / wanted to know how many hours a day I work(ed).*

2 ....

3 ....

4 ....

5 ....

6 ....

7 ....

8 ....

b ◉ **24.1 Listen again and answer the questions so that they are true for you.**

◀ B, C **4** The participants on a training course are unsure about some of the course details. Complete their questions using an expression from each box. You will need to use the expressions in Box A more than once.

A	Can you tell me	I've no idea
	Do you know	I'm not sure
	Could I just ask you	I wonder

B	how many	how long	how much
	if	when	whether
	which	who	

1 ...*Do you know if*.... we get a certificate at the end of the course?

2 .... department will do the training first?

3 .... will be running the sessions?

4 .... we have to take a final exam or not.

5 .... each training session will last?

6 .... the course starts and finishes.

7 .... previous knowledge we need to have?

8 .... sessions we have to attend.

◀ A–C **5** Find and correct seven mistakes with the questions in this article about the dangers of internet shopping.

How safe is internet shopping?

Finance companies always say they offer security that allows customers to conduct most internet financial transactions safely. But no system is infallible, as 25,000 customers of an American online travel company discovered recently.

Daniela Robertson was one of those affected but she had no idea her card details had been stolen until she tried to buy a sofa and was refused credit. She immediately called her credit card company and asked ~~to them~~ what the problem was.

The company did the usual security checks. They asked what was her password. They also wanted to know how often she paid off her credit card in full?

They asked to her when she had last visited Rome, because someone had just used her card to spend £2,500 on clothes there. She wondered how that could happen when she was not there?

They also wanted to know her if she had bought anything on the Internet recently. She remembered she had booked a hotel room online the previous month for her holiday in New York.

When she realised her details had been stolen, Daniela asked the credit card company what should she do and whether she could get a new credit card.

1 ...*asked them*....   3 ....   5 ....   7 ....

2 ....   4 ....   6 ....

Make it personal

Think of an interview or some market research you were involved in and report some of the questions.

24 Write for business: Making polite requests in business letters

When you make written requests in English, you need to use appropriately formal and polite language. Here are some useful expressions for making polite requests in business letters.

I/We would be grateful for *any information you could send us concerning this matter.*

I/We would be grateful if you could *send us details of schedules.*

I/We would appreciate it if you could *send us further details.*

I/We would welcome *any advice on local markets.*

Would you consider *send**ing** us some free samples?*

Would you be willing to *offer us a discount?* (would you be happy/prepared to offer us a discount)

Please let us/me know when *we can expect delivery of our latest order.*

Please let us/me know if *you require any further information.*

Please inform us/me of/about *any possible delays.*

Please inform us/me if *you are approached by any other interested companies.*

6 Rewrite these written requests in a more formal style using the words in brackets.

1 Please confirm receipt of our order. (*grateful if*)

   We would be grateful if you could confirm receipt of our order.

2 Please send your payment on receipt of the goods. (*appreciate*)

   ....

3 Are there any job opportunities in your company? (*inform*)

   ....

4 Can you offer us a reduced price for bulk orders? (*consider*)

   ....

5 Are you bringing out any new products this year? (*inform*)

   ....

6 When will this year's price list be out? (*let*)

   ....

7 Can you accept workers on a temporary basis? (*willing*)

   ....

8 Will there be any changes to my insurance policy? (*let*)

   ....

9 Please give us some feedback on our services. (*welcome*)

   ....

10 Can I have the opportunity to meet your personnel manager? (*grateful for*)

   ....

Make it personal

Look at a business letter that you or a colleague has written recently in English. Rewrite any requests using the expressions above.

If you do not have a recent letter, then write one of your own. Try to include at least four formal requests.

Checking information

Read this conversation between a shop assistant and a customer.

How does the customer check what the shop assistant says?

Shop assistant

We could order them. They'd be about two, three weeks.

You could try Blackstone's.

Two or three weeks? Mm. So you don't know any other bookshops?

Customer

Blackstone's?

A Checking information

You can use these expressions to ask someone to repeat what they said:
What? Sorry? I'm sorry? Pardon? What did you say? Sorry, I missed that. Can you say that again?

A: *I need the sales pack by next Tuesday.*
B: **Sorry, I missed that. What did you say?**

⚠ Be careful to say *What?* softly or it can sound rude. Use *Sorry?* if you're in doubt.

B Repeating words and phrases

B1 You can repeat the important words you hear with rising intonation to check something. You can also add *did you say?*

A: *Let's meet at ten o'clock.*
B: **Ten o'clock? Ten o'clock, did you say?**

B2 You can repeat words with falling intonation to confirm or agree something.

A: *Let's meet at ten o'clock.*
B: *OK.* **Ten o'clock,** (*then*).

🔘 **SS 6.1 Listen and notice the difference.**

C Using statements as questions

C1 You can repeat a whole statement as a question to check what you heard.

A: *He's selling his shares.*
B: **He's selling his shares?**

C2 You can also use statement questions to check your understanding of a situation.

A: *They said they could do it.*
B: **So, they're confident about finishing by May? The complete rewrite of the software?**

⚠ Don't use a statement question if you want to ask about a new topic that you haven't talked about before.

D Using echo questions

You can use 'echo questions' to check one key piece of information. These are words or whole sentences with a question word at the end.

A: *Tim went to **Oslo** last week.* B: *He went **where**?*
A: *We're holding a conference **in May**.* B: *You're holding it **when**?*
A: *He's **giving a presentation**.* B: *He's doing **what**?*
A: *They're about **€300**.* B: *They're **how much**?*

⚠ Don't use *why* in echo questions.

A: *He went to Paris* B: *Why did he go?* (**not** He went why?)

◀ See also Unit 21 (Business talk) and Unit 22 (Question tags) for questions to check information.

Practice

◀ A, B **1** a ⦿ **SS 6.2** Listen to six extracts from a conference call.

For each one tick the checking expressions you hear.

	1	2	3	4	5	6
What?						
Pardon?						
Sorry? I'm sorry?	✓					
(What) did you say?						
Can you say that again?						
Sorry, I missed that.						
Repeated words	✓					

SORRY?

b ⦿ **SS 6.3** Listen and use the expressions in Exercise 1a to check what you heard.

◀ C **2** Complete these conversations using the correct form of the words in brackets. Where appropriate, write statement questions. Otherwise write questions with normal question word order.

1 HAZEL: I started my new job last month. So far so good!

ODILE: (*you/enjoy/it*) So, ...you're enjoying it....?

HAZEL: Yes, a lot and the boss, he's really nice.

ODILE: (*you/like/him*) .... then?

HAZEL: Yeah, a lot. He's very organised. So how are things with you? (*you / sell / your house / yet*)

....

ODILE: No, we haven't. Our buyer changed his mind and pulled out.

2 PEGGY: Hi. You're back! (*you / enjoy / the course*) ....

ROSS: Yeah, I learned a lot. I'm now an expert in managing change!

PEGGY: (*it/useful*) So, ...?

ROSS: Yes, very useful. And the people were a laugh too.

PEGGY: (*you / have / a good time*) ...., then?

ROSS: Certainly did. (*everything/OK/here*) ....

PEGGY: Yeah, fine, Not much has happened.

ROSS: (*it/be/quiet?*) So, ...?

PEGGY: Yes, it's been extremely quiet. But now that you're back, I suppose it's all going to change, isn't it?

◀ D **3** a Complete these echo questions using the words in the box to check the information in italics.

how long	how much	~~what~~	what	when	where

1 MANAGER: Now first of all I'd like to talk about *the auditors'* visit.
COLLEAGUE: I'm sorry – you'd like to talk about ....what....?

2 MANAGER: They'll need *six days* to do a complete audit.
COLLEAGUE: They'll need ....?

3 MANAGER: We hope they'll be able to start *on 22 March*.
COLLEAGUE: So, they'll be coming ....?

4 MANAGER: I'm going to let them work *in the first-floor conference room*.
COLLEAGUE: They're going to work ....?

5 MANAGER: They're going to *check all staff* expenses again.
COLLEAGUE: They're going to do .... again?

6 MANAGER: Last year they found *£800* of fraudulent claims.
COLLEAGUE: They found ....?

b ⦿ **SS 6.4** Practise the conversations with the recording. Take the role of the colleague.

1 Make questions by putting the words in the correct order.

1 for / do / who / work / you / ? ...Who do you work for?...

2 worked / another / you / for / have / company / ever / ? ....

3 your / you / to / near / live / work / do / ? ....

4 partner / does / what / do / your / ? ....

5 you / week / did / manager / see / last / your / ? ....

6 is / job / what / your / title / ? ....

7 company / how / is / your / old / ? ....

8 many / does / employ / how / people / it / ? ....

9 your / happy / you / are / in / job / ? ....

10 at / which / with / do / person / you / most / time / spend / work / ? ....

11 starting / how / was / your / much / salary / ? ....

12 good / school / student / were / you / a / at / ? ....

2 Complete this conversation between two colleagues using suitable question tags.

ANNE: Carlos is retiring soon, **1** ...isn't he?...

MELANIE: Yes, he's worked for this company for 30 years, **2** ....

ANNE: He used to work as an assistant in the early days, **3** ....

MELANIE: He had a lot of original ideas back then, **4** ....

ANNE: Yes, so he was promoted very quickly, **5** ....

MELANIE: I bet he won't miss us all when he leaves, **6** ....

ANNE: Maybe not, but we'll miss him, **7** ....

MELANIE: He's planning to do a lot of travelling, **8** ....

ANNE: He hasn't visited many countries before, **9** ....

MELANIE: He can't speak any other languages, **10** ....

ANNE: So, he needs to learn some, **11** ....

MELANIE: We haven't got him a leaving present yet, **12** ....

ANNE: No, not yet. And we should organise a party for him, **13** ....

MELANIE: Yes, he might be sad if we don't do anything special, **14** ....

3 Correct the mistakes in these sentences. One sentence is correct.

1 He told me ~~be careful~~. ...to be careful...

2 She asked me can you help me. ....

3 I didn't realise it is so expensive. ....

4 She said I will be here tomorrow. (this was three days ago) ....

5 They said they might reduce the price. ....

6 She told to me to call back later. ....

7 We said you that the design could be ready in 48 hours. ....

8 Didn't you know the meeting starts ten minutes ago? ....

4 Read these comments about an e-book posted on the author's blog. Report them, changing the tense whenever possible.

1 What Des Walsh has done is fantastic. His book makes blogging easy and helps you do it yourself. [Andy]

Andy said that what Des Walsh ....*had done was fantastic.*.... He told us that his book ....

2 We're in the process of doing a blog. Until a week ago, we knew nothing about blogging. It's amazing what a person can learn in a week. [Ron]

Ron said .... He said that until a week ago .... He added that ....

3 It is a book you can easily read in one afternoon. But you'll go back to it again and again. [Bill]

Bill said it .... He added that ....

4 I love the book! [Jean]

Jean said that ....

5 If you are looking for a basic understanding of blogging, this is the book for you. Des delivers a message that all bloggers will appreciate. [Sam]

Sam said that if .... He also said that Des ....

5 **a** Delete any unnecessary words or punctuation.

1 He asked ~~to~~ me what I did in my free time.

2 He wanted to know me if I liked Mexican food.

3 He asked how many holidays do the managers have.

4 He asked where I had been on my last holiday?

5 He wondered if whether I travelled a lot in my job.

b Insert one word in each sentence.

1 Can you tell ⋏ which your favourite country is? *(me)*

2 I'm sure if it is Turkey or Peru.

3 I wondering when the best time to visit South America is.

4 I would appreciate if you could email me the information.

5 I would grateful for any advice you can send me.

6 Complete the written requests using the words in brackets so that they are more polite.

1 Email us your latest price list. (*appreciate*)

....*I/We would apreciate it if you could*.... email us your latest price list.

2 Can you work weekends when necessary? (*willing*)

.... work weekends when necessary?

3 Can you give us any suggestions to help improve our training programme? (*welcome*)

.... suggestions to help improve our training programme.

4 Will there be any changes to the schedule? (*inform*)

.... any changes to the schedule.

5 When can we expect to receive your proposal? (*let*)

.... we can expect to receive your proposal.

6 Could you let me know your decision by the end of the week? (*grateful*)

.... let me know your decision by the end of the week.

Verbs and objects

Read these comments by people who are talking about what motivates them at work.

a Which of the verbs in italics have objects? What are the objects?

b Which verbs do not have objects?

> I *have* job security.

> Conflicts and disputes with management seldom *happen*.

> They *encourage* us to *use* our skills.

> We have to *work* hard but we *get* lots of breaks.

> The company *offers* fantastic opportunities for promotion.

> My boss really *appreciates* me and *praises* me when I *do* good work.

A Verbs with or without an object

A1 The object comes immediately after the verb and before any adverbs of place, manner or time. An object can be one word or several words.

subject	verb	object	adverbs
I	**phoned**	<u>him</u>	yesterday morning.
We	**use**	<u>a different system</u>	overseas.

A2 Some verbs need an object to complete their meaning.

> ⊙ Here are some very common verbs used in business with an object:
> *bring, buy, call, contact, find, get, keep, like, make, need, produce, raise, sell, spend use, take, want.*

We should **contact** <u>the manufacturer</u> as soon as possible.
At present I think we **sell** <u>about two hundred units</u> per month.

A3 Some verbs almost never take an object.

> ⊙ Here are some very common verbs used in business without an object:
> *agree, arrive, come, fall, go, happen, live, rise, stay, talk, work.*

Motivation usually increases when a person's salary **rises**.
Do you **agree**?
Can you let me know when the new Sales Director **arrives**?

A4 Some verbs can be used with or without an object. These verbs include:
begin, decrease, finish, grow, increase, meet, return, start, stop.

The meeting **began** at 2 pm.
We **began** <u>our discussion</u> yesterday.
Employee numbers have **increased/decreased**.
We need to **increase/decrease** <u>expenditure</u>.

B Verbs with two objects

B1 Some verbs need two objects, a direct object and an indirect object. The indirect object receives or is the goal of the direct object. It comes before the direct object.

	verb	indirect object	direct object
They	**don't give**	their workers	enough time off.
Can you	**send**	me	the flight details?

> ⊙ Here are some common verbs that take two objects:
> *ask, bring, buy, find, give, hand, make, sell, send, show, tell.*

Can you **send** <u>the delegates</u> <u>that list of names</u>? And **make** <u>me</u> <u>a copy</u>, too.
We **showed** <u>the visitors</u> <u>the new machines</u>.

B2 You can also use a preposition + noun structure for the indirect object. The direct object comes before the indirect object in this case.

Can you send <u>the list of names</u> **to** <u>the delegates</u>? And make <u>a copy</u> **for** <u>me</u>, too.
We showed <u>the new machines</u> **to** <u>the visitors</u>.

B3 You must use a preposition when the direct object is an unstressed pronoun (e.g. *it, them*) and the indirect object is a noun.

A: *What did you do with the agenda?*
B: *I sent <u>it</u> **to** <u>Francesca</u>.* (**not** ~~I sent Francesca it.~~)
*I took some photos and showed <u>them</u> **to** <u>our client</u>.*
(**not** ~~showed our client them~~)

If both objects are pronouns, you can use the indirect + direct object structure.

A: *Did you send Harry the insurance document?*
B: *Yes, I sent <u>him</u> <u>it</u> yesterday.* (**or** *I sent <u>it</u> **to** <u>him</u> yesterday.*)

With most verbs use the preposition *to*. Some verbs use *for* (e.g. *book, buy, design, find, make, reserve*).

A: *I've reserved <u>you</u> <u>a room</u> at the Plazatel.*
B: *Can you find <u>me</u> <u>a new marker pen</u>, please, Terry?*

A: *I've reserved <u>a room</u> **for** <u>you</u> at the Plazatel.*
B: *Can you find <u>a new marker pen</u> **for** <u>me</u>, please, Terry?*

Practice

◄ A2–3 **1** Complete these sentences by adding a suitable object where necessary. If the verb doesn't need an object, leave the sentence as it is.

1 My laptop is being repaired. Can I use ....*your laptop?*....

2 We need to look at the sales figures. Can we fix a time to talk ....?

3 We must try to have short meetings. Nobody likes ....

4 I'm going to make coffee. Do you want ....?

5 I think generally motivation among the staff has fallen ....

6 I've lost that list of names for the staff dinner. I hope I can find ....

7 In the last year our costs have risen ....

8 Mr Pavlevski's coming today. Do you know what time he's arriving ....?

9 Do you have Maria Senara's email address? I need to contact ....

10 Some people are going for a meal after work. Do you want to come ....?

◄ A **2** Put the objects in brackets into these sentences in the correct order and position.

1 Can I keep for a few days? I'll return after my presentation. (*it, the projector*)

   ...*Can I keep the projector for a few days? I'll return it after my presentation.*...

2 When they increased last year I bought the following month. (*a new car, my salary*)

   ....

3 We spent and improved for the staff, and noticed that motivation increased very rapidly. (*a lot of money, the facilities*)

   ....

4 Handmade Cars Ltd sold in 2005 and made, which was good news. (*1,000 vehicles, a huge profit*)

   ....

5 They have promised to produce for us so that we can check before we make. (*a decision, the details, some drawings*)

   ....

6 Can you take to the mailroom? We need to send immediately. (*it, this package*)

   ....

7 I have to phone today but I can't find anywhere. (*his number, Charles Braun*)

   ....

8 We need to find because we want to take into new markets. (*a good supplier, our products*)

   ....

9 We must increase immediately. (*our sales force*)

   ....

10 Let's begin by looking at our sales figures. Orders for the new model have decreased sharply. (*the meeting*)

   ....

◄ B1　**3**　**Complete these sentences using the objects in brackets in the correct order.**

1　Lisa bought ....*Hannah a scarf*................... to celebrate her promotion. (*a scarf, Hannah*)

2　Melissa showed .... (*her new PA, the meeting room*)

3　Roy handed .... so that she could see what we had to discuss. (*Laura, the agenda*)

4　Karen asked .... (*the time, Ursula*)

5　Hilary gave .... so they could finish the task. (*some brochures, the visitors*)

6　David sent .... (*flowers, Pamela*)

◄ B2–3　**4**　**a**　**Rewrite these sentences using the preposition in brackets. Replace the direct object with *it* or *them*.**

1　She gave her assistant the customers' addresses. (*to*)

.....*She gave them to her assistant.*..

2　Henrik sent Zepak the consignment last week. (*to*)

....

3　They bought Charlie the golf clubs when he retired. (*for*)

....

4　We didn't show all the teams the new design. (*to*)

....

5　They sold the customer the wrong model without realising. (*to*)

....

b　**Rewrite sentences 4 and 5 with two pronouns instead of a pronoun and a noun.**

4　...

5　...

◄ A, B　**5**　**Find and correct six mistakes with direct and indirect objects in this article.**

During the credit crisis that began in 2008, there was a risk that banks would stop lending ∧ to small businesses ~~money~~, so governments all over the world gave public funds the banks to enable them to continue to offer loans in small businesses and private individuals. Some economists did not like, and believed it was better to let the market operate freely. Meanwhile, the banks had to find new products to their customers which would stop them taking their cash out and spending it. The basic problem was a lack of confidence in the banks, and many people felt that the government and economists were not telling the whole truth them.

(money written above the caret)

Make it personal

Write four sentences using verbs from the exercises. Write two about things that motivate you and two about things that demotivate you in your job.

25 Business talk: Typical business uses of verbs and objects

Some verbs that normally have an object in everyday language are often used without an object in business language, especially in spoken business contexts. This is because the object is usually clear from the context. These verbs include: *buy, cancel, confirm, delay, deliver, dispatch, launch, order, produce, sell, ship*.

Everyday use	Business use
They couldn't **deliver the goods** on time, so we had to **cancel the order**.	They couldn't **deliver** on time, so we had to **cancel**.
The 25th is too soon, so we'll have to **delay the contract**.	The 25th is too soon, so we'll have to **delay**.
You should never **launch a new product** in the winter.	You should never **launch** in the winter.
They **produce lines** for some of the big supermarkets.	They **produce** for some of the big supermarkets.

6 Read this extract from a senior management group meeting. Cross out the object after the verbs in italics if you think the speaker didn't use it.

BOB: I wanted to make the point that we shouldn't *launch* ~~the new model~~ in April – there are too many other things happening. I think we should *delay* the launch until May. We can *produce* the brochure in January, samples in February or March, then be ready to *ship* the goods in May. That gives us plenty of time. If we haven't prepared the launch properly and have to *cancel* the launch events, that would be far worse.

ANDREW: OK, thanks, Bob. That sounds sensible. All agreed? Right. Vanessa, anything you want to report on the financial side?

VANESSA: I wanted to talk about our investments in Zamrac. If we *sell* our shares now, we may be at a disadvantage. I think we should continue to *buy* more shares over the next few months and then *sell* them in the autumn when we have a clearer picture. If we all agree, I can *confirm* our decision with the brokers.

ANDREW: Right. Well, any comments?

🔘 **25.1** Listen and compare your answers.

7 Write sentences for these situations using the verbs in italics without an object.

1 Tell a colleague that you think the date for the sales conference is too soon and that it should be later. (*delay*)

   I think the date for the sales conference is too soon. I think we should delay.

2 Tell a friend that your company makes items mostly for the international market. (*produce*)

   ....

3 Tell a colleague that you and your team can be ready to send out an order tomorrow. (*dispatch*)

   ....

4 Tell a customer that your company can only send items to addresses within the EU. (*deliver*)

   ....

5 Tell a colleague you don't know if Kepra and Co. want to purchase some goods, because they haven't sent an order yet. (*buy, order*)

   ....

Make it personal

Which of the verbs in the Business talk section would you be likely to use in your job? Think of a context in which you would use three of them and make sentences using them without an object.

-ing and infinitives after verbs

Read this comment from a manager talking about her managerial style.

a Find an example of a verb + a verb.

b Find an example of a verb + an object + a verb.

> I want my staff to know it is okay to fail [...]
> I try to help people succeed because if they are successful, then I am successful.

A Using *-ing*

A1 You can use *-ing* after these verbs:
can't help, consider, enjoy, feel like, finish, involve, imagine, keep, mind, spend (time).

> I **enjoy working** here, but I **can't help wondering** if I made the right career choice.
> Would you **mind opening** the window? I'm quite hot.

A2 Use *-ing* after prepositions and most phrasal verbs.

> We **insist on recruiting** graduates from the best universities.
> Have you **given up going** to French classes?

B Using *to*-infinitive

You can use *to*-infinitive after:
can afford, agree, arrange, decide, expect, hope, manage, offer, tend, want, would like/love.

> We **decided to attend** the conference but we **couldn't afford to book** a stand.
> People **tend to be** multi-skilled these days – they **expect to change** jobs more often.

C *-ing* or *to*-infinitive?

C1 You can use *-ing* or *to*-infinitive after these verbs:
begin, bother, can't bear, continue, hate, intend, like, love, prefer, start.

> Don't **bother waiting / to wait** for me after the meeting.

> In spoken English, *-ing* is more frequent after *bother, can't stand, like, love, hate, start*, and *to*-infinitive is more frequent after *begin, can't bear, continue, intend, prefer.*

C2 If the first verb is an *-ing* form, *to*-infinitive is more common for the second verb.

> We're **starting to work** as a team. (rather than *We're starting working*)

C3 You use *like, love, hate, prefer* + *-ing* to talk about level of enjoyment. Use *to*-infinitive to talk about a habit or preference.

> I **hate doing** my expenses, but I **like to get** them in on time. (I make sure I get them in on time)

C4 Some verbs have a different meaning when they are followed by *-ing* or *to*-infinitive. In each of these examples the first sentence contains the more frequent form.

> I **forgot to call** the accountant. (I forgot and didn't do this)
> I'll never **forget walking** into the office party. (a memory now about the past)

> I **remember taking** a price list.
> (1 I took a price list 2 I remember that now)
> I **remembered to take** a price list.
> (1 I remembered 2 then I took the price list)

> I **stopped working** there last year. (I no longer work there)
> Sorry I'm late. I had to **stop to get** petrol. (in order to)

> Let's **try to boost** sales this year. (attempt to)

> A: My email's not working.
> B: **Try restarting** the computer. (experiment)

> People often say *try and do* something.

D Verb + object + verb

D1 You can use an object + *to*-infinitive after these verbs:
allow, ask, encourage, help, get, need, remind, want, would like, tell, teach.

> How can I **encourage my staff to make** their own decisions?
> My boss **wanted me to take** the visitors to dinner.
> (**not** ~~My boss wanted that I take~~)

D2 After *let* and *make* you can use an object + infinitive without *to*. When *make* is passive, use the *to*-infinitive.

> Just **let me know** if you need help.
> What **made you say** that?
> What efforts **have been made to find** new clients?

D3 After *help* + object the infinitive without *to* is more common than *to*-infinitive.

> I can **help you** (to) **install** the software.

E Sense verbs

You can use object + *-ing* or infinitive without *to* after *feel, hear, notice, see, watch*, but the meaning is slightly different.

> We **saw oil prices rise** last year. (suggests a single or complete action)
> We **saw oil prices rising** last year. (suggests a repeated, incomplete or ongoing action)

▶ See Appendix 6 (Verb patterns).

Practice

◄ A, B **1** **Complete this conversation between two colleagues about a competitor. Use the correct form of the verbs in brackets.**

ALAN: Any news of Mounts? Are they managing **1** ....*to take*.... (*take*) much business from us?

TIM: I'd say that around here we're still doing OK. Customers tend **2** .... (*come*) to us first. But we've ended up **3** .... (*lose*) customers in Scotland because that's always been their area.

ALAN: So, should we spend a lot of time **4** .... (*try*) to win back that business?

TIM: I'd say not, no. We decided **5** .... (*focus*) on other areas for now so that we can concentrate on **6** .... (*build*) our business round here. We can't afford **7** .... (*ignore*) the local area.

ALAN: I guess Mounts have considered **8** .... (*move*) into our area here, though. Are they still relying on **9** .... (*be*) the cheapest?

TIM: Yeah. If they do target this area, I expect **10** .... (*get*) a lot of calls from customers about prices. It's a worry – I don't mind **11** .... (*tell*) you.

ALAN: Well, we'll just have to keep **12** .... (*offer*) a better service.

◄ C **2** **Complete the comments some people made about their careers using the correct form of the verbs in italics. Sometimes more than one answer is possible.**

1 I try ......*to be*........ focused about my career, but I'm so busy. Like on an average day, I never have time to stop ....*think*........, 'What am I learning? Where am I going?'

2 The best career advice I ever read was to stop ....*be*........... a job seeker and start ....*think*....... of yourself as an investment. I did and it's beginning ....*work*........ .

3 I remember ....*meet*....... my boss for the first time. I said, 'How can I get your job?' But I respect her and I like ....*think*....... that she respects me, too.

4 I really don't bother ....*try*........... to impress my assistant any more. I tried ....*buy*........ him lunch and stuff when I got here, but I think he's jealous of me.

5 I like my job and I like ....*go*........... into work every day. I'm probably a bit of a workaholic. Sometimes I forget ....*have*....... lunch. I have to remember ....*make*....... time for myself.

6 I intend ......*change*...... jobs every two or three years till I have lots of contacts. My aim is to start ....*run*........... my own business. I can't stand ....*work*........ for a boss.

◄ C **3** **a** **Complete these questions using the correct form of the verbs in the box.**

feel give up ~~have~~ leave make up offer take tell use work

1 Should employers encourage staff ....*to have*.... a healthy lifestyle?

2 Can an employer make you .... smoking?

3 Does your boss let you and your colleagues .... work early if you need to?

4 Does your employer allow staff .... from home?

5 What would you like your employer .... you: more time off or a higher salary?

6 Does your boss ever remind you .... time off work?

7 Have you ever been made .... guilty for taking a holiday?

8 Does your boss ever want you .... excuses for him or her?

9 Would you ever get a colleague .... a white lie for you?

10 Do you ever have to help your boss .... his or her computer?

b **Write answers that are true for you to five questions. Give examples from your own experience.**

◀ A–D **4** **a** Match the beginnings (1–8) with the endings (a–h) of these sentences.

1 My job involves   a thinking I'm in the wrong job.

2 No one ever taught me   b sort out their personal problems.

3 My boss often wants me   c throwing out old papers and files.

4 My boss is great. I can't imagine   d to type properly.

5 On bad days I can't help   e to buy presents for her family.

6 You should keep quiet, even if you feel like   f working for anyone else.

7 I never seem to get round to   g writing software and training programmers.

8 I often help my colleagues   h complaining about your job to your boss.

b ⊙ **26.1** Listen and answer the questions your hear.

◀ A–E **5** Find and correct 12 mistakes in these emails.

1

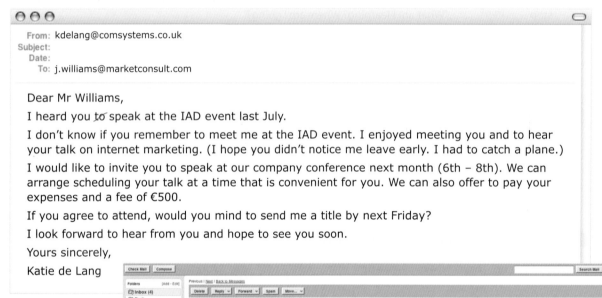

From: kdelang@comsystems.co.uk
Subject:
Date:
To: j.williams@marketconsult.com

Dear Mr Williams,

I heard you to speak at the IAD event last July.

I don't know if you remember to meet me at the IAD event. I enjoyed meeting you and to hear your talk on internet marketing. (I hope you didn't notice me leave early. I had to catch a plane.)

I would like to invite you to speak at our company conference next month (6th – 8th). We can arrange scheduling your talk at a time that is convenient for you. We can also offer to pay your expenses and a fee of €500.

If you agree to attend, would you mind to send me a title by next Friday?

I look forward to hear from you and hope to see you soon.

Yours sincerely,

Katie de Lang

2

From: j.williams@marketconsult.com
To: kdelang@comsystems.co.uk
Subject:
Date:

Dear Kate

Good to hear from you. Of course I remember – in fact I keep meaning to get in touch. And I didn't mind you leaving early – I saw you to look at your watch all the time in the last 15 minutes!

Thanks for invite me to speak at your conference. I would love coming – any day is fine. I can easily spend a day or two to look around the city. I feel like taking a few days' off actually, as I've just finished to write my book on relationship marketing.

Just let me to know where I'm staying and I'll see you next month.

John

PS Don't forget to send your phone number.

Make it personal

1 Choose six sentences from Exercises 3 and 4 that are not true for you or that you disagree with. Write sentences that are true for you or that you agree with.

2 Write a letter inviting a consultant to give a talk in your work place.

You can use *to*-infinitive:

- to give a reason for doing something.

  *The Service Department should email the customer **to say** which engineer is coming.*

  *Sofia is going to Switzerland on Friday **to interview** for a new rep in Zurich.*

- after an adjective to say how you or other people feel about doing something.

  *We are **pleased to announce** the appointment of a new regional Sales Manager.* (formal)

  *The directors were **unwilling to invest** more in the product.*

- after *it* + *be* + adjective to make a general statement, or to give a general view.

  *It is **difficult to predict** the success of any new product.*

  *It has been useful for us **to meet** our key customers on a regular basis.*

6 a Complete this letter to an employee about their performance using the correct form of the words in the box.

agree   arrange   confirm   discuss   happy/answer   important/keep   ~~pleased/inform~~   prepare

Dear Kim

I am **1** _pleased to inform_ you that you have successfully completed your probationary period with the company. The next step is that we will shortly hold a Job Appraisal meeting with you and your line manager **2** .... your performance and **3** .... your objectives for the next year.

4 .... for the meeting, please fill out the enclosed form and return it to me.

It is **5** .... a copy for yourself for the appraisal meeting. After the meeting your manager will write up a summary. The purpose of the summary is **6** .... the main points we discussed for the meeting.

I will be contacting you soon **7** .... a time. In the meantime, I would be **8** .... any questions you may have.

Yours sincerely

Joanna Lee

HM Manager

b Complete Kim's appraisal form using the correct form of the words in the box.

help   improve   ~~increase~~   interesting/see   happy/use   ready/take on   update   willing/contribute

Job Appraisal Meeting Form

Name ... Kim Ahn ....   **Manager** ... Martin Cheng ....

What has been your main achievement in the last year?

I designed a new workflow system **1** ... to increase ..... the efficiency of the department. The implementation went well and staff were
2 .... the new software. It was **3** .... their reactions.

What do you think you can do 4 .... **your performance?**

I feel I need some more training **5** .... my technical skills. I would also like to go on a spoken Mandarin course
6 .... me communicate with local staff in Beijing. (I would be **7** .... to the cost of this.)

What objectives do you want to set for the next 12 months?

I now feel **8** .... more management responsibility. I also want to set up a mentoring scheme.

Make it personal

Write a self-assessment for yourself or a description of what you said last time you a had a performance review, using five verbs from the unit.

Phrasal verbs

Read this phone conversation.

a How many words does each verb in italics consist of?

b Which verbs in italics have an object?

c Where does the object go in relation to the verb?

> Hi Leo. I'm sorry but my car's *broken down* so I'm going to be late for the meeting. Can we *put* it *off* until this afternoon?

> No, sorry, Josh, but I'll make detailed notes so you can *catch up on* the main points we discuss.

A What are phrasal verbs?

A1 Phrasal verbs are verbs used with one or more particles (e.g. *down, off, out, through, up*).

*We need to **set off** very early tomorrow.* (start our journey)
*It's not easy to **come up with** original ideas.* (create / think of)

> 👁 The most common verbs used in phrasal verbs include: *come, get, give, go, look, make, put, set, take, turn, work.*

> ► See Business talk for examples using *get*.

A2 It is not always easy to guess what phrasal verbs mean as the meaning is often unconnected to the meaning of the verb and particle(s) on their own.

*I decided to **turn down** the job.* (refuse)
*Could you **put** me **up** when I'm in town?* (Could I stay at your house?)

A3 Phrasal verbs can have more than one meaning.

*I think we'll have to **put** the meeting **off** until next week.* (postpone)
*The annual fee of £60 **put** me **off**.* (discourage)

B Using phrasal verbs with objects

B1 Some phrasal verbs do not need an object.

*Do you know how long this meeting will **go on** for?* (last)
*Sales have **dropped off** dramatically since last year.* (reduced)

> 👁 Common examples: *break down, carry on, drop off, get back, get through, go on, hang on, hang up, set off*

B2 Some phrasal verbs need an object. The object can go between the verb and the particle (separable phrasal verbs) or after the particle (inseparable phrasal verbs).

> ► See examples below.

B3 With separable phrasal verbs, you can put a noun object before or after the particle.

*You can't just **make up** a price. / You can't just **make** a price **up**.* (invent)

You must put a pronoun object (*me/them/us* etc. or *this/that/these/those/something/anybody* etc.) between the verb and the particle.

*If you have a mobile phone, please **turn it off** during this presentation.* (**not** *turn off it*)

Longer objects and verb + *-ing* go after the particle.

*Make sure you **back up whatever you do on your computer**.* (make a copy of)
*Are you going to **carry on working** much longer? It's very late.* (**not** *carry working on*)

> 👁 Common examples of separable verbs: *back up, call up, carry on, find out, finish off, give up, look up, make up, put forward, put off/on, ring up, set up, shut down, sort out, take on, turn on/up/off/down, work out, write down*

> 👁 Although *find out* can be separable, it is much more commonly used with the object after the particle; *give up* is usually only separated by pronouns.

B4 With inseparable phrasal verbs, the object always goes after the particle.

*If you **come across my pen**, please tell me. / If you **come across it**, let me know.* (inseparable)
*I've never **come across a PA who is as efficient as Sylvie**.* (+ longer object)

> 👁 Common examples of inseparable verbs: *come across, go on, go through, look after*

B5 With verbs with two particles, the object usually comes after the second particle.

*They're going to **come up against fierce competition** in Eastern Europe.* (meet a problem)
*BG says it will **make up for the shortfall in sales** by increasing prices.* (compensate for)

> 👁 Common examples: *carry on with, catch up on, come up against, come up with, do away with, look forward to, look out for, make up for, put up with, watch out for*

⚠ Use *-ing* (not the infinitive without *to*) after verbs with two particles.

*I look forward to **meeting** you.* (**not** *look forward to meet*)

Practice

◀ B1–2 **1** Read these comments from an online discussion about call centres. Complete the phrasal verbs in the text using the correct particle: *back, down, off, on, out, through, up.*

COMMENTS

A couple of months ago I rang **1** ....up.... my bank to tell them where to send my new debit card. I got **2** .... to an operator. She was very friendly but I had to hang **3** .... for 15 minutes while she tried to contact my bank in Birmingham. In the end, I gave **4** .... and sent an email! I'm not at all surprised that the number of companies using call centres has dropped **5** .... dramatically in recent years!

Sidonie, Birmingham

What puts me **6** .... using call centres is when the staff appear not to have the information I need. It makes me want to hang **7** .... immediately when they put me on hold and make me listen to that awful music. Why don't they just write my number **8** .... and call me **9** .... when they have the information I want? Haven't companies worked **10** .... yet that customer satisfaction increases profits?

Bruce, London

◀ B2–4 **2** Complete this advice for sales people using the verbs and objects in brackets. Where possible, put the object between the verb and the particle.

In the selling situation, salespeople often think they should fill any silence with the sound of their own voices. However, I recently **1** ...came across a very effective use of silence.... (*came across / a very effective use of silence*). It happened during a sales presentation that I attended last year in Vienna.

The client worked in the family fashion business and had a problem with stock control. Near the end of the session, the salesperson asked her, 'When you **2** .... (*sort out / these problems*),' and then he paused for 20 seconds before continuing, 'what improvements will you expect to see?' Amazingly, the client responded immediately and was able to **3** .... (*go through / her own detailed solutions*).

When it came to question time, I wanted to **4** .... (*find out / something*). I asked what the client had been doing during the silent pause. She said that she had **5** .... (*carried on / thinking*) while lots of ideas were moving about in her head and then she had suddenly been able to see a solution.

You see, when we interrupt the thinking of others to **6** .... (*put forward / our solutions*), we stop them **7** .... (*coming up with / their own ideas*). If you stay silent, you don't have to sell your products or ideas to your clients – you just **8** .... (*back up / them*) in their own decision to buy!

◀ B5 **3** Complete these employees' comments about a new manager using the correct form of the verbs in the box.

catch	come	come	do	look	look	make	put

1 I hope the new manager will ....come..... up with a business plan that'll work.

2 I'm .... forward to hearing about any changes she's going to make.

3 I expect she'll .... up against resistance from some of the employees.

4 She seems to think the solution is not to .... away with the old systems but to improve them.

5 I wonder if she'll be .... out for new opportunities for us to expand.

6 I hope she doesn't have to .... up with too much opposition from other managers.

7 Profits were down this quarter, but I'm confident that with her new strategies, we'll have .... up with last year by December.

8 She has promised to .... up for any losses incurred during the restructuring.

◄ A, B   **4** **a** **Underline the correct phrasal verbs in these conversations.**

CAMILLE: OK, we're going. Are you ready?

GIACOMO: No, I'm trying to **1** <u>*get through to*</u> / *hang up* a client before I leave but their line is always busy.

CAMILLE: You work too hard! Can't you **2** *carry that on* / *put that off* until tomorrow?

GIACOMO: No, I've got to **3** *make up* / *set up* a meeting with them for tomorrow.

CAMILLE: That's a pity. Well, don't forget to **4** *shut down* / *finish off* your computer and **5** *break down* / *turn off* the lights when you leave.

DENISE: Hurry up. We need to **6** *set off* / *go on* in the next few minutes.

NIGEL: **7** *Give up!* / *Hang on!* I'll be ready in a couple of minutes.

DENISE: OK, I'll just **8** *back up* / *look up* the address again so that we don't get lost.

NIGEL: Right, I'm ready. I'm really **9** *looking forward to* / *looking after* meeting our local clients socially.

DENISE: Yes, it should be good as long as we don't have to **10** *put up with* / *catch up on* too many boring speeches at the beginning of the party!

     b **Write your own sentences using each of the phrasal verbs you did not underline.**

◄ A, B   **5** **a** **Write answers to these questions that are true for you, using the phrasal verbs in italics.**

   1 What's the biggest contract your company has *taken on* recently?

      We took on a contract with Nucorps last month, so we are all working very hard now.

   2 What kinds of things do you *put off* doing at work?

   3 Has your company ever *taken over* another company?

   4 Is your company going to *set up* a branch in another country?

   5 Is it a good idea for businesses to *cut back* their training during a recession?

   6 What do you think people should *watch out for* when buying an insurance policy?

   7 Do you know anyone who has ever been *laid off*? Why and when did this happen?

   8 Has demand for your products ever *dropped off*? If so, why?

   9 Have you ever *turned down* the offer of a job? Why?

 10 What kinds of things would *put you off* applying for a particular job?

     b 🔘 **27.1 Listen to the questions and say your answers.**

Make it personal

Use the phrasal verbs *ring up, hang up, get back, hang on, get through, write down* to write six sentences about telephoning you do at work.

27 Business talk: Phrasal verbs with *get*

Phrasal verbs are very common in spoken business English. Some verbs are used in many different phrasal verbs. Here are some common examples with *get*.

*When you're working hard, try to **get away**, even if it's only for a few days.* (take a break/holiday)

*Household goods is one area where retailers can **get away with** raising prices.* (do something without any bad result / penalty)

*With some funds you can **get back** less than you originally invest.* (receive something you had before)

*We'd like to **get into** the Asian market.* (start working in or with)

*What do you think is the best way to **get on** in business?* (be successful)

*People work better as a team if they **get on with** each other.* (have a good relationship with)

*I wish I could **get over** my fear of flying.* (overcome illnesses/problems/worries/fears)

*I wonder if I'll ever **get round to** learning Chinese.* (do something that you have intended to do for a long time)

*Small businesses often find it hard to **get through** a recession.* (survive)

*It is the advertiser's job to **get through to** target audiences.* (communicate with)

Phrasal verbs often have a synonym (another word that means the same), so if you do not understand a phrasal verb, ask for an explanation.

◀ See Speaking strategies 6 (Checking information) for ways of doing this.

6 Look at this advice about setting up a new business. Complete the sentences using phrasal verbs with *get*.

Starting out in business

Whatever kind of business you'd like to **1** ....*get into*...., there are a number of things you need to think about first. Here is some advice to help you to **2** .... any worries you may have about setting up a new business.

- Choose a business area where you know you can **3** .... more money than you put into it.
- Don't wait too long to **4** .... learning any new skills – it'll be too late once you've started the business.
- Be aware that the first stage is the hardest. Once you **5** .... that, it usually gets easier.
- Banks sometimes try to **6** .... charging you too much for loans, so invest as much of your own money as you can initially.
- Be aware that you'll be working very long hours and it's unlikely that you'll be able to **7** .... for more than a day or two in your first year.
- If you want to **8** .... the local markets, choose your advertising well and learn what people in your area really want.
- Recruit sensibly. Choose people who will **9** .... you, each other and your customers.
- Finally, if you want your business to **10** ...., know your market, the competition and your product.

Make it personal

Answer these questions.

1 How often do you get away and where do you go?

2 Have you ever got back a large amount of money from an investment?

3 Which skills would you like to get round to learning?

4 Is there a business area you'd like to get into?

5 Who do you get on best with at work?

Prepositions

Read this extract from a university's website and underline the prepositions.

a Which two prepositions describe time?

b Which preposition describes location?

c Which preposition follows a verb?

d Which preposition follows a noun?

home	contact us	about us	research	courses

For over 100 years, research at Birmingham University has contributed to scientific knowledge. We are determined to be a leader in scientific research well into the twenty-first century.

A Using prepositions

A1 Prepositions are usually followed by nouns or noun phrases. If a preposition is followed by a verb, you must use the *-ing* form.

*Our offices are **in the east end of London**.*

*Are you thinking **about investing**? (not thinking about invest)*

► See Appendix 7 (Prepositions).

B Prepositions of place and movement

B1 Most prepositions of place and movement are one word (e.g. *about, among, around, at, before, between, by, from, in, into, off, on, over, through, under, up, within*). Some are two or three words (e.g. *ahead of, away from, close to, next to, out of, on top of*).

B2 Prepositions of place tell you where people or things are.

*We have several outlets **around** China, including Tiananmen Square **in** Beijing, **next to** McDonald's.*

B3 Prepositions of movement tell you where people or things are going (direction).

*We're currently flying **over** Moscow.*

C Prepositions of time

Prepositions of time tell you when something happens or how long something lasts (e.g. *after, at, before, between, by, during, for, from, in, on, over, since, to*). They are followed by a time expression.

*People work **from** 7 am **to** 7 pm **in** the week and **between** 9 am and 3 pm **at** weekends.*

⚠ Don't use a preposition with time expressions beginning with *next, this* or *last*.

*Your presentation is **next Tuesday**. (not on next Tuesday)*

D Verbs and prepositions

D1 Some verbs are followed by prepositions (e.g. *apply for, compete with, consist of, contribute to, depend on, focus on, lead to, talk to, work for*). Sometimes you can put an object between the verb and preposition (e.g. *divide something into, invest money in*).

*Why did you **apply for** this job?*

D2 Some verbs can be followed by different prepositions (e.g. *agree **with** someone **on** something, complain **to** someone **about** something, work **for** someone **on** something*).

*We **complained to** the manager **about** the poor service.*

⚠ Some verbs (e.g. *discuss, emphasise, lack, meet, show, stress*) are never followed by prepositions.

*We need to **discuss** the trip. (not discuss about the trip)*

◄ See Unit 25 (Verbs and objects).

E Adjectives and prepositions

Some adjectives can be followed by prepositions (e.g. *concerned with, consistent with, different from, interested in, involved in, responsible for, similar to, worried about*).

*Who is **responsible for** IT support in your company?*
*The fall in car sales was **consistent with** expectations. (was as expected)*

F Nouns and prepositions

F1 Some nouns can be followed by prepositions (e.g. *alternative to, interest in, lack of, price of, reason for, reference to, result of, solution to*). This can be the same preposition as the related verb or adjective.

*Increased competition is the **reason for** the price cuts.*
*There's no **interest in** this idea. (people aren't interested in)*

F2 Some nouns can be followed by different prepositions.

*The EU reached **an agreement with** China **on** trade tariffs.*

F3 The preposition *between* is often used to link two (or more) nouns with *and*.

*The alliance **between** Serfin, Habitat **and** Citibank is the latest in a series of pension fund partnerships.*

F4 People often use prepositional phrases (preposition + noun) in business (e.g. *for sale, in advance, at risk, in writing, in general, in stock, on the phone*).

*Payment **in advance** is preferred. This property is **for sale**.*

Practice

◀ A–C **1** Underline the correct preposition.

1 Sorry I didn't call sooner, I've been _in / on_ a presentation all afternoon.

2 There's a meeting _in / at_ 3 pm – that's _in / at_ two hours' time.

3 Perhaps you went _to / at_ the wrong place – we're _in / on_ the second floor.

4 I think we met _in / at_ this conference last year, didn't we?

5 To find us, go north _over / up_ Oak Hill Road, turn left and walk _to / by_ the end of the road. You'll see us _in / on_ the right. If you walk _under / before_ a bridge, you've gone too far.

6 I noticed it was broken when I took it _out of / into_ the box.

7 Our new, flat structure means nobody has more than three managers _over / on_ them.

8 Our advisors are available _between / from_ 10:00 and 16:00 every day. You can also call the helpline number (08452452423) _from / since_ 16:00 _to / by_ 22:00.

9 _After / From_ I left university, I worked _for / by_ six months _in / at_ Paris.

10 The stores are _in / among_ the production area, _next to / ahead of_ the machine shop.

11 A: Can you get the package _over / on_ to us _by / on_ 12:00?
B: Yes, but I'll have to send it _by / on_ courier.

12 Andre's worked here _for / since_ 1980. I think he's going to retire soon.

◀ D **2** Complete this article using the prepositions in the box where necessary, or put a dash (–) if no preposition is needed.

about	~~for~~	for	in	into	of	on	on	to	with

Do women avoid competition?

Research shows that, in business, most senior positions are still held by men. Also, few women work **1** ....._for_..... engineering or science-based employers or even apply **2** .... jobs in these areas. What exactly has led **3** .... this situation?

Explanations for these differences between men and women have often focused **4** .... discrimination against women, or the difficulty of working and finding time for the family. But a new study says that women are also more likely to dislike competition, even if they have the same ability as men. In an experiment, researchers took 80 managers and divided them **5** .... teams of men and women. The experiment consisted **6** .... a variety of business tasks and the teams received rewards which depended **7** .... how successful they were in completing their tasks. Although women performed well, the experiment suggested that women were likely to avoid direct competition or conflict.

This may make women less successful when they are competing **8** .... men for promotions and jobs. In one experiment where teams had to invest **9** .... high or low risk shares, men showed they were more likely to take higher risks. The study also found that men were less likely to lack **10** .... confidence than women. However, before anyone writes to complain **11** .... this study, it is worth remembering that other studies have shown **12** .... how effective women managers are. Women-managed companies in the UK are up to 14% more profitable than those with men-only management.

◀ E **3** Complete these sentences using the words in the box with a similar meaning to the words in italics.

> concerned with   consistent with   different from   interested in
> involved in   responsible for   similar to   ~~worried about~~

1 35% of executives are ..._worried about_.. a recession in the next year. (*frightened there will be*)

2 Portugal's business culture is .... Spain's. (*quite like*)

3 My report is .... the future strategic development of this organisation. (*discusses*)

4 Japanese taste in mobile-phone design is .... European taste. (*not the same as*)

5 Many European companies are already .... joint ventures in China. (*operating*)

6 Sales growth last year was .... our predictions. (*the same as*)

7 Shareholders are .... paying tax on any investment profits they make. (*should*)

8 Customers who are .... learning more about our products should call us on 0845 124 354. (*wanting to*)

◀ F **4** Complete these messages on a company noticeboard using suitable prepositions.

1 I'm pleased to announce that we have signed an agreement ....._with_.... Provost et Fils to use their distribution network in Northern France. The alternative .... this agreement was to set up our own system. With the price .... fuel so high at present, this agreement seems to be a solution .... our problems. This agreement was the result .... two months of hard work, so thanks to all those involved.

2 .... sale: Sony laptop $300

3 Cancelled: keyboard skills training Thursday @ 17.00 due to a lack .... interest.

4 With reference .... recent requests for longer opening hours for the canteen, I am happy to announce that it will now close at 18.00. These longer opening times will continue as long as there is interest .... using the facilities.

5 The inter-office football tournament .... us and the Queen's Road and Livermore Street branches will be on Saturday 11 June.

◀ A–F **5** Complete this presentation on positioning your brand using suitable prepositions. Sometimes more than one answer is possible.

1 ....._With/For_.... most of the companies I work **2** .... , I'll ask someone to think **3** .... this question: if you could put one message directly **4** .... the mind of a prospective customer, what would it be? **5** .... thinking for a moment, they'll mention something. Then I'll talk **6** .... a different person and I'll get a different answer. In fact, I get as many different answers as there are people working **7** .... the company! That's bad.

8 .... general, the only messages that customers are interested **9** .... are short, powerful and repeated. So every single employee has to focus **10** .... what the company's message is, and then they have to take responsibility **11** .... sharing it – **12** .... conversation, **13** .... the company website, **14** .... writing and **15** .... the phone. Consistently.

This is called positioning. It means thinking **16** .... your customers, your competitors, and your goods or services while you look **17** .... the most powerful words to describe your business. It's worth it: good positioning may improve your marketing **18** .... years!

◉ **28.1** Listen and compare your answers.

Make it personal

How does your company market its products? Write a short paragraph explaining the process.

28 Business talk: Describing change

You can use prepositions to describe change in terms of numbers. For example, you can use prepositions with words like *rise, fall, increase, decrease* to say if numbers (e.g. sales, profits) went up or down.

With noun phrases, use *in* to say what has changed and *of* to say how much it has changed.

*There has been **a rise in** sales **of** 5%.* (**not** *by 5%*)

*Marks and Spencer announced **pre-tax profits of** £35 million.*

In verb phrases, use *by* to say how much something has changed.

*Last night on Wall Street the Dow Jones **fell by** 48 points.*

You can use *from* and *to* to give the starting and final numbers in a series or period.

*Pre-tax profits climbed **from** £8.6m **to** £20.2m in the year to 1 April.*

6 **Complete these sentences using *in, of, by, from* and *to*.**

1 Revenues climbed ....*from*.... $175 million ....*to*..... $273 million in the final quarter of the year.

2 The company said its poor results reflected a sharp rise .... natural gas and oil prices.

3 Last year GDP grew .... about 7%, which is not high by China's standards.

4 The USA trade deficit with Japan fell .... more than $6 billion for September, a decrease .... 0.3%.

5 International business was heavily affected by the decrease .... sales of software products, down 18% .... the same quarter last year.

7 **Complete the descriptions of these two graphs with suitable prepositions.**

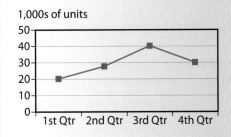

1,000s of units

There was a steady rise **1** ....*in*..... productivity, **2** .... 20,000 units **3** .... the first quarter **4** .... a peak **5** .... 40,000 **6** .... the third quarter. Productivity then fell **7** .... 10,000 units **8** .... the fourth quarter.

$m Export sales (Q1)

Export sales rose **9** .... $15m in February, **10** .... $60m **11** .... the start of the year. This was due to a favourable exchange rate. In March we benefited from further decreases **12** .... the exchange rate, which resulted in a further rise **13** .... sales **14** .... $10m. Since the beginning of the year, sales have risen **15** .... $25m, a year-on-year increase **16** .... 10%.

Make it personal

Prepare a presentation slide showing some of your company's results.
Write a short description of it using language from this page.

Organising what you say and highlighting information

Read this comment by a manager.

Which point is she trying to emphasise or highlight?

> We don't have much time. We have to be aggressive. What we need is a new campaign slogan.

A Organising what you say

A1 You can use *first(ly)*, *first of all*, *second(ly)*, *third(ly)* to organise the points you make, or to go through a list of items. The forms with *-ly* are more formal. People don't normally go further than *second* or *third* in informal situations.

*Well, **first** (**of all**), we should talk about market research, then we need to look at design samples.*
*There are three reasons for delaying the launch: **firstly**, February is not a good month to launch; **secondly**, we really do need more time to run tests; and **thirdly**, the sales force need more training.*

A2 You can also use numbers (*one, two, three*) or the letters of the alphabet (*A, B, C*) to organise what you say. People normally don't go further than *three* or *C* in informal situations.

*I can think of two reasons not to buy shares now: **one / A**, the US market is unstable; and **two / B**, nobody really knows what's going to happen in Asia.*

A3 When you make your last point or come to the last item in a list, you can say *lastly/finally*.

*And **lastly/finally**, I want to remind you of the date of our next meeting.*

⚠ Don't confuse *first(ly)* with *at first* (which means *in the beginning / initially*), or *lastly* with *at last* (which means *eventually / in the end*).

***At first** (**not** ~~firstly~~) I didn't really like my new boss, but now I like her a lot. (the situation has changed)*
*I looked everywhere for my keys and **at last** (**not** ~~lastly~~) I found them on my desk. (after a long time)*

A4 If one point or item is much more important than the rest, you can say *first and foremost*. If your last point is just as important as the rest, you can say *(and) last but not least*.

***First and foremost**, we should be thinking of how to expand our customer base.*
***Last but not least**, I want to thank Graham for coming all the way from Warsaw today.*

B Highlighting what you say

B1 You can use clauses starting with *What ...* to highlight important information.

- To highlight the object:
  They want more information. → ***What they want is** more information.*
  We need more desks. → ***What we need is** more desks. (**not** ~~What we need are more desks~~)*

- To highlight the action:
  We contacted Westons right away. → ***What we did was** contact Westons right away. (**not** ~~What we did was contacted~~)*

- To highlight what someone says or thinks:
  I told them / said / thought / meant that the date had been changed. → ***What I told them / said / thought / meant was** (**that**) the date had been changed.*

B2 You can also use *This is what* and *Here's what* to highlight a whole sentence.

We'll set up group a mailing list. → ***This is / Here's what we'll do:** we'll set up a group mailing list.*
They hired a team of consultants. → ***This is what / Here's what they did:** they hired a team of consultants. (Or ***What happened was**, they hired ...*)*

Practice

◀ **A** **1** Add the words *firstly*, *secondly*, *thirdly* and *finally* to this presentation at a training seminar so that the organisation is clear to the participants.

Firstly,
Let's have a look at the objectives of an effective PR strategy. ⋀ PR adds to the good image and reputation of the organisation – organisations can use PR to send out positive messages about their activities and performance. With good PR you attract and keep not only good customers, but also other parties such as employees, shareholders, etc. These other parties are the people that the organisation interacts with – I'll come back to that with an example in a minute. PR also deals with negative publicity, especially when something goes wrong, and can help overcome false ideas people might have about the organisation. You can also create good relations with the wider community.

🔘 **SS 7.1 Listen and check your answers.**

◀ **A** **2** An advertising agency is expanding into Ireland. Complete this extract from a meeting at the company using the words in the box.

A at last   at first   B   first   First and foremost   ~~First of all~~   last but not least   lastly   secondly   thirdly

LUCY: Right. Let's start. **1** ......*First of all*...... let's welcome Bryan Murphy from Dublin to our meeting. Now, there are several things we need to do. **2** ...., we must find out what Irish customers really want. That's the most important thing of all. As you know, there are two reasons for opening up in Ireland: **3** ...., it's got a good economy, and **4** ...., Dublin is a great city to work in.

JAMES: Before we go on, I just want to raise the concerns over the Ireland plan that we discussed at the last meeting. So, **5** .... there was the issue of health insurance, **6** .... public holidays in Ireland, **7** .... Irish tax laws and **8** .... the exchange rate. We've looked at all four and now **9** .... I think we've solved all the problems we raised in that meeting.

LUCY: That's good to hear. Now Bryan, **10** .... we found it difficult to make contacts in the west of Ireland, but we've made lots of progress since you joined the team. Thank you for all your help. And I'd also like to thank Benny and Hilda for getting the Irish website ready so quickly, and **11** ...., thanks to Joseph for doing the photographs. Thank you, everybody. Dublin, here we come!

🔘 **SS 7.2 Listen and check your answers.**

◀ **B1, B2** **3** Rewrite these sentences using the words in brackets so that you highlight the words in bold.

1 They need **a new CEO**. (*What / need*) ...*What they need is a new CEO.*...

2 They manufacture **lifting equipment**. (*What / manufacture*) ....

3 **We should send a questionnaire** to some of our biggest customers. (*What / do*) ....

4 We had a problem with our packing line. So **we completely redesigned the entry and exit points.** (*this is what*) ....

5 I told everyone that **we couldn't afford any more delays**. (*What / told*) ....

6 **I'll call a meeting of everyone concerned with the Krypak project.** (*Here's what*) ....

7 **They closed every branch** except the one in the capital city. (*What happened was*) ....

8 I said that **I'd be ready to travel at short notice**. (*What / said*) ....

9 **We should check all the figures again.** (*This is what*) ....

10 **They hope to expand** into Latin America. (*What / hope to do*) ....

Test 7: Units 25–28

1 Complete these sentences using an object from the box where necessary. If the verb doesn't need an object, leave the sentenes as it is.

| interest rates | money | productivity | the results | the way | ~~your CV~~ | your office |

1 We're always looking for talented staff and we very much liked ....your CV..... .

2 I've just seen the market research survey and I'd like you to check ....

3 Ms L'Huillier? Someone rang while you were in the meeting. Can you contact ....?

4 Following the restructuring, around 40 middle managers will go ....

5 Inflation is rising .... and Central banks must decide whether to increase
....

6 A report says insurance companies shouldn't do genetic testing. Many scientists agree
....

7 I'm looking for the canteen. Do you know .... ?

8 If we don't raise .... by 20% next year, we'll have problems meeting demand.

9 Can you help me, please? I can't get the new printer to work ....

10 My forecast for next year? I expect blue-chips to continue to make ....

2 Complete this conversation by putting the words in italics in the correct order.

A: Have you *the / CFO / yet / the / report / sent?*

B: I'm *a / giving / presentation / Sam* about it today.

A: I *it / to / her / showed* yesterday. The CFO needs it now.

B: OK. *him / a / make / I'll / copy.*

A: Thanks. If you *me / bring /* one, I'll / *buy / a / drink / you* too.

1 ....Have you sent the CFO the report yet?....

2 ....

3 ....

4 ....

5 ....

3 Complete these sentences using the correct form of the verbs in brackets.

1 As a consultant, I enjoy ....meeting..... (*meet*) such a wide range of people.

2 Do you want anything .... (*drink*) before we start the meeting? Tea? Coffee?

3 After 14 years I have decided .... (*step down*) as managing director. I will, however, carry
on .... (*manage*) the company until my successor takes over in May.

4 We're beginning .... (*involve*) the staff more in the decision-making process.

5 If you agree .... (*order*) over 100, we'll give you a 10% discount.

6 How long did you spend .... (*prepare*) this report? Five minutes?

7 The Internet has really helped consumers .... (*compare*) prices easily.

8 My job involves a lot of time .... (*read*) the financial press.

9 Will Saudi Arabia continue .... (*dominate*) oil production?

10 I'm like you – I don't like .... (*make*) presentations; I prefer .... (*be*) in
the audience.

11 You cannot afford .... (*miss*) this fantastic investment opportunity.

12 Personally, I hate .... (*ask*) for help, but I always expect my staff
.... (*ask*) me for help when they need it.

13 The UK Post Office tried .... (*rebrand*) themselves as Consignia, but without success.

14 Sorry I'm late. I stopped .... (*get*) some petrol on the way.

4 Match the phrasal verbs (1–6) with the meanings (a–f).

1 I *came up with* the idea yesterday.

2 Barkers *turned down* our merger offer.

3 We've *put* the meeting *off* for too long.

4 Thanks for calling. Can I *get back* to you in a minute?

5 Union leaders claim the pay talks have *broken down*.

6 Many graduates see an MBA as the best way to *get on* in business.

a reply

b postponed

c failed

d succeed

e rejected

f thought of

5 Put the objects in brackets in the best position. Sometimes two positions are possible.

1 A: Can we turn .... off ...*the aircon*.... in the meeting room? It's really cold.

B: I'd rather not. Can't we just turn .... down .... ? (*the aircon / it*)

2 A personal advisor looks .... after .... in our bank. (*each client*)

3 Unemployment is so bad that many people have given up looking .... for .... (*a job*)

4 Regarding next year's budget, I'd like you to put .... forward .... (*your proposals*)

5 With plenty of cash in the bank, private equity funds are looking .... out .... for .... (*new acquisitions*)

6 I've got some messages for you, Adrian. I wrote .... down .... somewhere … here they are! (*them*)

6 Underline the correct prepositions in these sentences.

1 I don't want to retire. I want to go <u>on</u>/out working until I'm at least 75.

2 Have my emails been getting *through/over*, because you haven't replied to any of them?

3 I'm afraid we're going to be late. We didn't set *up/off* until five minutes ago.

4 I didn't know the answer to one of the questions after my presentation so I made it *up/out*.

5 We are looking forward *by/to* meeting you on Wednesday.

6 As a company expands it comes up */against/with* bigger, stronger competitors.

7 Complete these extracts from the business news using the correct preposition.

a As an alternative **1** ....*to*.... fossil fuels such as oil, there is growing interest **2** .... wind and solar energy. Until now the lack **3** .... government spending on alternative energy sources has kept the price **4** .... renewable energy high. Some people believe that pressure from the oil industry is the reason **5** .... this. However, as a result **6** .... the fall in oil supply, the government is now determined to find a solution **7** .... the problem.

b In the US, Ford sales have fallen **1** .... 21% **2** .... the last month and, despite a fall **3** .... 4% in September, Toyota has remained the market leader, ahead **4** .... GM. Toyota has lowered its sales forecast **5** .... 9.85 million **6** .... 9.5 million vehicles in the worsening economic climate.

c There are many more companies investing **1** .... direct recruitment through their corporate websites. But they have to compete **2** .... specialist job websites that focus **3** .... a single industry. Since the dramatic growth **4** .... job websites first started **5** .... 2000, the industry has grown **6** .... value **7** .... around £300 million. There are quality issues, however: 73% **8** .... HR directors complain **9** .... the low quality **10** .... CVs that these job websites supply.

d In India, the markets were closed **1** .... an hour **2** .... Tuesday **3** .... 10 am and 11 am as trading was halted **4** .... an 8% fall, the largest-ever share-price drop **5** .... the Bombay Exchange **6** .... one morning.

Adjectives

Read this advertisement.

a Which words describe US magazine?

b Which word describes US magazine's readers?

> US Magazine is a young, cool and fresh entertainment magazine, which focuses on the artists and achievers that the new generation of youthful consumers really cares about.

A What are adjectives?

Adjectives give more information about nouns or pronouns. They can describe a person or thing, or they can tell you about the class or group something belongs to.

*The **new** CEO is **effective**, **flexible** and **helpful**.* (this tells us about the CEO's qualities)

*He's a **civil** engineer by profession.* (this tells us what kind of engineer he is)

B Forming adjectives

B1 You can often form adjectives by adding suffixes to other words (e.g. *-able, -ed, -ful, -ic, -less*).

*a market**able** product   a success**ful** firm   a qualifi**ed** doctor*

B2 You can often make opposite forms by adding prefixes to the adjective (e.g. *dis-, im-, in-, ir-, un-*).

*a **dis**honest trader   an **in**effective leader an **un**comfortable office*

B3 ⚠ Don't confuse pairs of adjectives like *interested/ interesting*.

*We built an **exciting product**.* (describes the product)
*'I'm **excited**,' said Tom.* (describes how Tom feels)

C Using adjectives

C1 Most adjectives go before the noun they are describing.

*China is an **important market** for our company.* (**not** ~~a market important~~)

C2 Some adjectives can also go after a noun (e.g. *affected, available, required, suggested*).

*Products **affected** by the new tax include electronics.* (**not** ~~Affected products by the new tax~~)

You can use *concerned, present* and *responsible* before and after the noun, but the meaning changes.

*There were four **managers present** at the meeting.* (four managers went to the meeting)

*The **present managers** are being replaced.* (the managers of the company at the present time)

You can use the adjectives *high, long, old, tall, wide*, etc. after a measurement noun (e.g. *metres, years*).

*The building is 30 **storeys high**.*
*He's 20 **years old**.*

C3 You can use adjectives after indefinite pronouns (e.g. *anybody, no one, something, everybody*).

*The iX451 is **something new** in mobile communication.*

C4 You can use an adjective after the verbs *be, become, feel, get, look, seem, remain* and *sound*.

*The new office furniture **looks good**.*

D Ordering adjectives

When there is more than one adjective before a noun, the most common order is:

quantity → opinion → size → quality → shape → age → colour → origin → material → purpose

*It's easy for **efficient**, **new**, **consulting** firms to enter the market.* (quality, age, purpose)

E Making adjectives stronger or weaker

E1 You can make adjectives that describe qualities stronger or weaker using adverbs like *a little, quite, rather, really, very* and *extremely*.

*The training costs this year are **very** high.*

E2 You can make adjectives with a very strong meaning (e.g. *essential, impossible*) stronger using *absolutely* and *totally*.

*It's **absolutely essential** to maintain that core market.* (**not** ~~very essential~~)

▶ See also Units 30 (Adverbs) and Unit 31 (Comparisons 1).

Practice

◀ B1, 3 **1** Complete this text using adjectives based on the words in brackets.

So, you want to be a Venture Capitalist?

In a highly **1** _competitive_ (*compete*) industry like this one, **2** .... (*succeed*) candidates for employment must have excellent **3** .... (*academy*) records. This means **4** .... (*qualify*) chartered accountants, or graduates who've had **5** .... (*response*) positions in industry and done an MBA.

It requires **6** .... (*consider*) stamina and a **7** .... (*flex*) mind, as **8** .... (*finance*) transactions are often completed in the middle of the night.

We're looking for people that see it as a **9** .... (*challenge*) career. We like people who are **10** .... (*ambition*) and **11** .... (*determine*).

Venture capitalism can be a **12** .... (*reward*) and **13** .... (*profit*) career. If you are **14** .... (*interest*), get in touch.

◀ B2 **2** Make the adjectives negative using the prefixes from the box.

> dis- il- im ~~in~~ in- ir- mis- un-

1 The London Stock Exchange fined Curden Securities £1m for filing _in_accurate accounts.

2 In the US, it is nearly ....possible to eat in restaurants, hire cars, or stay in a hotel without a credit card.

3 New technology has been developed to prevent ....legal copying of software.

4 In a ....managed business, it is not just staff who suffer; customers suffer, too.

5 In my job, I can't afford to be ....decisive. I have to react instantly to the markets.

6 The supermarket's strategy of opening superstores and closing ....economic branches has paid off in record profits.

7 InSat TV checks all its installers for quality, and has set up a complaints procedure for ....satisfied customers.

8 People who work ....regular hours are four times more likely to have health problems than those in 9 to 5 jobs.

◀ B3, E **3** Underline the correct adjectives in italics in these market reports.

1 GM's share price dropped by $2.125 yesterday due to the announcement of _disappointing/disappointed_ results for the last quarter of this year. A series of damaging strikes meant that September was a very _bad/terrible_ month for GM in terms of output. The management believe that a new corporate structure is absolutely _essential/important_ for the future success of the company.

2 The share price of restaurant chain Michels & Butler climbed nearly 19.5¢ to $5.44, after rumours spread of a takeover by rival Enterprise Catering. Reports have suggested that Enterprise is _interested/interesting_ in M&B after it failed to buy Star Restaurants last year.

3 UCS analysts are said to be _satisfying/satisfied_ with recent sales figures from Holt Telecom. 'There are still risks,' they said, 'but these results are _pleasing/pleased_ for us as we know Holt have spent a lot on quality improvements.'

4 Finally, there are _exciting/excited_ investment opportunities at Hedge Oil. The markets have previously seen the company as a rather _boring/bored_ investment. However, Hedge are expected to announce new discoveries of oil in the North Sea, perhaps as much as 100 million barrels, which would see their share price climbing rapidly.

4 Complete this article about customer care. Put the adjectives in brackets in the correct position.

Customer service is **1** .... absolutely ....vital.... (*vital*) for small businesses. Why? Well, anyone who **2** .... is .... (*keen*) to compete with **3** .... companies .... (*other*) needs customers who want to come back again and again.

So, how can businesses improve their service? The answer **4** .... is .... (*simple*): make sure the **5** .... people .... (*responsible*) for customer service **6** .... feel .... (*valued*), because they are your **7** .... customer service .... (*main*) asset. How does this help? Obviously, when staff **8** .... are .... (*happy*) with their work, customers **9** .... feel .... (*welcome*). And how can you help staff enjoy their work? By using **10** .... feedback .... (*positive*). Managers usually only thank employees when they do **11** .... something .... (*special*). Why not thank them for doing what they're supposed to do? It certainly can't hurt.

What next? Well, just more of the same. Thanking staff for doing a **12** .... job .... (*good*) can mean the difference between **13** .... employees .... (*motivated*) and **14** .... employees .... (*demotivated*). Which do you want serving your customers?

◄ D **5** Complete these conversations by putting the adjectives in brackets in the correct order.

1 CUSTOMER: What's on the menu today?
WAITER: Well sir, we have some ...lovely fresh Scottish... (*fresh/lovely/Scottish*) salmon. I can also recommend the .... (*spicy/tomato*) soup.
CUSTOMER: They sound good. I'll have the soup to start and then the salmon.

2 RECEPTIONIST: Good morning, how can I help you?
PAULA: Hello, it's Paula from Seymour Ltd. Can I just double-check our order, please?
RECEPTIONIST: Of course. You wanted .... (*black/fifty/personalised*) pens, didn't you?

3 SALES REP: Where's your office?
NEW CLIENT: It's on Lausanne Road, in that .... (*old/stone*) building – number 62.
SALES REP: Oh yes, I know it, next to the .... (*luxury/sports*) car dealer.

4 PROPERTY DEVELOPER: So, if you look at this part of the diagram, you can see we've got a .... (*square/thousand*) metres of storage space in the basement. Above that there's a .... (*huge/shopping*) area and behind the shop we have the .... (*customer/underground*) car park.
COLLEAGUE: Sounds good, doesn't it?
PROPERTY DEVELOPER: Yeah, and don't forget the .... (*busy/pedestrian*) area out front. Thousands of potential customers per hour!

◉ **29.1** Listen and check your answers.

Make it personal

Look around you. How would you describe each object in the room where you are?
Use as many adjectives as you can.

29 Write for business: Describing your products and services

Compound adjectives are often used to describe companies, their products and services, and their performance. They are formed by linking two words. Here are some common types of compound adjectives.

- *well* + past participle

  Coke is the most **well-known** brand in the world.

  We are a **well-established** firm, founded in 1912.

  AmTel is **well-run** by its excellent management.

  Our website is **well-designed** and easy to navigate.

- *fast* + -ing

  Primark is a **fast-growing** retail business.

  Good research is vital in a **fast-moving** market.

- *high/low* + noun

  This laptop displays **high-quality** images.

  As a **high-tech** company, R&D is vital to us.

  This is a **high-yield** investment returning 8% pa.

  Our **high-profile** clients include oil companies.

  Low-cost airlines made travel cheaper.

  Bonds are **low-risk** compared to shares.

6 Complete these extracts from business reports using the words in the box.

> cost   designed   established   known   moving   profile   ~~quality~~   tech

1 Today's telecoms companies face increasing demand for high-....*quality*.... internet services.

2 Feedback from customers indicates that they think our products are well-.......................... .

3 Samsung is a world leader in the fast-.......................... area of high-.......................... products such as memory chips and mobile phones.

4 Many well-.........................., high-.......................... business leaders, including the Microsoft board, attended the conference.

5 Online retail is now a well-.......................... way of shopping and most problems were solved years ago.

6 Our new, low-.......................... solar powered laptop computer is selling well in Africa.

7 Read this email from a financial advisory service to its clients. Rewrite the words in italics using a suitable compound adjective.

Dear Investor,

This month we are recommending Nevills, **1** *an old British estate agents*, with a strong record of growth. Nevills is **2** *an expanding company* with profits up 20% to £48m last year. Its strong management team make it **3** *an efficient company*. It regularly pays a good dividend and could become **4** *a profitable investment* if the property markets recover as expected. Don't buy while the shares remain above 120p, but any fall below that price is a good opportunity to buy into this **5** *famous company*. For those who prefer **6** *safe investments*, consider buying government securities as a safe, secure home for your money. However, as the **7** *dynamic stock market* hits record highs, and the US markets seem happier about **8** *advanced IT stocks*, there seems to be no need to play safe yet. The problem with government securities is that they are only returning 4% – not exactly a way to get rich quickly.

Thank you for your support and we look forward to helping you again soon.

---

1   *a well-established British estate agents*

2   ....

3   ....

4   ....

5   ....

6   ....

7   ....

8   ....

Make it personal

Think about your company and its products and services. How would you describe them in English? Use some of the adjectives from this unit.

30 Adverbs

Read this advertisement.

a Which word tells you where the food is grown?

b Which word tells you how the food is grown?

c Which word tells you when the food is sent to customers?

> ## Greenerway Organic foods
>
> All our food is produced **locally** and grown **organically**.
> Orders are dispatched **immediately**, fresh to your home.

A What are adverbs?

Adverbs add information about verbs, adjectives and adverbs. They tell us how, where, when or how often something happens, or about the speaker's attitude.

*We need to look at this **carefully**.* (tells us **how**)
*My car is parked **outside**.* (tells us **where**)
*We haven't had any complaints **recently**.* (tells us **when**)
*Does she visit you **often**?* (asks **how often**)

B Forming adverbs

B1 You can form many adverbs by adding *-ly* to an adjective. If the adjective ends in *-y*, the adverb ends in *-ily*. If the adjective ends in *-ic*, the adverb ends in *-ically*.

Adjective	Adverb
It's a **direct** way of contacting customers.	We can contact customers **directly**.
We were **lucky** and found a new supplier.	**Luckily**, we found a new supplier.
Economic development is taking place in the region.	The region is developing **economically**.

► See Appendix 1 (Spelling).

⚠ Don't confuse adjectives and adverbs.

*We must look **carefully** at the cost before we decide.* (**not** ~~We must look careful at the cost~~)

B2 Some short adverbs do not end in *-ly*. These include: *far, fast, hard, late, long, often, soon, well.*

*The company's doing **well**.* (**not** ~~good~~)
*Everyone's been working very **hard** recently.* (**not** ~~hardly~~)

C Position of adverbs

C1 These adverbs come after the verb (and object):

- most adverbs of time, place and manner.

  *I don't want to arrive **late** at the airport.*

  *Please send the invoice **immediately**.* (**not** ~~send immediately the invoice~~)

- adverbs of frequency (e.g. *daily, monthly, annually*).

  *The conference takes place **annually**.*

C2 These adverbs come between the subject and main verb:

- adverbs of frequency which have an indefinite meaning (e.g. *often, rarely, seldom, sometimes*).

  *We've **rarely** had any orders from Moldova.*

- adverbs which describe possibility (e.g. *possibly, probably, certainly*).

  *Her flight has **probably**/**definitely** left by now.*

- adverbs which show the speaker's attitude (e.g. *actually, honestly, sincerely, personally*).

  *I **honestly** think we should postpone the sales conference.*

- short adverbs (e.g. *also, always, just, only, really, never*).

  *We **just** need more time, but we **also** need more staff.*

If there are auxiliary or modal verbs, these adverbs come after the first verb.

*I **have often** wondered why part-time staff are badly paid.*
***Could** you **also** make a copy of the letter for me?*

If the main verb is *be*, the adverb comes after the verb.

*We **are always** ready to discuss any special requirements.*

C3 Adverbs can come at the beginning of the sentence for extra emphasis.

***Unfortunately**, we've been having problems with our server.*
***Yesterday**, we had a visit from Head Office.*

⚠ Don't use *always* at the beginning of a statement or question.

*I **always** prefer morning meetings.* (**not** ~~Always I prefer~~)

D Adverbs + adjectives/adverbs

D1 You can use adverbs before adjectives, and before other adverbs, to make them stronger or weaker.

*The new office building was **extremely expensive** to build.*
*I thought that meeting went **really well** even though it went on **slightly longer** than usual.*

D2 Some adverb and adjective combinations are typical in a business context (e.g. *heavily dependent, entirely different, remarkably/broadly similar, highly competitive/profitable/successful/skilled, greatly reduced/increased/improved, totally different/new/unexpected*).

*The markets are **heavily dependent** on currency movements.*
*The two reports are **remarkably similar**.*

Practice

◀ A, B **1** Complete these sentences using adverbs formed from the adjectives in the box.

annual complete economic efficient global lucky internal primary ~~recent~~ sudden

1 We've had two progress meetings ....*recently*...., one last week and one the week before.

2 Worsman's Bank had a crisis and had to close within 24 hours. It all happened very ....

3 This document should only be circulated .... – it's not for outsiders to read.

4 We have to stop thinking just about Europe and start thinking ....

5 I needed to speak to Pietro in private. ...., he was alone in his office.

6 We waste so much time. We must learn to do things more ....

7 This filing system doesn't work at all. I think we should change it ....

8 The building is inspected .... by the health and safety people.

9 We .... offer consultancy about web development, but we can also offer general IT services.

10 We are dependent on Europe politically as well as ....

◀ B **2** Complete these sentences using an adjective from the box in one gap and the related adverb in the other gap. It may be the same word in both cases.

bad early economical fast ~~good~~ hard late long normal total

1 **a** We had a very ....*good*.... year last year. Congratulations, everyone!

  b The company performed ....*well*.... last year. Congratulations, everyone!

2 **a** Today is just a .... day – meetings, writing reports, all the usual things.

  b We .... spend our day having meetings, writing reports, all the usual things.

3 **a** We apologise for the .... delivery of your order.

  b We apologise for the fact that your order was delivered ....

4 **a** The Zarison is a very .... car – it uses very little fuel.

  b The Zarison performs very .... – it uses very little fuel.

5 **a** We took the .... train to Brussels and were there in an hour.

  b The train we took to Brussels travelled very .... and we were there in an hour.

6 **a** I have a very .... flight tomorrow. I've ordered a taxi for 5 am!

  b My flight leaves very .... tomorrow. I've ordered a taxi for 5 am!

7 **a** Their marketing strategy was a .... failure.

  b Their marketing strategy failed ....

8 **a** She did a lot of .... work designing the website. We must thank her officially.

  b She worked so .... designing the website. We must thank her officially.

9 **a** The software has a .... record of crashing during periods of high demand.

  b The software is known to perform ...., and it often crashes during periods of high demand.

10 **a** It wasn't a .... journey; we were only on the plane for 45 minutes.

  b The journey didn't last very .... ; we were only on the plane for 45 minutes.

153

30

◄ C1　**3**　Complete this article about automated telephone systems by using the words in brackets in the correct order.

In many large companies nowadays the telephone network is connected to a computer that acts as an electronic receptionist. **1** ....*The system takes incoming calls automatically*.... (*automatically / takes / the system / incoming calls*) and checks the caller's details, using information from its database. This means that, for example **2** .... (*the customer service department / instantly / the customer information / can / view*) when they take a call. The customer is greeted by someone who **3** .... (*them / correctly / can / address*). This person speaks to them as if **4** .... (*they / the caller / personally / remember*) and any previous calls they made. In this way **5** .... (*the computerised receptionist / helps / the customer / directly*) and **6** .... (*immediately / them / connects*) to the person who **7** .... (*them / best / can / assist*).

◄ C2–3　**4**　Complete these sentences by putting the adverbs in brackets in the correct position.

1 She has ....*often*..... done .... training sessions for new staff. (*often*)

2 We .... need to search .... the old customer database. (*probably*)

3 .... I .... am .... here to answer any questions you may have. (*always*)

4 It's .... been .... a good year for us. Let's hope we can repeat it next year. (*certainly*)

5 The company's .... done .... well in the last three years. (*actually*)

6 Does .... your company .... employ .... temporary staff? (*sometimes*)

7 .... I .... bring .... back useful information from my trips abroad. (*always*)

8 .... I didn't get .... the contract. (*unfortunately*)

9 .... I .... have three days' holiday left this year. (*only*)

10 .... I .... attend meetings .... these days. .... I'm .... too busy. (*seldom, usually*)

◄ D　**5**　Two colleagues are discussing possible locations for expanding their business. Complete their conversation by putting the adverbs in the box before or after the words in italics.

entirely　heavily　highly　probably　quickly　rapidly　~~really~~　remarkably

ROGER: Twainhill is a **1** ....*really*.... *interesting* .... town. And it's big. Ninety thousand people!

CHARLES: Ninety thousand, wow! Now, Brigmouth also looks interesting. In fact Twainhill and Brigmouth are **2** .... *similar* .... The population of both towns has **3** .... *grown* .... in the last five years, so we should **4** .... *give* .... them serious consideration. They could be **5** .... *profitable* ....

ROGER: I'm surprised they're so similar. I thought they'd be **6** .... *different* .... Well, if we could open **7** .... *outlets* .... , we could really get an advantage over the competition.

NORA: They're not retirement towns, are they? Because we're **8** .... *dependent* .... on young professionals, out at work all day.

ROGER: No, I think there's a good population mix there.

Make it personal

Think of something in your job that you always do, something that you occasionally do (e.g. once a month) and something you rarely do (e.g. once a year, once every two or three years). Write three sentences about those things, using the three adverbs.

30 Business talk: Giving your personal perspective

⊙ The ten most common adverbs used in spoken business English fall into two groups. They show the speaker's attitude or viewpoint, or how certain the speaker is. People often use them to soften what they say, or to make it less direct.

- These adverbs show the speaker's attitude or way of looking at things:
  actually, basically, hopefully, obviously, really.

  Note that *actually* means *in fact / in reality*. It does **not** mean *at present / now*.

  Actually, *Poland is a new venture for us.* (in fact / in reality)

  Hopefully, *Felix will be able to visit some new equipment stores.* (this is what I/we hope)

  Basically, *we need to re-think our strategy.* (this is the most important thing)

- These adverbs show how certain the speaker is about things:
  certainly, definitely, maybe, perhaps, probably.

  Perhaps *you'd like to see our catalogue?* (softer / less direct / more polite)

  I'll **probably** *go to Warsaw next month.* (I'm not 100% certain)

  Are you **definitely** *considering resigning?* (how certain are you?)

In informal spoken language people use these adverbs much more flexibly, often at the beginning or at the end of the sentence (as well as between the subject and verb).

◄ See sections C2 and C3.

6 A market researcher, Lena, is talking to a sales and marketing manager, David, about European consumer attitudes. Underline the most suitable adverbs in italics.

DAVID: Lena, tell me a little bit about recent projects you've been working on.

LENA: Well, **1** *perhaps/basically*, we've created a system for monitoring attitudes, preferences and needs across Europe, which manufacturers of fast-moving consumer goods, such as cosmetics or paper products, can use. **2** *Definitely/Hopefully*, this will give them reliable information to support their products.

DAVID: But customer attitudes towards fast-moving consumer goods have **3** *really/probably* been tested on a country-by-country basis in Europe many times before now, haven't they?

LENA: Yes, they have. But in the early days market researchers tried to identify the differences between one country and another. Nowadays, the fast moving-consumer goods sector is **4** *actually/maybe* looking at the similarities with our friends across the rest of Europe. That's why, for example, we've seen pan-European and global marketing and advertising campaigns from the leading brands.

DAVID: Yes, there have **5** *certainly/basically* been changes in advertising policy. But is there an advantage in targeting a marketing campaign at just one country, **6** *obviously/perhaps*?

LENA: Yes, **7** *maybe/really*. But I think that what our research **8** *really/probably* shows is that we have to think very carefully. **9** *Definitely/Obviously*, we are now one trading community in Europe, but there are **10** *definitely/hopefully* still some important differences between the countries.

⊙ **30.1** Listen and check your answers.

Make it personal

Write five sentences about your company's future. Use adverbs from this unit to express how certain you are about these things and what your attitude to them is.

31

Comparisons 1 (comparatives, *as … as*)

Read this extract from a letter on a website.

a Which words show the difference between the old and the new company?

b Which words show the difference between the writer and his colleagues?

> My company merged with a larger and more dynamic one some months ago. Its culture is quite different to ours, which was pretty conventional. I find this attractive but my colleagues are more resistant to change than I am. I'm feeling isolated.

A Forming comparative adjectives and adverbs

A1

one-syllable adjectives and adverbs	add *-er*	*cheap → cheaper* *fast → faster*
adjectives and adverbs of two or more syllables	*more …*	*expensive →* **more** *expensive* *often →* **more** *often*
two-syllable adjectives ending in *-y*	drop *-y* and add *-ier*	*happy → happier*
adverbs ending in *-ly*	*more …*	*easily →* **more** *easily*

► See Appendix 1 (Spelling).

Some adjectives and adverbs have irregular comparative forms.

good/well → **better**   *bad/badly →* **worse**   *far/far →* **further** ⊙ *farther* is possible but less frequent

A2 Some two-syllable adjectives have two comparative forms (e.g. *friendlier / more friendly*). One form is usually more frequent.

⊙ The more frequent forms are: *cleverer, easier, quieter, simpler; more likely, more costly, more friendly*.

B Using comparative adjectives and adverbs

B1 Comparative adjectives and adverbs compare two people or things. Use *than* before the second one if you mention it.

Smaller companies can often change **more quickly** (**than** *large corporations*). (**not** ~~more quickly that large corporations~~)

B2 When you compare two different people or things with the same quality, or doing the same activity, you can use an object pronoun or a verb phrase after *than*.

Do they supply orders more quickly **than us**? */* **than we do**?

⊙ With possessives, a pronoun is normally used, not a verb phrase.

Last year their prices were higher **than ours**. (*than ours were* is possible but rare)

C *as … as*

C1 You can use *as … as* with an adjective or adverb to say things are equal.

We try to keep our fees **as low as** *our competitors*. (**not** ~~as lower as~~)

C2 *Not as … (as)* and *less … (than)* are the opposite of *more … than*. ⊙ *Not as … as* is much more frequent than *less* in spoken English. *Less* is not common before *-ly* adverbs or one-syllable adjectives.

*This year's sales are***n't as good as** *last year's. Clients are ordering* **less often**.

D Comparing measures

D1 You can compare measures with *twice / three times as … as*, and *three/four times more/-er* (**not** ~~twice more/-er~~).

My new laptop was **twice as expensive as** *my old one, but it's* **four times faster**. (or **four times as fast**)

D2 You can compare percentages with *more/-er*.

Growth this year is **12% higher** *than last year*.

Practice

◄ A **1** Complete this magazine article about changes in business travel using the comparative form of the adjectives and adverbs in brackets.

> Business travel is growing **1** ....*faster*.... (*fast*) than ever, as we travel **2** .... (*far*) to do business. But in many ways air travel is becoming increasingly difficult for the executive traveller. Long security checks mean we have to get to the airport **3** .... (*early*) than before. As a result, airports are **4** .... (*busy*), with **5** .... (*long*) queues and **6** .... (*frequent*) delays. With the arrival of budget air travel, the departure lounges are **7** .... (*crowded*). Things will only get **8** .... (*bad*), as now they are introducing **9** .... (*large*) aircraft with over 800 passengers. Travel will be **10** .... (*stressful*). Airlines should take business travellers **11** .... (*seriously*) and work **12** .... (*hard*) to keep us happy.

◄ A, B1 **2** Complete this review of two mobile phones using comparative forms of the words in the box. Add *than* where necessary.

	Dimensions (mm)	Memory card	Standby time	Talk time	Weight	Price
Plexia	L100 x W46 x D15.5	8GB	400 hours	8 hours	83g	€499.99
Tanyo	L88 x W48 x D13.5	1GB	350 hours	10 hours	101g	€259.99

> big   cheap   easily   easy   expensive   good   heavy   ~~long~~   long   suitable   thin   wide

As far as size is concerned, the Plexia is **1** ....*longer than*.... the Tanyo, but the Tanyo is **2** .... and **3** .... the Plexia. The Plexia fits into a shirt pocket **4** .... You can talk on the Tanyo for **5** .... on the Plexia before charging the battery, but you get a **6** .... standby time with the Plexia. The Plexia's memory card is **7** .... the Tanyo's. At 101g, the Tanyo is **8** .... the Plexia, so the Plexia is **9** .... to carry around. However at €499.99 the Plexia is **10** .... the Tanyo, which is **11** .... other phones of this type. The Tanyo is therefore **12** .... for business people on a budget.

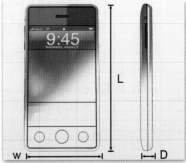

◄ B2 **3** An employee is talking about a competitor. Complete the second sentence so that it means the same as the first sentence. Use a comparative form of the word in brackets and *than* + a pronoun or verb phrase.

1 The sales team at Marston's all speak French fluently. We don't.

   They speak French ...*better than us / than we do*... . (*good*)

2 Our average delivery time is three days. At Marston's, it's five days.

   We deliver .... (*quickly*)

3 My colleagues are very friendly. The people at Marston's aren't.

   My colleagues are .... (*friendly*)

4 Our sales team is very successful. The sales team at Marston's isn't.

   We can sell .... (*effectively*)

5 The marketing department at Marston's has ten people. Ours has two!

   Their marketing department is .... (*big*)

6 We had a great year last year. Marston's results weren't very good.

   Our end of year results were .... (*impressive*)

◄ C **4 a** Read these interview notes on two candidates for a sales manager position. Complete the phone conversation between the personnel manager (PM) and sales director (SD). Use (*not*) *as ... (as)* or *less ... (than)* and the words in brackets. Sometimes both are possible.

	Paola Lombardi	Gisela Meyer
Age	31	42
Education	Degree, MBA	Degree
Years in sales	3	7
Managerial experience	Just over a year	4 years
Personality	Quiet but confident	Talkative, possibly a bit insecure?
Internal test results	95/100	95/100

PM: So what do you think? I mean, they're both good but I think Gisela is the better candidate. Paola was
1 ...*less impressive than* / *not as impressive as*... (*impressive*) Gisela.

SD: Um, I think they're about equal. For me, Paola was just **2** .... (*strong*) Gisela.

PM: But Paola's **3** .... (*old*) Gisela and she's **4** .... (*experienced*).

SD: True, but on the other hand Gisela's qualifications are **5** .... (*good*) Paola's. Paola hasn't worked for **6** .... (*long*) Gisela, but Gisela is **7** .... (*well-qualified*) Paola.

PM: How about personality? I mean Gisela was **8** .... (*shy*) and **9** .... (*quiet*) Paola.

SD: Well, Paola was **10** .... (*talkative*) Gisela, but I actually think Gisela was
11 .... (*confident*). And Paola's test results were also **12** .... (*high*) Gisela's.
I'd like to offer her the position.

🔘 **31.1** Listen and compare your answers.

b 🔘 **31.2** Practise the conversation with the recording. First take the role of the sales director.

🔘 **31.3** Then take the role of the personnel manager.

◄ D **5** Complete this extract from a handout at a training seminar using the correct comparative form of the words in brackets.

The ABC of Selling

A Look after your existing customers.

1 A customer's lifetime value is ...*many times greater*.... (*many times* / *great*) than the value of their first purchase.

2 It's .... (*six times* / *expensive*) to sell to a new customer than an existing one.

3 It can take .... (*three times* / *long*) to get a new customer than to keep one you have.

4 Existing customers spend their money .... (*33%* / *fast*) than new customers.

B Make your customers part of your sales team.

5 Existing customers are .... (*three times* / *likely*) to recommend you to their friends.

6 Customers are .... (*twice* / *likely*) to talk about bad experiences as good ones.

C Use your customer's own language.

7 People are .... (*four times* / *likely*) to buy if they can do it in their own language.

8 Internet users spend .... (*twice* / *long*) on a website in their native language.

Make it personal

Write about changes you have noticed in travelling or commuting to work.
Or compare two candidates you have interviewed, or two colleagues you work with.
Or compare two phones or pieces of equipment that you have looked at recently.

31 Business talk: Modifying comparisons

Business people often make comparative adjectives and adverbs stronger or weaker with these expressions.

Stronger:	*Living costs are*	***much / far / a lot***	*higher / more expensive.*
Weaker:	*The future is*	***slightly / a bit / a little / a little bit***	*less certain.*

⚠ **In very formal contexts don't use *a lot* or *a (little) bit*. Use *much/far/significantly/considerably* or *slightly/little*.**

Sometimes people repeat comparative forms to emphasise big changes, or changes over a period of time.

*Property is getting **more and more** expensive, so it's becoming **harder and harder** to recruit staff.*

*People are **less and less likely** to work near to their homes*

6 **A manager is talking about his business over the last year. Make the words in italics stronger (+) or weaker (–) by using an expression from the presentation above. Sometimes more than one answer is possible.**

It's been a really tough year. We've had to work **1** (+) ....*a lot / much / far*.... *harder* to achieve the same results as last year. And it's been **2** (+) .... *more difficult* for me personally because my boss is **3** (+) .... *less involved* with day-to-day tasks – I hardly ever see her. And I also meet with my assistant **4** (–) .... *less often*. Everything is changing **5** (+) .... *faster* than we realise – it's hard to keep up. With all the new systems the company has become **6** (+) .... *more bureaucratic* – they say it's to cut costs. I'm not sure it's made a difference. Maybe we are working **7** (–) .... *more efficiently*, but not much. Every little helps, I suppose.

7 **Rewrite the words in italics in the same manager's written report using more formal expressions.**

1 ....

This has been an extremely difficult year for the department, and staff have had to work **1** *a lot* harder to achieve the same results as last year. The new accounting system was **2** *a lot* more difficult to use than we had anticipated. It was also **3** *a lot* more expensive. Although it has made our department **4** *a bit* more efficient, we have spent a great deal of our time on software problems. In addition, changes to the reporting structure have made staff **5** *a bit* less confident about their own responsibilities. In future I recommend that as a management team we should try **6** *a lot* harder to communicate the aims of all these changes **7** *a bit* more effectively.

2 ....*much/far/significantly/considerably*....

3 ....

4 ....

5 ....

6 ....

7 ....

Make it personal

Write about recent changes in your workplace, using the expressions in the presentation above.

1 Compare one aspect of your company's performance this year with last year.

2 Compare the computer you use now with the one you used five years ago.

3 Compare two jobs or two bosses you have had.

Comparisons 2 (superlatives, comparing with verbs)

Read this extract from a blog.

a Which adjectives describe Wal-Mart?

b Does the writer think any other stores are bigger and more profitable than Wal-Mart, with lower prices?

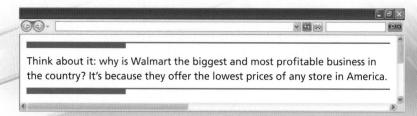

Think about it: why is Walmart the biggest and most profitable business in the country? It's because they offer the lowest prices of any store in America.

A Forming superlative adjectives and adverbs

A1

short adjectives and adverbs	add *-est*	*cheap* → **cheapest** *fast* → **fastest**
adjectives and adverbs of two or more syllables	*most/least …*	*expensive* → **most/least expensive** *carefully* → **most/least carefully**
two-syllable adjectives ending in *-y*	drop *-y* and add *-iest*	*busy* → **busiest**

◄ See Unit 31 (Comparisons 1) and ► Appendix 1 (Spelling).

Some adjectives and adverbs have irregular superlative forms.

good/well → **best**   *bad/badly* → **worst**   *far/far* → **furthest**   ⊙   farthest is possible but less frequent

A2 Some two-syllable adjectives have two superlative forms (e.g. *friendliest / most friendly*). One form is usually more frequent.

⊙ The more frequent forms are: **-est**: *costliest, friendliest, simplest, wealthiest;* **most**: *most common, most (un)likely.*

B Using superlative adjectives and adverbs

B1 You can use a superlative to compare three or more people or things. The superlative shows that one person or thing has more (or less) of something than the others.

*We bought the **best** and **most efficient** air conditioners on the market.*

In spoken English people often use superlatives to compare two people or things.

⊙ *I've got two designs to show you. The blue one's the **cheapest**, but which do you like **best**?*

B2 You can use a superlative adjective with *the* or a possessive (e.g. *your, the company's, Italy's*). With a superlative adverb, you do not have to use *the*.

*Sales in June were **the / our highest**. Sales to Asia are growing (**the**) **fastest** even though we go there (**the**) **least often**.*

B3 After a superlative, use *in* (**not** *of*) before places and organisations (e.g. *in the country/world/company/department*).

*Walmart is **the biggest** business **in the US**. (**not** ~~of the US~~)*

⚠ **Use *of* to introduce other things you are comparing and time periods (e.g. *of my life / the last ten years / the century*).**

*Hyundai is the largest **of the conglomerates** in South Korea.   Leaving my job was the worst decision **of my life**.*

B4 You can use superlative adverbs before adjectives that are present or past participles (e.g. *developing/developed*).

*Mobile communications is **the fastest growing** area in the telecom sector.   Our logo is probably **the best known** in the world.*

B5 You can use ordinal numbers (*second, third* etc. but **not** *first*) before a superlative to order things.

*Intel is the world's **second most successful** computer company after Microsoft.*

C Making comparisons with verbs

You can use *more, less* and (*the*) *most* and (*the*) *least* as adverbs.

*Computers cost **less** now **than** (they did) in 2004.   Unemployment hurts young people (**the**) **most**.*

► See Unit 35 (Quantifiers) for comparisons with nouns.

Practice

◄ A

1 **a** Complete these questions using superlative adjectives and adverbs. Use *least* where you see ↓.

Thinking of relocating in the EU to cut costs, or to improve your business prospects, or even your lifestyle? How much do you know about the EU? Do the quiz and find out.

1 Which country has ....the largest.... (*large*) population in the EU?

2 Which three countries have the EU's .... (*expensive*) workforce?

3 Which country in the EU has Europe's .... (*old*) population?

4 In which country do people live .... (*long*)?

5 Which two countries have .... (*low*) retirement ages?

6 Which EU country is .... (*wealthy*) in terms of per capita GDP?

7 Which capital cities in the EU have .... (*happy*) citizens? On the other hand, which have .... (↓ *satisfied*)?

8 In which EU cities do the public transport systems run .... (*efficiently*)?

9 In which EU countries do citizens feel .... (*secure*)?

b ⊙ 32.1 Do you know the answers to the questions in Exercise 1a? Listen to a radio programme and check your answers.

◄ A, B1–3

2 Find and correct the mistakes in this consultancy report for AC Transport. There is one mistake in each sentence.

the

1 AC Transport is ∧ largest transport company in the UK. **2** We are also the most respected company of the country. **3** Customers say we are still the most best transport company in the North. **4** In the last 20 years we have grown the fastest in all our competitors. **5** However, we have recently lost our most big contract. **6** Last year was our least good since we began. **7** AC Transport could become least competitive transport company in the region if this continues.

8 Analysis has shown that the personnel department greatest problem is keeping experienced drivers. **9** These drivers travel most far and take the most time off for sickness. **10** This is especially true in the busyest months of the year. **11** Various solutions have been discussed and the effectivest one is to reorganise operations so that drivers drive shorter distances between stops. **12** We also need to ensure that our best drivers are away from home the less often.

◄ B4

3 Complete these sentences using the correct superlative adverb and adjective form of the words in the box.

bad/pay   common/ask   dense/populate   environmental/damage   good/protect
heavy/regulate   physical/demand   rapid/expand   wide/use

1 British business is not ....the most heavily regulated.. in Europe and its workers are not .... either.

2 The Consumer Price Index, which is prepared by the US Bureau of Labor Statistics, is .... measure of inflation in North America.

3 Tourism is one of the biggest and .... business sectors in the world. But in many regions it is also one of ....

4 'Why are you applying for this position?' is probably .... question at job interviews.

5 .... countries in the world are Rwanda, Monaco and Singapore.

6 Why are .... jobs such as fishing, mining and construction often some of .... ?

◄B5 **4** Complete this business report using the correct superlative form of the adjectives *profitable* and *large*. Use ordinal numbers (*second*, *third*, etc) where necessary.

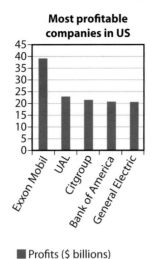

Most profitable companies in US

■ Profits ($ billions)

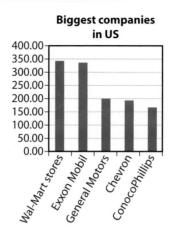

Biggest companies in US

■ Revenues ($ millions)

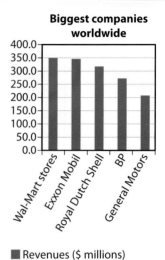

Biggest companies worldwide

■ Revenues ($ millions)

In 2007 Walmart remained **1** ....the largest.... company in the US, and was also **2** .... company in the world. However, Exxon Mobil was **3** .... company in the US by far, earning $39.5 billion. It was also **4** .... company in the world in terms of revenues. Other oil giants followed close behind: Royal Dutch Shell was **5** .... company in the world and BP was **6** ....

7 .... company was UAL with a net income of $22.9 billion. Profits at Citigroup fell by 12% to $21.5 billion, but the banking giant still ranked as **8** .... company in the US. General Motors was **9** .... company in the US and **10** .... company worldwide, but it made losses of almost $2 billion.

◄C **5** Read the information about an accountant, Karim. Complete what he says about the recent changes to his job using *more*, *less*, *the most* or *the least*.

Karim didn't use to enjoy his job. He travelled a lot and didn't spend much time with his family. Then a new manager changed the work of the auditing team, which affected Karim more than anyone else. He's now happier. His colleagues travel more often, but he's able to concentrate on key customers.

1 I'm enjoying the job ....more...... now.

2 Basically I'm travelling .... – in fact I'm probably travelling .... of all us.

3 It's nice for me. It means I can be at home .... , see the kids, you know.

4 The changes my manager brought in affect everybody, but they probably affect me ....

5 I'm dealing with the big accounts .... They need looking after ....

6 I guess I like her .... than my old boss. She understands customer care .... than him.

Make it personal

Answer these questions and give reasons for each answer.

In your department …
● who works hardest?
● who handles problems most or least successfully?
● who comes to work late most often?
● who's the most efficient person? And the least?
● who's the best at managing their time? Who's the worst?

32 Write for business: Using *most* in formal correspondence

In formal business letters and emails people often use *most* instead of *very* with adjectives or adverbs that describe reactions and feelings. This makes the text sound formal and polite, so use it with people you do not know well or at all.

*I would be **most grateful** if you could return the enclosed questionnaire.* (**not** ~~the most grateful~~)

*It was **most unfortunate** that I was unable to see you on your last visit.*

People often also use a past tense with this structure to describe how they feel now.

*I **was most pleased** to hear that you had accepted our quotation for the construction work.* (I am feeling very pleased now)

⚠ **Don't use this too often in one letter or email. Two examples are enough.**

6 Complete these formal written expressions so that they have a similar meaning to the informal spoken expressions. Use *most* and a word from the box.

| concerned | disappointed | grateful | impressed | interesting | sincere | ~~sincerely~~ | thoughtful |

1 'Thanks very much for the present.' →
   I wish to thank you ...*most sincerely*... for the gift.

2 'I was really worried when you said the product wasn't working.' →
   I was .... to learn of the problems you have experienced with our product.

3 'Thanks for dinner. It was nice of you to think of us.' →
   Thank you for your hospitality – it was .... of you to invite us.

4 'Well done!' →
   We would like to send you our .... congratulations.

5 'I'm sorry you're going.' →
   I was .... to learn that you are leaving the company.

6 'What you're working on is really fascinating.' →
   Your new project sounds ....

7 'Your reps seem really good.' →
   We were .... by your sales team.

8 'Can you send me a catalogue?' →
   I would be .... if you could send me a catalogue.

7 Write a formal sentence for each of these situations. Use the examples from Exercise 6 to help you.

1 Tell a job applicant that you're sorry he has withdrawn his application.

   ....

2 Ask for a brochure from a hotel.

   ....

3 Thank a new consultant for lunch on a recent visit.

   ....

4 Congratulate a competitor on an industry award.

   ....

Make it personal

1 Has your job changed in any way, like Karim's in Exercise 5? Write a paragraph about the changes.

2 Write two sentences with *most* + adjective that you could use in your business correspondence.

Being an active listener

Read this conversation.

Who is the more active listener, Tony or Diana? Why?

Rita: We've just heard we've got the Hong Kong contract!

Diana: Mm.

Tony: That's great news!

A Showing you are actively listening

You can show you are actively involved in a conversation by responding to what people say with these expressions.

congratulating someone	A: *I've just been promoted to senior manager.* B: **Congratulations! That's great (news)! That's wonderful/fantastic.**
wishing someone good luck	A: *I've got an interview at Westrak tomorrow.* B: **Good luck!**
to someone who is about to travel	A: *Right. I'm leaving for the airport now.* B: OK. **Have a good trip. / Safe journey.**
reacting to problems and bad news that affect you and others	A: *We've lost a lot of customers because of the strike.* B: **That's a shame/pity. / That's awful/terrible. / That's bad news.** A: *The server's crashed again. That's the second time this week!* B: **Oh dear! / Oh no!** (*Oh no!* is stronger than *Oh dear!*)
reacting to bad news that affects others	A: *We didn't get the Agraspec contract after all.* B: **Oh, I'm sorry (to hear that). / Never mind. / Better luck next time!**
showing general interest	A: *We sell more plastic containers in Moldova than any other country.* B: **That's interesting. / How interesting! / Interesting.**
showing surprise	A: *Timson's have gone bankrupt!* B: **(Oh), really! / Wow! / You're joking!** (These can all be used together. *Wow!* and *You're joking!* are more informal than *Really!*)

B Responding positively using *That's ...*

🔘 The ten most common words which people use after *That's* when they respond positively to what someone says are: *all right, correct, excellent, fine, good, great, interesting, OK, right* and *true.*

general positive reactions	A: *We've had a record year so far.* B: **That's good/great/excellent!**
agreeing with someone's point or opinion	A: *Obviously, there's more margin on some products than on others.* B: **That's right. / That's true.**
agreeing to an arrangement or a decision	A: *We're aiming for the 30th of this month for the new web pages.* B: **That's fine/OK. / That's great.**
confirming a fact or a piece of information	A: *So, that's 30,000 units by end of March?* B: **That's right. / That's correct.** (more formal)
saying that something is not a problem	A: *We may need about five days.* B: **That's OK/all right.**

People often use these words on their own, without *That's.*

A: *We're aiming for the 30th of this month for the new web pages.*
B: **Fine/Great/OK.**

Practice

◄ A **1** Match the statements (1–8) with a suitable response (a–h). Sometimes more than one answer is possible.

1 I just heard I've been promoted to area manager!
2 I didn't get the job at Winntek after all.
3 Two major UK banks have just collapsed!
4 Dolmora have three branches in South America.
5 We're going to get a big bonus this year, I heard.
6 I'm flying to Berlin tomorrow. See you next week.
7 I've got my driving test tomorrow.
8 I won't be able to join you for lunch today.

a That's a pity.
b Good luck!
c Congratulations!
d Oh, no! You're joking!
e Never mind. Better luck next time.
f OK, safe journey.
g That's wonderful.
h That's interesting.

◄ A **2** a Complete these responses using a suitable expression from A. Sometimes more than one answer is possible.

1 A: I've failed one of my accountancy exams.
   B: Oh, I'm sorry to hear that. Never mind. ....Better luck next time.............

2 A: Three new electronics factories have opened just in that one small town this year!
   B: Wow! ....That's amazing!

3 A: Right. I'm setting off for Madrid now.
   B: OK. Safe journey. .... Bye.

4 A: We're going to have to close some branches – we're losing money.
   B: Oh dear! ....

5 A: We've just heard we've won a design gold medal!
   B: Oh! Congratulations! ....

6 A: We won't be able to exhibit at Expoenergy this year. The dates don't fit.
   B: Oh dear! ....

b ○ SS 8.1 Practise the conversations with the recording. Take the role of B.

◄ B **3** Write positive reactions to what these people say using expressions with *That's*. Sometimes more than one answer is possible.

1 A: So, shall we say 4 pm on Wednesday 26th for our next conference call?
   B: That's ....great/fine/OK.......

2 A: So I can contact you on 745 538, and that's a direct line?
   B: That's ....

3 A: Sales are up for the third quarter running.
   B: That's ....

4 A: I'm afraid delivery is going to be delayed by a day.
   B: That's .... It's not a problem.

5 A: Customer support is just as important as selling.
   B: That's ....

6 A: They're giving me a lovely big new office all to myself!
   B: That's ....!

7 A: OK, so we'll have two more meetings before the launch date.
   B: That's ....

8 A: So the current rate is $1.45 to the pound, yeah?
   B: That's ....

○ SS 8.2 Listen and compare your answers.

Test 8: Units 29–32

1 Complete these descriptions from an office supplies catalogue using the positive or negative adjective forms of the words in brackets.

The Marbella chair (£29.99): A **1** ....*beautiful*.... (*beauty*), **2** .... (*luxury*) leather chair. We only have **3** .... (*limit*) stock of this model, so hurry while stocks last.

Floorex Chair Mat (£19.99): This is an **4** .... (*economy*) and **5** .... (*ease*) way to protect your office floors. (Warning: for hard floors only; it's **6** .... (*suit*) for carpet)

Bisworth storage cabinet (£129.99): This is an **7** .... (*expense*) solution for storing office supplies, ideal if your budget is limited. (This model is installed by our **8** .... (*profession*) **9** .... (*assemble*) team).

Office Finance 2.1 (£138.98): This software package makes **10** .... (*finance*) management simple, letting you pay employees and safely store **11** .... (*value*) records for customers, suppliers, products and employees.

For more **12** .... (*excite*) offers, visit our website.

2 Put the adjectives in italics in the correct order and add commas where necessary.

1 Align Technology, a *medical / Californian* products company, produces *plastic / removable / dental* appliances manufactured for each individual patient. (with handwritten *2* above *medical*, *1* above *Californian*)

2 The BISYS Group is a *US / independent / leading* provider of information and investment outsourcing solutions to *financial / international / 20,000* institutions.

3 Callaway Golf produces and markets *golf / innovative / high-quality* clubs, balls and other accessories.

4 Earthcoat makes *environmentally-friendly / industrial / new* coatings, as well as *organic / traditional* paint.

3 Complete these sentences by putting the adjectives in brackets in the correct position.

1 The failure of the project was a ∧ shock to all team members ∧ . (*great, concerned*) (with handwritten *great* above first ∧ and *concerned* above second ∧)

2 The owners have decided to sell the company, but it will be a process. (*present, long*)

3 Product lines by the economic downturn include luxury goods such as perfumes. (*affected*)

4 Some money is missing from the safe and I want to know who is. (*responsible*)

5 Rising energy costs have forced us to keep prices. (*high*)

4 Complete these sentences using the adverb form of the words in brackets in the correct position.

1 I'm flying to Moscow ∧ after I get back from New York. (*immediate*) (with handwritten *immediately* above ∧)

2 The Sub-Saharan energy project went. We ran a similar project in Asia. (*also, good*)

3 Have you worked here? (*long*)

4 What's the best advertisement you've seen? (*late*)

5 I can't come to this week's meeting, but I can make next week's. That's a promise. (*definite, unfortunate*)

6 In a job interview, try to answer any questions. (*honest*)

7 Your appraisal is due, isn't it? Are you nervous about it? (*soon*)

8 I've seen such impressive results. You deserve your bonus. (*rare, real*)

5 Look at the words in italics. If they are correct, tick (✓) them and correct them if they are wrong.

The Association of Chartered Certified Accountants believes that UK companies need to ensure that their
1 *annually reports* are 2 *meaningful and accurate* for readers. Presentation is 3 *importantly*, but shareholders
4 *will read always* these reports more for business than for their 5 *well design*.

Company reports 6 *just should not focus on* the past year's achievements but 7 *should think about also* the
future. 8 *Unfortunately*, 9 *reports often focus* on 10 *well news* and avoid addressing future challenges.

Companies 11 *need to think careful* about how they can 12 *effectively inform* shareholders and provide them
with the information they require. Our advice to companies is to 13 *work hardly* at explaining the things that
14 *real matter* to the people reading their reports.

1	*annually reports*	5	....	9	....	13	....
2	✓	6	....	10	....	14	....
3	....	7	....	11	....		
4	....	8	....	12	....		

6 a Make the comparative and superlative forms of these adjectives and adverbs.

big	*bigger*	*the biggest*	cheap	....	....
good	....	....	cheaply	....	....
bad	....	....	easy	....	....
expensive	....	....	easily	....	....

b Read these extracts from an article about locating a business in different North American cities.
Complete the sentences using the correct form of the words in Exercise 6a. Use *much / far / a lot / slightly
/ a bit / a little / a little bit* or *second, third* etc. when appropriate.

	New York City	Chicago	Los Angeles
Population (m)	8.1	2.9	3.8
Office costs ($ per m^2 per month)	110	99	85
Salary ($000)	47,395	46,250	41,245
Apartment rent ($ per month)	1,600	910	941
Easy to do business* (world ranking)	2nd	5th	17th

*Mastercard survey of world cities

Where should we locate our business?

1 If you want a big potential market, choose New York; it has ....*the biggest*.... population of the three.

2 If you want to keep office costs down, go to LA; office leases are not as .... as Chicago or New
York. Chicago has .... leases of the three cities at $99 per m^2. New York offices are ....
at $110.

3 Salaries in New York are only .... than in Chicago. Salaries in LA are ....

4 Compared to New York, you can live .... in both Chicago and LA. Rents in Chicago are
.... at $910 per month.

5 Finally, in Mastercard's survey of cities around the world, New York was ranked .... place to do
business (London was number one). Both New York and Chicago are .... places to do business
than LA, which only came seventeenth.

Countability and number

Read this introduction to a presentation about market research.

a Which nouns in italics are singular (one thing)?

b Which nouns in italics are plural (two or more things)?

> *Market research* is essential to understanding your *customers* and your *competition*. Market research can also identify *trends* that affect *sales* and *profitability*. But successful market research takes *planning* and *strategy*.

A Countable and uncountable nouns

A1 Countable nouns are people or things you can count as separate, individual items.

a **manager**   *a* **job**   *an* **idea**   *a few* **ideas**   *two* **women**   *ten* **computers**

A2 👁 Uncountable nouns are things that you cannot divide or count. Here are the most frequent in spoken business English:

accommodation	documentation	feedback	health	luggage	paperwork	research	transport
advertising	employment	furniture	help	machinery	permission	software	travel
advice	equipment	guidance	information	marketing	progress	traffic	weather
cash	evidence	hardware	literature	money	publicity	training	work

B Using countable and uncountable nouns

B1 Countable nouns can be singular or plural. Uncountable nouns do not have a plural form.

This new job is a great **opportunity** *for me.   I have lots of* **opportunities** *to travel.*
Can you arrange (some) **accommodation** *for ten visitors?* (**not** *accommodations*)

B2 You can use *a/an* with singular countable nouns but not with uncountable nouns.

We had **a** *meeting and made (some)* **progress**. (**not** *a progress*)

B3 Singular countable nouns need a determiner (e.g. *a/an*, *my*). You can use an uncountable noun without a determiner.

Research *is expensive. We paid £6,000 for* **this report**. (**not** *for report*)

B4 Countable nouns can take a singular or plural verb. Uncountable nouns always take a singular verb.

My boss has *a PhD.* **My colleagues are** *all graduates.*
This **software is** *out of date and* **needs** *updating.*

C Nouns that are countable and uncountable with a different meaning

Countable
Small **businesses** *are our future.* (companies)
Do you want **a coffee**? (a cup of coffee)
Going to Asia was **a great experience**.
Do you get **a local paper**? (a newspaper)
We're short of meeting **rooms**.
We run **competitions** *as part of promotion.*

Uncountable
We do **business** *all over the world.* (the activity)
No, thanks, I don't drink **coffee** *or* **tea**.
I have no **experience** *in sales.*
I didn't have any **paper** *so I couldn't take notes.*
Our office is full. There's no **room** *to expand.* (space)
Is there much **competition**? (companies/products)

D Talking about amounts and measures

You can use these expressions to talk about an amount or an example of an uncountable noun.

measures and containers: **a litre of** *oil,* **15 tonnes of** *cement;* **a bottle of** *water,* **two tins of** *paint*
a piece of / a bit of + *advice, equipment, evidence, furniture, luggage, machinery, news, paper, publicity, research, software, work*
a bit of + *advertising, cash, feedback, fun, luck, money, progress, traffic, travel*

⚠ Don't use *a bit of* in formal writing.

► See Unit 35 (Quantifiers) and Appendix 3 (North American English).

Practice

◀ A, B1–3 **1** Complete these sentences using a pair of words from the box. Use plural forms where necessary.

bag – luggage	document – paperwork
brochure – literature	~~accommodation – hotel~~
chair – furniture	equipment – projector
comment – feedback	advertisement – publicity

1 It was difficult to find ....*accommodation*.... as all the ...*hotels*.... were full.

2 There was a lot of .... to do to get visas. I forgot a vital .... the day we went to the embassy and we had to go back the next day.

3 We had to wait ages at the airport for our ...., and the airline lost one of my ....

4 Our .... didn't arrive and we had to borrow a .... for our presentation.

5 There weren't enough .... in the room, so people were sitting on other ....

6 We got good .... on our presentation – we didn't get a negative .... from anyone.

7 Unfortunately, we left all our promotional .... on the plane, so we only had one .... between us.

8 We had put .... in the local papers, which gave us good ....

◀ A, B1–3 **2** Find and correct ten mistakes with articles and plurals in these extracts from websites.

1

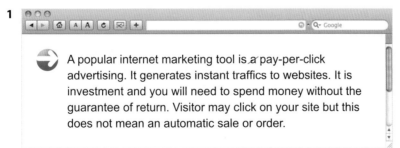

A popular internet marketing tool is a pay-per-click advertising. It generates instant traffics to websites. It is investment and you will need to spend money without the guarantee of return. Visitor may click on your site but this does not mean an automatic sale or order.

2

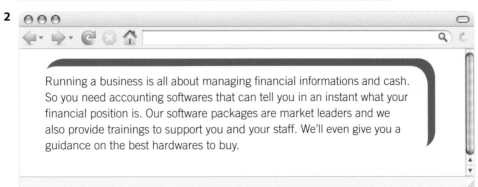

Running a business is all about managing financial informations and cash. So you need accounting softwares that can tell you in an instant what your financial position is. Our software packages are market leaders and we also provide trainings to support you and your staff. We'll even give you a guidance on the best hardwares to buy.

33

◀ **A, B** **3** Complete these extracts from a staff handbook using the correct present simple form of the verbs in brackets.

> Work **1** ...*is*.... (*be*) important in all our lives but some people **2** .... (*find*) their jobs a major cause of stress, especially when unemployment **3** .... (*be*) high. Research **4** .... (*show*) that stress can be a major contributor to ill health. Ill health often **5** .... (*lead*) to absenteeism and poor performance. The evidence for this **6** .... (*be*) overwhelming. So the health of your employees **7** .... (*be*) directly linked to the health of the company. Managers **8** .... (*need to*) watch for signs of extreme stress.
> * * * *
> Some of the machinery in the workshops **9** .... (*be*) dangerous, so use with care. All equipment **10** .... (*be*) checked daily and there **11** .... (*be*) documentation for each machine on file. Make sure machines **12** .... (*be*) turned off after use. Permission **13** .... (*be*) required to borrow tools for personal use. Permits **14** .... (*be*) available from the office.
> * * * *
> Transport to and from the city centre **15** .... (*be*) provided free of charge. Coaches **16** .... (*leave*) every half an hour between 5 pm and 7 pm. The last coach **17** .... (*depart*) at 7:15. Employees who **18** .... (*wish*) to use the bus service must contact personnel.
> * * * *

◀ **A–C** **4** Underline the correct words in italics in these extracts from an interview at an advertising agency.

1 INTERVIEWER: What an awful *weather* / *day*!
CANDIDATE: Yes, it's been so wet lately.

2 I: What's the hotel like?
C: Nice, thank you. I have *nice room* / *a nice room*.

3 I: How was your journey here today?
C: Well, there *were* / *was* bad traffic in the centre.

4 I: Do you travel much as part of your current job?
C: Yes, I do about four *trips* / *travels* a year.

5 I: How many *jobs* / *works* have you had?
C: About five.

6 I: Do you have *experience* / *an experience* in TV advertising?
C: Yes, I once got an agency to do *a marketing* / *a campaign* for the launch of a shampoo.

7 I: Tell me about your company.
C: Well, we're *small business* / *a small business*.

8 I: Who are your *competitions* / *competitors*?
C: There's a lot of competition in our business.

◀ **D** **5** Complete this business lunch conversation between friends using *a bit of*, *a piece of* or an appropriate container or measure.

ARIANNA: Would you like to share **1** ....*a bottle of*.... mineral water?

BRONA: Yes, OK. Can I get **2** .... orange juice, too?

ARIANNA: Sure. Now, I'd like to ask you for **3** .... advice, actually. I've had **4** .... luck on the stock market and I've made **5** .... cash, and I want to start my own company.

BRONA: And you need **6** .... help from me?

ARIANNA: Yeah. I've developed **7** .... software that searches the web. I'd like you to help me do **8** .... advertising. We could both make **9** .... money on it and have **10** .... fun, too.

🔘 **33.1 Listen and compare your answers.**

Make it personal

Answer these questions.

In your company who is the market research done by? How about the advertising?

How is training organised?

Do you feel you are making progress in your career?

33 Write for business: Checking verbs after singular and plural nouns

When you edit a document, letter or email, check for mistakes with verbs after nouns.

Use a singular verb with:
- a singular countable noun.
  This **report looks** at our position in the US.
- an uncountable noun.
  Our **advertising has** not been successful.

- these nouns ending in –s: economics, electronics, maths, news, physics, public relations (PR).
  The **news isn't** good. (**not** ~~The news aren't~~)

Use a plural verb with:
- a plural countable noun.
  Sales in Greece **have** grown rapidly this year.
- two (or more) nouns joined by and – even if they are uncountable nouns.
  Advice and training are important for new staff.
- these nouns ending in –s: clothes, earnings, goods, jeans, premises, scissors, (sun)glasses, trousers, tights.
  The **premises are** locked at night.

Politics and headquarters can take a plural or singular verb.

Office **politics are** unavoidable. (or **is** unavoidable)

You can often use a plural or singular verb after nouns for groups of people or company names (e.g. board, company, committee, firm, government, management, staff, team, union, BP, Microsoft).

The **board was/were** unanimous.
BP is/are investing in new technology.

Use a plural verb if you think of the noun as individual people, not one group.

All my **staff are** graduates.

---

6 a Find and correct eight mistakes with the verbs in italics in these minutes from a meeting.

Health and safety

Ms Gera said that safety glasses *is* [are] now available in the workshops. She reminded the meeting that work clothes *are* provided and that shorts *is* not allowed in any work area.

New furniture and audio equipment *has* been bought for the recreation room. The staff *are* reminded to treat this with care. The union *has* asked staff to report any misuse.

The premises *are* now patrolled at night by NB Security.

Company performance

The management team *is* pleased to announce that earnings from investments *was* 10% up on last year. The news in Asia *are* especially encouraging. In contrast, exports to the EU *was* 2% down.

Staff benefits

Mr Binder said that the company *is* taking advice from ALD Insurance on the pension scheme, which *have* a shortfall. Changes to the current scheme *is* inevitable. ALD Insurance *is* due to report next month.

b Find four verbs in italics where a plural is possible as well as the singular form.

7 Underline the correct words in italics. Sometimes both are possible.

1 *Is/Are* office politics a problem where you work?

2 *Is/Are* the people you work with nice?

3 *Is/Are* your company headquarters in the EU?

4 *Is/Are* maths important in your job?

5 *Is/Are* jeans considered acceptable to wear to work?

Make it personal

Write answers to the questions in Exercise 7 that are true for you.

34 Articles

Read this extract from a website.

a Which nouns are used with articles?

b Which nouns are used with no article?

◄ See Unit 33 (Countability and number).

Business.gov is the official business link to the US Government. It is managed by the US Small Business Administration. It provides an access point to government services and information to help the nation's businesses with their operations.

A The indefinite article: *a/an*

A1 You can use *a/an*:

- to talk about something for the first time.
  *Sam met **an interesting contact** at the conference.* (Sam did not know this person before the conference)

- before someone's job and type of workplace (but not to describe their area of business).
  *My wife's **a consultant**. She works for **a large consultancy** in Bristol. She works in marketing.* (**not** ~~in a marketing~~)

- to say when something is one of many / a group.
  *They're looking for **a new supplier**.* (there are many possible new suppliers)

- in measurements or frequency expressions (*per* can often also be used).
  *We produce 3,000 units **a/per day**.*

⚠ You can only use *a/an* with singular countable nouns.

*I'd like **some** information about your courses.* (**not** ~~an information~~)

A2 Use *a* when the word after it begins with a consonant sound.

*a **b**usiness / a **c**omputer / a **r**etailer / a **s**uccessful business*

⚠ Some written vowels have a consonant sound when you say them.

*a **u**niform / a **U**S company / a **E**uropean company*

A3 Use *an* when the word after it begins with a vowel sound.

*an **o**pportunity / an **A**merican / an **M**BA* (pronounced em)

⚠ Sometimes the first written consonant is silent.

*an **h**our / an **h**onest woman*

B The definite article: *the*

You can use *the*:

- when there is only one of something.
  *The **finance director** is giving a presentation tomorrow.*

- when the listener or reader knows what we are talking about. This may be something you have already mentioned in the conversation or text or something you both know about already.
  *We have an outlet in Paris and one in Lyon. We've decided to close **the store** in Paris to cut costs.* (mentioned before)
  *Where's **the meeting** today?* (we know which meeting)

- with superlative adjectives.
  *UBS is **the biggest bank** in Switzerland.*

- with groups, categories and nationalities.
  the rich** / **the laptop (a category of computer) / ***the French***

- with some institutions.
  the UN** / **the World Bank

- with some countries (e.g. with *Republic, Kingdom, States*), place names and geographical features.
  the UK** / **the Atlantic** / **the Middle East** / **the White House

- with points of the compass.
  *We're based in **the north/south/east/west**.*

- with some time expressions.
  the past** / **the present** / at **the moment

🔘 *The* is more than twice as frequent as *a/an*.

C No article

When we talk about plural or uncountable nouns in a general way, we do not use an article.

***Lawyers** often work very long hours.* (lawyers in general)
***The lawyers** we use are very expensive.* (specific lawyers)

We do not use an article for:

- most company names.
  *He works for **BP/Microsoft/Sony**.*

- days, months, years and some festivals.
  *on **Tuesday** / in **May** / in **2010** / at **Christmas***

- means of transport.
  *by **plane/car/bus**, on **foot***

- some types of buildings.
  *He's in **hospital/prison/court**.* (**but** *the office*)

Practice

◀ A2–3 **1** Underline the correct words in italics.

1 All our staff wear *a/an* uniform – a black jacket and grey trousers or skirt.

2 *A/An* government report says that we spent $320bn doing paperwork last year.

3 You need *a/an* university degree to work here, but *a/an* MBA would be better.

4 Can you start your presentation now? I have *a/an* meeting in *a/an* hour and I mustn't be late.

5 I think she's *a/an* successful sales person because she has such *a/an* honest face.

6 It's *a/an* Australian company, but it employs *a/an* European advertising agency.

◀ A, B **2** Complete these sentences using *a*, *an* or *the*.

1 Apart from saving money, ...*an*.... unexpected result of ...*the*.... job cuts we made was that ...*the*.... productivity rate actually rose.

2 Staff will receive .... big bonus this year. We will shortly announce how big .... bonus will be.

3 Is it true that .... new general manager is .... friend of yours?

4 I'm glad to tell you that we plan to open .... branch office in Moscow and there will be .... opportunity for some of you to transfer there. If you are interested in working in .... new branch, send me .... email.

5 .... new packing machine that I told you about processes 3,000 units .... hour.

6 With .... record turnover of $40m, last year was .... most profitable in .... company's history.

7 Pete? He's retraining as .... IT consultant. He's always wanted .... job in computers.

8 Sales in .... Italian market continue to rise, but .... French are turning more to domestic producers.

9 There has been .... 27% increase in people who said they had .... skills to start .... business.

10 'Shareholders have rejected .... takeover offer,' .... SG spokesman said.

◀ B, C **3** For each pair of sentences, write *the* in one gap and – (no article) in the other gap.

1 A: It took ages to get ....*the*.... photocopier repaired.

B: I know. We're trying to cut ......‾...... maintenance costs and that means delays.

2 A: Sorry I'm late. I had to finish .... marketing report you asked for.

B: That's OK. I had loads of .... emails to deal with.

3 A: What's .... best time to discuss your plans for tomorrow's presentation?

B: How about .... Tuesday at 3 o'clock?

4 A: I've just spoken to Parkers and $60 is .... lowest price they'll give us.

B: Well, ... prices are going up everywhere. I can't say I'm surprised.

5 A: I need .... help with finding our delivery schedule. Where can I find it on the system?

B: Didn't you receive .... information I emailed you yesterday?

🔘 **34.1 Listen and check your answers.**

◀ **A–C** **4** Complete this presentation using *a*, *an*, *the* or – (no article).

My name is Dr Francis Li and I'm **1** ....*a*.... consultant psychiatrist at **2** .... Brookfield Hospital in London. Today, I'm going to be talking about how **3** .... motivation affects our lives. I'm going to talk briefly about **4** .... subject, and then I'm going to show you **5** .... film of me playing in **6** .... chess tournament with **7** .... £10,000 prize, where I was one of **8** .... last four people in quite **9** .... large competition. I'll be using this experience to illustrate some of my ideas about motivation psychology.

I believe that **10** .... motivation is **11** .... most important factor in your success in **12** .... life, whether that means being happily married, or being **13** .... big success in your career. Psychology has ignored this feature of **14** .... personality and focused on other things that I believe are less important. It is often claimed that **15** .... intelligence is **16** .... main reason for being successful. I think that **17** .... motivation has much more of **18** .... effect than intelligence.

◀ **A–C** **5** Underline the correct words in italics in this business news story (– means no article).

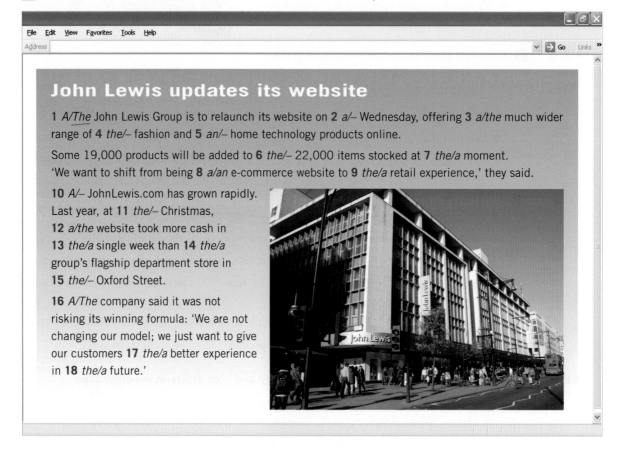

John Lewis updates its website

1 *A/The* John Lewis Group is to relaunch its website on **2** *a/–* Wednesday, offering **3** *a/the* much wider range of **4** *the/–* fashion and **5** *an/–* home technology products online.

Some 19,000 products will be added to **6** *the/–* 22,000 items stocked at **7** *the/a* moment. 'We want to shift from being **8** *a/an* e-commerce website to **9** *the/a* retail experience,' they said.

10 *A/–* JohnLewis.com has grown rapidly. Last year, at **11** *the/–* Christmas, **12** *a/the* website took more cash in **13** *the/a* single week than **14** *the/a* group's flagship department store in **15** *the/–* Oxford Street.

16 *A/The* company said it was not risking its winning formula: 'We are not changing our model; we just want to give our customers **17** *the/a* better experience in **18** *the/a* future.'

Make it personal

Write a short news story about your company or a company that has been in the news recently. As you write, check that you are using articles correctly.

34 **Write for business:** Not using *the*

When referring to sections within documents such as reports or formal letters, you sometimes do not use *the* to refer to specific parts of that document.

Don't use an article:

- when the page or section number is specified.

  Please turn to **page 28**. (**not** *the page 28*)

  Compare with:

  On **the next page** *there is a map of the conference centre.*

- when the section or part is labelled.

  In **Part C** *you will find details of the sales figures.* (**not** *the Part C*)

  Compare with:

  I thought **the part about** *recent changes in working practices was very helpful.*

- When the page is divided into sections.

  Paragraph 2 *refers to our cashflow problems.* (**not** *The paragraph 2*)

  Compare with:

  The second paragraph *needs to be amended.*

  Remember to use *the* with ordinals (e.g. *first, second*) or *next, last*.

---

6 Complete these sentences using *the* or – (no article).

1 I was very interested in what you wrote in ....*the*.... second paragraph.

2 For a fuller explanation see .... paragraph 8 below.

3 You forgot to insert .... page number on .... page 42.

4 A copy of the plans for the new building can be found in .... Appendix 2.

5 That issue is covered in .... section D of this report.

6 There was something about the takeover in .... business section of *The New York Times*.

7 Complete this conversation using *a, an, the*, or – (no article).

RAJ: So, we've nearly finished our new brochure. I just have a couple of queries. On **1** ....*the*.... first page …

LYNN: Sorry, do you mean **2** .... page 1, or **3** .... introduction page, which isn't numbered?

RAJ: Er… **4** .... introduction page. In **5** .... paragraph 3 – you know, **6** .... section about **7** .... design team – it needs amending to include Max Janssen. His work was really important on this project.

LYNN: OK, I'll change it. Anything else?

RAJ: Yes, can you turn to **8** .... fourth page? What do you see on **9** .... opposite page?

LYNN: Nothing … Oh, hang on. **10** .... page 4 again. I'll change that too.

RAJ: Thanks. I think that's it.

LYNN: Actually, I'd just like to mention something. Wouldn't it be **11** .... good idea to include **12** .... extra section of photos of team members, our factory and so on. They could go on **13** .... last page with **14** .... part about contact details

RAJ: Good idea. **15** .... page won't look so empty.

Make it personal

Does your language have articles or use articles in the same way as English? Look back at some of the examples on page 172. Would these sentences use articles in the same way in your language?

Quantifiers

Read this extract from a newspaper article.

Do the words in italics tell you what/who, how many/much, or where/when?

Pensions in crisis

A new survey reveals that *a lot of* companies have not set aside *enough* money to pay for pensions. Several schemes have now closed as *more and more* employers consider them too expensive.

A What are quantifiers?

Quantifiers go before nouns to tell you how much or how many (e.g. *a few, a little, a lot of, all, enough, lots of, many/ much, more, most, no, some/any, several*).

*I do **a lot of** travel – **several** trips a year.*

👁 People often use *a few* with time words (e.g. *hours, days*).

*I spent **a few months** working in Brazil last year.*

B Using quantifiers with countable and uncountable nouns

B1 You can use plural countable nouns with *a few*, (*not*) *many*, *several*.

*I have **a few questions** to ask you.*

B2 You can use uncountable nouns with *a little*, (*not*) *much*.

*We did **a little research** via the website.*

B3 You can use plural countable nouns and uncountable nouns with *a lot of, all, enough, lots of, most, some/any, no*.

A: *Do you have **enough work** at the moment?*
B: *Yes, I've got **lots of orders**.*

👁 In spoken English, people use *much* and *many* in negative statements and questions, especially with *how*. In affirmative statements they use *so, too, as* or *that* before *much* and many.

*I have **so/too much** work to do. (**not** I have much work)*

C some and any; no

C1 As a general rule, use *some* in affirmative statements and *any* in negative statements.

*We have made **some** improvements to our software.   Staff are **not** allowed **any** holiday pay in the first year.*

C2 In questions, use *any* to ask about quantities and use *some* for offers and requests.

*Do we have **any** urgent orders for this month?*
A: *Do you want **some** coffee? (offer)*
B: *Erm, can I have **some** tea, please? (request)*

C3 *No* means *not one/any*. Don't use *no* after a negative verb.

*We had **no** feedback/comments on the newsletter. (**not** We didn't have no feedback)*

D Using quantifiers with and without of

D1 You can use quantifier + noun (but *a lot of*, *plenty of*) to talk about things in general.

***All CEOs** have to take risks.*
*We're not making **any progress**.*

D2 You can use quantifier + *of* + determiner / possessive determiner / pronoun to talk about specific things.

***Most of those teams / my colleagues / us** work flexitime.*

⚠ You can use *all* without *of* except before pronouns.
***All my staff / of them** have annual appraisals. (**not** All them)*

⚠ For *no* use *none* + *of*.
***None of** them can speak English.*

👁 People use *none of* with a plural verb when they speak, but a singular verb in writing.

***None of** the workers **have** had eye tests. (spoken)*
***None of** the workers **has** had eye tests. (written)*

E Making comparisons

E1 You can compare plural countable nouns with *more, fewer*, (*not*) *as many … (as), the most, the fewest*.

*We took **fewer/more orders** this month. Which airline has **the fewest cancellations**?*

E2 You can compare uncountable nouns with *more, less*, (*not*) *as much … (as), the most, the least*.

*We did**n't** have **as much work** this month (**as** last month). It generates **the most revenue** of any product.*

👁 *Fewest* and *fewer* are rare in spoken English. People often say *less* before plural nouns, but do not write this.

Practice

◄ A, B **1** Replace the words in italics in this article with suitable quantifiers. Sometimes more than one answer is possible.

Stress and the Chief Financial Officer

There are **1** ~~one or two~~ familiar techniques to cope with stress, and stress is the biggest problem for **2** *the majority of* CFOs. Everyone knows the usual advice about eating well, getting **3** *an adequate amount of* sleep etc. but it's often ignored. **4** *Hundreds of* CFOs don't even take **5** *the total of* their holiday days or they check email and voice mail while they're away and don't get **6** *a large amount of* rest.

7 *A number of* CFOs give themselves **8** *additional* stress by eating in front of the computer. 'Bad idea,' says one expert, who suggests looking at a photograph of a favourite place **9** *about six or seven* times a day, even if it's just for **10** *two or three* minutes. 'It's important to take **11** *a small amount of* time for yourself in a 12-hour day,' she says, 'but **12** *a great number of* senior executives, especially CFOs don't do this.'

1 ...*a few*...
2 ....
3 ....
4 ....
5 ....
6 ....
7 ....
8 ....
9 ....
10 ....
11 ....
12 ....

◄ C **2** Complete this conversation using *some*, *any* or *no*.

SAM: OK, well I see that we've got **1** ....*some*..... time left, so do we have **2** .... other business? Or would you like to go and get **3** .... lunch?

CAROL: I have an item. David, can we have **4** .... feedback on the new catalogue?

DAVID: It's a bit early to say just yet. I haven't heard **5** .... negative comments at least. But, um, actually I've got **6** .... bad news. It looks as if one of our biggest customers, DDE, is going out of business. They're not paying **7** .... suppliers by the looks of things. They're generating profit but they've got **8** .... cash.

SAM: Do they owe us **9** .... money?

DAVID: Ten thousand. And, you know, there was **10** .... warning either. I mean we haven't had **11** .... problems with them in the past. But we're going to have to make **12** .... big changes to the budget forecast.

🔘 **35.1 Listen and check your answers.**

◄ A–C **3 a** Cross out the incorrect quantifier in each group.

1 A: Do you have ~~many~~ / *much* / *a lot of* foreign currency in your wallet?

B: I usually have *a few* / *some* / *a little* sterling and *any* / *a few* / *some* euros.

2 A: Do you do *any* / *many* / *much* travelling in your job?

B: I used to, but I don't make *a lot of* / *many* / *some* trips these days.

3 A: Have you had *any* / *much* / *several* training this year?

B: Well, yes. I've been on *a few* / *a little* / *several* courses since the summer.

4 A: Do you usually have *a few* / *enough* / *a lot of* time to have lunch?

B: Not really. I usually have *a lot of* / *much* / *some* work to do at lunchtime.

b 🔘 **35.2 Listen and answer the questions so that they are true for you.**

◀ D **4** Look at the information on two corporate websites. Complete these extracts using the quantifiers in the box with or without *of*. You will need to use some quantifiers more than once.

| a few | all | any | most | no | none | some |

a Employee profile
20% managers have MBAs.
100% employees are graduates.
2% researchers have PhDs.
70% staff are in job-related training.

Are you ready to join our highly skilled workforce?

1 ...Some of... our managers have MBAs.
2 .... our employees are graduates.
3 .... researchers have PhDs.
4 .... the staff are in job-related training.

b

Sweetie Syrups nutritional information

	Chocolate	Fruit	Nut	Golden
contains nuts?	✗	✗	✓	✗
E numbers?	✗	✗	✗	✗
milk?	✓	✗	✗	✗
gluten free?	✓	✓	✓	✓

About our syrups:

1 There are .... E numbers in .... our products.
2 .... them are nut-free - except Hazelnut!
3 Apart from Chocolate syrup, ... the syrups contains milk.
4 .... them are gluten free.

◀ E **5** Complete this report comparing three airlines using *more, fewer, less, (not) as many, (not) as much, the most, the fewest* and *the least*.

Jet Off had a mixed year. They had **1** ...more... passengers than close rival Sun Set and in fact had **2** .... passengers of the three airlines. However, there are danger signs for the company. Jet Off generated **3** .... revenue than Sun Set, and Flyaway made almost **4** .... profit as Jet Off with half the passenger numbers. Sun Set had a good year, making **5** .... profit of all three airlines and giving away **6** .... free seats. Although they didn't fly **7** .... passengers as their big rival Jet Off, Sun Set generated **8** .... revenue than Jet Off, probably because it gave away **9** .... free seats. Flyaway generated **10** .... revenue, and gave away **11** .... seats, but they have the best revenue-to-profit ratio of any of the airlines. Jet Off, the biggest carrier, made **12** .... profit in relation to revenue.

	Jet Off	Sun Set	Flyaway
Passengers	41.8 million	36.4 million	22.1 million
Free seats	800,000	700,000	850,000
Revenue	€1,756 million	€1,965 million	€1,109 million
Profit after tax	€319 million	€432 million	€318 million

Make it personal

Add quantifiers to these sentences to make them true for you.

1 .... my colleagues are looking for other jobs right now.

2 In my workplace .... us have degrees.

3 .... my work involves dealing with the general public.

4 My employers have given me .... training this year.

5 There are .... advantages of working for my current employers.

6 I send .... emails now than I used to and I make .... phone calls.

35 Write for business: Levels of formality

Some quantifiers are more common in formal or written English.

- *many* and *much*
  In formal, written English you can use *many* and also *much*, especially with *of*, in affirmative sentences. This is less common in spoken English.
  *In recent years **many companies** have been forced to cut costs.*
  ***Much of the meeting** involved discussing the investment plans.*

- *few* and *little*
  Few and *little* (not *a few / a little*) mean *not much/many* or *almost none*. This use without *a* is much more frequent in formal English.
  Compare:
  *There's **little** competition for this product.* (there's almost no competition)
  *There's **a little** competition for this product.* (there is some competiton)

- *no*
  In formal or written English you can use *no* as the subject of a sentence. This is less common in spoken English.
  ***No claim**(s) can be made on the policy for losses less than €100.* (from an insurance policy)

6 Make this text more formal by rewriting the words in italics using the quantifiers in the box. Use *of* where necessary.

| a few   a little   few   little   many   much |

Business interruption insurance

There are **1** *lots of* different types of business interruption insurance. This protects a business owner against loss of income, for example after a fire or other disaster, if there is **2** *a lot of* damage to the premises. It can also cover **3** *a lot of* the other things that can stop a business from operating, including external events such as a flu pandemic. Surprisingly, **4** *not a lot of* small businesses have this kind of insurance. **5** *A lot of* small business owners underestimate the time it will take to get the business running normally again, but it is critical to resume normal business with **6** *not a lot of* or no delay. It is worth spending **7** *some* time researching the best policy for your business. **8** *Some of* the bigger insurers now offer advice on interruption insurance to their business customers. It is also important to review all policies regularly as **9** *a lot of* the information about a business can change in a short time. There are **10** *lots of* times when the unexpected does happen. While having the right policy may be **11** *not a lot of* comfort, it will take away **12** *a lot of* the financial anxiety when the worst happens.

1	many
2	
3	
4	
5	
6	
7	
8	
9	
10	
11	
12	

7 Rewrite these sentences so that they sound more formal. Start with *No* + a singular noun.

1 Company executives don't like to think about disaster recovery.

   No company executive likes / to think about disaster recovery.

2 There isn't a perfect insurance company.

3 A company can't be without a disaster recovery plan.

4 A small company can't afford to ignore its insurer's advice.

Make it personal

Write about the use of the Internet in your workplace.

Are there many rules about it? Do all employees know them? Can you use social networking sites?

Possessives and reflexive pronouns

Read this extract from an article about self-confidence.

a Which words in italics are followed by a noun?

b Which words in italics are not followed by a noun?

90% of *your* success depends on *your* level of confidence.

Expanding *your* comfort zone can make you feel good about *yourself* and it gives you confidence. Success can be *yours* if you just say 'yes'.

A What are possessives?

A1 You use possessive adjectives, pronouns and *'s* to talk about something that belongs to someone or an organisation.

*Have you got **Alison's/her** report? I've lost **mine**.*

A2 You use *whose* + noun to ask about who owns something.

***Whose** laptop is this?*   ***Whose** keys are those?*

B Possessive determiners

B1 Possessive determiners (*my, your, his, her, its, our, their*) come before nouns (without other determiners e.g. *the, this*).

*This is **my** office. (**not** the my office)*

B2 You can use *own* after possessive adjectives for emphasis.

*Each product has **its own** bar code. (**not** an own)*

C Possessive pronouns

Possessive pronouns (*mine, yours, his, hers, ours, theirs*) are not followed by a noun.

*If you don't have an accountant, I can recommend **mine**.*

⚠ Don't use *its* as a possessive pronoun.

*I wanted a high-interest account so my bank recommended its **eSavings account**. (**not** … so my bank recommended its)*

D Possessive 's

D1 You can use *'s* to talk about something that belongs to a (named) person or organisation.

***Rita's** boss has just phoned.*

⚠ If the noun ends in an *s*, don't add a second *s* after the apostrophe (').

*When is the **shareholders'** meeting? (**not** shareholders's)*

D2 You can use *'s* and *'* with time expressions.

*Let's meet again in **a day's / two weeks' time**.*

D3 You can use *'s* after a name to talk about someone's house or a shop. You can also use it after jobs (e.g. *dentist's, doctor's, chemist's*) to talk about the place of work.

*Shall we meet at **Andy's** tonight?*
*Don't forget I will be in late tomorrow morning. I am going to the **dentist's**. (**not** dentist's surgery)*

⚠ Don't use an apostrophe (') with possessive pronouns.

*She's a customer of **ours**. (**not** our's)*

E Reflexive pronouns and *each other / one another*

E1 You use reflexive pronouns (*myself, yourself, himself, herself, itself, ourselves, yourselves, themselves*) when the subject and object of a verb are the same. They are common with some verbs (e.g. *behave, call, convince, enjoy, introduce*) and verbs with prepositions (e.g. *be sure of, believe in, feel good about, help yourself to, look after, pay for, think for*).

*Do **they** still **call themselves** 'Nubiz'?*

⚠ Don't use reflexive pronouns with *get changed, concentrate, feel, hurry, relax, sit down* or *wonder*.

*I **feel** happy. (**not** I feel myself happy)*

E2 You can use reflexive pronouns for emphasis.

*I haven't met him **myself**, but people say he's reliable.*

E3 You use *by* + reflexive pronoun to mean 'alone' or 'without help from another person'.

*Can you find your way back to the car park **by yourself**?*

E4 There is a difference between reflexive pronouns and *each other / one another*. Compare:

*The London and Paris offices talk to **each other / one another** every day. (London talks to Paris; Paris talks to London)*
*Matt often talks to **himself** when he's alone. (Matt talks to Matt)*

Each other / one another are common with contact, criticise, email, get to know, know, like, live near / next to, remind, see, sit near / next to, talk to, understand and work near / next to.

E5 You can use *'s* with *each other / one another*.

*Both operating systems run **each other's** programmes.*

Practice

◀ B, C **1** Underline the correct words in italics in these comments by Sir Terence Conran, a businessman, restaurateur and designer, about his business.

All companies have a core ethos. **1** *Our/Ours* is to use design to improve quality of life. Conran & Partners consists of an experienced team of creative and professional people, who understand design and how it creates value for **2** *our/ours* clients.

Architecture ↘

Over the past 20 years **3** *our/ours* buildings have made a big difference to **4** *their/theirs* surroundings. Have you heard of the Longman Headquarters, the greenest building of **5** *its/it's* time? Or Roppongi Hills, an 11-hectare urban quarter in the heart of Tokyo? Both of these projects are **6** *my/mine*. In terms of design, there is no doubt that each building improves **7** *its/it's* location.

Product and graphic design ↘

8 *My/Mine* approach is to create a successful relationship between clients and customers by developing products that have character, are simple to manufacture and easy to use.

If you employ several companies for the packaging, marketing and brand development of **9** *your/yours* products, you may have problems when there are differences between **10** *their/theirs* ideas and **11** *your/yours*. We offer a full range of services so that clients do not need to deal with many different service companies, all with **12** *their / their own* creative ideals.

◀ A–C **2 a** Answer these questions using the possessive form of the correct name in brackets.

1 Whose company is called Virgin? (*Richard Branson / Madonna*) ..... Richard Branson's .....

2 Whose web address is ba.com? (*British Aerospace / British Airways*) ....

3 Whose product is iPhone? (*Vodafone / Apple*) ....

4 Whose logo is this? (*Lexus / Honda*) ....

5 Whose shop is called Harrods? (*Mohamed al-Fayed / Philip Green*) ....

6 Whose soft drink was first sold in 1886 as a medicine? (*Pepsi / Coca Cola*) ....

7 Which country's railways are called SNCF? (*France / Poland*) ....

8 Where would you go if you had bad toothache? (*the doctor / the dentist*) ....

b Write answers for these two questions that are true for you.

1 Whose coffee do you prefer – Starbucks' or Subway's? ....

2 When will you have your next holiday? In .... time.

◀ D **3** Put an apostrophe (') in the correct position in eight of these sentences.

1 If anyone calls, can you tell them I'll be back after lunch. I'm going to the doctor's.

2 Whose laptop is this? Is it Susannas?

3 Are you looking forward to tomorrows report into the banking sector?

4 I'm just going to the newsagents. Can I get you anything?

5 What's that product called? I can never remember its name.

6 I'm planning to retire in about ten years time.

7 Their new logo is an exact copy of ours!

8 We're going to Mikes tonight. Do you want to come too?

9 What are the unions latest demands about working conditions?

10 Please visit the companys website at www.tarnproducts.com

◀ E **4** Complete these sentences using the words in the box. In one sentence, you do not need to write anything.

by myself	by yourself	each other's	himself	myself	one another	ourselves	themselves	yourself

1 I prefer travelling ....by myself.... on business.

2 It's hard to relax .... when you have a busy work life.

3 My colleagues and I like .... so much that we often go out together socially after work.

4 I'm quite shy and find it hard to introduce .... to new people.

5 In my company, the employees make a lot of the policy decisions ....

6 The two managers in my department always agree with .... proposals.

7 Do you prefer to work .... or in a team?

8 The CEO .... attends all of our meetings.

9 We feel good about .... and the work we do in our company.

10 Do you think it's quicker to delegate or do tasks ....?

◀ A–E **5** Complete this conversation between a financial advisor (FA) and a new client. Use a suitable possessive or reflexive form.

FA: Many investors prefer to make **1** ...their own... investment decisions, but if you would like some help with **2** ...., then we can certainly provide that.

CLIENT: That's great.

FA: I can assure you that my company **3** .... financial advisors are among the best in the UK. We also work well as a team, always keeping **4** .... informed of any financial opportunities that we find.

CLIENT: That's good. Well, I have made these decisions **5** .... in the past, but with last week **6** .... news about the problems in the stock market, I've lost confidence.

FA: Yes, many people have had the same reaction, but I'm sure we can help. First, we need to look at **7** .... attitude to risk. Do you like to take risks, or do you prefer to be safe with your money? All investors should ask **8** ...., 'Do my investments reflect **9** .... feelings about risk?' We all want to maximise **10** .... income from investments, but we also want to feel comfortable with how much risk we're taking, don't we?

🔘 **36.1** Listen and check your answers.

Make it personal

Rewrite these sentences so that they are true for you.

1 In my office we often answer each other's emails when someone is away.

2 I think business people should pay for themselves when they go out with clients.

3 If I could have any job in the world, I'd like my boss' job!

4 The most interesting job in my company is mine.

You can often use *of* instead of possessive *'s*. This tends to be more common in written business English. Sometimes you can use either structure with little or no change in meaning.

the name of your company = *your company's name*

the economic policy of Britain = *Britain's economic policy*

the decision of the committee = *the committee's decision*

⚠ Compare *a list of customers* (belonging to a company) with *a customer's list* (belonging to the customer).

You always use *of*:

* with long noun phrases.

  *Please could you send me **the names of the delegates who are coming tomorrow**. (**not** ~~the delegates who are coming tomorrow's names~~)*

* to talk about position.

  *Please sign and date **at the end of the document**. (**not** ~~the document's end~~)*
  *Offices **in the centre of London** are very expensive. (**not** ~~London's centre~~)*

* to link a member to its group, or a part to the whole.

  *There are 12 **members of the board**, all reporting directly to the CEO.*
  *Production starts in **the first month of next year**. (**not** ~~next year's first month~~)*
  *I disagree with **several parts of the proposal**. (**not** ~~the proposal's several parts~~)*

* with possessive pronouns to talk about relationships between people.

  *They're friends **of mine**. (they're my friends)*
  *She's a client **of theirs**.*

6 A marketing consultant is advising a food manufacturer about one of their products, bottled water. Underline the correct words in italics. Sometimes both are possible.

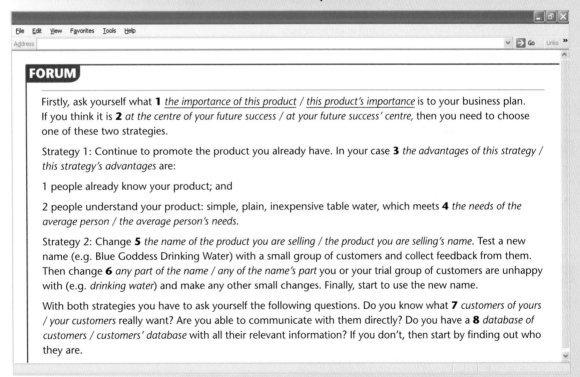

> **FORUM**
>
> Firstly, ask yourself what **1** *the importance of this product* / *this product's importance* is to your business plan. If you think it is **2** *at the centre of your future success* / *at your future success' centre,* then you need to choose one of these two strategies.
>
> Strategy 1: Continue to promote the product you already have. In your case **3** *the advantages of this strategy* / *this strategy's advantages* are:
>
> 1 people already know your product; and
>
> 2 people understand your product: simple, plain, inexpensive table water, which meets **4** *the needs of the average person* / *the average person's needs*.
>
> Strategy 2: Change **5** *the name of the product you are selling* / *the product you are selling's name*. Test a new name (e.g. Blue Goddess Drinking Water) with a small group of customers and collect feedback from them. Then change **6** *any part of the name* / *any of the name's part* you or your trial group of customers are unhappy with (e.g. *drinking water*) and make any other small changes. Finally, start to use the new name.
>
> With both strategies you have to ask yourself the following questions. Do you know what **7** *customers of yours* / *your customers* really want? Are you able to communicate with them directly? Do you have a **8** *database of customers* / *customers' database* with all their relevant information? If you don't, then start by finding out who they are.

Make it personal

Look at internet discussion forums and notice when they use possessives with *of*. Match them to the rules above.

Vague language 1

Read this conversation between two colleagues who are arranging to go to a conference.

What do you think the words in italics mean?

> What time do you want to leave for *this thing*?

> About ten. Do you want to get a coffee *or something* first?

> OK. I'll just get my *stuff* and I'll meet you by the back door.

A General words: *thing(s)* and *stuff*

You can use the words *thing(s)* or *stuff* to talk about objects, activities, states or ideas.

*The most important **thing** for people here is job satisfaction.* (issue, question, factor)
*The building has to be secure or somebody will be in there stealing **stuff**.* (equipment, tools)

⚠ *Stuff* is an informal word. Don't use it in formal writing or with people you don't know well.

B Adding ideas

B1 You can use these vague expressions to avoid giving a long list of things:
and stuff (*like that*), *and that sort of thing/stuff*, *and what have you*, *and things* (*like that*), *and that kind of thing/stuff*.

*We've invested a lot of money in equities **and things like that**.* (and other types of investments)
*Do you want to talk about the budgets **and stuff** now?*
*My office is full of old files and folders **and what have you**.*

B2 Here are more formal expressions for adding ideas: *and so on*, *and so forth*, *etcetera* (*etc.* is the written form). People often use more than one.

*Do you get benefits like health insurance **and so on** (**and so forth**)?*
*We need to look at our spending on postage and stationery **etcetera** (**etcetera**).*

C Completing a list of ideas

You can use these vague expressions to suggest a complete list of ideas:
and all that sort of thing/stuff, *and all sorts of things/stuff*, *and everything*, *and all the rest of it*.

*We need ways of measuring our market impact **and all that sort of stuff**.*
*Managers do all the thinking and planning **and everything** on major contracts.*

D Giving alternatives

D1 You can use these vague expressions to give alternatives:
or something (*like that*), *or anything* (*like that*).

Use *or something* in a positive statement or a question. Use *or anything* after a negative or in a question.

*She did a degree in food manufacturing **or something**.*
*The computer wasn't connected **or anything** so we couldn't use it.*

D2 You can use *or something* (*like that*) to make offers and suggestions more open, to include other possibilities.

*Do you want a cup of tea **or something**?* (tea, coffee or any drink)
*Let's go out for a curry **or something like that** after work.* (an informal meal)

Practice

◀ **A** **1** Replace the words in italics with *stuff*, *thing* or *things* without making any other changes. Sometimes more than one answer is possible.

Now that I'm more senior, I do mainly consultancy-type **1** *work* these days. And **2** *my activities* have been going well recently. I've got lots of interesting **3** *jobs* to do – it's good. The main **4** *point* I like about my job is the freedom and all the **5** *benefits* that come with a senior job.

1 ...*things / stuff*............   3 ....   5 ....

2 ....   4 ....

◀ **B** **2** Complete these conversations using suitable formal or informal expressions from B. Use a variety of expressions.

1 CHRIS: So the summary plan, the one with the objectives **1** ...*and so on*...., is almost done?

LINDSAY: Yes. I just want to add a bit more on market positioning **2** ....
Then I'll email it to everyone with all the forecast documents **3** ....

CHRIS: Good. So now we can concentrate on other issues like recruiting new staff **4** ....

2 JO: Hi there. So, can we have a chat about next year's conferences **5** ....?

SAM: Yeah. I've just got all the dates and costs **6** ....

JO: Then there's the budget for the website **7** .... to look at.

SAM: Yeah. We need somebody to keep it up-to-date, change the photographs **8** ....

🔘 **SS 9.1 Listen and compare your answers.**

◀ **C** **3** Complete this informal talk about recycled materials using expressions from C. Sometimes more than one answer is possible.

There's a new European directive – it's just come in actually – for packaging and packaging waste **1** ...*and all that sort of thing*.... Basically, it's all about creating a market for recycled products **2** ...., but it also affects marketing and the colours you can have **3** ...., and we'll have to think more about our use of paper, plastic **4** .... We've had a working party look at this **5** .... and they've come up with a plan which is long term and strategic **6** ....

◀ **D1** **4** Complete these comments from guests at a hotel reception using *or something* (*like that*) or *or anything* (*like that*). Sometimes both are possible.

1 Do you have any leaflets ...*or anything / or something*.... about the hotel? I can't see a price list .... here.

2 I heard there's a theme night .... at the restaurant – Dutch night ....

3 No, I don't want a newspaper, thanks. I don't read newspapers, or listen to news ....

4 Is there like a snack bar .... where I can just get a coffee?

◀ **D2** **5** Make these offers and suggestions more open.

1 Would you like a coffee?

...*Would you like a coffee or*...
...*something?*...

2 Do you fancy a snack?

....

3 Maybe we should get a sandwich?

....

4 Do you feel like seeing a film tonight?

....

5 Do you want to check your email?

....

6 Would you like to get some fresh air?

....

Test 9: Units 33–36

1 Underline the correct words in these sentences. Sometimes both are possible.

1 A customer wants *an information* / <u>*some information*</u> about our returns policy.

2 There's *a message* / *some message* for you. John thinks there was *a mistake* / *some mistake* with *a price* / *price* you quoted him.

3 We can't hire him because he lacks *an experience* / *any experience*.

4 I'd appreciate *a feedback* / *some feedback* on my presentation, please.

5 With *a bit of luck* / *luck*, we'll have finished the meeting by 4 o'clock.

6 I'm looking for *work* / *a work* in London. I'd like *a job* / *some job* in marketing.

7 Let me give you *a piece of advice* / *an advice*, don't be late again.

8 A: Would you like *a drink* / *drink*? A cup of tea perhaps?
B: No, thanks, I don't drink *tea* / *a tea*.

9 We've done *some research* / *research* into the market and we're very confident.

10 So, you say you placed *an order* / *some order* for *a machinery* / *some machinery* from us, but it arrived without *documentation* / *a documentation*. OK, I'll check and when I have *some news* / *a news*, I'll call you back.

2 Complete these sentences using the words in the boxes.

~~a few~~   a little   a lot of   not many   much

1 Do you want to be a better negotiator? Take ...*a few*.... minutes to read these tips.

2 Research shows that .... people know our firm. How can we improve this?

3 Your presentation was good, but I think you should speak .... slower.

4 Entering the US market means you have .... competition to face.

5 So, how .... did the whole project cost?

all   any   enough   no   several

6 They wrote to .... the shareholders calling for a meeting.

7 We'll probably launch the product nationwide if there's .... demand.

8 In the last month .... customers have cancelled orders. Why was this?

9 My previous company gave me .... support and I was forced to leave.

10 The new laptop has sold so well it hasn't needed .... expensive advertising.

a little   any   many   more than   most of

11 Overseas sales now account for .... 20% of our total revenue.

12 Apparently .... analysts feel that the economy is beginning to recover.

13 Our Berlin office handles direct sales for .... Europe.

14 The CFO has promised me that we have .... money available for investment.

15 Have we got .... printer paper left?

3 Complete this article about blogging using *a*, *an*, *the* or – (no article).

The business of blogging

Not long ago, blogs were seen as **1** ....a.... collection of cyberspace chat, read mainly by **2** .... young. Now advertisers are realising there is **3** .... market developing in **4** .... online community. Already, **5** .... online advertising growth is faster than any other sector of the media world. In addition, **6** .... fact that about 11% of Internet users today read blogs makes **7** .... blogging world look financially important for marketers.

8 .... estimated 48 million blogs now exist in **9** .... cyberspace and many bloggers are putting advertisements on their blogs, or getting corporate sponsorships and writing blogs for companies. **10** .... Marcom, for example, **11** .... communications-software maker in **12** .... USA, recently began paying several bloggers $10,000 per year to talk about its products. **13** .... best paid bloggers can earn more than $10,000 **14** .... month.

4 Complete these extracts from an article about doing business with friends using the words in brackets.

1 Adam Fairfax started ....his.... consultancy in partnership with .... sister Martha. It was .... marketing expertise that helped the company achieve .... early successes. (*her*, *his*, *his*, *its*)

2 Adam has been a client of .... for many years now. Over that period, he has also become one of .... closest friends. (*mine*, *my*)

3 I know many people say you shouldn't do business with .... friends, but we have managed to keep .... business and personal relationships separate. Most relationships – business or personal – have a few disagreements and .... has been no exception. (*our*, *ours*, *your*)

4 Adam and Martha are currently preparing a takeover bid for one of .... rival companies. I'm not sure it is a good idea, but the decision is .... , of course. (*their*, *theirs*)

5 Put an apostrophe (') in the correct position in five of these sentences.

1 What's your company͵s website address?

2 There were 4,000 people at the shareholders meeting.

3 Are you going to Charles leaving party tonight?

4 We're holding our annual conference in four weeks time.

5 Sorry I'm late, I had to go to the dentists.

6 You can have any colour car you want; the choice is yours.

6 Complete these sentences using the words in the box.

each other	herself	himself	itself	myself	one another	ourselves	themselves	~~yourself~~	yourselves

1 Sorry, I haven't got time to call the suppliers. You'll have to do it ....yourself..... .

2 Ann works part-time as an accountant and finds .... managing different roles as mother and a professional working woman.

3 We operate an internal market where different departments buy and sell services from ....

4 He worked so hard last month that he made .... ill.

5 The meeting starts in five minutes. Do you all want to get .... a coffee first?

6 The new packing machine is so efficient, it'll pay for .... in another month.

7 I'm really in favour of delegation. It encourages staff to think for ....

8 My worst business decision? I managed to convince .... that I should invest in property, just before the market collapsed.

9 As partners, we only pay .... a small salary. We put most of the profits back into the business.

10 Every three months we take the staff to a restaurant so that people from different departments can meet .... face-to-face for a change.

37

Relative clauses 1 (*who, whose, which, that*)

Read this extract from an article about Sir Richard Branson.

a Which words in italics refer to people?

b Which words in italics refer to things?

c Which word in italics refers to possession?

Sir Richard Branson, *whose* company Virgin started as a mail-order record retailer, opened his first record shop in Oxford Street in 1970. Mike Oldfield, *who* was the first Virgin artist, recorded 'Tubular Bells' in 1973, *which* became a huge hit. In 1967, at the age of 17, Branson also set up a charity that helped young people.

A Defining relative clauses

A1 Defining relative clauses make it clear exactly who or what you are talking about. They often begin with a relative pronoun (e.g. *who, which, that*).

A2 You can use *who/that* to refer to people.

*The security guard **who works on the main gate** used to be a policeman.* (who works on the main gate tells us which security guard)
*The person **that set off the fire alarm** apologised to everyone in an email.*

A3 You can use *which/that* to refer to things. *That* is much more common.

*The logo **which the CEO prefers** comes from Saatchi and Saatchi.*
*The company **that won this year's Queen's award** is a little-known manufacturer of solar heaters.*

⚠ Remember to use *who/which/that* not *he/she/it/they*.

*The job went to the candidate **who** had the most programming experience.* (**not** ~~the candidate who she had / the candidate she had~~)

B Subject and object relative clauses

B1 You can leave out *who, which* or *that* when they are the object of the defining relative clause.

*The operator (**who**) **we hired last week** has already resigned.*
*Where's the email (**that**) **I wrote yesterday**?*

B2 You must use *who, which* or *that* when they are the subject of the defining relative clause.

*Investors **who want a secure fixed rate** should choose our eSaver account.* (**not** ~~Investors want a secure fixed rate should~~)
*The person **that discovered the theft** informed the security guard immediately.* (**not** ~~The person discovered the theft informed~~)

C Non-defining relative clauses

C1 You can use non-defining relative clauses to give extra information about a person or thing.

*Mr Premji, **who was India's richest man in 2004,** drives an old Ford Escort.* (We know which person we are talking about: Mr Premji. The fact that he *was India's richest man in 2004* is extra information.)
*Racing Green, **which is headquartered in Regent Street,** has just opened a new shop in Bath.*
*The CEO's job, **which no-one has applied for,** is still being advertised.*

⚠ Use commas around this type of relative clause.

C2 You must always use *who/which* in non-defining relative clauses. You can use *who* or *which* to talk about companies.

⚠ Don't use *that* in non-defining relative clauses.

*Tesco, **who control over 30% of the UK grocery market,** are now entering the housing market.* (**not** ~~Tesco, that control over 30%~~)

D *Whose*

You use *whose* in defining and non-defining relative clauses to show possession (instead of *her/its/their* etc.).

*What was the name of the delivery company **whose website we looked at yesterday**?* (the delivery company's website)

*Mme Cathiard, **whose parents own the Chateau Smith Haut Lafitte wine estate**, started the world's first wine spa.* (Mme Cathiard's parents)

188

Practice

◀ A **1** Join these pairs of sentences using *who*, *which* or *that*.

1 The woman answered the phone. She told me you were out.

.....The woman who/that answered the phone told me you were out.....

2 The photocopier arrived two days ago. It has already broken down.

....

3 The customer telephoned this morning. She's waiting to see you.

....

4 A colleague has never taken a day off. He called in sick this morning.

....

5 The model was launched nine months ago. It isn't doing very well.

....

6 We need to discuss the candidates. They came for interview this morning.

....

7 Some customers received faulty goods. They may want a refund.

....

8 We've decided to close two of our power plants. They are old and becoming dangerous.

....

◀ B **2** Read this article about outsourcing. Put brackets ( ) round *that*, *who* or *which* when they are not necessary.

Finding the right person for the job

Are you, like many entrepreneurs, overworked but unable to find an employee to do work **1** (*that*) you feel you could do much better yourself? You don't need to be! In this article we reveal the secrets of how to find the perfect person for the job.

First you need to identify a task in your business **2** *that* you would like to hand over to someone else, so you can focus on more important parts of your business. Then place an advertisement to attract someone **3** *who* can do the task. You will get a number of responses, **4** *which* you will need to decide between. Choose the ones **5** *which* you think look the most interesting and invite those candidates for interview.

In the interviews you will probably ask the sorts of questions **6** *which* everyone asks, for example, 'Do you have experience or knowledge of this area?' Everyone **7** *who* wants the job you offer will say 'yes', of course, so then ask the question **8** *that* only good candidates will be able to answer well: 'Tell me a little more about that.' If the candidate doesn't have anything to say, finish the interview and keep interviewing, until you find someone **9** *who* you think is going to do the job well.

Once you've found the right person, you'll finally have time to answer all those emails **10** *that* are filling up your inbox.

◀ C **3** Complete this extract from DHL's website using *which* or *who*.

DHL, **1** ....*which*..... is 100% owned by Deutsche Post World Net, is the global market leader in international express, overland transport and air freight, and is also the world's number one in ocean freight and contract logistics. DHL offers a wide variety of customised solutions, **2** .... range from express document shipping to supply chain management.

Our shipments, **3** .... arrive rapidly, safely and on time all over the world, are sent via a combination of air, sea and ground transport. Our global customers, **4** .... demand the highest standards, frequently choose us because we have a strong local presence and unique understanding of local markets and customers. We also offer a wide range of standardised postage services, **5** .... include express and worldwide mail deliveries, as well as tailor-made industry solutions.

We continue to meet the growing demands of globalisation, **6** .... are creating more and more complex supply chains. DHL's international network, **7** .... links more than 220 countries and territories worldwide, is core to our business. As well as this, our 285,000 employees, **8** .... are dedicated to providing fast and reliable services, ensure that we exceed customers' expectations in 120,000 destinations in all continents.

◀ A–D **4** Complete these extracts from a newsletter giving investment advice using *who, whose, which* or *that*.

1 Caulfield Capital, ...*who*..... provide impartial information about finance, produce three newsletters a year.

2 This newsletter is for investors .... want to make their own investment decisions.

3 My client, ... business partner recommended Caulfield Capital, is happy with their advice.

4 25% of this pension fund is tax free. The rest is used to provide an income .... is taxable.

5 Does your company pension scheme guarantee an income .... you would lose if you changed pensions?

6 You can also call our pensions team, ... will be happy to answer your questions.

7 I have two monthly pension plans .... I started when I left college.

8 My father, ... advice I always listen to, suggested I start my pension.

◀ A–D **5** Match the beginnings (1–8) with the endings (a–h) of these sentences from a discussion about women in the workplace. Complete the sentences using a suitable relative pronoun.

1 Welcome to today's discussion,

2 There are many talented women

3 There are still too many managers

4 The first thing

5 I remember one manager

6 It is important to set specific targets

7 We need a system of rewards

8 We should congratulate employers

a .... attitudes have not changed.

b .... all employers can try to meet.

c .... said that women shouldn't have a job and a family.

d ......*which*..... is 'Women in the workplace'.

e .... are not being paid as much as men.

f .... record of employing women is good.

g .... are given to the best employers.

h .... needs to be done is to publicise the issue.

🔘 **37.1** Listen and check your answers.

Make it personal

Complete these sentences so that they are true for you.

My boss, whose ....

I've always worked with people who ....

I would hate to have a job that ....

37 Business talk: Commenting on what people say

You can use a relative clause with *which* to comment on something someone else has just said.

A: *We'll have to find a hotel for 50 people next month.*
B: **Which won't be easy.**

A: *If we don't advertise now, it means we'll be short of people.*
B: **Which is not a good thing.**

You can use also use a relative clause with *which* to comment on something that you have just said.

We've made budget for the year, **which is excellent.**

A: *I've just made my biggest sale this year …*
B: *Well done.*
A: **Which I'm very pleased about.**

6 Match the beginnings (1–6) with the endings (a–f) of these sentences.

1 He was rude to the CEO at the opening party,

2 House prices are going down at last,

3 Debenhams is being considered for a retail award,

4 Humphreys is monopolising the fast food industry,

5 J K Rowling has helped to get millions of children reading,

6 The return on my shares was minimal,

a which I think they deserve to win.

b which was very disappointing.

c which I don't think should be allowed.

d which is good news for first time buyers.

e which was a really stupid thing to do.

f which is great for the book trade.

7 Complete this discussion about two candidates for a job using the relative clauses (a–h).

a which seems reasonable

b which makes her seem to be the weaker candidate

c which makes me wonder why she wants to leave them

d which would make working overtime difficult for her

e which seems unlikely as she's only 38

f Which she needs to be in this job

g ~~which makes her the stronger candidate~~

h Which makes the decision easy for me

SUE: So let's talk about Lesley first. She certainly has all the right qualifications for the job, 1 ....g.... .

JON: True, but she also claims to have twenty years' experience, 2 ....

NICK: Yes, and she's already working for a very prestigious firm, 3 ....

SUE: Well, she says she wants to move back to this area to be nearer her elderly parents, 4 ....

JON: What about the other candidate – Jennifer? Her qualifications are not as good as Lesley's, 5 ....

SUE: But she seemed more outgoing and open to new ideas.

JON: 6 ....

NICK: Mm. Lesley did seem a little inflexible. For example, she said she had several regular fixed commitments in the evenings, 7 ....

JON: 8 .... , because we definitely need someone who can work overtime in busy periods. I vote for Jennifer.

NICK: So do I.

SUE: Fine, so Jennifer it is.

Make it personal

Try to include six *which* … relative clauses in conversations with colleagues or clients over the next week.

Relative clauses 2 (*whom, where, when, -ing, -ed*)

Read this text about business success from a consultant's website.

What do the relative pronouns in italics refer to?

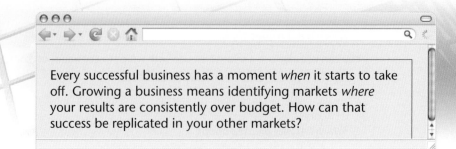

Every successful business has a moment *when* it starts to take off. Growing a business means identifying markets *where* your results are consistently over budget. How can that success be replicated in your other markets?

A *Whom*

A1 *Whom* is often used immediately after a preposition. The six prepositions most commonly used with *whom* are *of*, *to*, *for*, *with*, *from* and *by*.

*Saverfone allows consumers to chose the retailers **from whom** they wish to receive special offers.*
*We understand the needs of our customers, **for whom** flexibility is a top priority.*

In spoken and informal written English, it is much more common to use *who/that* (or no relative pronoun) and to put the preposition at the end of the relative clause.

*Let me introduce you to Clare, **who** I worked **with** at Nicholson's.* (with whom I worked)
*Are you the person (**who/that**) **I should speak to** about hiring the meeting room?*

◀ See Unit 37 (Relative clauses 1).

A2 You can sometimes use *whom* for people when they are the object of the relative clause. This is very rare in spoken English and is mostly used in very formal written contexts. It is more common to use *who/that* in informal contexts.

*Managers should keep in touch with potential clients **whom** they meet at conferences.* (who they met)

◀ See Unit 37 (Relative clauses 1)

B *Where*

B1 You can use *where* in relative clauses about places, including non-physical ones (e.g. financial markets).

*Our new chocolate drink will be launched in regions **where** our brand is already established.*
*Italy is the country **where** we face the biggest challenge.*

⚠ **Don't use *where* with prepositions (e.g. *in, for, at*).**

*The office (**which/that**) I work **in** is very cold.* (**not** ~~The office where I work in~~)
*The hotel (**which/that**) I stayed **at** was very near the Paris office.* (**not** ~~The hotel where I stayed at~~)

B2 You can also use *where* after words like *situation*, *point* and *stage*.

*They've reached **a situation where** they'll have to negotiate.*
*We're at **a stage where** things can still be changed.*
*We're at **a point where** we can take a break to think about the options.* (*when* is also possible with *point*)

C *When*

C1 You can use *when* in relative clauses about time.

*I look forward to a time **when** we are the market leaders.*
*It's not possible to upgrade so often these days **when** machinery costs millions of pounds to put in.*

C2 You can also often use *that* (or no relative pronoun) in relative clauses about time.

*Do you remember the time (**when/that**) I spilled coffee over a client?*

D Using participles in relative clauses (*-ing/-ed*)

When the verb in the relative clause is a continuous (*-ing*) or passive form (often *-ed*), you can leave out the relative pronoun when it is the subject of the clause and the verb *be*.

*Can I speak to the person **who is running** the conference?* →
*Can I speak to the person **running** the conference?*
*The items **which were reduced** are selling quickly.* →
*The items **reduced** in the sale are selling quickly.*
*Port is from grapes **which are grown** in the Douro valley.* →
*Port is from grapes **grown** in the Douro valley.*

Practice

◄ A **1** Underline the correct words in italics. In one sentence both are possible.

1 Dammann's, with *who/whom* we do most of our business, is based in France.

2 Thanks to Mike Bailey, *who/whom* we have worked with for years, we have created many original designs.

3 The personnel in the home deliveries department, about *who/whom* we have had the most complaints, need to be retrained.

4 We've got a fantastic IT manager called Brenda Lynch, *who/whom* we couldn't survive without.

5 Mr Baughen, *who/whom* the CEO has named as his successor, joins the company in August.

6 Our report shows that labour market reforms have encouraged firms to employ more young, part-time and unskilled workers, *who/whom* they could not afford to hire previously.

◄ B1 **2** Complete these questions using *where*, *which*, *that* or – (nothing). Sometimes more than one answer is possible.

1 Is there a tailor's near your office ....*where*.... I could get a suit made?

2 Do you work in a sector .... there's a lot of competition?

3 In your building, is there a place .... you can get a good view of the city?

4 Can you recommend a good hotel .... I could stay at in your city?

5 Do you know a good restaurant .... we could get Japanese food?

6 Do you have one particular desk .... you always work at, or do you 'hot desk'? [share different desks at different times]

7 Does your company have a restaurant .... employees can get meals or coffee?

8 Could you tell us about the regions .... your company has been most successful in?

◄ A–C **3** Two people are talking about their work experience. Complete these extracts using the relative clauses (a–h) and *whom*, *who*, *where*, *when* or – (nothing). Sometimes more than one relative pronoun is possible.

a .... I got on very well with

b .... I was living at the time

c for ....*whom*.... I was working

d .... I thought that I'd never get another job

> I used to be a successful high flyer, but the company **1** ....*c*.... went out of business and I was made redundant. Being unemployed for a long time really destroys your confidence and I was getting to the point **2** .... Eventually, a suitable job came up near to the place **3** .... I went to meet the technical manager, **4** .... , and she offered me the job immediately.

e .... you don't do any technical work any more

f .... I worked with

g .... I didn't really have enough to do

h .... I became a full-time manager of a small section of the factory

> When I first started, I loved my job on the factory floor and I became very good and fast at it. Unfortunately, this meant that I was disliked by the people **5** .... because they weren't as efficient as me. But on a more positive note, I was promoted several times, until there came a time **6** .... The funny thing is that when this happens you get to a point **7** .... and I found myself in a situation **8** ....!

🔘 **38.1 Listen and check your answers.**

◀ D **4** Complete this extract from a booklet about management using the present or past participle of the verbs in brackets.

As a manager, how open should you be with your staff? Many managers **1** ..*asked*.. (*ask*) this question replied that they always tried to be as open and honest as possible. But we need to think what 'as possible' really means. Look at the example situations **2** .... (*list*) below.

Would you always be totally open when …

- you have been asked by your company to keep something confidential, or when you don't want to pass on confidential information **3** .... (*tell*) to you by a colleague?

- being open will make your team unhappy? For example, you might not want to tell your team about every new cost-cutting idea **4** .... (*suggest*) by head office, as they may not actually happen. Would you want to give possible bad news to staff **5** .... (*try*) to get on with their work? How much information would you share with any team members **6** .... (*ask*) questions?

- being open could cause unnecessary pain? For example, should managers **7** .... (*dissatisfy*) with an employee's performance discuss all their weaknesses at the same time with that staff member?

- you are very busy? You will never have enough time to communicate with your team as much as you would like. People **8** .... (*want*) to discuss everything with you can use up a lot of your valuable time. So teach your staff to prioritise and limit what they expect from you.

◀ A–D **5** Read the following advice from a guide to setting up a new business. Decide if the sections in italics are correct or not. If they are correct, tick (✓) them. If they are wrong, correct them.

Setting up a new business

Experts **1** *asking for advice* about setting up new businesses always encourage clients to begin by researching their new market carefully. Here are seven questions you should ask yourself when you do your market research.

- Would you buy your product? Think about a time **2** *you went shopping for a similar product* and ask yourself if you'd pay the price you're asking and, if not, why not?

- Would customers buy it? Consider the people **3** *to who you are selling*. Don't just imagine what they like. Ask them!

- Who already does it? Check websites **4** *where companies already sell a similar product*. How can you be different?

- Does no competitors mean no market? If there is no one else **5** *already sold your product*, does this mean there is no market demand?

- Where is it done best? Visit places **6** *that your competitors have had the most success in*.

- Would you be my 'mystery shopper'? Ask friends to pretend to be customers and contact the competition. Their feedback, **7** *basing on their experience with these companies*, will help you to make your business different and more successful.

- Does this feel right to me? Be honest with yourself. Have you reached a point **8** *you are just trying to persuade yourself* that this is going to be a success?

1	.*asked*.	5	....
2	.✓.	6	....
3	....	7	....
4	....	8	....

Make it personal

In your business is there someone you'd like to work with? Have you ever been in a situation where negotiations broke down? Is there a manager whom you'll never forget? Have you ever refused a job offered to you? Have you ever interrupted a person giving a presentation?

38 **Write for business:** Writing about quantity

In writing, you can often use *whom* and *which* after phrases with *of* that talk about quantity: *two/£50/800 of, (a) few of, all of, any of, both of, half of, many of, most of, much of, neither of, none of, one of, some of, the (vast) majority of.*

*I've had two great bosses in my career, **both of whom** were women.*

*Next week I'm going to Russia with two colleagues, **one of whom** can speak Russian.*

*This year we made a profit of £400,000, **£30,000 of which** we gave to our usual charities.*

In spoken English it is more common to say *and all of them, and both of them,* etc.

*The committee has six members, **and all of them** are elected by the staff.* (all of whom are elected)

---

6 The CEO of a toy manufacturer is making a presentation about the company. Match the beginnings (1–8) with the endings (a–h) of these sentences.

1 We have an exceptionally young management team,

2 There are two senior managers,

3 We have two sites,

4 We have 200 employees,

5 We launched two new toys this year,

6 We produce very cheap products,

7 We have an excellent reputation,

8 We have a very large number of satisfied customers,

a both of which are selling extremely well.

b none of whom are over 50.

c many of whom return to us year after year.

d most of which are manufactured in Africa.

e neither of which is far from the centre of town.

f both of whom approach the job in different ways with different personal styles.

g 80 of whom are based in our Croydon office.

h much of which is due to the quality of our products and our after-sales service.

---

7 Look at the results of a recent survey of employees at Global Ltd. Complete the report using the quantity expressions in the box.

| 54% of whom a third of whom all of whom few of whom half of whom ~~most of whom~~ |

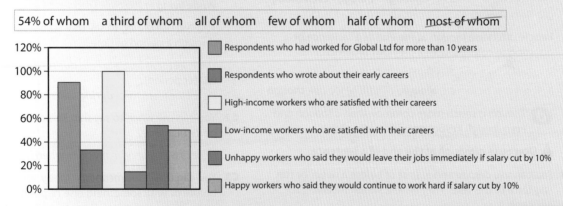

The survey was conducted with employees at Global Ltd, 1 ....*most of whom*.... had worked there for over ten years. The employees, 2 .... wrote about their early careers, were often very disappointed with how their later careers had developed.

The highest-income workers, 3 .... were satisfied with their careers, tended to be happier at work than those with lower incomes, 4 .... said that they were satisfied with how their careers had developed. So, do people in this first group enjoy higher pay because they're happier at work, or are they happier because they're better paid?

To find out, we asked employees if they would remain loyal to Global Ltd. if their salaries were cut by 10% during a difficult economic period. It seems that unhappy workers would not, 5 .... said that they would start looking for new work immediately. In contrast, satisfied workers, 6 .... said that they would work as hard as before, would not consider leaving their company in these circumstances.

Make it personal

Look back at Exercise 6. Write similar sentences that describe your place of work.

Conjunctions and linking words 1

Read this market analysis.

a Which word in italics adds information?

b Which words in italics show something unexpected?

c Which word in italics describes something happening at the same time as something else?

Market Analysis: Textiles

Despite supply problems, Europe's producers have had a boom year. *However,* margins remain under pressure. *Meanwhile,* US exporters report strong demand from Africa. The summer has *also* seen growth in the domestic market. *In spite of* good demand, prices remain stable.

A Contrasting ideas or information

A1 You can use *but* and *however* to say that something contrasts with or is different to what was said before. *However* often comes at the beginning of a sentence.

The product was designed in the UK, **but** *it is made in China. Productivity was terrible last year.* **However,** *things have changed recently.*

A2 You can use *although*, *though* and *even though* to say that something is surprising or unexpected compared to another thing. You can use them in different positions.

Although / Though / Even though the location of the office is good, it's too noisy.
The economy is still strong, although / though / even though growth is slowing.

People often use *though* at the end of a sentence or question to contrast with a previous sentence.

A: *We'll have to postpone the launch for a week.*
B: *Won't that be too late,* **though**? */ That'll be too late,* **though**.

⊙ *Though* is much more common than *although* and *even though* in spoken business English.

⚠ Don't use *although* at the end of a sentence.

A3 You can use *despite* and *in spite of* before a noun, or the *-ing* form of the verb. They have a similar meaning to *although*.

Despite / In spite of their cost, training courses are well attended. Molyco continues to dominate the market, **despite / in spite of** *making a loss last quarter.*

⚠ Don't say *despite of.*

Despite climbing 9% in early trading, the shares closed down $2. (**not** *Despite of climbing*)

⊙ *Despite* is much more common than *in spite of* in business contexts.

B Adding ideas or information

You can add information with *also*, *too* and *as well*. *Too* and *as well* come at the end of a sentence.

'Mastering Presentations' is now available online. It is **also** *out on CD-ROM.*
May sales are better than April and I think they're better than last year's **too / as well**.

⊙ *As well* and *too* are more common in speaking than writing. People use *also* very often in speaking, but even more in writing.

C Time expressions

C1 You can use *while* before a clause or the *-ing* form of a verb to link actions that happen at the same time.

I want to talk to you **while** *Jason is out of the room.*
While living *in Toulouse, I decided to set up my own business.*

You can use *during* to say that something happens in or through a period of time.

There are fewer flights to Paris **during** *the winter.* (through the winter period)
He left the room twice **during** *the meeting.*

C2 You can use *when* to say that something happens at a particular time.

Richard was waiting in my office **when** *I arrived.*

C3 You can use *in the meantime* to say something happens before or until something else happens.

It took me two years to find a new job. **In the meantime,** *I retrained as an IT engineer.*

C4 You can use *afterwards*, *then* and *before/after that* to say that one event follows another and *eventually* to say that something happens after a long period of time. *Afterwards* sometimes follows words like *soon*, *shortly* and *not long*, or time words (e.g. *days*, *months*, *years*).

He became CEO at 64, but **then** *retired* **shortly afterwards**.
His meeting is at 10.30, but (**before/after that**) *he's free* (**before/after that**).
The UK factory is very expensive to run. **Eventually,** *all our production will be moved abroad to cut costs.*

C5 You can use *before + -ing* and *after + -ing* to show the order of two actions in time.

Please clear your desks **before going** *on holiday.*
He worked full-time **after leaving** *college.*

Practice

◀ A ☒1 **Read this extract from a podcast about working more effectively and underline the correct words in italics. Sometimes both answers are possible.**

Improving productivity is a constant battle in business. Working longer hours is a depressing option, **1** *though / despite* many of us choose it. How can we get the same results quicker: how can we work smarter?

My advice may not be very original, **2** *but / even though* it could be useful for business people who have no time to think about their lives and working styles. First, multi-tasking. **3** *Although / But* many people say they are good at multi-tasking, trying to do lots of things at once is distracting. Try closing your office door, diverting calls to voice mail and doing some real work. **4** *Despite / However*, making you feel busy, multi-tasking often means switching from task to task rather than making real progress.

Email is a great invention. **5** *In spite of / However*, it is also a great distraction. **6** *Even though / Although* it may only take up an hour or two a day, it's a significant proportion of your working time. If you double the time you spend on activities which produce real results and stop doing the others, you will double your output, **7** *despite / but* only working for the same length of time.

Concentrate your time on the customers who really matter. You might think you are treating some of your customers badly, **8** *but / however*, don't forget that 80% of your profits come from 20% of your customers.

Delegation also improves results. When delegating a task, **9** *however, / although* it doesn't mean you can sit back and relax; get on with another task.

Working faster, identifying 80/20 tasks and delegating will all improve your efficiency. They all benefit from careful planning, **10** *although / though*. That's my final tip.

🔘 **39.1 Listen and check your answers.**

◀ B ☒2 **Complete this article from a financial website about IT spending using the words in the box. Sometimes more than one answer is possible.**

also	Although	as well	but	Despite	Even though	~~However~~	In spite of

The IT industry experienced record spending levels last year. **1** ....However...., a recent fall in IT share prices shows that the good times may be over and reports of a possible recession have started to appear in the media.

2 .... many companies say that they have not yet had any drop in sales, cuts in spending are likely. Bigger companies in all sectors say they are still very confident about the future. **3** .... this confidence, they are quietly already cutting IT costs. The number of small and medium companies with reduced IT budgets is **4** .... expected to grow.

If there is an economic downturn, it is unlikely to be a disaster, **5** .... there is one factor which could slow any recovery for developed economies: India. **6** .... its enormous cost advantage, Indian IT providers do not only compete on price. They match Europe and the US on expertise, **7** .... Many Indian IT firms are leading the way in terms of software development.

8 .... it will take them time to enter Western markets, it is clear that India is the place to invest in the IT future.

◀ A, B ☒3 **Rewrite these financial reports using the linking words in brackets. Make any other changes necessary.**

1 In the US, the Dow Jones index fell. The decline was less sharp than expected. (*but*)

  In the US, the Dow Jones index fell, but the decline was less sharp than expected.

2 The Tokyo Stock Exchange closed down 30 points and Germany's Dax index closed 0.7% down. (*as well*)

....

3 The UK's FTSE 100 index was up 3.2% and France's CAC rose. (*also*)

....

4 Apart from share prices, commodities such as oil and gold fell. (*too*)

....

5 Some analysts recommend a cut in interest rates. This could lead to inflation. (*however*)

....

6 The dollar remained steady. Some experts have predicted a drop in its value. (*although*)

....

7 'These problems might seem bad for investors. They are also an opportunity,' said a spokesperson. (*though*)

....

8 The poor performance of the stock market continued. US investors remain confident. (*despite*)

....

◀ C **4** Read about an executive's career history and future plans. Join these pairs of sentences from a career plan using the linking expressions in brackets. Make any other changes necessary.

1 I left university. I started working for ASOC Technologies. (*when*)

   When I left university, I started working for ASOC Technologies.

2 I had been with the company for five years. I became Head of UK Sales. (*after*)

....

3 I took a part-time MBA. I was working for the company full time. (*while*)

....

4 I passed my MBA. I was promoted to head of department. (*soon afterwards*)

....

5 I am planning a career break next year. I am teaching at the university. (*and in the meantime*)

....

6 My career break will be in Kenya. I will teach at a school there. (*during*)

....

7 I will come back to the UK. I hope to have some time to travel around Africa. (*before*)

....

8 I want to save a lot of money during my career. I would like to retire and live in the country. (*eventually*)

....

◀ A–C **5** Read this article about the biggest mistake an investment fund manager made and the lessons he learned. Find and correct six mistakes with linking words.

Patrick Everlast: New Horizon Select fund

Patrick says he learned his hardest lesson more than 30 years ago, ~~also~~ *but* he still remembers it well. He was a broker in the early 1970s when there was a mining boom. 'People really wanted to buy these shares. You could buy $400 of shares on a Monday, and sell them for $1,000 two days before that – a lot of money in those days,' he adds. Everlast too got involved with his own money. Despite the risks, he invested every cent he had.

Although, people soon discovered that their shares were almost worthless. The mining companies did not have as much gold as they had claimed. Everlast lost half his money. Almost 30 years later, eventually Everlast was working as a fund manager, he noticed something very similar to the mining boom. People were paying crazy prices for shares in technology companies, though many did not have a realistic business plan.

This time, although, he sold at the top of the market, avoiding the massive collapse.

Make it personal

What was your biggest mistake in business or at work? Write a short summary of what happened.

39 Write for business: Linking ideas in formal reports

In written business reports people often use formal linking expressions that are rare in spoken business English.

Informal (spoken)	Formal (written)
also / too / as well	*furthermore / moreover / in addition*
as well as	*in addition to*
but	*whereas*
but / however	*nevertheless*
then	*subsequently*
while	*meanwhile / while at the same time*

You can add information in formal business reports with *furthermore*, *moreover* and *in addition*. They usually come at the beginning of a sentence. You can use *in addition to* before a noun or *-ing*.

Business training materials are getting cheaper. **Furthermore / Moreover / In addition,** *their quality is improving.*

In addition to *the basic price, there is a 0.5% tax.* (**not** ~~Furthermore/Moreover the basic price~~)

You can use *whereas* to contrast two ideas with opposite meanings.

Imports grew sharply, **whereas** *exports rose much more slowly.*

You can use *nevertheless* at the beginning of a sentence to say something is unexpected.

Our new range of professional laptops is not cheap. **Nevertheless,** *sales have been excellent.*

You can use *subsequently* to show that something happened after something else.

Consumer confidence rose in the new year. **Subsequently,** *demand increased.*

You can use *meanwhile* at the beginning of a sentence. It means *while* (at the same time).

European markets remain quiet. **Meanwhile,** *in the US, business is good.*

---

6 **Underline the correct words in italics.**

1 *Furthermore / <u>In addition to</u>* its Tokyo headquarters, ADAL has offices in Korea and China.

2 Jon has a strong business background, *whereas / moreover* the other managers all have technical expertise.

3 Higher oil prices lead to inflation and rising interest rates and, *meanwhile, / subsequently*, upwards pressure on salaries.

4 The BN3000 Notebook is designed with the business user in mind. *Nevertheless, / Whereas*, it has more than enough performance and battery life to satisfy mobile gamers too.

5 Consumer spending rose 6% in the first quarter. *Meanwhile, / Subsequently*, inflation remained at 2.2% for the same period.

7 **Make this report about problems with a supplier more formal by replacing the words in italics with a suitable formal expression. Sometimes more than one answer is possible.**

Our problems with GT Engineering have been increasing for some time. Prices have risen, **1** *but* quality standards have seriously declined. **2** *Also,* they have been late with 24 deliveries in the past six months - more than during the whole of the previous year. **3** *Also,* we have received 17 letters of complaint from our own customers complaining about the quality of our products which use GT components. **4** *On top of* these problems, our secretary has found seven errors with invoices so far.

5 *While this continues*, our company image is being damaged by the problems described above. We have been working with GT for a long time. **6** *But,* something must be done now. I recommend meeting GT's sales manager to discuss the situation. If the situation does not improve after this meeting we will review the situation. **7** *After that,* we may have to look for a new supplier.

1 ....*whereas*.... 3 .... 5 .... 7 ....

2 .... 4 .... 6 ....

Conjunctions and linking words 2

Read this comment from a business traveller.

a It takes the speaker a long time to get to Frankfurt. What is the result of this?

b What is his purpose in staying two nights?

> It takes me half a day to get to Frankfurt, so I need to spend two nights there in order to justify the travel time.

A Giving reasons

A1 You can use *because*, *as* and *since* to explain the reason why things happen(ed). The reason may come first or second in the sentence.

***Because/As/Since** I didn't know the password, I couldn't log on to the server.*

*They cancelled the flight **because/as/since** the weather was so bad.*

⚠ **Don't start a new sentence with *because* to give a reason for something you wrote about in the sentence before.**

*Competition is healthy **because** it forces firms to improve their products.* (**not** ~~Competition is healthy. Because it forces firms to improve their products.~~)

A2 If you are guessing or want to find out why something happens, use *because*, not *as* or *since*.

*Are you working late **because** you enjoy it, or **because** you have to?* (**not** ~~Are you working late as/since you enjoy it …?~~)

👁 In spoken language, *because* is the most common and *since* is the least common.

B Talking about results

B1 You can use *so* to talk about the result of something. The result comes second in the sentence. *So* is often used after *and*.

*Kevin was on holiday, **so** we couldn't contact him.* (**not** ~~So we couldn't contact him, Kevin was on holiday.~~)
*I'm not happy with these costs (and) **so** I think we should look at them again.*

B2 *Therefore*, *as a result*, and *consequently* can link two sentences to show results. They most often come at the beginning of the second sentence. Less commonly, they can come at the end of the second sentence or between the subject and verb.

*The airline has a huge volume of passengers taking out car hire. **Therefore** / **As a result** / **Consequently** they get a good deal from the car hire firms.*

*The server crashed and was down for a whole day. We lost a lot of business **as a result**.*

*The latest web technology will make markets more efficient and will **therefore** boost competition.*

👁 All of these are more common in formal business contexts. *Therefore* is the most common, and *consequently* is the least common, in both speaking and writing.

C Stating purposes and goals

C1 You can talk about someone's purpose or goal by using a *to*-infinitive.

*We decided to share a taxi to the airport **to keep** the cost down.* (**not** ~~for keeping / for keep~~)

***To clear** the backlog of orders, we took on a part-time assistant.*

C2 We can also use *so that* instead of a *to*-infinitive. We must use *so that* if the subject is different in the two parts of a sentence.

*I'll just copy this list **so that** you can look at it before the meeting.*

👁 *So that* is more common in spoken language than in writing.

C3 You can also use *in order to* and *so as to*. These are more formal than the *to*-infinitive.

*The government split up the national rail system **in order to** / **so as to** create competition.*

👁 *In order to* is much more common than *so as to*.

You can give a negative purpose using *in order not to* or *so as not to*.

*We should despatch the consignment now **in order not to** / **so as not to** cause further delays.*

Practice

◄ A   **1** **Join these pairs of sentences using *because*, *as*, or *since* in the position shown by the box. Sometimes all three linking expressions are possible.**

1 I worked on my day off. I wanted to finish my report.

.... I worked on my day off as/because/since I wanted to finish my report. ....

2 The weather was so bad. I decided to take the train.

[........................] ....

3 I decided to invite Galina to lunch. I wanted to find out more about Russia.

[........................] ....

4 We changed our insurance. The premiums had become too expensive.

We .... [........................] ....

5 Why did he change his job? Was he unhappy at PGC?

Did .... [........................] .... ?

6 We are expanding so quickly. We need to look again at our distribution network.

[........................] ....

7 We decided to meet again the next day. It was getting late.

[........................] ....

8 Nobody had an address for him. We couldn't contact him.

We couldn't .... [........................] ....

9 Why did you turn down the job? Wasn't the salary good enough?

Did .... [........................] .... ?

10 I couldn't access my emails. My computer had crashed.

[........................] ....

◄ B   **2** **Complete this story using your own ideas. Then compare your ideas with the suggested answers in the key.**

1 There was snow at the airport. As a result, a lot of flights were cancelled. **2** ....
Therefore I had to go back to the city and find a hotel for the night. **3** .... , so I went
out and looked for a restaurant. **4** .... Consequently, I had to go back to the hotel
and try to get room service. **5** .... I had to go to bed hungry as a result.

6 .... , so I went back to the airport. **7** .... I therefore had
to ring Nikoleta in our Athens office and cancel my meeting with her. **8** .... , so
fortunately, she and I were able to meet after all.

◄ A, C   **3** **Find and correct five mistakes with linking expressions in this newspaper article about e-commerce. .**

Webstores do not have some of the advantages of traditional retail stores. Consequently, they often face financial problems. Firstly, any new web-based business has to work hard to establish brand recognition among so many competitors, as a result, new online stores need to spend large amounts of money for establishing their brand name. Traditional retail outlets who want to move into internet retail do not have to invest so heavily in promoting their brand. Because they already have a recognised brand name. Secondly, since sales and marketing costs are so high, costs per customer for new online stores are much higher than for traditional stores; it costs the average webstore well over €150 to get one customer. Therefore a number of webstores have been re-thinking their strategy, for reduce costs. They have done this as so to avoid having to close down.

1 ~~, as~~ . As

2 ....

3 ....

4 ....

5 ....

◀ C **4** **Match the sentences and join them using the linking expressions in the box. Sometimes more than one expression is possible.**

| in order to | in order not to | so as not to | ~~so as to~~ | so that | *to*-infinitive |

1 ~~The bank has decentralised.~~

2 The company has chosen a brand which suggests quality.

3 Gas Co. offers a range of different price options.

4 We always give returning customers good discounts.

5 Could you give us a reference number?

6 You should liaise with Mona.

a They want to ensure best value for consumers.

b You don't want to duplicate work.

c Then we can refer to it in our documentation.

d They want to appeal to high-income groups.

e ~~This gives local managers more freedom.~~

f We don't want to lose them to the competition.

1 *The bank has decentralised, so as to give local managers more freedom.*

2 ....

3 ....

4 ....

5 ....

6 ....

◀ A–C **5** **Put the extracts (a–i) in the text in the correct position (1–9).**

a Consequently, the airline can reduce in-flight services to a minimum and save money.

b so cabin attendants have to clean the aircraft and act as gate agents.

c Since they allow only internet and telephone booking,

d ~~in order to ensure profitability while keeping fares low.~~

e And because they only raise fares as the flight fills up,

f in order not to have to pay high landing and parking fees.

g As there are no reserved seats and a single class,

h so as to keep costs down by having no connecting services.

i They can therefore reduce training and maintenance costs.

BUDGET AIRLINES

Low-cost airlines all work to approximately the same business plan, **1** ...d....

• They tend to use smaller airports further away from big city centres, **2** ....

• They offer only point-to-point flights **3** ....

• They only use one type of aircraft. **4** ....

• Passengers pay extra for meals and other services. **5** ....

• Staff are made to do extra tasks, **6** ....

• **7** .... agents' fees and commissions are kept to a minimum.
  8 .... the airline can offer very attractive, low fares to those who book early.

• **9** .... passengers board early and quickly.

These measures have resulted in a very profitable, worldwide industry.

Make it personal

Write a few sentences about the business model of your own company.

40 Business talk: Reasons, results and consequences

Here are some more expressions for talking about reasons, results and consequences that are common in spoken business language. People often use them to explain or justify their position in a discussion.

- *seeing as/that / given that*

  You can use *seeing as/that* or *given that* when the reason for something is quite clear to everyone. *Seeing as/that* are more informal than *given that*.

  *Let's leave it till next week, **seeing that/as** we can't find a day to meet this week.*

  ***Given that** we've only got two weeks, we'd better order the materials we need today.*

- *or else / otherwise*

  You can introduce something bad that may happen if something else does not happen with *or else / otherwise*.

  *We need to cut our costs **or else / otherwise** we'll have to raise our prices.*

- *in that / which case*

  You can use *in that case / in which case* when you accept that something is true and state the consequences.

  A: *March is too late for the final test – we're launching in April!*

  B: ***In that case / In which case,** we should change the test to January.*

6 **A trainer, Clare, is talking to a trainee, John, about organising focus groups for market research. Complete their conversation using the expressions in the box. Sometimes more than one answer is possible.**

given that   In that case   In which case   or else   otherwise   ~~seeing as~~   seeing that

JOHN: Focus groups are not just groups of people who answer prepared questions, then?

CLARE: No. 1 ...~~Seeing as~~... you want the group just to talk freely about how they use a product, it's a good idea to ask them simple, general questions first and just let them talk, 2 .... you run the risk of focusing too much on your own ideas. But in the second stage it's important to test out your own ideas. 3 ...., you'll probably use a questionnaire. Now, 4 .... a lot of people find questionnaires difficult, and 5 .... you want to get the best out of people, it's important to allow them plenty of time to fill them in properly.

JOHN: 6 ...., we always have to have two main goals in planning a focus group, is that what you're saying?

CLARE: Yes. You want to collect both spontaneous comments and answers to the questions that you've prepared in advance, 7 .... you're only doing half the job you set out to do. That's very important.

🔊 **40.1 Listen and check your answers.**

Make it personal

Search online for articles or blogs of interest to you that contain these expressions. For example, search for 'webstores' and 'seeing that'. Read some of the results to see how they use these expressions.

Vague language 2

Look at these two statements.

What's the difference between them?

> It's only 20 kilometres, so if I give you a ring at half past three, we can leave at four.

Jeroen

> It's only about 20 or so kilometres, so if I give you a ring about half past three-ish, we can leave around four.

Howard

A Time

People use these vague expressions to talk about approximate times: *about, around, just before/after, -ish; a couple of, a few, … or two, … or so; ages, a while.*

*Let's meet **about** one / **around** one / at one-**ish**. It'll only take us **a couple of** minutes / a minute **or two**.*

People often use more than one vague expression in a sentence when they talk informally.

B Prices and measurements

People use these vague expressions to talk about approximate prices or measurements: *about, around, (a)round about, (somewhere) in the region of, approximately, roughly, … or so, … or thereabouts; (just) under / short of (less than), (just) over (more than).*

*A new laptop will cost **just over** / **under** / **short of** €800.*
*You can pay twenty pounds **or so** / **or thereabouts** for a new printer cartridge.*
*Bedford's **about** / **around** / **roughly** 60 miles from here.*

C Quantities

People use these vague expressions to talk about approximate quantities.

Countable nouns (smallest first): *a couple of, a few, a number of, a lot of / lots of, loads of*
Uncountable nouns (smallest first): *a little, a bit of, a lot of / lots of, a great deal of, loads of*

*We still have **a couple of** issues to discuss, but there's **loads of** time.*

People often exaggerate numbers and say *hundreds/thousands/millions of*.

*There were **millions of** people at the reception. You couldn't move.*

D Vague numbers in formal speaking and writing

People use these expressions in formal contexts: *approximately, in the region of, in excess of, up to, upwards of, over/under; some, a great deal of, a (large/small) number of, a considerable number/amount of, (a great) many.*

*Our forecast for next year's spending is **in the region of** €60,000. There are **a number of** reasons for this.*

E Descriptions

People often use these vague expressions to describe things or people: *kind of, sort of, more or less,* adjectives + *-ish,* colours + *-y* or *-ish*.

A: *What colour's your new car?*   B: *It's green**ish**. It's **sort of greeny** brown.*
*My report is **more or less** finished. (nearly)*

⚠ In very formal speaking or writing avoid using *ages, loads of, sort of, -ish*.

Practice

◄ A–C **1 a** ◉ **SS 10.1 Listen to a manager answering these questions. Complete his answers using vague expressions.**

A: How long does it take you to get to work in the morning?

B: It takes **1** ....*ages*.... . Well, **2** .... an hour.   *It takes about half an hour.*

A: How far is it?

B: 60 **3** .... kilometres. Yeah, 60 **4** ....

A: What time do you start work?

B: It depends, usually **5** .... 8:30 or **6** ....

A: And when do you leave usually?

B: I usually finish at **7** .... six.   ....

A: How much do you think you spend a month on commuting?

B: **8** .... €200.   ....

A: How many hours a week do you work, roughly?

B: **9** .... 45.   ....

A: How many people work in your company?

B: **10** .... 560.   ....

A: How often do you meet with your boss?

B: **11** .... times a day, but only for **12** .... minutes.   ....

A: How many emails do you get a day, would you say?

B: **13** .... 30.   ....

A: How much time do you spend answering them?

B: **14** .... ! **15** .... an hour **16** .... every day.   ....

b Write answers that are true for you in the column on the right using vague expressions.

c ◉ **SS 10.2 Practise the conversation with the recording. Use your answers from Exercise 1b.**

◄ D **2 Make this report from an online retailer more formal. Replace the informal expressions in italics with two more formal expressions in the box.**

> a great deal of time   A great many   ~~approximately~~   A large number of
> in excess of   in the region of   some time   upwards of

1 Although the final figure's not confirmed, sales for the last month are estimated to be *about* €500,000.
   a ...*approximately*... **b** ....

2 We plan to invest *a bit more than* €5 million in new warehousing facilities next year.
   a .... **b** ....

3 *Loads of* customers are now turning to the Internet as their primary shopping experience.
   a .... **b** ....

4 It has taken us *ages* to achieve a 24-hour turnaround time for 90% of our orders.
   a .... **b** ....

◄ E **3 Change each adjective in this description of a laptop to use a vague expression. Sometimes more than one answer is possible.**

newish

I bought my computer about nine months ago so it's **1** ~~new~~ – well, it's not that old yet. I like the colour. It's **2** *silver and grey*, you know, it's **3** *silver-grey*. The only thing I don't much like about it is its size, it's a **4** *large* bit of kit compared to other laptops on the market. Am I happy with it? Well, **5** *happy*. I suppose it's nice, well **6** *nice*.

Test 10: Units 37–40

1 Underline the correct words in italics. In two sentences both are possible.

1 We manufacture many products <u>*which*</u>/*who* are well known for their reliability.

2 The people *who / who they* work in our factories are very well trained.

3 Our main product, *that/which* is sold worldwide, has been in the top five best sellers for over ten years.

4 Our customers, *–/who* are very loyal, often recommend us to other buyers.

5 We sometimes offer discounts *which/who* encourage even more people to buy our products.

6 The suppliers *who/–* we always use are local.

7 Our biggest rivals, *that/whose* turnover is £12 million a year, are based in the South East.

8 The factory *which/that* makes the largest profit for us employs only 100 people.

2 Complete this report using the words in the box. You need to use some words more than once.

> held   <u>living</u>   showing   that   where   which   who   whom   whose   working

Serving the world's poorest consumers

There are billions of people **1** .....*living*..... in relative poverty in the world. The World Resources Institute, **2** .... with the International Finance Corporation, has released a study **3** .... estimates the size of this consumer market, **4** .... includes four billion people with incomes below US$3,000, is worth US$5 trillion.

We have now reached the point **5** .... we should enter this market.

Following a discussion we **6** .... with consultants and manufacturers, we have produced guidelines **7** .... how companies can develop successful products and services aimed at poorer consumers. For practical examples **8** .... show how companies have developed such products and services, see our website.

Respond to specific needs

Firms should try hard to consider local conditions and culture, rather than just repackaging a product or service **9** .... was developed for another market.

Use a wider range of business partners

An important role can be played by non-governmental organisations, many of **10** .... know a lot about the market **11** .... a product or service is designed for.

Find the right people to work on projects

Companies **12** .... recruit from the best business schools often employ people **13** .... know very little about the problems **14** .... poor people have. Companies recruiting new staff should hire people from the area or region of the project, **15** .... knowledge of their local communities would be very useful.

Think big

Projects targeting markets like these need to be large in size because, in many cases, the margins on individual products are very small. Often, these projects are run in areas in **16** .... a company's supply and distribution networks are already well developed.

3 **a** Add the words in brackets to these sentences, making any other changes necessary.

                                               but

   1 Quite a few people go into town for work ⋀ there is still quite a large majority that work out of town. (*but*)

   2 There are many big employers locally and quite a lot of smaller factories. (*as well*)

   3 Some companies get involved in the area and sponsor or support local charities. (*also*)

   4 Some talented local students find jobs easily. It's harder for older people to get a job. (*however*)

   5 They are often not even asked to interview by some companies having more experience. (*despite*)

b Use the words in brackets to join the sentences. Make any changes necessary to the punctuation.

   1 I called you last week. You told me my order would be ready last Friday (*when*)

      When I called you last week, you told me my order would be ready last Friday. ....

   2 Sorry, but we couldn't continue working. We were waiting for these parts. (*while*)

      ....

   3 We waited all day. They arrived at 6 pm. (*and eventually*)

      ....

   4 We installed them as quickly as possible. We realised we still needed another part. (*but afterwards*)

      ....

   5 We worked for eight hours on that order. Three more big orders came in. (*and in the meantime*)

      ....

4 Tick the correct sentence in each pair.

   1 **a** We are moving offices. Because we need larger premises.

      b We are moving offices because we need larger premises. ✓

   2 **a** Are you learning English as it is useful for your job or as you want to travel?

      b Are you learning English because it is useful for your job or because you want to travel?

   3 **a** I am not feeling very well and so I am going home early.

      b I am going home early and so I am not feeling very well.

   4 **a** Our sales to dealers are up about 11%. As a result we gained one point of market share.

      b As a result our sales to dealers are up about 11%, we gained one point of market share.

   5 **a** We are attending the conference to raise our profile.

      b We are attending the conference for raise our profile.

   6 **a** You can improve your financial health by selling assets in order pay off debts.

      b You can improve your financial health by selling assets in order to pay off debts.

Key

Contracted forms are given in the key unless it is a written or formal speech context.

Unit 1

Introductory exercise

a *Provides* and *helps* give you facts. **b** *Search* and *browse* tell you to do something.

1

2 Come to our first Fairtrade market on 16 July at Cutty Sark Gardens. **3** Listen to our guest speakers talking about Fairtrade and development issues. **4** Learn how you can improve the lives of farmers in developing countries. **5** Take part in lots of games and fun activities. **6** Win some great prizes in our raffle to raise funds for Afghan women. **7** Buy some wonderful presents for yourself and those you love. **8** Make a real difference to many of the world's poorest people.

2

2 Have **3** Don't forget **4** Try / Let's try (either option is possible here, as it could be an instruction to someone else – *Try* – or a suggestion – *Let's try*) **5** Don't call **6** Let's walk **7** Check **8** Don't worry **9** Let's get **10** Let's think

3

2 is **3** allows **4** Does Skype have **5** don't cost **6** includes **7** don't have **8** does Skype have **9** writes **10** talk

4 a

2 Who do you work for? **3** Is your office near your home? **4** How many offices does your company have? **5** Where do you work? **6** Do you like your job? **7** How often do you travel? **8** How many days' holiday do you get?

5

2 needs **3** think **4** try **5** helps **6** start **7** make **8** be **9** don't like **10** suggest **11** don't forget **12** Don't tell

6

3 comes **4** ✓ **5** ✓ **6** ✓ **7** it always has **8** is (the subject *Another global leader* is singular) **9** ✓ **10** are not **11** produce **12** ✓

Unit 2

Introductory exercise

a *we are currently looking for* describes a temporary activity
b *we are growing* describes a changing situation

1

2 's not working / isn't working **3** 's getting cold **4** 'm expecting **5** aren't going; aren't paying; 're having (it would be difficult to pronounce *Sales're not …* or *Customers're not*) **6** 'm sitting; 're repairing; 's leaking

2

1 Is it going **2** What projects are you working **3** Are you hoping **4** Are your colleagues learning **5** Is anyone in your department looking **6** How is your company doing **7** Is it achieving **8** What is your company investing **9** Is your boss making **10** Is he or she running

3

(Spoken items (questions 5, 7, 8 and 9) are likely to have contractions. Full forms are used for the written text.)
2 are finding **3** are going **4** are having to **5** 's costing **6** are paying (it would be difficult to pronounce *supermarkets're paying*) **7** is planning **8** 's getting **9** 's not doing / isn't doing **10** are concentrating **11** are running **12** are opening

4

2 When I'm having lunch with a friend, I don't talk about work. **3** I always switch off my mobile phone when I'm talking to a client. **4** When I'm negotiating a deal, I never make my best offer right at the beginning. **5** I don't chat to my colleagues when I'm writing a report or something like that. **6** When my team is working on an important project, we often come into the office at the weekend. (*When my team are working* is also possible)

5

(The form that the original speaker or writer used is given first.)

a **2** are not doing **3** is/are investing (you can use either a singular or plural verb after a fraction) **4** are not helping **5** are/'re being
b **1** 're still working **2** are/'re making **3** are/'re putting **4** isn't / is not going **5** are/'re looking **6** are/'re doing
c **1** are introducing **2** are demanding **3** are finding **4** is/'s taking

6 a

2 're always looking for **3** 're always complaining **4** 'm always reading **5** 're always sending **6** are always changing **7** are always breaking down **8** 'm always thinking about **9** 's always saying **10** is always borrowing

Unit 3

Introductory exercise

a *imagine* = imperative (◄ see Unit 1); *makes, exists, is* = present simple; *is growing* = present continuous
b The verbs in the present simple give general factual information. The verbs in the present continuous describe change.

1

2 Do you hold* **3** 're looking for (we usually use the continuous with *currently*) **4** talks* **5** doesn't make* **6** 's trying (we usually use the continuous with *at the moment*) **7** 's Mark doing **8** isn't taking **9** 's changing **10** Does he always come* (*these are all routines/habits, so are in the present simple)

2

2 is expanding (a trend/change) **3** rely **4** lets **5** are growing (a trend/change) **6** makes **7** produce

3

2 manage **3** does that mean (state verb) **4** try **5** 're holding **6** 're displaying **7** are you working on **8** need (state verb) **9** fit (state verb) **10** do you enjoy **11** don't like (state verb) **12** look forward to (habit)

4

3 Are you enjoying **4** I go **5** ✓ (*seem* is a state verb) **6** ✓
7 do you think **8** I have (*have* here means *possess* so is in the present simple) **9** ✓ **10** the waiter is coming

5

2 is expecting **3** is losing **4** sells **5** has **6** is **7** are giving **8** is falling **9** falls **10** is benefiting

6

2 They say (that) the expansion project isn't going well.
3 I believe (that) you're having difficulties with the prototype of your new fuel pump. **4** Revenue is down so I guess (that) the advertising campaign needs a rethink. **5** I see (that) you're replacing the CEO. Are you thinking of an internal or external candidate?

7

2 seems **3** 's not / isn't selling **4** reckons/thinks/says
5 're losing **6** need **7** are complaining **8** says **9** 's visiting
10 comes **11** are thinking **12** guess

Unit 4

Introductory exercise

a They describe the past.
b present perfect simple = *has/have* + past participle; present perfect continuous = *has/have been* + *-ing*

1

2 've never managed **3** 've run **4** has your company ever sent **5** 've been **6** 's asked **7** 've said **8** haven't planned
9 Have you ever done **10** has never asked

2

2 just **3** just **4** for **5** yet **6** first **7** since **8** still

3

2 haven't been charging; since **3** 's been visiting; for
4 Have you been working; for **5** 's been giving; for **6** hasn't been sleeping; for **7** 's been contacting; since **8** 've been discussing; since

4

2 a (*lose* is a short, single action and also a past action with a present result) **3** a (*crash* is a short, recent past action)
4 a (we are interested in the result – *doubled sales*)
5 b (*talking* is a long activity) **6** a (*arrive* is a short single action and here it is also recent past) **7** b (*waiting* is a long action)
8 a (*understand* is a state verb)

5

(This is a formal spoken presentation so both the contracted and the full forms are possible.)
2 've/have just completed **3** 's/has been supplying / 's/has supplied **4** have been working / have worked **5** 've/have already exchanged **6** have looked / have been looking
7 has ever taken (*have* is also possible, although *none of* is usually used with a singular verb in formal English)
8 has now moved **9** hasn't / has not been **10** 's/has been
11 has had **12** 've/have learned

6

2 has (have) announced **3** has (have) bought **4** have fallen
5 has (have) launched **6** has (have) cut (it is possible to use a singular or a plural verb with companies, or words which refer to groups of people e.g. *government*, *team*, but the singular verb is more common)

7

Suggested answers:
2 There has been a fall in the price of Microtel shares. / The price of Microtel shares has fallen. **3** Sales of DVDs have reached a new high. / The number of DVDs sold has reached a new high. **4** The US and China have met to discuss a new trade agreement. **5** The cost of insurance has risen following the recent bad weather. / Insurance premiums have gone up following the recent bad weather.

Speaking strategies 1

Introductory exercise

Ana says *Absolutely!* to show she agrees.
Tina says *though* and *actually* to show she disagrees.

1 a

2 personally **3** To be honest **4** Basically / Really **5** In fact / As a matter of fact, **6** to be honest **7** Fortunately **8** Obviously
9 To be honest **10** clearly; unfortunately; of course / obviously

b

2 in my opinion **3** I would say **4** in my opinion **5** as far as I'm concerned **6** I would have thought that **7** As a matter of fact / In fact **8** I feel **9** as far as I'm concerned **10** I'd say

c

You can use any of the expressions in sections B and C.
Suggested answers:
2 That's true. / On the other hand, some people find them useful.
3 Definitely. / I take your point, but everyone knows that.
4 I agree. / That's a valid point, but you need time between reviews, too.
5 Absolutely. / I think most managers do that already, actually.
6 Exactly. / That's very time consuming, though.
7 That's true, they do. / On the other hand, you can give feedback in other ways too.
8 Definitely. I agree with that. / Yes, but it doesn't need to be in a formal interview.
9 I agree with you. / I take your point, but I think it's the manager's job to make the staff feel relaxed.
10 That's right. / That's a fair point.

2 a

Suggested answers (use one of the expressions in brackets):

2 (On the other hand,) face to face contact is more personal (though). Do you know what I mean?

3 (However,) it helps to understand the culture (, though. / if you know what I mean?)

4 That's true. That's a (very) good/fair/valid point.

5 That's partly true but (actually) you can work on planes (though).

6 Well, it's (actually) hard work. (only say *I don't agree* if you are sure the other person won't be offended)

Test 1

1

2 look after **3** are **4** are **5** Keep **6** Don't write **7** don't tell **8** Make **9** is **10** doesn't allow **11** contact **12** call

2

2 Is your manager watching (happening at the time of speaking) **3** Do you always work (habit + *always*) **4** Are you studying (happening around the present time) **5** Do you understand (state verb) **6** does your manager talk (habit/routine) **7** Is your company making (change/trend) **8** Does your salary go up (fact) **9** aren't speaking; do you doodle (*aren't speaking* is a longer action after *when*) **10** Do you listen

3

2 have **3** 'm sharing (temporary situation) **4** 're redecorating (longer action with *while*) **5** Do you like (state verb) **6** hate (state verb) **7** are always talking (annoying habit with *always*) **8** smells (state verb) **9** 's always eating **10** does he eat **11** cycles (habit) **12** doesn't have **13** gets **14** don't want

4

3 ~~is liking~~ likes **4** ~~has~~ is having **5** ✓ **6** ~~'m agree~~ agree **7** ✓ **8** ~~think~~ are thinking **9** ~~isn't seeming~~ doesn't seem **10** ~~are appearing~~ appear

5

2 We haven't had a training manager for a long time. **3** We've been asking our line managers to get someone to do this for over a year. **4** She's made a lot of changes already. **5** For example, she's introduced regular training sessions already. **6** I've been to three sessions this month. **7** I've just come from a session about Excel spreadsheets. **8** I've never understood how to use them before. **9** I've learnt/learned a lot since the sessions started. **10** She hasn't given us a session on team building yet. **11** She's been promising to do that since she arrived. **12** Have you ever been to any of her sessions?

Unit 5

Introductory exercise

a Enron was a US corporation that went bankrupt in 2001.

b Yes, the concerns started before they reported the earnings in July.

1

2 didn't want; stayed **3** planned; introduced; grew **4** could; had to **5** didn't find **6** replied; was **7** Did you buy; began

2

2 weren't you answering **3** was having **4** was driving **5** was answering (*nobody* takes a positive verb) **6** was looking **7** were preparing **8** were using **9** were practising **10** wasn't feeling

3

2 The auditors arrived when he was having his lunch. **3** Share prices were increasing daily until the market crashed. **4** My taxi arrived as I was leaving the office. **5** I told her about her new role while we were travelling to the conference. **6** The Board announced the name of the new CEO while the staff were celebrating the opening of the new office. **7** He was thinking of retiring when they offered him promotion. (*thinking* = considering, not a state verb)

4

2 did you ever think **3** was enjoying / enjoyed **4** were you doing **5** applied **6** worked **7** wanted **8** left **9** wasn't **10** learnt / learned **11** were working (*worked* is also possible) **12** negotiated

5

Suggested answers:

2 When I was a child, I wanted to be an actress. **3** I started my first job in 1991. I really enjoyed it. **4** After school, I lived in my parents' house / university accommodation / Paris. **5** While I was studying, I met the man who later gave me my first job. **6** Yesterday, I wrote 20 emails before lunch. **7** When I was trying to decide where to work, my friends helped me a lot / didn't help me much. **8** When I was a teenager, I decided to study economics at university / decided that I wanted to be a lawyer.

6

Suggested answers:

2 I was wondering if you could tell me about places to stay in Kiev. **3** I was hoping (that) you would/could finish the report by lunchtime. **4** I wanted to talk to you about the standard of your work in your first three months. **5** I was thinking maybe you could / I thought you could talk me through the figures in the report.

7

2 were hoping **3** were wondering **4** could **5** did you want **6** were thinking **7** might **8** wanted **9** did you want **10** was wondering **11** could **12** were

Unit 6

Introductory exercise

a produced **b** have been spending; have made **c** has decided

1

2 haven't heard **3** exploded **4** 've been negotiating **5** 've been going **6** 's it been going **7** made **8** 've reached **9** only got back **10** Didn't you go **11** opened **12** was

2

3 a 4 b 5 b 6 a 7 a 8 b 9 b 10 a

3

2 last 3 for 4 earlier 5 ago; at 6 since 7 in; never 8 ever

4

2 What subject did you study at university or college?
(if you are still a student or have just finished your studies,
What subject were you studying? or *What subject have you
been studying?* are also possible)
3 How many jobs did you apply for when you left university
or college?
4 When did you start working for this company?
5 Has your company expanded / been expanding since
you joined them? (*expanded* focuses on the result; *been
expanding* focuses on the process)
6 Have you worked / been working on any interesting
projects this year?
7 Have you ever spoken at a conference? If so, what did you
talk about? (*What were you talking about?* is also possible)
8 Have you had a pay rise this year? If so, how much did
you get?
9 How much time have you spent abroad in your working life
so far?
10 Is this the first time you've studied another language?

5

2 owned / has owned (use the present perfect if you think
the situation is still unfinished) 3 have now reached 4 has
acquired (the text uses singular verbs with company names
so *have acquired* is unlikely) 5 signed 6 booked / have
booked 7 flew 8 have used / have been using (use the
continuous form if you think the action is the most important
thing) 9 recently introduced / have recently introduced

6

2 were considering; thought; didn't believe 3 have you
decided / did you decide; 've been spending / were spending
4 've been working; didn't get 5 was having; told 6 was
she complaining / has she been complaining (if you use
the present perfect continuous, it sounds like she is still
complaining now); didn't get

7

2 ~~We checked~~ We were checking 3 ~~I had~~ I've been having
4 ~~I told~~ I was telling 5 ~~I've tried~~ I've been trying 6 ~~you chaired~~
you were chairing

Unit 7

Introductory exercise

Sentence b makes it clear that Zetac accepted an offer from
Kronos *before* E-Linx made their offer.

1

2 'd expected/predicted 3 hadn't received 4 had decided
5 'd already spoken 6 'd suffered 7 Had you predicted/
expected 8 hadn't sold 9 'd only asked 10 had fallen

2

2 had already made; made 3 closed; 'd heard (*we'd heard* is a
reason or explanation) 4 'd already discussed; didn't want
5 had only started; arrived 6 was; 'd phoned 7 did you know;
Had you spoken 8 had risen (a reason or explanation); had to
(*had* cannot be abbreviated here) 9 hadn't left; was 10 said;
'd ever given

3

2 the banks' shares had been falling before the
announcement. 3 the directors had been negotiating the
terms of the agreement. 4 some people had said it would
create one of the biggest financial groups in Europe.
5 the financial sector had been unstable in recent weeks.
6 it had been predicted in a popular financial blog.

4

2 had you been working 3 'd been thinking 4 hadn't seen
5 'd been working / 'd worked 6 had been living 7 'd been
studying / 'd studied 8 hadn't found 9 'd been considering / 'd
considered 10 'd been doing 11 'd begun 12 had just started
13 'd already realised 14 had missed / been missing

5

1 had been rising; had been falling (had fallen); had already
  dropped; introduced; expected; reported
2 grew; took; had started; became; had become; had left / left
3 looked; had; had improved; had cut; had gone; was

6

2 If only they'd booked their flights earlier; they would have
  got a better deal.
3 Julio wishes he'd taken the job in Bucharest.
4 I had intended / had been intending to meet each new
  member of staff individually, but there wasn't time.
5 I wish I'd realised the figures were wrong. I could have
  corrected them sooner.
6 We had been planning / had planned to meet up at six
  o'clock, but the traffic was very bad and Henry didn't arrive
  till 7:30.
7 If only Rosa had been here when Vladimir arrived; she
  speaks Russian.
8 They had been hoping / had hoped that property prices
  would drop so that they could carry out their expansion
  plans.

7

1 ~~If only you let~~ If only you'd let; ~~I planned~~ I had planned / had
been planning (*had* is not abbreviated here as it is stressed);
~~I bought~~ I'd bought 2 ~~I expected~~ I had expected / had been
expecting (*had* is not abbreviated here as it is stressed); ~~you
were~~ you'd been

Unit 8

Introductory exercise

a State: I *was* in the music business
b Habits: I *used to go* to America regularly; I *would always
  come back* with lots of ideas

1

1 What things did you use to do in your first job? **2** Did you use to have a weekend job when you were younger? **3** Which companies did you use to want to work for? **4** How did you use to keep in touch before you had a mobile phone? **5** Did you use to work in London?

2

2 used to need **3** took over, got; was (these verbs refer to specific events, not habits) **4** didn't use to enjoy; decided; got (*decided* and *got* both refer to single events) **5** used to be **6** did you use to keep; used to make **7** used to **8** was (this refers to how long he was at the company, not a habit); left (a single event)

3

2 Didn't they use to work **3** didn't use to do / wouldn't do **4** used to go / would go **5** never used to get / would never get **6** always used to work / would always work **7** didn't use to have **8** used to have to / would have to **9** used to be **10** used to make **11** used to work **12** always used to make / would always make

4 a

2 used to / would earn; £14,000 **3** used to be; fewer **4** used to / would stay; longer **5** majority; didn't use to have

5

2 backed up / used to back up / would back up **3** didn't back up / didn't use to back up / wouldn't back up **4** didn't know / didn't use to know (not *would* because it describes a past state) **5** wasn't / didn't use to be **6** was / used to be **7** occasionally saved / occasionally used to save / would occasionally save **8** used to work (not ~~would work~~ because there is no clear time reference or context) **9** were / used to be **10** stored / used to store / would store **11** never did / never used to do / would never do **12** always wrote / always used to write / would always write

6

2 is used to (*80 years* sounds too long to be in the process of getting used to something.) **3** 'm slowly getting used to (the process is not yet complete) **4** wasn't used to **5** weren't used to **6** never got used to

7

2 a 'm used to writing; 'm getting used to speaking **3 d** get used to; used to put **4 e** wasn't used to getting up / didn't use to get up; used to get **5 b** 've got used to; 'll get used to seeing

Speaking strategies 2

Introductory exercise

OK. Right. So.

1

2 Can I ask you something? **3** Busy day? / Are you busy at the moment? **4** Could I talk to you for a minute? / Have you got a minute/moment? / Do you have a minute/moment? **5** I was wondering **6** How are things? / How's it going? / How are you? **7** Could I have a word with you?

2

2 Can you all hear me? / Can everyone hear me? **3** stay on the line / hold the line **4** Are you there **5** OK. So. Right. / OK. Let's make a start. / Let's get started. **6** Could you speak up a little **7** Anyway, getting back to my trip / as I was saying **8** Sorry, can I just **9** OK. So / Right. Well. Anyway. Now (or various combinations of these words) **10** I want to bring in

3 a

2 Speaker 6 **3** Speaker 4 **4** Speaker 1 **5** Speaker 2 **6** Speaker 5

b

Speaker 2 *What about you? What do you think?*
Speaker 3 *Getting back to*
Speaker 4 *Right then. So. Let's get started*
Speaker 5 *Well, thanks for your time, all of you.*
Speaker 6 *How's it going? Horrible weather, isn't it? Busy day?*

Test 2

1

2 started **3** 've been doing **4** missed; wasn't working; rang **5** Have you finished; 've been **6** were you going; seemed **7** were planning; decided **8** appointed **9** wanted; was wondering **10** was leaving; called **11** was sitting **12** Did you have; Have they signed

2

2 made **3** were having **4** were looking for **5** weren't having **6** decided **7** interviewed **8** promoted **9** were looking for **10** taught **11** needed **12** has generated **13** 's been **14** 's attracted / 's been attracting

3

2 went **3** included / had included **4** needed **5** 'd been overspending / 'd overspent **6** didn't use **7** decided **8** 'd been offering / 'd offered **9** realised **10** 'd made **11** received **12** didn't help **13** arrived **14** did I learn **15** saw **16** 'd lost **17** wasn't / hadn't been **18** 'd saved

4

2 used to need / needed **3** used to take **4** would involve / used to involve / involved **5** used to have / had **6** never used to need / never needed **7** are getting used to being **8** knew / used to know **9** is used to working **10** are used to using

5

2 last **3** ago **4** When **5** for **6** In **7** earlier **8** before **9** already **10** since

Unit 9

Introductory exercise

Are you going to be; I'm not leaving

1

2 Are you going to need to borrow money? **3** How much money are you going to need? **4** Who is going to buy your product or service? **5** How well is it going to sell? **6** Where are you going to sell it? **7** How much are you going to charge for it? **8** Why are customers going to buy your product and not a competitor's? **9** How are your competitors going to react? **10** Are they going to be able to copy your product easily?

2

2 's not / isn't going to be **3** 're not / aren't going to be able to **4** 're going to have to **5** 's not / isn't going to like **6** are going to explain **7** 'm not going to lie **8** 'm going to say

3

2 'm going **3** 'm giving **4** are you doing **5** Are you coming **6** are you doing **7** 's showing **8** are coming **9** 's taking **10** are you starting

4

2 's not / isn't going to rain (a prediction) **3** 're going to leave / 're leaving (both forms are possible here as this is a plan *and* an arrangement) **4** are they coming back / are they going to come back (a plan and an arrangement) **5** 's moving / going to move (a plan and an arrangement) **6** 'm going to research (a plan or intention) **7** 'm going to find out (a prediction) **8** 'm going to have to (state verb) **9** 're not going to be able to (a prediction) **10** are you going to give (an intention, not an arrangement) **11** 's not / isn't going to be (a prediction) **12** 're going to travel / 're travelling (a plan and an arrangement)

5 a

(These are predictions, so use *be going to* here.)
3 ~~going to might happen~~ going to happen / might happen
4 ~~Is unemployment rising~~ Is unemployment going to rise
5 ~~Is your company having~~ Is your company going to have
6 ✓ **7** ~~you're going to can change~~ you're going to change / you can (will be able to) change **8** ✓

b

Suggested answers:
1 No, I think inflation is going to fall next year. **2** Yes, I think house prices are going to go down. **3** I think interest rates are going to rise a little. They're not going to go down in the near future. **4** I think unemployment is going to go down. **5** I think we're going to have a good year. **6** They're going to invest in new communications technology. **7** I'm definitely not going to change jobs next year. **8** I hope I'm going to get a pay rise. I'm not going to be promoted because I was just promoted last month.

6

It's important to vary the phrases that you use, and not to use too many *what*-clauses as these should only introduce key points.
Suggested answers:
2 I'm/we're going to focus on / what I'm/we're going to focus on is **3** I'm/We're going to look at / talk about **4** I'm going to talk about / we're going to look at **5** I'm/we're going to look at / talk about **6** what I'm going to do **7** I'm going to ask **8** I'm going to ask

Unit 10

Introductory exercise

The present simple (*launches*), the present continuous (*is providing*) and *will* (*will talk*) are all used to talk about the future.

1

2 Shall (suggestion) **3** 'll **4** won't **5** 'll **6** 'll **7** shall **8** won't **9** Shall **10** shall **11** 'll **12** 'll

2

2 arrives / will arrive **3** will meet (this is a future fact, not a timetabled event) **4** begins / will begin **5** ends/end (you don't have to repeat *will*) **6** arrives (use present simple with *before*) **7** will take **8** will not eat (written context) **9** will eat **10** lasts / will last **11** will be / is **12** departs / will depart

3

2 will rise (the speaker thinks it is a fact; *going to rise* is also possible, as it could be a prediction based on evidence) **3** 're going to find / 'll find **4** will small businesses be able to **5** 'll be (*'s going to be* is also possible, but this is personal opinion so *will* is more natural) **6** probably won't / probably aren't going to put up **7** 'm seeing / 'm going to see (a future arrangement) **8** 'll let **9** is probably putting up / is probably going to put up / will probably put up (a future plan or a prediction) **10** 'll have (a personal opinion) **11** 's going to grow **12** Will you survive (a personal opinion)

4

2 will sit / are going to sit **3** are rewiring (a scheduled arrangement) **4** 'll take (use *will* with *think*) **5** 'll need (state verb) **6** 'll have to (state verb) **7** 'm meeting (a scheduled arrangement) **8** will ask (prediction) **9** meet (use present simple with *when* to refer to the future) **10** won't forget (the speaker believes that this promise is a future fact) **11** leaves (schedule) **12** 'll miss (use *will* with *expect*)

5

2 What will you do first when you arrive at work tomorrow? **h** I'll check my emails. **3** How old will your company be this year? **e** It'll be 42 years old. **4** What do you expect will happen to your salary next year? **g** I don't expect I'll get a pay rise, unfortunately. **5** Are you chairing any meetings this week? **b** No, but I'm making a presentation to the Board on Tuesday. (don't use *will* to talk about an existing plan) **6** Do you think it'll be a good year for your business? **a** No, our sales so far are poor so we probably won't hit our targets. **7** What do you think will happen to unemployment in your country this year? **f** I think it'll continue to rise. **8** Will you have more free time next year? **d** No, I expect I'll spend more time at work than last year.

6

2 will cover / will deal with / will look at **3** 'll take **4** 'll cover / 'll deal with / 'll look at **5** 'll show **6** 'll look at / outline **7** 'll cover / 'll deal with / 'll look at **8** 'll sum up **9** 'll make **10** 'll answer
You could also use *going to* in answers 1–9. Use *will* for **10** because it means 'I'll be happy to answer any questions *if there are any*'.

7

2 I'll come on to that point later / in the next section / in a second. Is that all right?
3 I'll go back to that point at the end. Is that OK?
4 I'll be pleased to answer your questions now.

Unit 11

Introductory exercise

a will be looking; will be asking
b will have found

1

2 will you be staying **3** 'll be staying **4** 'll be doing **5** will be taking **6** 'll be trying **7** won't be joining **8** 'll be thinking

2

2 won't have made **3** 'll have chosen **4** 'll have had **5** 'll have announced **6** 'll have started **7** 'll have joined **8** will we have achieved

3

3 ✓ **4** ✓ **5** 'll also be taking on (*during the next four months*)
6 'll be publishing (future plan) **7** ✓ **8** ✓

4

2 by then **3** tomorrow **4** all night **5** in a few minutes **6** by the end of the month **7** by lunchtime **8** for the whole week

5

Suggested answers
2 By 30 January, I'll have set up a team of employees to lead our green programme. **3** From January to March, they'll be investigating sourcing raw materials more locally. **4** Between February and June, they'll be looking for greener suppliers who provide sustainable products. **5** From now on, I/I'll be encouraging people to print less. **6** By April, we'll have created 20 reserved parking places for car poolers. **7** By this time next year, we'll have reduced business travel by 40–50%. **8** By 2016, we'll have transferred 30% of our energy to wind power.

6

2 b How will you be paying? **3 i** How long will you be staying?
4 c Will you be needing anything for your presentation?
5 g Will you be needing a wake-up call? **6 a** Will you be wanting to use the sports facilities? **7 e** When will you be arriving? **8 d** Will you be wanting room service? **9 f** How will you be travelling? **10 h** What will you be doing while you are in London?

Unit 12

Introductory exercise

is expected to; is set to; is likely to

1

2 is likely to begin **3** Is next week likely to be **4** 'm unlikely / not likely to be **5** 're likely to make **6** Is anyone likely to need **7** 'm unlikely / not likely to finish **8** are likely to enter **9** are unlikely / are not likely / aren't likely to change **10** are likely to become

2

2 It is/seems unlikely that digital camera sales will decline before 2020. **3** It is/seems likely that China will be the world's biggest Internet user in 2015. **4** It is/seems unlikely that the USA will be the world's biggest Internet user in 2015. **5** It is/seems likely that the population of the EU will rise to 470m in/by 2025. **6** It is/seems unlikely that the population of the EU will continue to rise after 2025. **7** It is/seems likely that more than 25% of households will own two cars in 2020. **8** It is/seems unlikely that car ownership will decline sharply over the next 20 years.
Other possible sentences:
It is/seems likely that sales of digital cameras will slow down a little after 2015.
It is/seems likely that Internet use in Japan will continue to grow/increase.
It is/seems likely that the population of the EU will be more than 465 million in 2015.
It is/seems likely that ownership of two cars in the UK will increase by around 2% between 2010 and 2025.

3

Suggested answers:
2 In the future, people are quite likely to have to work till they are 70 or 75. **3** It seems very/ likely that organic food production will increase worldwide. **4** It's most likely that it will rain in London in the next five days. **5** The English language seems extremely unlikely to die out in the next 20 years. **6** It's very likely that internet shopping will continue to expand rapidly.

4

2 is expected to (there is no reason to think it will not continue) **3** is about to (it is going to happen very soon – this Friday) **4** is to (this is often used for announcements about official decisions) **5** is set to (it is already planned and decided) **6** is expected to (this is what the analyst thinks; it is not 100% certain)

5

1 ~~about sending~~ about to send; ~~I going to ask~~ I was going to ask **2** ~~is due arriving~~ is due to arrive; ~~we were supposing to meet~~ we were supposed to meet; ~~is expect to finish~~ is expected to finish

6

2 in the short term **3** in the immediate future **4** in the foreseeable future **5** going forward **6** looking ahead **7** In the long/longer term

Speaking strategies 3

Introductory exercise

a really, do
b sort of, a bit

1

2 It's completely different from what I expected. **3** I do like it a lot. **4** It'll make such a difference, going into work.
5 It's absolutely wonderful. It's just fabulous. **6** I won't miss the old offices at all. **7** The furniture looks extremely

expensive. **8** I'm really looking forward to working here.
9 They've planned the space really well. / They've really
planned … **10** I must say thank you very much to the design
team.

2

2 don't really **3** Not really. **4** just **5** not really **6** I think
7 a bit **8** sort of **9** kind of **10** Perhaps that's **11** probably
12 very clear **13** slightly **14** a little bit **15** maybe

3

2 Maybe/Perhaps/Probably **3** just so / so / very / really /
extremely **4** totally/completely/absolutely/really **5** sort of /
kind of / a little bit / slightly **6** just so / very / really / extremely
7 at all / very much **8** such **9** really/just **10** really

Test 3

1

2 will **3** won't **4** will **5** will **6** will **7** will **8** won't

2

2 is going to rise (prediction based on evidence) **3** 'll help
(decision at time of speaking) **4** 'm meeting (arrangement)
5 arrives (with *as soon as*) **6** I don't think the meeting will
finish **7** I don't expect the CEO will freeze **8** Shall we start
(suggestion) **9** Is the company going to make **10** will be
(with state verb)

3

2 'll have given **3** won't be working **4** 'll be advertising
5 won't have sent **6** Will you have finished **7** Will you be
staying **8** 'll have delivered

4

2 are expected to **3** is set to **4** were supposed to **5** are due
to **6** Looking ahead (notice that this phrase usually comes at
the start of a sentence) **7** is likely that **8** is extremely unlikely
that **9** in the foreseeable future (notice that this phrase
usually comes at the end of a sentence)

5

2 was supposed to start **3** starts **4** are marking **5** Looking
ahead **6** is not due to finish **7** happens **8** will be organising
9 seems likely that **10** won't be **11** will be **12** will have
recruited and trained **13** is **14** are going to invite **15** is
expected to host **16** will be

6

2 How many people do you think will attend (use *will* after
think) **3** what time does the conference start (timetabled
future) **4** Shall I come along (an offer or suggestion) **5** What
time are we supposed to leave **6** Will the presentations have
finished (future perfect with *by*) **7** Will they be signing (an
action in progress at a specific time in the future – *during the
breaks*) **8** Are you likely to need

Unit 13

Introductory exercise

b something is possible and it does actually happen

1

2 can create (*creates* is also possible) **3** is **4** are / can be
5 like **6** can lead **7** can have (*has* is also possible) **8** have
9 can result (*results* is also possible) **10** is (this always happens
so *can* is not possible)

2

2 Can you add dates to cells in a spreadsheet? Because I
certainly can't (do it)! **3** Iris was able to persuade Philip to
speak at the sales conference. (**not** ~~could~~ as it is a specific
occasion) **4** I couldn't / wasn't able to get hold of Flavio
yesterday; it was a public holiday in Brazil. **5** Could they /
Were they able to hear what we were saying? It was a terrible
line! **6** Small, local stores were unable to / could not compete
with the new superstore and were forced to close. (the
situation seems more formal, so *be unable* or *could not* are
more suitable than *couldn't*) **7** The weather can be very hot
and humid in New York in August. **8** The assistant I had at
Mantech could speak four languages.

3

2 e **3** g **4** h **5** d **6** i **7** c **8** b **9** a

4

2 Will you be able to speak at the sales conference? (*Could
you / Can you* are also possible, but they are more likely to be
heard as a request rather than a question about whether it
is possible) **3** Could you give me a price for a business-class
flight to Bangkok (please)? (*Can* is also possible) **4** May I
have a room with a sea view (please)? (*Can* and *Could* are also
possible) **5** Yes, of course (you can). (**not** ~~Yes, you could~~)
6 Are you able / Would you be able to attend our group
meeting today? **7** Can you come to our showroom
personally? (*Are you able to* and *Could you* are also possible)
8 I'm sorry, (but) I'm / we're / the company is not able to offer
credit. (you can also say *unable to*)

5

2 Mr Rundaf is a very busy person but I am delighted to say
that we were able to find an evening when he was free.
3 We will be able to spend two hours with him to discuss
international business trends. **4** We have been able to book
the Chesham Room, which is a wonderful venue for such an
important meeting. **5** We hope to start at 7:30, so could you
all make / could I ask you all to make a special effort to be
punctual? **6** I cannot say at the moment how many questions
Mr Rundaf will take, but do prepare any questions you would
like answers to.

6

2 allow you to design **3** is known to increase **4** lets you
upload **5** permits you to complete **6** makes it possible (for
you) to find

7

2 enables us to access **3** ~~knows to~~ is known to **4** makes it
possible to **5** allows us ~~tracking~~ to track **6** ~~permission~~ permit

Unit 14

Introductory exercise

a There are three suggestions or pieces of advice: *You should talk to our trained advisors; You might want to drop in for a chat; You could give us a call or email us.*

b *should* + infinitive without *to*; *might want* + *to*-infinitive; *could* + infinitive without *to*

1

2 You should / ought to do some research into the job and the company. **3** You could / might want to take extra copies of your CV. **4** You could / might want to avoid discussing salaries before you get an offer. **5** You shouldn't / ought not to forget to ask questions. **6** You shouldn't / ought not to be negative about yourself.
Suggested answers for **7** and **8** You should wear smart clothes / be friendly and polite / be positive about yourself.
You could / might want to read the company's annual report beforehand.

2

2 A Shall I phone them? B should **3** A What should I do B might **4** A Should I wear a suit and tie B could; could **5** A Should I practise answering questions? B shouldn't

3

3 ✓ **4** ✓ **5** ~~might as well~~ should/ought to (it's essential) **6** ~~could~~ should/ought to (it's essential) **7** ✓ **8** ✓ **9** ~~couldn't~~ shouldn't **10** ~~might like to~~ should/ought to (very important advice)

4

You can use *should* or *ought to* for all these answers. Other possibilities are also shown.
2 should / ought to buy **3** should / ought to use **4** could install (not essential, one idea of several) **5** should / ought to carry / might consider carrying (use *might consider* when you think it is a good idea, but not essential) **6** could / might like to / might want to lock (a good idea rather than essential) **7** shouldn't make (use *shouldn't* to show it is essential not to do something) **8** should try (this is very important – do it if you can)

5

2 You should go (this is a strong recommendation) **3** Shall we do (*We might as well do* doesn't sound like a very friendly way to speak to a colleague) **4** should talk / might want to talk **5** You ought to talk / Could you talk (both are possible but *Couldn't you talk* is more indirect) **6** Could we arrange (*we should arrange* is probably too direct)

6

Suggested answers:
2 give (people) more responsibility **3** I'd turn it off and on again **4** using the Internet **5** to try Wednesday **6** the new restaurant on Pail Street

7

2 Why not start / How/What about starting / Why don't we start **3** Why don't we link / Why not link / How/What about linking **4** Why not talk / How/What about talking / Why don't we talk **5** Let's arrange **6** If I were you, I'd wait

Unit 15

Introductory exercise

You must make; you need to say; don't give; You don't need to tell; Remember; you have to give

1

Suggested answers:
2 You need to fax your order to us as soon as possible. (*must* or *have got to* would be too strong for a new customer)
3 You must / 've (got) to / need to pay attention to the feedback after your presentation. **4** You must / 've got to get a visa before your trip to Australia. **5** You need to email the address list to the CEO. (*need* is less strong than *must* or *have got to* here, so it will probably create a better relationship with your PA!) **6** We must check the exchange rate every day.

2

1 must **2** has to; must; has to / 's got to **3** have to / 've got to; must **4** have to **5** must / have to **6** have to / must

3

Suggested answers:
2 You can / might want to think **3** you can / might want to consider **4** Do you want to / Can/Could/Will/Could you invite …? **5** you can all come up with **6** Can/Could/Will/Would you / Do you want to organise…? **7** you'd better / you might want to make **8** everyone needs to attend

4

2 You need to make sure you have the correct email addresses in the database. **3** You (or *we*) must follow up every meeting with a courtesy phone call! Is that clear? **4** Could you let me know immediately if Mr Madureira calls? **5** You'd better cancel your group meeting tomorrow. Something urgent has come up. **6** Would you make ten photocopies of this, please?

5

2 don't have to (not necessary) **3** mustn't (forbidden) **4** mustn't (forbidden) **5** don't have to (not necessary)

6

Suggested answers:
2 You definitely need to / have to keep an eye on the exchange rate. (stronger) **3** Personally, I think we need to / 'd better take on more staff during the busy period. (more polite) **4** Could / Would you try to sort it out today, perhaps? (more polite) **5** Actually, you don't need to / have to use the same spreadsheet for both orders. (more polite) **6** We/You really must finish the meeting by 4 pm. (stronger) **7** If you would/could switch off the lights, please. (more polite) **8** Could/Can/Will/Would you just wait another week or so before you call them again? (more polite)

7

2 If you'd / you could come this way, please. **3** If you'd / you could just close the door, please, Robert. Thanks. OK, let's begin the meeting. **4** If you could / you'd get James Hartley on the phone for me, please. I'll return his call.

Unit 16

Introductory exercise

Sentence d is definitely true.

1

2 a should **3 d** should **4 g** can't **5 b** ought to **6 e** ought to **7 h** shouldn't **8 f** must

2

2 should/ought to (Andy isn't as certain as Phil) **3** should/ought to (he thinks this is probably true) **4** might/could/may **5** can't (he is certain this is not true) **6** might/may (*not* so *could* is not possible) **7** might/could/may **8** must (or *should / ought to* if you think Andy is not absolutely certain) **9** must (or *should / ought* to if you think Andy is not absolutely certain) **10** might/could/may **11** might/could/may **12** might/could/may

3

2 might **3** may **4** might / should (*should* is less likely because it is repeated later in the sentence) **5** should **6** might **7** could (this is possible but not certain) **8** can't

4

2 should / ought to be open **3** must have the key **4** may/might/could have it **5** might/could/may be in my office **6** could/might/may (well) still have it **7** should / ought to be in her desk drawer (*could/may/might* are also possible) **8** shouldn't/ought not to take long

5

Suggested answers:
2 They may/might/could go up, too. **3** It should / ought to cost about £25. **4** It shouldn't take more than 15 minutes. **5** Yes, I should / ought to / might be free at 10 o'clock. **6** It must be the server. We're having problems with it at the moment. **7** You can't find a good hotel for that price. / You could try the budget hotel near the station. **8** He may/might be in a meeting right now.

6

2 must be pleased/relieved **3** must be furious **4** must be pleased/relieved **5** must be joking **6** must be surprised

7

Suggested answers:
2 That must be a relief / a good feeling.
3 That must be upsetting/frustrating/annoying.
4 That must be really frustrating/annoying/irritating.

Speaking strategies 4

Introductory exercise

The conversation sounds informal and friendly because the speakers are using shorter forms of the grammar structures.

They are not using the 'full structures' – see the words in italics below.

A: *Are you going* to the party tonight?
B: Yeah. *Are you going*?
A: *I might* do. *It depends* what time I leave work.

1

2 ~~Are~~ you in Hannah's team? **3** ~~Are (you)~~ going with them? **4** ~~Do you~~ need a personal assistant? **5** ~~Are (you)~~ busy these days? ~~Have you~~ been anywhere interesting? **6** ~~Do you~~ like my new travel bag? **7** ~~Are~~ you the lucky person who gets all those trips to California? **8** ~~Have you~~ heard the news? **9** ~~Are (you)~~ ready for lunch? **10** ~~Are (you)~~ hungry?

2

1

… <u>I</u> must tell you in case you don't know: Richard Wilson's going to be there. <u>I</u> can't be with you myself, though. <u>I</u> really should be, I know – <u>the</u> problem is, I'll be in Milan …

2

… <u>Holly</u> tells me you were having trouble with the sound files for your presentation. <u>It</u> might be because they're in a different folder from the main presentation. <u>It</u> depends on the file location. If you like, <u>I'll</u> come and have a look at it for you. <u>I</u> won't be free till 3. <u>Is</u> that OK? …

3

2 ~~I~~ can't find **3** ~~It~~ must be **4** ~~Do you~~ want **5** ~~Have you~~ got **6** ~~I~~ might as well just mention **7** ~~It's~~ something **8** ~~The~~ trouble is **9** ~~I~~ don't know **10** ~~It~~ could be **11** ~~It~~ depends **12** ~~I~~ think so **13** ~~I'm~~ not sure **14** ~~It~~ must be

Test 4

1

1 can **2** can; be able to **3** be unable to; can **4** could you; would you mind (+ *-ing*) **5** May; can

2

2 will enable people to reach **3** lets borrowers have (**not** ~~lets borrowers to have~~) **4** makes it possible to save money **5** is known to be

3

2 Should **3** shouldn't **4** could **5** might **6** Shall **7** might

4

2 must (an obligation) **3** have to (less direct obligation) **4** don't need to (not necessary) **5** must **6** need to (*must* is too direct; not the use of *we* instead of *you*)

5

2 have to (*company rules* = external obligation) **3** Could (polite request) **4** need (a less direct order) **5** must not (very strong order)

6

1 must; must (you are sure this is true); might (this is possible); shouldn't (the speaker expects this *won't* happen)
2 may/could (*may* is more formal); might not; should (an expectation); ought to (an expectation)

7

2 can/could **3** can/could **4** Change **5** Don't **6** could/can **7** needn't **8** able to **9** can/could/should (*can* = is able to; *could/should* = this is expected) **10** might want **11** can/could **12** have to **13** How about **14** need **15** shouldn't **16** couldn't **17** enables **18** Could **19** must / have to (*must* is more direct) **20** let's

Unit 17

Introductory exercise

a Sentence 1 is offering something.
b Sentence 2 is giving advice / making a suggestion.

1

2 pick up **3** is **4** flashes **5** do/should I do **6** 's **7** get **8** have to **9** are **10** don't waste

2

2 sign; 'll get **3** 'll have to; don't get **4** won't charge; order **5** 'll feel; take **6** meet; 'll get **7** don't give; won't be **8** will you do; offer **9** finishes; 'll go **10** have to; don't arrive

3

2 If you're self-employed, you might have to hire an accountant. **3** You could print this page out to read later if you don' want to read all the information online. **4** You may have to pay taxes on goods if you import them from outside the European Union. **5** If your turnover reaches £67,000 a year, register for VAT. **6** We may need to see your VAT records if there are any questions about your tax. **7** If you don't have storage space in your offices for your VAT records, you should arrange alternative secure storage. **8** The police could arrest you if you don't keep any records, as this is a legal requirement. **9** If you have an accountant, you might want to get their advice on keeping VAT records. **10** If you need any help with your taxes, contact your local Advice Team.

4

2 in case **3** in case **4** If **5** Unless **6** If **7** As long as **8** unless **9** provided that **10** If

5

Suggested answers:
2 Whenever the price of oil goes up, we increase our product prices too. (use the present because this is what normally happens)
3 Providing the economy remains strong, we will consider opening a new office in the Far East. (use *will* because we are not sure if this will happen)
4 We won't change our corporate branding unless customers feel it's old fashioned. (don't use *will* in the *if*-clause)
5 As long as customers give us positive feedback, we will continue to provide the same service as we have always done.
6 We may employ more staff if we win this new contract.
7 If a rival company opens in our city, it shouldn't be a problem for us because we have very loyal customers.
8 If our company makes a large profit this year, they may decide to move to premises nearer the centre of town.

9 We offer special incentives to staff providing they promise to stay with the company for at least two years.
10 Our company will do well this year if we continue to meet the increased demand for our product.

6

2 providing **3** if **4** unless **5** as long as

7

Suggested answers:
2 … you stock our full range. **3** … you stay with the company for two years after you pass. **4** … you increase the size of your order. **5** … you put it into our bags and leave it outside the office before 7 am on Thursdays. **6** … you sign a five-year contract

Unit 18

Introductory exercise

a Yasmina is talking about a problem in the past (the new assistant didn't get better training and didn't stay).
b Omar is talking about a problem now (there isn't one point of contact and customers don't know who to talk to).
c You can tell that Yasmina is talking about the past because they use a past hypothetical conditional: *if* + past perfect (*if we had given*) and *would have* + past participle (*would have stayed*).
You can tell that Omar is talking about the present because they use a present hypothetical conditional: *if* + simple past (*if there was*) and *would* + infinitive without *to* (*would know*).

1

2 worked **3** would I do **4** 'd invest **5** owned **6** 'd treat **7** was **8** would have to **9** didn't work **10** was

2

2 had a company car, I wouldn't take **3** spent (more) time building client relationships, you'd have **4** did a presentations course, I'd speak **5** 'd fly business class if it didn't cost **6** didn't work in an open plan office, people wouldn't interrupt me **7** had a PA, she'd be **8** sent us the final order, we'd be able to close their account.

3

3 ~~it gave~~ it would have given **4** ✓ **5** ~~If interest rates would go up~~ If interest rates went up **6** ~~I have to sell~~ I'd have to sell **7** ✓ **8** ~~If they wouldn't have spent~~ If they hadn't spent

4

2 would've been able to **3** Would you have got **4** 'd organised **5** Would it have helped **6** had taken **7** would've been **8** hadn't known **9** 'd learnt **10** wouldn't have had **11** 'd had **12** would've succeeded

5

2 wouldn't have had **3** 'd established (*'d* = had) **4** wouldn't have experienced **5** received **6** would have to be **7** was **8** would be **9** would be

6

2 if it hadn't been for; wouldn't have come back **3** If it hadn't been for; would've shown **4** if it wasn't/weren't for; 'd be able to **5** If it hadn't been for; 'd have had to **6** If it wasn't/weren't for; 'd make

7

2 If the USA were to suffer a recession, it would possibly mean bankruptcy for a company like Airserve.

3 If the EU were to raise taxes on carbon emissions, European airports would lose business.

4 If Skyplan were to pull out of the negotiations with Swallow Air, Swallow Air's future would be in doubt.

5 If more countries were to join the EU, it would open the possibility of new routes.

6 If airlines were to spend more time finding out what customers actually want, they would probably see an increase in revenues.

Unit 19

Introductory exercise

a You can't answer questions 2 & 3. (1 The news about the factory is that it is going to close.)

b The writer didn't include this information as he or she wanted to focus on other information. In sentence 2 the writer focuses on the workers and what happened to them, not who told them the news (probably the management of the company). In sentence 3, the focus is on the company not getting paid, not the people who owed the money (the writer may or may not know who they are).

1 a

(As this is a written text full forms of *be* are used, not contractions.)

2 is logged **3** is mailed **4** are sent **5** are read **6** are categorised **7** are passed on **8** is forwarded **9** is answered **10** are sorted out **11** is known **12** are not left

b

(Look at the assistant's answers to help you choose between present perfect and past simple.

2 was it received **3** was it sent **4** Has an acknowledgement been mailed out **5** was it sent **6** was it forwarded to **7** Have the customers been contacted **8** Were they asked

2

2 's being sacked **3** aren't being replaced; 's being upgraded **4** were being paid **5** was being bullied **6** are being audited **7** 're being asked **8** are being criticised

3

2 was found **3** is swallowed **4** – (active verb) **5** – (active verb) **6** had been ignored **7** had not been followed **8** have been suspended **9** are being put **10** are (currently) being redesigned

4

2 had been working **3** was doing **4** states **5** applied **6** was invited **7** asked **8** was told **9** showed **10** sacked

11 was escorted **12** was informed **13** had been installed **14** had not been told

5 a

2 is searched by security staff **3** are checked by the receptionists **4** are tested randomly for drugs by an outside agency **5** are scanned by antivirus software **6** is backed up by the IT group **7** is tested by fire safety officers on Fridays **8** are trained by their manager in fire safety procedures

b

The lifts are monitored by cameras.

Visitors aren't allowed into the building without a member of staff.

Drivers are tested for drugs and alcohol weekly.

Staff are tested on fire safety procedures regularly.

6 a

2 the goods in your last order were damaged during transportation

3 the goods had not been packed securely / had not been securely packed

4 The matter has been investigated

5 our packing procedures are being reviewed

6 you were treated (by our Order Department)

7 the matter was not handled properly (the writer may decide not to name the person who caused the problem)

8 the sum of $300 is being credited to your account

9 you have been caused (the writer may not wish to say that their company caused the problem)

b

The writer may decide to leave sentences 4 and 8 in the active form to show that he has personally taken action and is responsible for giving the customer some good news.

7

2 … I was educated at Bristol Grammar School and the University of Manchester, where I was awarded a first-class honours degree … I was elected President of the Debating Society.

3 … I have been employed by Directions plc … I was appointed Senior Auditor.

Unit 20

Introductory exercise

The speaker does not say exactly who is responsible for the problem. The speaker uses the passive (*won't be finished, can't be done*) which avoids saying who is respoonsible. The person responsible could be the speaker or someone else. It is probably not Angela, since the speaker asks if she should be told.

1

2 The new store will be opened by the Regional Director on 15 May.

3 Do you think the building works might be delayed by the bad weather?

4 The payment may not have been sent to the right department .

5 The fire exits must be kept clear at all times.

6 Couldn't the meeting be held in a bigger room next time?
7 This invoice should be paid by Friday.
8 Some of the technical problems can't be avoided.

2

2 will be completed **3** will be needed **4** may not be done
5 mustn't be forgotten **6** could things be improved
7 ought to be changed **8** could the next project be completed **9** should be informed

3

2 she was given **3** that information is given **4** she's been sent (or more formally *she has been sent*) **5** she's been offered (or more formally *she has been offered*) **6** 1,000 units were sold
7 I was promised **8** Examples of our new product range will be sent

4

2 Elena **3** Ulla **4** Yunis **5** Giacomo **6** Kirsten

5

2 will be picked up **3** should be detected
4 getting the same searches done **5** could be applied
6 have predictions made **7** can be done **8** could be marketed **9** had the same prediction made **10** get awarded

6

Suggested answers:
2 As can be seen from the flowchart, (note the comma after *flowchart*) **3** Our environmental responsibilities should not be forgotten **4** As might be expected, **5** As will be seen on page 40 of this report, … it should be noted that (note the comma after *report*) **6** The current slowdown in the housing market must be taken into account **7** It could be argued that **8** 2009 can be regarded / can be seen as

Speaking strategies 5

Introductory exercise

Howard uses these expression so that he doesn't offend Lucy:
I'm sorry.
I think there may have been a slight misunderstanding.

1

2 mean **3** I mean is / I'm trying to say is / I'm saying is
4 mean **5** other words **6** mean **7** me put it this way

2

Suggested answers:
2 I think you may have got that wrong. / I'm not sure that's right. I think it was in the low season. **3** I mean / sorry, March. **4** Really? Are you sure? I thought they went down 0.2%. **5** sorry. / I think I've got that wrong. / I don't think that's right. / my mistake! **6** What I actually meant was / I meant / I should have said **7** sorry, I mean Streamjet
Don't forget: people often use more than one of these expressions together.

3

2 What does that mean, exactly? / What is that exactly?
3 Could you explain that a bit more (for me)? **4** Perhaps I've misunderstood you? / Maybe I've got it wrong? (*Perhaps* and *maybe* are interchangeable. *Maybe* is more informal than *perhaps*.) **5** I'm not sure I know what you mean. Could you explain that? / Could you explain that for me? **6** I think we may have misunderstood one another. / I'm afraid there's been a slight misunderstanding.

Test 5

1

2 wants **3** need **4** get **5** 'll have to **6** spend **7** won't have
8 won't need **9** break **10** contacts **11** can do **12** don't waste
13 need **14** 'll find **15** isn't **16** may be **17** can't sell
18 will be able to **19** wants **20** ask

2 a

2 would~~n't~~ want **3** ~~must be~~ would have to be **4** ~~would choose~~ could choose / chose **5** ~~volunteered~~ would volunteer

b

1 would <u>have</u> sold **2** ~~would be~~ 'd been **3** <u>would have</u> started **4** ~~I'd had started~~ I'd have started **5** ~~would have started~~ 'd started

3

2 arrive; will show **3** gave; would place **4** wasn't; wouldn't be asking **5** 'll offer; contacts **6** won't take; want **7** are; can
8 would be; were **9** would've offered; 'd been able to
10 'd won; wouldn't

4

2 was voted **3** were opened **4** were sold **5** have been opened **6** have been welcomed (*were welcomed* is also possible) **7** were recruited **8** has been made up **9** has been created **10** have been used

5

2 should be wrapped **3** were promised **4** hasn't had the central heating checked **5** get the air conditioning fixed **6** used to be refilled **7** will the report be finished **8** might we be offered

Unit 21

Introductory exercise

a You can answer the first question 'yes' or 'no' (*Can I ask you a question?*)
b The questions with question words *How much* and *What* need a longer answer (*If you had no internet access for a day, how much would it cost your business? What would the effects be?*)

1 a

2 Do **3** Are (present passive) **4** Does **5** Does **6** Does
7 Is (present passive) **8** Do **9** Are **10** Is

b

2 was 3 Did 4 Was 5 was 6 were 7 Has 8 Were 9 have
10 Have

2

2 Why do you want to leave your current job?
3 What are your strengths and weaknesses?
4 Are you applying for other jobs? (*What other jobs are you applying for?* is also possible)
5 Why do you want this job?
6 Are you happy to travel?
7 Can you work well under pressure?
8 How did you get on with people in your last job?
9 What have you achieved in your career so far?
10 How do you see your future career?

3

2a Who told Ana b Who did Ana tell 3a Who did Beth email
b Who emailed Beth 4a Who wants to see Sue b Who does Sue want to see

4

2 How bad is it?
3 whose photo does it have?
4 Which guy (is it)? (You could also say *Which one is it?* but not *What* for people.)
5 What else did you find?
6 What colour is it?
7 How quickly can we do it?
8 How expensive will it be? (You could also say *How much will it be?*)
9 Well, whose fault was it?

5

(Do not forget capital letters at the start of the questions and question marks at the end.)
2 What projects are you involved in?
3 How many jobs have you applied for in the last ten years?
4 Which colleagues do you have lunch with?
5 Have you ever complained about a colleague?
6 Who did you complain to?
7 Does your salary depend on your performance?

6 a

2 Don't you think it's (very) memorable? / Isn't it memorable?
3 Why don't we / Can't we use it for the new campaign?
4 Aren't the colours a bit bright? / Don't you think the colours are a bit bright?
5 Don't you think the teddy bear looks a bit silly? / Doesn't the teddy bear look a bit silly?
6 Can't we do some market research on it? / Why don't we do some market research on it?
7 Don't you think the teddy bear is childish? / Isn't the teddy bear childish?
8 Can't you make it a bit less bright? / Why don't you make it a bit less bright?

b

The four questions could all have two meanings. It depends on the situation and what everyone understands about it. Lee's colleagues could just be asking Lee to confirm things he said earlier or they could be criticising him.
1 Meaning 1 (confirming): I think you told me you have tested this with customers – is this correct?
  Meaning 2 (criticism): You should have tested this with customers.
2 Meaning 1 (confirming): I'm sure we asked for a different colour – is this correct?
  Meaning 2 (criticism): I think it should be a different colour.
3 Meaning 1 (confirming): I think you told me you were going to change it – is this correct?
  Meaning 2 (criticism): I think we should change it.
4 Meaning 1 (confirming): I think you told me they do research – is this correct?
  Meaning 2 (criticism): I think they should do research (and it looks like they haven't).
  Lee's colleagues could ask these questions to make them more neutral:
1 Have you tested this with customers?
2 Did we ask for any different colours?
3 Are you going to change it?
4 Do the design people do research?

Unit 22

Introductory exercise

Conversation 2 sounds more natural and friendly because the speakers use question tags (*isn't she?* and *is she?*). People use question tags when they want to involve one another more in the conversation and when they want to sound more friendly.

1

2 do 3 did 4 doesn't 5 didn't 6 does 7 don't 8 didn't
9 does 10 do

2

People often answer a question tag with another question tag. However, it is unlikely they would continue doing this sentence after sentence, so some question tags are in brackets to show they are possible, but might not be used.
2 KIM: They delivered the order on time, didn't they?
  LUCA: Yes, but they didn't deliver it for free, did they?
  KIM: No, That's true.
3 ALAN: The meeting lasted a long time, didn't it?
  PILAR: Yes, marketing meetings always last for hours, don't they?
  ALAN: Yes, and they're so boring, (aren't they?)
  PILAR: I need a coffee! Let's go to the cafeteria, shall we?
4 RAJIV: We don't have a distributor in Moldova, do we?
  NUALA: No, but we've got some contacts there, haven't we?
  RAJIV: Oh yes, Vimala was there last year. I'd forgotten.
5 ANGIE: The delivery hasn't arrived yet, has it?
  BILL: No. It never arrives on time, (does it?)
  ANGIE: No, never.

6 BLAKE: Michelle isn't working at the Paris office any more, is she?

KIARA: No. She works with Gosia in Warsaw now, doesn't she?

BLAKE: Yes, I think you're right.

7 NORA: You've got the agenda for the meeting, haven't you?

ELSA: Yes, and you have the presentation on your laptop, don't you?

NORA: Yes. So everything's ready. See you later.

8 JAN: We weren't advertising much in the Italian press, were we?

ZOË: No, but we had web pages in Italian, (didn't we?)

JAN: Yes, I guess the website was enough.

3

2 hasn't it (we don't use *doesn't* with *have got*) **3** haven't you **4** won't I **5** mightn't we **6** didn't it **7** can you **8** wouldn't you **9** shouldn't I **10** must I

4

2 You don't need the spreadsheet any more, do you?
3 I should book a room for my meeting, shouldn't I?
4 Your firm has a branch in Amsterdam, doesn't it?
5 Linda doesn't work on Mondays, does she?
6 You used to work in sales, didn't you?
7 The Board seemed interested in further talks, didn't they?
8 Photo paper can't be used with this printer, can it?

5

2 sure **3** not sure **4** sure **5** not sure

6

2 is it **3** did they **4** does it (*does* is much more frequent than *has*) **5** have they **6** can we

7

She's going to use them at the Commercial Vehicle Show, is she?
And we ordered some stickers, did we?
We can get them made in time, can we?
OK. You'll see to that, will you?

Unit 23

Introductory exercise

The employers' actual words were probably: 'Temporary workers *are not required* to speak and understand English, even for health and safety purposes.'

1 a

2 49% said (that) they had seen only part of the benefit they had expected from outsourcing.
3 39% said (that) they would renew their outsourcing contract with their existing supplier.
4 15% said (that) they planned to bring the service back in-house. (*they plan* is also possible if the report is published before they carry out their plan)
5 78% said (that) they were satisfied with the service provided by their main outsourcing supplier.

Here is the original survey report from The Financial Times.
As many as 66% of respondents said they were disappointed with the results of their outsourcing contracts. Of the companies polled, 49% said they had seen only part of the benefit they

had expected from outsourcing. An extraordinary 17% said they had seen no benefits from outsourcing. Only 26% said that outsourcing had been everything they had expected.
According to the survey, only 39% of the companies surveyed said they would renew their outsourcing contract with their existing supplier. As many as 15% said they planned to bring the service back in-house.
(…)
As many as 78% in the survey said they were either satisfied or very satisfied with the service provided by their main outsourcing supplier.

b

2 83% of employers and 21.9% of employees thought that employees were involved in decisions and could influence them.
3 31.6% of employers and 18.8% of employees believed that employers worked in close partnership with the union.
4 87% of employers and 30.9% of employees said that employers had taken steps to improve the working environment.
5 54.3% of employers and 84.7% of employees stated that the management needed to do more to improve the working environment.

Here is the original survey report extract from The British Printing Industries Federation.
Communication
83% of employers stated that employees in their companies were involved in and could influence decisions that impacted on them. By contrast only 21.9% of employees shared this view. 71.2% of employers said that their employees were briefed on the company's performance on an on-going basis, whereas only 37.6% of employees said so.
Partnership Working
31.6% of employers believed that they worked in close partnership with the union, but only 18.8% of employees were of this view. 54% of employers and 69% of employees believed that there were practical steps the BPIF, SPEF and GPMU could take to help companies and their employees to work in partnership successfully at company level.
Working Environment
Contrasting opinions were found between employers and employees in relation to improvements made to the working environment. 87.5% of employers said that they had taken steps to improve this in the previous two years, whereas only 30.9% of employees thought that their companies had done so. 84.7% of employee respondents thought that additional steps needed to be taken to improve the working environment, whereas only 54.3% of employer respondents thought this.

2

Used to, *could*, *should* and *might do* not change in the reported minutes. Use *we* because the person writing the minutes is part of the company.
… had been looking at the catalogues and (that) he hadn't found anything. He said (that) we could give the client a clock. Klara said (that) we used to give people clocks years ago but (that) they were bad luck in some cultures. She said (that) she might do some research on that.
Yuri said (that) we should give something fun, like an electronic sudoku. He said he would look online.

Fatma said (that) we had to be careful because we couldn't give things like wine coolers or penknives. She said that if we chose the wrong gift, we might run into cultural problems.

3

2 said (that) / told me/us (that) they hadn't slept well
3 said (that) / told them (that) I'd order coffee **4** told him not to worry about it **5** asked/told me to show them round the building **6** told them not to leave their valuables in the meeting room **7** asked/told her not to smoke **8** asked me to speak a little slower **9** said (that) we'd met before
10 said / told us (that) they were/are definitely going to place an order (here you can use *are* or *were* as the information is still true)

4

2 didn't enjoy (*weren't enjoying* is also possible) **3** was
4 didn't use **5** was **6** 'd done / did

5

2 that morning **3** to check **4** had **5** that afternoon **6** was / 'd been **7** the day before / the previous day **8** had **9** that day **10** wasn't working / hadn't been working **11** had
12 the next day / the following day **13** 'd cancel
14 was **15** 'd try **16** that evening

6

1 was saying; was asking; was telling
2 was saying; was saying; was telling; were saying
3 was saying; was saying; was telling
4 was asking; was telling

Unit 24

Introductory exercise

The original questions could be *Will you become a board member?* (*Would you like to become …* is also possible) and *What is your schedule for the coming year?*

(◄ See Unit 23 for tense changes in reported speech.)

1

2 how many days a year he/she could take off sick
3 when he/she would get a pay rise
4 how much I earn(ed)
5 why I ('d) kept him/her waiting before the interview
6 who the worst candidate was (that) I'd interviewed that day / who the worst candidate I'd interviewed that day was
7 which 5 star hotels he/she would stay in when he/she travels/travelled on business
8 where he/she could get the best lunches near to the office

2

Remember you can use the same tense as the original speaker used if it is soon after they spoke or if you want to show that their comments are still relevant now.
2 if/whether all our products are/were organic
3 if/whether we do/did home deliveries
4 if/whether they can/could order their shopping online
5 if/whether we are/were open on Sundays
6 if/whether we offer/offered reusable bags instead of plastic bags

7 if/whether there is/was disabled access
8 if/whether we sell/sold our own branded products
9 if/whether someone will/would help with packing
10 if/whether we are/were going to ask them for their comments again in a few months

3

2 He asked (me) / wanted to know who our biggest clients are/were. (you use *our* to refer to the company *I/we* work for; you can also say *my biggest clients* if you are just talking about your own clients, not your colleagues' clients)
3 He asked (me) / wanted to know who set up the company.
4 He asked (me) / wanted to know why I joined the company.
5 He asked (me) / wanted to know what I like/liked most about my work.
6 He asked (me) / wanted to know if/whether I live/lived near my work.
7 He asked (me) / wanted to know if/whether I went / 'd gone to university or college.
8 He asked (me) / wanted to know how long I've/'d worked for the company.

4

2 Do you know / Can you tell me / Could I just ask you which
3 Do you know / Can you tell me / Could I just ask you who
4 I'm not sure / I've no idea / I wonder whether **5** Do you know / Can you tell me / Could I just ask you how long **6** I'm not sure / I've no idea / I wonder when **7** Do you know / Can you tell me / Could I just ask you how much **8** I'm not sure / I've no idea / I wonder how many

5

2 ~~what was her password~~ what her password was **3** how often she paid off her credit card in full? (do not use a question mark with reported questions) **4** They asked ~~to~~ her (do not use *to* with *ask*) **5** how that could happen when she was not there? (do not use a question mark after *wonder*) **6** They also wanted to know ~~her~~ if (do not include the person asked after *want to know*) **7** ~~what should she do~~ what she should do

6

2 We would appreciate it if you could send your payment on receipt of the goods.
3 Please inform me of / if there are any job opportunities in your company.
4 Would you consider offering us a reduced price for bulk orders?
5 Please inform us if you are bringing out any new products this year.
6 Please let me/us know when this year's price list will be out.
7 Would you be willing to accept workers on a temporary basis?
8 Please let me know if there will be any changes to my insurance policy.
9 We would welcome any/some feedback on our services.
10 I would be grateful for the opportunity to meet your personnel manager.

Speaking strategies 6

Introductory exercise

The customer checks information on two occasions by repeating the last words of the salesperson (*Two or three weeks?* and *Blackstone's?*) The customer also asks a statement question to check how much the sales person knows about other bookshops in the area (*So you don't know any other bookshops?*) This may follow on from an earlier part of the conversation or it may be because the sales person hasn't offered this information and the customer is checking if the sales person knows it.

1

	2	3	4	5	6
What?					✓
Pardon?		✓			
Sorry? I'm sorry?	✓		✓		
(What) did you say?		✓	✓		
Can you say that again?	✓				✓
Sorry, I missed that.				✓	
Repeated words			✓	✓	

2

1 You like him; Have you sold your house yet? (use normal question word order because this is a new topic which doesn't come out of the previous conversation)

2 Did you enjoy the course? (use normal question word order because this is a new topic); it was useful; You had a good time; Is/Was everything OK here? / Has everything been OK here? (use normal question word order because this is a new topic which doesn't come out of the previous conversation); it's been quiet / it was quiet

3

2 how long **3** when **4** where **5** what **6** how much

Test 6

1

2 Have you ever worked for another company? **3** Do you live near to your work? **4** What does your partner do? **5** Did you see your manager last week? / Did your manager see you … **6** What is your job title? **7** How old is your company? **8** How many people does it employ? **9** Are you happy in your job? **10** Which person do you spend most time with at work? (or … *most time at work with?*) **11** How much was your starting salary? **12** Were you a good student at school?

2

2 hasn't he? **3** didn't he? **4** didn't he? **5** wasn't he? **6** will he? **7** won't we? **8** isn't he? **9** has he? **10** can he? **11** doesn't he? **12** have we? **13** shouldn't we? **14** mightn't he?

3

2 ~~can you help me~~ to help her/ if I could help her **3** it ~~is~~ was so expensive **4** ~~I will be here tomorrow~~ she would be there the next/following day **5** ✓ **6** told ~~to~~ me **7** said <u>to</u> you / told you **8** started

4

1 had collected together the latest ideas and best practices about blogging; made blogging easy and helped you start to do it yourself; started a blog yourself, you wouldn't fully understand their power or potential

2 they were in the process of doing a blog; they'd known nothing about blogging; it was amazing what a person could learn in a week

3 was a book you could easily read in one afternoon; you'd find yourself referring back to it again and again

4 she loved the book

5 you were looking for a basic understanding of blogging, this was the book for you; delivered a message that all bloggers would appreciate

5 a

2 ~~me~~ **3** ~~do~~ **4** ?<u>.</u> **5** if *or* whether (not both)

b

7 I'm <u>not</u> sure **8** I <u>was</u> wondering **9** appreciate <u>it</u> if **10** would <u>be</u> grateful

6

2 Would you be willing to **3** We would welcome **4** Please inform me/us of/about **5** Please let us/me know when **6** I would be grateful if you could

Unit 25

Introductory exercise

a have (*job security*); encourage (*us*); use (*our skills*); get (*lots of breaks*); offers (*fantastic opportunities for promotion*); appreciates (*me*); praises (*me*); do (*good work*)

b *happen, work*

1

Suggested answers:

2 – **3** long meetings/ones **4** some / a cup / one **5** – **6** the list / it **7** – **8** – **9** Maria / her **10** –

2

2 When they increased my salary last year I bought a new car the following month.

3 We spent a lot of money and improved the facilities for the staff, and noticed that motivation increased very rapidly.

4 Handmade Cars Ltd sold 1,000 vehicles in 2005 and made a huge profit, which was good news.

5 They have promised to produce some drawings for us so that we can check the details before we make a decision.

6 Can you take this package to the mailroom? We need to send it immediately.

7 I have to phone Charles Braun today but I can't find his number anywhere.

8 We need to find a good supplier because we want to take our products into new markets.

9 We must increase our sales force immediately.

10 Let's begin the meeting by looking at our sales figures. Orders for the new model have decreased sharply.

3

2 her new PA the meeting room **3** Laura the agenda
4 Ursula the time **5** the visitors some brochures
6 Pamela flowers

4 a

2 Henrik sent it to Zepak last week. **3** They bought them
for Charlie when he retired. **4** We didn't show it to all the
teams. **5** They sold it to the customer without realising.

b

4 We didn't show them it. **5** They sold them (or *him/her*) it
without realising.

5

During the credit crisis which began in 2008, there was a risk
that banks would stop lending ~~to small businesses money~~
money to small businesses, so governments all over the world
gave ~~public funds the banks~~ the banks public funds to enable
them to continue to offer loans ~~in~~ to small businesses and
private individuals. Some economists did not like this (*like*
must have an object), and believed it was better to let the
market operate freely. Meanwhile, the banks had to find new
products ~~to~~ for their customers (or *had to find their customers
new products*) which would stop them taking their cash out
and spending it. The basic problem was a lack of confidence
in the banks, and many people felt that the government and
economists were not telling ~~the whole truth them~~ them the
whole truth.

6

BOB: I wanted to make the point that we shouldn't *launch*
~~the new model~~ in April – there are too many other things
happening. I think we should *delay* ~~the launch~~ until May. We
can *produce* the brochure in January, samples in February or
March, then be ready to *ship* ~~the goods~~ in May. That gives us
plenty of time. If we haven't prepared the launch properly
and have to *cancel* ~~the launch events~~, that would be far
worse.
ANDREW: OK, thanks, Bob. That sounds sensible. All agreed? Right.
Vanessa, anything you want to report on the financial side?
VANESSA: I wanted to talk about our investments in Zamrac. If
we *sell* ~~our shares~~ now, we may be at a disadvantage. I think
we should continue to *buy* ~~more shares~~ over the next few
months and then *sell* ~~them~~ in the autumn when we have a
clearer picture. If we all agree, I can *confirm* ~~our decision~~ with
the brokers.
ANDREW: Right. Well, any comments?

7

2 We produce mostly for the international market.
3 Our team / We can dispatch tomorrow.
4 (I'm sorry.) We can only deliver to addresses within the EU.
5 I don't know if Kepra and Co. want to buy because they
haven't ordered yet.

Unit 26

Introductory exercise

a I try to help (verb + verb) **b** I want my staff to know (verb +
object + verb)

1

2 to come **3** losing (after phrasal verb *end up*) **4** trying
5 to focus **6** building (after the preposition *on*) **7** to ignore
8 moving **9** being **10** to get **11** telling **12** offering

2

1 to think (= I never stop working in order to think; *I never stop
thinking* = I do this all the time) **2** being; thinking / to think;
to work (*-ing* is less likely after *beginning*) **3** meeting; to think
(= I prefer to think this way) **4** trying / to try; buying (I did buy
him lunch) **5** going (= I enjoy going); to have; to make
6 to change (*-ing* is less likely after *intend*); running (*to* is less
common after *start*); working (*to* is less common after *can't
stand*)

3a

2 give up **3** leave **4** to work **5** to offer **6** to take **7** to feel
8 to make up **9** to tell **10** use / to use

4

2 d **3** e **4** f **5** a **6** h **7** c **8** b

5

1 remember ~~to meet~~ meeting; enjoyed meeting you and ~~to
hear~~ hearing; arrange ~~scheduling~~ to schedule; would you
mind ~~to send~~ sending; look forward to ~~hear~~ hearing
2 saw you ~~to look~~ looking (repeated activity, not a single
event); Thanks for ~~invite~~ inviting; would love ~~coming~~ to
come; spend a day or two ~~to look~~ looking; finished ~~to write~~
writing; let me ~~to~~ know

6 a

2 to discuss **3** to agree **4** To prepare **5** important to keep
6 to confirm (*confirming* is also possible here) **7** to arrange (*to
confirm*, *to discuss* and *to agree* are also possible here)
8 happy to answer

b

2 happy to use **3** interesting to see **4** to improve **5** to
update **6** to help **7** willing to contribute **8** ready to take on

Unit 27

Introductory exercise

a Two or three parts (1 verb and 1 or 2 particles)
b put it off (object = pronoun *it*); catch up on the main points
(object = *the main points*)
c The pronoun object comes between the verb and the
particle with *put off* (*put it off*); the object comes after the
particles with *catch up on* (*catch up on **the main points***).

1

2 through **3** on **4** up **5** off **6** off **7** up **8** down **9** back (*up* is
also possible but unlikely. If you *call someone back*, they called
you first. If you *call someone up*, it is not usually in response to
their call.) **10** out

2

2 sort these problems out **3** go through her own detailed solutions **4** find something out **5** carried on thinking **6** put our solutions forward **7** coming up with their own ideas **8** back them up

3

2 looking **3** come **4** do **5** looking **6** put **7** caught **8** make

4 a

2 put that off **3** set up **4** shut down **5** turn off **6** set off **7** Hang on! **8** look up **9** looking forward to **10** put up with

b

Suggested answers:
1 Don't hang up yet! We still need to discuss the Blackmoor contract.
2 I love my job so much that I'd like to carry on working until I am 75 years old!
3 Your password has expired. You need to make up a new one / make a new one up.
4 It can be noisy in the office so I sometimes prefer to finish off my work / finish my work off at home.
5 Team building activities help to break down barriers / break barriers down and strengthen team spirit and understanding.
6 Our weekly strategy meetings go on for much too long. I'd manage the time better if I was in charge.
7 This is a very busy time at work, so I've had to give up my evening class / give my evening class up for the last two months.
8 I make sure I back up all my files / back all my files up at the end of every day so that I don't lose anything important.
9 We believe it is very important to look after our customers.
10 I'm going to have to study all weekend to catch up on the classes I missed when I was ill.

5

Suggested answers:
2 I always put off answering difficult emails for as long as I can!
3 No, it hasn't. But one of our competitors was taken over recently by a big American conglomerate.
4 We've just set up a new branch in Croatia, which is very exciting.
5 I understand why businesses do cut back their training during a recession but I don't think it's a good idea in the long term.
6 I think they should always read the small print and watch out for the things that are not covered.
7 Unfortunately nowadays I think it is quite common to be laid off and it has happened to several of my friends in the last two years because of the recession.
8 We produce beauty products at the top end of the market, so I don't think demand will ever drop off.
9 Yes, I turned down a job in Istanbul a few years ago because I didn't speak the language. Now I wish I'd taken it!
10 A drop in salary and reduced holidays would definitely put me off applying for a job.

6

2 get over **3** get back **4** get round to **5** get through **6** get away with **7** get away **8** get through to / get into **9** get on with **10** get on

Unit 28

Introductory exercise

a *For* over 100 years (a period of time); *into* the 21st century (from now to the future.)
b *at* Birmingham University (location)
c contributed *to* (this is a common verb + preposition combination)
d a leader *in* (this is a common noun + preposition combination)

1

2 at; in **3** to; on **4** at **5** up; to; on; under **6** out of **7** over **8** between; from; to **9** After; for; in **10** in; next to **11** over; by; by **12** since

2

2 for **3** to **4** on **5** into **6** of **7** on **8** with **9** in **10** – **11** about **12** –

3

2 similar to **3** concerned with **4** different from **5** involved in **6** consistent with **7** responsible for **8** interested in

4

1 to; of; to; of **2** For **3** of **4** to; in **5** between

5

2 for/with **3** about (= consider) **4** into **5** After **6** to **7** for/at/in **8** In **9** in **10** on **11** for **12** in **13** on **14** in **15** on **16** about **17** for (*look for* = try to find) **18** for

6

2 in **3** by **4** to/by; of **5** in; from

7

2 from **3** in **4** to **5** of **6** in **7** by **8** in **9** by **10** from **11** at **12** in **13** in **14** of **15** by **16** of

Speaking strategies 7

Introductory exercise

The manager is emphasising the fact that they need a new campaign slogan. She stresses this by using the expression *What we need is*.

1

… <u>Secondly</u>, with good PR you attract …; <u>Thirdly</u>, PR also deals with …; <u>Finally</u>, you can also create …

2

2 First and foremost **3** A **4** B **5** first **6** secondly **7** thirdly **8** lastly (= the last point) **9** at last (= eventually / after a long time) **10** at first (= in the beginning) **11** last but not least (Joseph is equally as important as Benny and Hilda)

3

2 What they manufacture is lifting equipment.
3 What we should do is send a questionnaire to some of our biggest customers.
4 This is what we did: we completely redesigned the entry and exit points.
5 What I told everyone was (that) we couldn't afford any more delays.
6 Here's what I'll do: I'll call a meeting of everyone concerned with the Krypak project.
7 What happened was they closed every branch except the one in the capital city.
8 What I said was (that) I'd be ready to travel at short notice.
9 This is what we should do: we should check all the figures again.
10 What they hope to do is expand into Latin America.

Test 7

1

2 the results 3 your office 4 – 5 –; interest rates 6 – 7 the way 8 productivity 9 – 10 money

2

2 giving Sam a presentation 3 showed it to her
4 I'll make him a copy 5 bring me one; buy you a drink

3

2 to drink 3 to step down; managing 4 to involve 5 to order
6 preparing 7 (to) compare 8 reading 9 to dominate
10 making (this describes the level of enjoyment); to be (this describes a preference; *being* is also possible) 11 to miss
12 asking; to ask 13 to rebrand (they did it, but unsuccessfully) 14 to get

4

2 e 3 b 4 a 5 c 6 d

5

1 Can't we just turn it down?
2 A personal advisor looks after each client in our bank.
3 … many people have given up looking for a job.
4 … I'd like you to put your proposals forward / put forward your proposals.
5 … private equity funds are looking out for new acquisitions.
6 … I wrote them down somewhere

6

2 through 3 off 4 up 5 to 6 against

7

a 2 in 3 of 4 of 5 for 6 of 7 to
b 1 by 2 in/during/over 3 of 4 of 5 from 6 to
c 1 in 2 with 3 on 4 in 5 in 6 in 7 to 8 of 9 about 10 of
d 1 for 2 on 3 between 4 after 5 on 6 in

Unit 29

Introductory exercise

a young, cool, fresh b youthful

1

2 successful 3 academic 4 qualified 5 responsible
6 considerable 7 flexible 8 financial 9 challenging
10 ambitious 11 determined 12 rewarding 13 profitable
14 interested (this describes how you feel)

2

2 impossible 3 illegal 4 mismanaged (*unmanaged* means that there is no management at all) 5 indecisive
6 uneconomic 7 dissatisfied (*unsatisfied* is also possible but is much less common) 8 irregular

3

1 bad (*terrible* has a strong meaning so you can't use it with *very*); essential (this has a strong meaning so you can use the adverb *absolutely*)
2 interested (*-ed* adjectives describe how someone feels about something)
3 satisfied (*-ed* adjectives describe how someone feels about something); pleasing (this describes *results*)
4 exciting; boring (both of these adjectives describe the investment)

4

2 is keen 3 other companies 4 is simple (use adjectives after *be*) 5 people responsible (*responsible people* describes the type of people) 6 feel valued (use adjectives after *feel*)
7 main customer service (*customer service* is an adjective of purpose here so it comes after *main* which describes quality)
8 are happy (use adjectives after *be*) 9 feel welcome (use adjectives after *feel*) 10 positive feedback 11 something special (use adjectives after indefinite pronouns) 12 good job 13 motivated employees 14 demotivated employees

5

1 spicy tomato (quality, material) 2 fifty black personalised (quantity, colour, purpose) 3 old, stone (age, material); luxury sports (quality, purpose) 4 thousand square (quantity, shape); huge shopping (size, purpose); underground customer (quality, purpose); busy pedestrian (quality, purpose)

6

2 well-designed 3 fast-moving; high-tech 4 well-known; high-profile 5 well-established 6 low-cost

7

2 a fast-growing company (change *an* to *a*) 3 a well-run company (change *an* to *a*) 4 a high-yield investment 5 well-known company 6 low-risk investments 7 fast-moving stock market 8 high-tech stocks

Unit 30

Introductory exercise

a locally **b** organically **c** immediately

1

2 suddenly **3** internally **4** globally **5** Luckily **6** efficiently
7 completely **8** annually **9** primarily **10** economically

2

2 a normal **b** normally **3 a** late **b** late **4 a** economical
b economically **5 a** fast **b** fast **6 a** early **b** early **7 a** total
b totally **8 a** hard **b** hard **9 a** bad **b** badly **10 a** long **b** long

3

2 the customer service department can view the customer
information instantly **3** can address them correctly **4** they
remember the caller personally **5** the computerised
receptionist helps the customer directly **6** connects them
immediately **7** can assist them best

4

2 We probably need to search **3** I am always **4** It's certainly
been **5** has actually done **6** Does your company sometimes
employ **7** I always bring back **8** Unfortunately, I
9 I only have **10** I seldom attend; I'm usually

5

2 remarkably similar **3** grown rapidly (*quickly* is also possible)
4 probably give **5** highly profitable **6** entirely different
7 outlets quickly (*rapidly* is also possible) **8** heavily dependent

6

2 Hopefully **3** probably **4** actually **5** certainly **6** perhaps
7 maybe **8** really **9** Obviously **10** definitely

Unit 31

Introductory exercise

a larger; more dynamic
b more resistant to change

1

2 further (or *farther*) **3** earlier **4** busier **5** longer **6** more
frequent **7** more crowded **8** worse **9** larger **10** more
stressful **11** more seriously **12** harder

2

2 wider **3** thinner than **4** more easily **5** longer than **6** better
7 bigger than **8** heavier than **9** easier **10** more expensive
than **11** cheaper than **12** more suitable

3

2 more quickly than they do / than them **3** more friendly
than them / than they are (*friendlier* is also possible) **4** more
effectively than they can / than them **5** bigger than ours (is)
6 more impressive than theirs (were)

4a

2 as strong as (= they are equally good) **3** not as old as (not
less old because *old* is a short adjective) **4** not as experienced
/ less experienced **5** n't as good as (not *less good* because

good is a short adjective) **6** as long as (there's a negative in
hasn't) **7** n't as well qualified as / less well qualified than
8 n't as shy **9** (as) quiet as (*was less shy and quiet than* is
possible) **10** n't as talkative as / less talkative than **11** n't as
confident / less confident **12** as high as (they are the same)

5

2 six times more expensive / as expensive **3** three times
longer / as long **4** 33% faster **5** three times more likely / as
likely **6** twice as likely **7** four times more likely / as likely
8 twice as long

6

2 much / far / a lot / more and **3** much / far / a lot / less and
4 slightly / a bit / a little / a little bit **5** much / a lot (*far faster*
isn't very common) **6** much / far / more and / a lot **7** slightly /
a bit / a little / a little bit

7

Do not use the same word (e.g. *much* or *slightly*) in every gap.
2 much/far/significantly/considerably **3** much/far/
significantly/considerably **4** slightly / a little **5** slightly / a
little **6** much/far/significantly/considerably **7** slightly / a little

Unit 32

Introductory exercise

a biggest, most profitable
b No. The form of the adjectives that the writer uses (the
   superlative: *the biggest and most profitable*; *the lowest prices*)
   shows that he or she thinks there are no other stores which
   are bigger etc.

1a

2 most expensive (you do not need *the* after the possessive
EU's) **3** oldest (you do not need *the* after the possessive
Europe's) **4** (the) longest (*the* is optional as this is an
adverb) **5** the lowest **6** the wealthiest (more common than
the most wealthy) **7** the happiest; the least satisfied **8** (the)
most efficiently (*the* is optional as this is an adverb) **9** (the)
most secure (*the* is optional as this is an adverb)

b

1 Germany **2** Germany, France and Austria **3** Italy **4** France
5 France and Italy **6** Luxembourg **7** Copenhagen,
Luxembourg and Tallinn; Athens, Bucharest and London
8 Munich, Helsinki, Hamburg and Vienna **9** Denmark, Sweden
and Finland

2

2 ~~of~~ in the country (use *in* for places) **3** the ~~most~~ best
transport company. (*best* is the superlative, without *most*)
4 the fastest ~~in~~ of all our competitors (use *of* before the
thing you compare with) **5** our ~~most big~~ biggest **6** our ~~least
good~~ worst (*least good* is rare) **7** the least competitive (the
superlative adjective needs *the*) **8** the personnel department's
greatest problem (the possessive *'s* is needed) **9** ~~most far~~
furthest/farthest (*far* is a short word with two superlative
forms) **10** the ~~busyest~~ busiest (spelling change: *y* to *i*)
11 ~~effectivest~~ most effective (*effective* is a longer word so uses
most) **12** the ~~less~~ least often (*less often* is also possible)

3

1 the best protected / the most well protected **2** the most widely used **3** most rapidly expanding (don't repeat *the*); the most environmentally damaging **4** the most commonly asked
5 The most densely populated **6** the most physically demanding; the most badly paid / the worst paid

4

1–3 do not need an ordinal because they are all about the first item in each graph.
2 the largest **3** the most profitable **4** the second most profitable **5** the third largest **6** the fourth largest
7 The second most profitable **8** the third most profitable
9 the third largest **10** the fifth largest

5

2 less; the least **3** more **4** (the) most **5** more; (the) most
6 more; more

6

2 most concerned **3** most thoughtful **4** most sincere **5** most disappointed **6** most interesting **7** most impressed **8** most grateful

7

Suggested answers:
1 I was most disappointed to learn/hear that you have withdrawn your application.
2 I would be most grateful if you could send me a brochure for the hotel.
3 It was most thoughtful of you to invite me to lunch on my recent visit.
4 We would like to send you our most sincere congratulations on your award.

Speaking strategies 8

Introductory exercise

Tony is the more active listener as he gives a longer reaction and responds with a positive comment to what is good news. Diana just shows she is listening with a brief response.

1

2 a/d/e **3** d **4** h **5** g **6** f **7** b **8** a

2

2 Really! **3** Have a good trip. **4** That's bad news. / That's a shame. / That's terrible. / That's awful. **5** That's great/good news! / That's great/wonderful! **6** That's a shame/pity. / That's bad news.

3

2 right/correct **3** good/great news **4** OK / all right **5** right/true **6** good/great/excellent **7** fine/OK/great **8** right/correct

Test 8

1

2 luxurious **3** limited **4** economical **5** easy **6** unsuitable
7 inexpensive **8** professional **9** assembly **10** financial
11 valuable/invaluable **12** exciting

2

1 removable plastic dental (quality, material, purpose)
2 leading independent US (opinion, quality, origin); 20,000 international financial (number, quality, purpose)
3 innovative, high-quality golf (opinion, quality, purpose)
4 new environmentally friendly industrial (age, material, purpose); traditional organic (quality, material)

3

2 The present owners have decided to sell the company, but it will be a long process.
3 Product lines affected by the economic downturn include luxury goods such as perfumes.
4 Some money is missing from the safe and I want to know who is responsible.
5 Rising energy costs have forced us to keep prices high.

4

2 The Sub-Saharan energy project went well. We also ran a similar project in Asia.
3 Have you worked here long?
4 What's the best advertisement you've seen lately?
5 (Unfortunately) I can't come to this week's meeting (unfortunately), but I can definitely make next week's. That's a promise.
6 In a job interview, try to answer any questions honestly.
7 Your appraisal is due soon, isn't it? Are you nervous about it?
8 I've rarely seen such impressive results. You really deserve your bonus.

5

3 important~~ly~~ **4** will <u>always</u> read ~~always~~ **5** ~~well~~ <u>good</u> design **6** ~~just~~ should not <u>just</u> focus on **7** should <u>also</u> look to ~~also~~ **8** ✓ **9** ✓ **10** ~~well~~ <u>good</u> news **11** need to think <u>carefully</u> **12** ✓ **13** work hard~~ly~~ **14** <u>really</u> matter

6a

good, better, the best; worse, the worst; expensive, more expensive, the most expensive; cheap, cheaper, the cheapest; cheaply, more cheaply, the most cheaply; easy, easier, easiest; easily, more easily, the most easily

b

2 expensive; the second most expensive (*the second cheapest* is also possible); the most expensive **3** a little / a bit / a little bit / slightly better (*bigger* is also possible); the worst **4** more cheaply; the cheapest **5** the second easiest; easier

Unit 33

Introductory exercise

a *Market research, competition, profitability, planning* and *strategy* are all singular. They are uncountable and so they do not have a plural form.
b *Customers, trends* and *sales* are all plural, countable nouns.

1

2 paperwork; document **3** luggage; bags **4** equipment; projector **5** chairs; furniture **6** feedback; comment
7 literature; brochure **8** advertisements; publicity

2

1 ~~traffics~~ traffic (uncountable); <u>an</u> investment; <u>a</u> return; Visitor<u>s</u> **2** ~~informations~~ information (uncountable); ~~softwares~~ software (uncountable); ~~trainings~~ training (uncountable); ~~a~~ guidance (uncountable); ~~hardwares~~ hardware (uncountable)

3

2 find **3** is **4** shows **5** leads **6** is **7** is **8** need to **9** is **10** is **11** is **12** are **13** is **14** are **15** is **16** leave **17** departs **18** wish

4

2 a nice room (a singular countable noun needs a determiner) **3** was (*traffic* is uncountable and and takes a singular verb) **4** trips (*travel* is uncountable) **5** jobs (this use of *work* is uncountable) **6** experience (this meaning of *experience* is uncountable); a campaign **7** a small business (this meaning of *business* is countable) **8** competitors (the countable meaning of *competitions* is games or contests)

5

2 a bottle/glass of **3** a bit/piece of **4** a bit of **5** a bit of **6** a bit of **7** a bit/piece of **8** a bit of **9** a bit of **10** a bit of

6 a

shorts ~~is~~ <u>are</u>; New furniture and audio equipment ~~has~~ <u>have</u>; earnings from investments ~~was~~ <u>were</u>; The news in Asia ~~are~~ <u>is</u>; exports to the EU ~~was~~ <u>were</u>; the pension scheme, which ~~have~~ <u>has</u>; changes to the current scheme ~~is~~ <u>are</u>

b

The union has/have; The management team is/are; the company is/are; ALD Insurance is/are

7

2 Are **3** Is/Are **4** Is **5** Are

Unit 34

Introductory exercise

a *The* official business link; *The* US Government; *The* US Small Business Administration; *an* access point; *The* nation's businesses
b *Business.gov*; *government services*; *information*; *operations*

1

2 A **3** a (*university* starts with a consonant sound /j/); an (*MBA* starts with a vowel sound /em/) **4** a; an (the *h* is silent in *hour*) **5** a; an (the *h* in *honest* is silent) **6** an; a (*European* starts with a consonant sound /j/)

2

2 a (first mention); the (second mention) **3** the (there is one general manager); a (you have more than one friend) **4** a (first mention); an (one of many opportunities); the (second mention); an (first mention) **5** The (I told you about this machine before); an (frequency expression) **6** a (first mention); the (superlative form); the (specific company) **7** an (type of job); a (one of many jobs) **8** the (there is one Italian market); the (a nationality) **9** a (first mention); the (specific skills); a (one of many) **10** the (we know which offer they are talking about); an (first mention; starts with a vowel sound /es/)

3

2 A the B – (a plural noun) **3** A the (superlative form) B – (day) **4** A the (superlative form) B – (plural noun) **5** A – (uncountable noun) B the (a specific noun; we both know about this)

4

2 – (a company name) **3** – (uncountable) **4** the (already mentioned) **5** a (first mention) **6** a (first mention) **7** a (first mention) **8** the (a specific category of people) **9** a (one of several) **10** – (uncountable) **11** the (superlative) **12** – (uncountable noun used in a general way) **13** a (first mention) **14** – (uncountable noun used in a general way) **15** – (uncountable noun used in a general way) **16** the (there is only one) **17** – (uncountable) **18** an (one of several effects)

5

2 – **3** a (first mention) **4** – (noun used in a general way) **5** – (plural noun) **6** the (a specific category) **7** the (a time expression) **8** an (*e-commerce* starts with a vowel sound) **9** a (first mention) **10** – (company name) **11** – (a festival) **12** the (previously mentioned) **13** a (one of many) **14** the (there is only one) **15** – (street name) **16** The (specific and already mentioned) **17** a (first mention) **18** the (a time expression)

6

2 – **3** the; – **4** – **5** – **6** the

7

2 – **3** the **4** the **5** – **6** the (they both know about this) **7** the (there is one design team) **8** the **9** the **10** – **11** a (one of many possible ideas) **12** an (first mention) **13** the **14** the **15** The (already mentioned)

Unit 35

Introductory exercise

The words in italics tell you how many/much.

1

2 most **3** enough **4** Many / A lot of* **5** all **6** much / a lot of* **7** Some / A lot of **8** more **9** several **10** a few **11** a little / some **12** many / a lot of*
* *Lots of* is possible but is less formal and therefore unlikely in a written context.

2

2 any (question) **3** some (offer) **4** some (request) **5** any (negative sentence) **6** some (affirmative sentence) **7** any (negative sentence) **8** no (negative idea after an affirmative verb) **9** any (question) **10** no (negative idea after an affirmative verb) **11** any (negative sentence) **12** some (affirmative sentence)

3 a

1 ~~a few~~ (*sterling* is uncountable); ~~any~~ (*any* is usually used with a negative verb) **2** ~~many~~ (*travelling* is uncountable); ~~some~~ (*some of* is not usually used with a negative verb) **3** ~~several~~ (*training* is uncountable); ~~a little~~ (*courses* is countable and plural) **4** ~~a few~~ (*time* is uncountable here); ~~much~~ (*much* isn't normally used in simple affirmative statements)

4 a

2 All / All of (*all* can be used with or without *of*) **3** A few (do not use *of* as it is before a noun) **4** Most of (use *of* before *the*)

b

1 no (do not use *of* before a noun); any of (use *of* before *our*)
2 All of (use *of* before a pronoun) **3** none of (use *none of*, not *no*, before a pronoun) **4** All of (*all* is used with *of* before a pronoun)

5

2 the most (*passengers* = countable noun) **3** less (*revenue* = uncountable noun) **4** as much (*profit* = uncountable noun) **5** the most (*profit* = uncountable noun) **6** the fewest (*seats* = countable noun) **7** as many (*passengers* = countable noun) **8** more (*revenue* = uncountable noun) **9** fewer / the fewest (*costs* = countable noun) **10** the least (*revenue* = uncountable noun) **11** the most (*seats* = countable noun) **12** the least (*profit* = uncountable noun)

6

2 much **3** many of **4** few **5** Many **6** little **7** a little **8** A few of **9** much of **10** many **11** little **12** much of

7

2 No insurance company is perfect.
3 No company can be without a disaster recovery plan.
4 No small company can afford to ignore its insurer's advice.

Unit 36

Introductory exercise

a your **b** yourself; yours

1

2 our **3** our **4** their **5** its **6** mine **7** its **8** My **9** your **10** their **11** yours **12** their own (*their* is also possible but does not show the emphasis that is needed here.)

2 a

2 British Airways' **3** Apple's **4** Lexus' (the name of the company ends in an *s* so you do not need to add another one to make a possessive) **5** Mohamed al-Fayed's **6** Coca-Cola's **7** France's **8** the dentist's

b

1 Subway's / Starbucks' **2** In x days'/weeks'/months' time

3

2 Susanna's **3** tomorrow's **4** newsagent's **5** No apostrophe necessary **6** years' **7** No apostrophe necessary **8** Mike's **9** union's **10** company's

4

2 – (*relax* doesn't need a reflexive pronoun) **3** one another **4** myself **5** themselves **6** each other's **7** by yourself **8** himself **9** ourselves **10** yourself (Note that *to do a task yourself* means you do not ask someone else to do it. Compare this with *to do a task by yourself*, which means that you do it alone.)

5

2 yours **3** my company's **4** each other / one another **5** myself **6** last week's **7** your **8** themselves **9** my **10** our

6

2 at the centre of your future success **3** the advantages of this strategy / this strategy's advantages **4** the needs of the average person / the average person's needs **5** the name of the product you are selling **6** any part of the name **7** your customers (*customers of yours* is also possible but very rare and rather formal) **8** database of customers (*a customers' database* would belong to the customers)

Speaking strategies 9

Introductory exercise

this thing = the event they are going to. This could be a conference, a meeting, an exhibition or some other work related event. The speaker can use *thing* because the listener obviously knows what he/she means here.
or something = a drink (coffee, tea, or maybe a cold drink) possibly with a small snack of some kind
stuff = possessions of some kind which the speaker needs to take to the event. It could be a bag or briefcase with papers and office equipment, or if they are staying away overnight, it might mean a small case with clean clothes and toiletries. Again both speaker and listener know what they are talking about.

1

2 things (*Things* often means 'life in general', e.g. *How are things? Stuff* isn't used in this way.) **3** things / stuff **4** thing (*Thing* is very common in spoken English in expressions which introduce a point or topic e.g. *the thing is, the main thing is, the best/worst/important thing is. Stuff* isn't used to mean issue or factor.) **5** things

2

People often use a mix of formal and informal expressions in the same conversation, though *stuff* should be avoided in very formal situations. The first conversation sounds more formal so any expression from B2 would fit here. The second one sounds more informal so the expressions from B1 would fit. The expressions the speakers actually used are:
2 and so forth **3** and what have you **4** and so on **5** and things **6** and stuff **7** and things like that **8** and that kind of thing

3

You can use all the expressions in section C in each sentence. Suggested answer (using some of the original speaker's choice of expressions):
2 and everything **3** and all that sort of stuff **4** and all the rest of it **5** and everything **6** and all the rest of it

4

1 or anything **2** or something; or something like that **3** or anything like that **4** or something / or anything

5

Suggested answers:

2 Do you fancy a snack or something? **3** Maybe we should get a sandwich or something? **4** Do you feel like seeing a film or something tonight? **5** Do you want to check your email or something? **6** Would you like to get some fresh air or something?

(You can also use *or anything* in all cases but *or something* is much more common.)

Test 9

1

2 a message; a mistake / some mistake; a price **3** any experience **4** some feedback **5** a bit of luck / luck **6** work; a job **7** a piece of advice **8** a drink; tea **9** some research / research **10** an order; some machinery; documentation; some news

2

2 not many **3** a little **4** a lot of **5** much **6** all **7** enough **8** several **9** no **10** any **11** more than **12** many **13** most of **14** a little **15** any

3

2 the **3** a **4** the **5** – **6** the **7** the **8** An **9** – **10** – **11** a **12** the **13** The **14** a

4

1 his; her; its **2** mine; my **3** your; our; ours **4** their; theirs

5

2 shareholders' **3** Charles' **4** weeks' **5** dentist's **6** yours (no apostrophe needed)

6

2 herself **3** each other / one another **4** himself **5** yourselves **6** itself **7** themselves **8** myself **9** ourselves **10** each other / one another

Unit 37

Introductory exercise

a who, whose
b which, that
c whose

1

2 The photocopier which/that arrived two days ago has already broken down.
3 The customer who/that telephoned this morning is waiting to see you.
4 A colleague who/that has never taken a day off called in sick today.
5 The model that/which was launched nine months ago isn't doing very well.
6 We need to discuss the candidates who/that came for interview this morning.
7 Customers who/that received faulty goods may want a refund

8 We've decided to close two of our power plants which/that are old and becoming dangerous.

2

2, **5**, **6** and **9** are not necessary (they are the object of the relative clause)

3

2 which **3** which **4** who **5** which **6** which **7** which **8** who

4

2 who/that **3** whose **4** which/that **5** which/that **6** who **7** which/that **8** whose

5

2 e who/that **3** a whose **4** h which/that **5** c who **6** b which/that **7** g which/that **8** f whose

6

2 d **3** a **4** c **5** f **6** b

7

2 d **3** c **4** a **5** b **6** f **7** e **8** h

Unit 38

Introductory exercise

when refers to *a moment*; *where* refers to *markets*

1

2 who **3** whom **4** who **5** both are possible (*who* is less formal) **6** whom (this is a formal written context)

2

2 where **3** where **4** that/which/– (do not use *where* with a preposition) **5** where **6** that/which/– (do not use *where* with a preposition) **7** where **8** that/which/– (do not use *where* with a preposition)

3

2 d where **3** b where/– **4** a who **5** f who/– **6** h when **7** e where **8** g where

4

2 listed **3** told **4** suggested **5** trying **6** asking **7** dissatisfied **8** wanting

5

3 to who<u>m</u> you are selling / who are you selling to **4** ✓
5 already ~~sold~~ <u>selling</u> your product **6** ✓ (*which/–* are also possible) **7** ~~basing~~ <u>based</u> on their experience … **8** <u>where/when</u> you are just trying …

6

2 f **3** e **4** g **5** a **6** d **7** h **8** c

7

2 a third of whom **3** all of whom **4** few of whom **5** 54% of whom **6** half of whom

Unit 39

Introductory exercise

a also
b Despite, However, In spite of
c Meanwhile

1

2 but (This is a contrast. *Even though* doesn't work here because the information that business people are very busy is not surprising or unexpected) **3** Although (use *although* at the beginning of sentences) **4** Despite (this contrasts two idea in the same sentence; *however* often contrasts with the sentence before) **5** However **6** Even though / Although **7** despite (use *despite* in front of the *-ing* form) **8** but (*however* is usually at the beginning of a sentence) **9** however (*however* is contrasting with the previous sentence) **10** though (use *though* at the end of a sentence to contrast with the previous sentence; *although* makes a contrast within the same sentence)

2

2 Although / Even though **3** Despite / In spite of **4** also **5** but **6** Despite / In spite of **7** as well **8** Although / Even though

3

2 The Tokyo Stock Exchange closed down 30 points and Germany's Dax index closed 0.7% down as well.
3 The UK's FTSE 100 index was up 3.2% and France's CAC also rose.
4 Apart from share prices, commodities such as oil and gold fell too.
5 Some analysts recommend a cut in interest rates. However, this could lead to inflation. / This could, however, lead to inflation. / This could lead to inflation, however. (*however* is used most often at the beginning of sentences)
6 Although the dollar remained steady, some experts have predicted a drop in its value. / The dollar remained steady, although some experts have predicted a drop in its value. (You can use *although* in both positions. In news reports people might use it in the middle position because *the dollar remained steady* is the main focus of the story.)
7 'These problems might seem bad for investors, though they are also an opportunity,' said a spokesman. / 'Though these problems might seem bad for investors, they are also an opportunity,' said a spokesperson.
8 Despite the (continued) poor performance of the stock market, US investors remain confident / US investors remain confident despite the (continued) poor performance of the stock market. (*continued* can be used as an adjective)

4

2 After I had been with the company for five years, I became Head of UK Sales. / After being with the company …
3 I took a part-time MBA while (I was) working for the company full time.
4 I passed my MBA. Soon afterwards, I was promoted to Head of Department.
5 I am planning a career break next year and in the meantime, I am teaching at the university.
6 During my career break in Kenya, I will teach at a school there.

7 Before coming / I come back to the UK, I hope to travel around Africa. (**not** *Before I will come back* ◄ See Unit 10 D2)
8 I want to save a lot of money during my career. Eventually I would like to retire and live in the country. / I would like to retire eventually and live in the country. / I would like to retire and live in the country eventually.

5

2 two days ~~before that~~ after that / afterwards **3** Everlast ~~too~~ also got involved **4** ~~Although~~ However, people soon discovered **5** ~~eventually~~ while/when Everlast was working as manager **6** This time, ~~although~~ though/however he sold

6

2 whereas **3** subsequently, **4** Nevertheless, **5** Meanwhile,

7

2 Furthermore / Moreover / In addition **3** Furthermore / Moreover / In addition **4** In addition to (before a noun) **5** Meanwhile **6** Nevertheless **7** Subsequently

Unit 40

Introductory exercise

a He needs to spend two nights there.
b He needs to be able to make it worth the travel time

1

2 As/Because/Since the weather was so bad, I decided to take the train.
3 As/Because/Since I wanted to find out more about Russia, I decided to invite Galina to lunch.
4 We changed our insurance because/as/since the premiums had become too expensive.
5 Did he change his job because he was unhappy at PGC? (the speaker is guessing why he changed his job so *as* and *since* are not possible)
6 As/Because/Since we are expanding so quickly, we need to look again at our distribution network.
7 As/Because/Since it was getting late, we decided to meet again the next day.
8 We couldn't contact him because/as/since nobody had an address for him.
9 Did you turn down the job because the salary wasn't good enough? (the speaker wants to find out why the other person turned down the job so *as* and *since* are not possible)
10 As/Because/Since my computer had crashed, I couldn't access my emails.

2

Suggested answers:
2 The hotels around the airport were all full. **3** I was very hungry **4** But I was too late, and all the restaurants were closed. **5** The hotel had no room service after midnight. **6** The weather was better the next morning **7** I couldn't get another flight. **8** Nikoleta came to our office a week later

3

2 ~~for establishing~~ to establish / in order to establish / so as to establish **3** promoting their brand. ~~Because~~ , because they already have **4** ~~for~~ to / in order to / so as to reduce costs **5** They have done this ~~as so~~ so as to avoid

4

2 The company has chosen a brand which suggests quality, (in order) to appeal to high-income groups.
3 Gas Co. offers a range of different price options (in order) to ensure best value for consumers.
4 We always give returning customers good discounts, so as not to / in order not to lose them to the competition.
5 Could you give us a reference number, so that we can refer to it in our documentation? (the subject is different in both sentences so *in order to / to-* infinitive are not possible)
6 You should liaise with Mona, so as not to / in order not to duplicate work.

5

2 f **3** h **4** i **5** a **6** b **7** c **8** e **9** g

6

2 otherwise / or else **3** In that case / In which case **4** seeing that / given that **5** given that / seeing that **6** In which case / In that case **7** or else / otherwise

Speaking strategies 10

Introductory exercise

In sentence **a** the speaker uses precise times and measurements. In sentence **b** the speaker uses vague expressions: *about 20 or so kilometres* (= not exactly 20 but something like 20); *about half past three-ish / around four* (= not exactly at 3:30 and 4:00, but just before or just after) Spoken English, especially informal spoken English, is full of vague expressions you can use when you can't be or don't need to be precise.

1 a

2 just over **3** or so **4** or thereabouts **5** about **6** just before **7** about **8** Somewhere in the region of **9** Around about **10** Roughly **11** A couple of **12** a few **13** Approximately **14** Loads! **15** About **16** or so

2

1 b in the region of
2 a in excess of **b** upwards of
3 a A great many **b** A large number of
4 a a great deal of time **b** some time

3

2 sort of / kind of silver and grey / silver and greyish **3** silvery/ silverish grey **4** largeish **5** Happyish **6** sort of nice / kind of nice / niceish

Test 10

1

2 who **3** which (you cannot use *that* in a non-defining relative clause) **4** who (you must use a relative pronoun in a non-defining relative clause) **5** which (*discounts* are things not people) **6** – / who (*who* is the object of a defining relative clause) **7** whose **8** which/what (the relative pronoun is the subject of a defining relative clause)

2

2 working **3** that/which **4** that/which **5** where **6** held **7** showing **8** which/that **9** which/that **10** whom **11** which/ that **12** who/which/that **13** who **14** which/that **15** whose **16** which

3 a

2 There are many big employers locally and quite a lot of smaller factories as well. **3** Some companies get involved in the area and also sponsor or support local charities. **4** Some talented local students find jobs easily. However, it's harder for older people to get a job. **5** They are often not even asked to interview some companies despite having more experience.

b

2 Sorry, but we couldn't continue working while we were waiting for these parts.
3 We waited all day, and eventually they arrived at 6 pm.
4 We installed them as quickly as possible, but afterwards we realised we still needed another part.
5 We worked for eight hours on that order and in the meantime three more big orders came in.

4

2 b **3** a **4** a **5** a **6** b

Recording script

1.1

1 What do you do?
2 Who do you work for?
3 Is your office near your home?
4 How many offices does your company have?
5 Where do you work?
6 Do you like your job?
7 How often do you travel?
8 How many days' holiday do you get?

2.1

1 Are you enjoying your job at the moment? Is it going well?
2 What projects are you working on at the moment?
3 Are you hoping to get promoted soon?
4 Are your colleagues learning English too?
5 Is anyone in your department looking for a new job?
6 How is your company doing this year?
7 Is it achieving its goals?
8 What is your company investing in?
9 Is your boss making any major changes this year?
10 Is he or she running your department well?

3.1

Market share of one of the world's top mobile phone makers, FinTel, is increasing faster than ever before. Meanwhile, its rival, WestCom, is expecting a second-quarter loss due to poor sales.

US-based WestCom is losing market share in several regions, including Europe and Asia. FinTel, which sells more than one in three of all mobile phones sold globally, has taken over much of this market.

'FinTel has a very strong product mix, and now there is a good opportunity for FinTel to consolidate its position as market leader,' according to FIM Securities analyst, Jeremy Hilton.

Weak sales in Asia and Europe this quarter are giving investors a real headache. 'WestCom's market share is falling rapidly and it could continue. As it falls, FinTel is benefiting from the market share that WestCom has lost,' said Danske Markets analyst, Thomas Simonsen.

4.1

… and as I'm sure you're all aware, over the past few years Eastern Water has diversified into other areas, including waste management and renewable energy.

In terms of our core business, I'm pleased to announce we've just completed the acquisition of Aqua NE, an American water company that has been supplying the consumers of New England since 1950. Eastern Water and Aqua NE have been working together closely for three years – we've already exchanged executives a few times!

Im personally very proud of this acquisition, our first step into the US market. Several other British water companies have looked into the US market, but none of them has ever taken it very seriously. With this acquisition, Eastern Water has now moved from being a regional-based company to being an international company. It hasn't been easy, but it has been exciting.

The water business has had its problems in recent years, but I think we've learned a lot from those problems.

SS 1.1

1 Basically, I think we should change the annual performance reviews.
2 You see, personally I'd say that they're not really effective in my opinion.
3 To be honest, the formal interview is a very artificial situation, I would say.
4 Really, twelve months is a long time between reviews, in my opinion.
5 In fact, as far as I'm concerned, as managers, we should always be looking at staff performance.
6 I would have thought that we should review performance monthly, to be honest.
7 Fortunately, staff tell me they'd prefer that too. As a matter of fact, some people ask for more feedback.
8 Obviously, I feel it would be better if we supervised staff more closely.
9 To be honest, as far as I'm concerned, the annual review is embarrassing for staff and managers who have a more informal relationship the rest of the year.
10 And I'd say, clearly some people exaggerate their achievements so they get good reviews. And then other people don't like to boast, so unfortunately, they don't do so well, of course.

SS 1.2

1 We need to cut down on travel costs.
2 We can use video conferencing. It's just as good.
3 We don't need to go to the branches to talk.
4 Travel is bad for the environment.
5 You waste so much time travelling.
6 People see travel as a mini-holiday.

5.1

PA: I wanted to book a return flight from London to Paris for two people.
AGENT: When would you like to travel?
PA: We were hoping to go on Tuesday the 21st, but we were wondering if we could book different days coming back – the 23rd for one and the 28th for the other.
AGENT: No problem. What time did you want to travel?
PA: We need to be there for a ten o'clock meeting on Tuesday and we were thinking we might leave the returns open. Is that possible?

AGENT: Of course. There's a flight out which would get you there for 9 am.

PA: We wanted to go business class. How much would that be?

AGENT: £332 per person each way. How did you want to pay?

PA: By credit card. Also, I was wondering if you could add these air miles onto my frequent flyer card?

AGENT: Certainly. I'll book the flights for you now. What were the names of the people travelling?

6.1

1 How many companies have you worked for?
2 What subject did you study at university or college?
3 How many jobs did you apply for when you left university or college?
4 When did you start working for this company?
5 Has your company expanded since you joined them?
6 Have you been working on any interesting projects this year?
7 Have you ever spoken at a conference? If so, what did you talk about?
8 Have you had a pay rise this year? If so, how much did you get?
9 How much time have you spent abroad in your working life so far?
10 Is this the first time you have studied another language?

7.1

1

In October 2006, Voltra International was in trouble. The price of raw materials had been rising steadily, its sales had been falling and the company's shares had already dropped in value by 30%. When the board introduced an emergency budget in January 2007, few people expected that it would transform things so quickly, but in September 2007, the company reported a record $15m profit.

2

The biotechnology industry grew out of university laboratories in the 1980s. The first successful gene transfer took place in the early 1970s, and by the end of the decade some pharmaceutical companies had started mass-producing some proteins. These later became the first drugs of the biotechnology industry. By the 1980s, scientists had become aware of the commercial potential of their work, and many had left the universities to set up their own companies.

3

In 2002, the country's economy looked very unstable. It had a budget deficit of 14% of GDP, high inflation and slow growth, and one of the highest unemployment rates in the OECD. By 2005, things had improved: government measures had cut the budget deficit to 7% of GDP, the inflation rate had gone down to 1.6% and was one of the lowest in the OECD.

8.1

Originally, only computer experts had some sort of tape drive in their home computer and backed up their hard drives. Other computer users wouldn't back up as they didn't know how to. And it wasn't relevant for people using computers at work, as their important data used to be on an office server. At most, people would occasionally save some of their important files on a floppy disc or CD.

So what has changed and why is it so important to back up your computer now? Firstly, we all used to work at large desktop computers, but now many people have laptops and the chances of them getting damaged are high. Secondly, hard drives are now much bigger than they used to be, and contain far too much data to store on CDs or DVDs. For example, we used to store a few favourite photos in albums, but these days we all have thousands of photos stored on our computers. Some of our most important memories are often stored on our hard drive. Thirdly, the number of people using computers, especially children, has risen dramatically in the past decade. Before then, children never used to do homework on a computer, they always wrote it. Today, the home computer is essential for completing homework, and backing up regularly makes sure this work isn't lost.

Today I want to talk to you about continuous back-up protection systems …

SS 2.1

1 Well, anyway, it was good to talk to you, Mick. I'll get back to you.
2 What about you, Hilda? What do you think we should do?
3 Getting back to health and safety, what should we do about the smell in the storeroom?
4 Good to see you all here today. Right then. So. Let's get started, shall we?
5 Well, thanks for your time, all of you. Maybe we can have another call on Monday?
6 How's it going, Oliver? Horrible weather, isn't it? Busy day?

9.1

So, how's the economy? I mean, what's inflation going to do over the next year?

YOU:

I see. And how about house prices – are they going to go up or down?

YOU:

Uh huh. I guess it's the same for interest rates too, right?

YOU:

Do you think unemployment is going to rise here?

YOU:

And how's your company doing? Are you going to have a difficult year next year?

YOU:

What investment plans do you have?

YOU:

Hmm. Interesting. And your own job? Do you feel you're developing – like, are you going to stay with the company or change jobs?

YOU:

Uh huh. Do you think you're going to get a pay rise or be promoted any time soon?

YOU:

I see. Well, I'm looking for a new person for the Madrid office. Think you might be interested?

10.1

My presentation will focus on our online sales strategy and will cover five main areas. It'll take about 45 minutes. In the first part we'll deal with why we needed a website. Secondly, I'll show you who designed the website. Then, I'll outline some of the technical problems we had. After that we'll look at the online sales so far. Finally, I'll sum up and I'll make some recommendations for the future development of the site. I'll answer any questions at the end of my presentation.

11.1

SIMONE: Are you OK? You're staring into space.

KARL: Sorry, I was just daydreaming about my holiday next week. I can't wait. This time next week I'll be flying to Mexico with my wife.

SIMONE: Wow, that sounds great! Where will you be staying?

KARL: We'll be staying with some friends near Mexico City for the first week, and then in Cancún for the second.

SIMONE: And do you have any particular plans for your trip?

KARL: Yes, we'll be doing a lot of sightseeing. Our friends will be taking us to see the Mayan pyramids – Palenque, Chichén Itzá and places like that. I've always wanted to see them.

SIMONE: Yes, me too. Lucky you! And what are your plans for Cancún?

KARL: Well, I'll be trying lots of different water sports but my wife won't be joining me. She prefers sunbathing!

SIMONE: Well, I'll be thinking about you while I'm stuck here working. I'm so jealous!

12.1

LYDIA: Andreas, what do you think growth is likely to be in your sector this year?

ANDREAS: Well, low interest rates are expected to stimulate consumer confidence by the second half of this year, so we're pretty optimistic in the medium term. But in the short term I think we'll continue to see a slight drop in the market, and in the immediate future I think we need to continue to be very careful to minimise risk for investors.

LYDIA: And what about the general financial picture in the foreseeable future? What's your view?

ANDREAS: Well, after a difficult start to the year, I think that things are likely to improve going forward. And actually, looking ahead, there is every reason to be optimistic about the general global situation. In the long term it's harder to predict, but I'm hopeful that the situation will continue to improve.

LYDIA: Well, it's good to hear that you're generally optimistic.

ANDREAS: Yes, I am.

SS 3.1

MIGUEL: It's a bit disappointing. I don't really like it. Do you?

ELENA: No. Not really.

MIGUEL: I just feel that as publicity it's not really projecting the image we want.

ELENA: I know. I think it looks a bit old-fashioned.

MIGUEL: It's sort of weird – it kind of looks like it's from the 1980s.

ELENA: Perhaps that's deliberate. It's called 'retro'.

MIGUEL: You're probably right.

ELENA: The marketing message isn't very clear.

MIGUEL: Yeah. Are the photos slightly out of focus?

ELENA: Yes, they are – a little bit.

MIGUEL: We maybe need to get some alternative designs.

SS 3.2

Have you got a minute? I just wanted to talk to you about Hannah. Maybe this is nothing to worry about, but I mean she used to be extremely efficient. And lately she's – well, if I'm totally honest, she's become a bit absent-minded. She's just so easily distracted, you know. Her mind is not on the job at all. But she's such a sensitive person – she really gets upset if anyone criticises her. I really don't want to take disciplinary action, but I don't know what to do.

13.1

1 I'll carry one of them.
2 Will you be able to speak at the sales conference?
3 Could you give me a price for a business-class flight to Bangkok please?
4 May I have a room with a sea view please?
5 Yes, of course you can.
6 Would you be able to attend our group meeting today?
7 Can you come to our showroom personally?
8 I'm sorry, but I'm not able to offer credit.

14.1

MANAGER: We want to pay our staff more money without increasing their salaries. Have you got any ideas?

COLLEAGUE: Why not introduce a bonus scheme?

MANAGER: It'll take too long. I mean, the results aren't out until the new year.

COLLEAGUE: How about starting it in January?

MANAGER: Well, maybe. Anyway, how do you think it should work?

COLLEAGUE: Why don't we link it to staff performance?

MANAGER: Mmm, I suppose that's the best option. How do you think we should begin?

COLLEAGUE: What about talking to the staff representatives as soon as possible?

MANAGER: What do you mean by as soon as possible?

COLLEAGUE: Let's arrange a meeting for next week, say Tuesday.

MANAGER: OK, if you think that's manageable. One more thing. Do you think we should announce this yet?

COLLEAGUE: If I were you, I'd wait until after the first meeting.

MANAGER: I agree. OK, we'll talk about this again tomorrow morning, shall we?

MANAGER: We want to pay our staff more money without increasing their salaries. Have you got any ideas?

YOU:

MANAGER: It'll take too long. I mean the results aren't out until the new year.

YOU:

MANAGER: Well, maybe. Anyway, how do you think it should work?

YOU:

MANAGER: Mmm, I suppose that's the best option. How do you think we should begin?

YOU:

MANAGER: What do you mean by as soon as possible?

YOU:

MANAGER: OK, if you think that's manageable. One more thing. Do you think we should announce this yet?

YOU:

MANAGER: I agree. OK, we'll talk about this again tomorrow morning, shall we?

15.1

We all have some idea of what a bad customer experience is. You need to find out the right customer experience that we want to deliver in our stores. You can think about this in the existing stores. And you might want to consider the new stores too, you know, in terms of training. Jean, you told us about the lady who set up the Excel store chain and who also worked at Prima. Do you want to invite her to talk to us about her own experience? Then you can all come up with some ideas about what the customer experience should be. Can you organise that for the next meeting? In fact, you'd better make a note of that, please, Chris. Then finally, don't forget, everyone needs to attend the planning meeting tomorrow at three.

16.1

SUZIE: This meeting shouldn't last long. It's a short agenda. Ah, here we are, room 4B. That's funny. The door's locked. It should be open. Robert must have the key. He was using the room yesterday afternoon.

ALEX: Sarah might have it. I thought I saw her with it earlier.

SUZIE: I know she used the room first thing this morning, but she said she'd leave it open. It could be in my office.

ALEX: She may still have it. Why don't you call her?

SUZIE: … She says it should be in her desk drawer. I'll go and look. It shouldn't take long … Found it! Now, shall we make a start?

SS 4.1

GRAHAM: Lost something, Tanya?

TANYA: Can't find my agenda. Must be on my desk.

GRAHAM: Terry made some extra copies. Want one?

TANYA: Oh, yes. Thanks.

GRAHAM: Right. Who'll start off? Archie? Got any technical problems to talk about? What about the databases and the emailing problem?

ARCHIE: Yes, OK, might as well just mention that. Something to do with the Filewiz programme. Trouble is, um, don't know what exactly.

GRAHAM: Mm. Maybe it's something to ask Gale in IT to come and look at?

ARCHIE: Could be, yeah. Depends whether it's a software problem or a server issue. Gale just deals with software, really.

TANYA: Michaela deals with server problems these days, doesn't she?

ARCHIE: Yeah. Think so. Not sure, actually. They're always changing people around in IT.

GRAHAM: Yeah. Must be really confusing for you when you don't know who does what!

ARCHIE: Yeah.

17.1

MARGARET: This is the procedure. If two calls come in at the same time, pick up the internal call first and put the other call on hold. If there is a call waiting, the light flashes.

SAM: What do I do if there is an external call for someone in the office?

MARGARET: If you get an external call for Joe Johnson, for example, you have to call Joe's extension number. When Joe answers, you usually say who's calling, but if there are other phone calls waiting, don't waste time telling him. Just put the call through.

18.1

CRISTINA: why do you think the project was so unsuccessful?

JEFF: Looking back, there were so many mistakes. If we'd started the project in January instead of May, we would have been able to launch at the right time for the buying season.

CRISTINA: OK, but I heard that there were delays in sending out stock even once the project was established.

JEFF: Well, yes, we had lots of problems organising the packing line.

CRISTINA: I see. Would you have got more stock out into the market on time if you'd organised the packing line better?

JEFF: Maybe. I think that's something that we should look at in future projects.

CRISTINA: What about the communication problems? Would it have helped if more people had taken Spanish classes before moving to the Guatemala office?

JEFF: Well, as you know, I studied Spanish for several months before moving. I certainly think it would've been difficult to communicate with my clients if I hadn't known any Spanish.

CRISTINA: It's really important to learn from our mistakes this time. If we'd learnt the lessons from our previous ventures in Latin America, we wouldn't have had so many problems establishing the business in Guatemala.

JEFF: Yes, if we'd had more support from our other offices, the project probably would've succeeded.

19.1

OFFICE SERVICE MANAGER: We take the safety of our staff very seriously here at the bank and the security of all our operations is very important to us.

NEW EMPLOYEE: Uh huh. I see there are a lot of cameras around.

OSM: Yes, the building is monitored by CCTV. The lifts are monitored by cameras, too.

NE: Well, that's worth knowing – I mean it's good to know you're always being watched. Um… And the security staff at the door are fairly strict, I've noticed.

OSM: That's right. All employees, um, every employee is searched by security staff both when they enter and when they leave the building.

NE: Yeah, I've been searched every time I've been here, so I suppose you're pretty strict on who comes in.

OSM: Right. We have to be very, um, careful about visitors. Their identities are always checked by the receptionists. Visitors aren't allowed into the building without a member of staff.

NE: That makes sense.

OSM: One of our more controversial safety measures is drugs testing.

NE: Yes, I heard about that. Is everyone tested?

OSM: Well, they could be, it depends. Members of staff are tested randomly for drugs by an outside agency.

NE: Right …

OSM: And our drivers are tested for drugs and alcohol weekly – they have to be safe, obviously.

NE: Of course. And what about data security?

OSM: Well, that's not my field – the IT group deals with that. I'm told that it's a secure system. I mean, for example, all the computer files are scanned by antivirus software every hour.

NE: Every hour?

OSM: Yes, and the data on the servers is backed up daily.

NE: I see.

OSM: So, what else can I tell you? Um, oh, fire alarms. The fire alarm is tested by someone in my department – Office Services – every Friday.

NE: Every Friday?

OSM: Yes, at 11 o'clock in the morning.

NE: I see, so let's hope there's never a fire on a Friday morning at 11.

OSM: And as a manager you need to know that you have to train your team in fire safety procedures.

NE: I have to?

OSM: Yes, that's your responsibility. And staff are tested on the procedures regularly.

NE: Hmm.

20.1

JOURNALIST: What are the main issues you deal with in the training you do?

JAKOB: Well, project management is very complex. It's mostly about asking the right questions. Before a project, you have to ask whether it can be done. Is it likely that everything will be completed within the timescale? What resources will be needed? And so on.

JOURNALIST: Yes, and even if people prepare before a project, the follow-up may not be done.

JAKOB: Yes, the follow-up mustn't be forgotten. We train people to ask the questions: How could things be improved next time? What ought to be changed in the future? Could the next project be completed more quickly? Which people should be informed of the results? So, you can see, there are a lot of complex issues.

SS 5.1

CUSTOMER: Could you explain the different car insurance policies you offer?

CLERK: Well, there are three basic types. OK? First, there's third-party insurance.

CUSTOMER: What does that mean, exactly?

CLERK: Basically, it means you're insured for damage to other people's cars. Then the second type is third-party, fire and theft.

CUSTOMER: Could you explain that a bit more for me?

CLERK: It's the same as the first type, but you're also insured if your car is stolen or if it's damaged in a fire.

CUSTOMER: Perhaps I've misunderstood you? So with the second type my car is insured against some things?

CLERK: That's right. And finally, there's fully comprehensive insurance.

CUSTOMER: I'm not sure I know what you mean. Could you explain that?

CLERK: It means you're insured against damage to your own and other people's cars. It basically covers everything. Why don't you give me your name and phone number and I can arrange for an agent to call you with more details?

CUSTOMER: I'm afraid there's been a slight misunderstanding. I'm not ready to buy a policy. I was just interested in the types there are.

21.1

1 Who are you working for at the moment?
2 What projects are you involved in?
3 How many jobs have you applied for in the last ten years?
4 Which colleagues do you have lunch with?
5 Have you ever complained about a colleague?
6 Who did you complain to?
7 Does your salary depend on your performance?

22.1

NARRATOR: Sure.
SPEAKER: We met in Paris, didn't we?

NARRATOR: Unsure.
SPEAKER: We met in Paris, didn't we?

NARRATOR: Sure.
SPEAKER: She's not in our group, is she?

NARRATOR: Unsure.
SPEAKER: She's not in our group, is she?

22.2

1 You're working on the Westin project, aren't you?
2 We're not using this version of the spreadsheet any more, are we?
3 Laila's got a new job, hasn't she?
4 We could send them our latest report, couldn't we?
5 They said they would finish by 4:30, didn't they?

22.3

A: She's the Human Resources Manager, is she?
B: No, she's the Financial Controller.

A: Paul Summers owns the company, does he?
B: Yes, he actually started it in 1997.

22.4

1 You work with Charles, do you?
2 This is your copy of the business plan, is it?
3 They sold their shares in Zetac, did they?
4 This voice recorder has a USB connection, does it?
5 The design team have sent us a drawing, have they?
6 We can get a price quote, can we?

23.1

1

A: I was just down in HR and Pam was telling me about the new training programme. She was saying that all members of staff are now entitled to five days' training a year.
B: Oh, it's funny you should mention that, because someone in Production was asking me about that the other day. I didn't know what to tell them as it was the first I'd heard about it.
A: Yeah, well as I was telling Pam – it's long overdue.

2

A: My bank manager was saying that the branch is very involved with the local community. She was saying it's so important these days.
B: Well, you remember I was telling you about that event I went to on social responsibility? All the speakers were saying it's high on the agenda in all the big companies these days.

3

A: How much are we paying for buildings insurance?
B: A lot! We're thinking about changing our insurer next year. Leslie was saying it's a good idea to shop around and get several quotes. He was saying we could probably get it much cheaper than we're paying now.
A: That's exactly what I was telling him last week but he wouldn't listen to me then!

4

A: John was asking me about the GHI exhibition. He wanted to know if we were going this year.
B: I don't know. Someone was telling me how expensive it was to exhibit there last year with the number of people attending.

24.1

1 How many hours a day do you work?
2 Who are your biggest clients?
3 Who set up the company?
4 Why did you join the company?
5 What do you like most about your work?
6 Do you live near your work?
7 Did you go to university or college?
8 How long have you worked for the company?

SS 6.1

A: Let's meet at ten o'clock.
B: Ten o'clock? Ten o'clock, did you say?

A: Let's meet at ten o'clock.
B: OK. Ten o'clock, then.

SS 6.2

1

ALISON: Did you send an agenda?
GREG: Sorry? Did I send an agenda? Yeah. I emailed it last night. Didn't you get it?
ALISON: Oh, I haven't checked my email this morning yet.

2

ALISON: You know, I don't think I've got all the papers here. I might want to print a few documents. Do you mind?
GREG: Sorry? The line just went a bit funny. Can you say that again?
ALISON: Do you mind if I print a few documents?
GREG: No, no, no. Go ahead. We'll have a chat while you're doing that.

3

JENNY: Did you hear about T&G Electronics? I heard that they're going bust.
GREG: What did you say?
JENNY: T&G. They're going out of business. They're getting rid of people and closing the head office, and I heard that their partners in Ireland are in the same position.
GREG: Pardon?
JENNY: Their Irish partners – they're closing down, too.
GREG: Is that the company that Michael Kelly went to work for?
JENNY: Yeah. That's right.

4

GREG: OK, let's start. Jenny, are you going to make an announcement about the new performance review procedures?
JENNY: Am I going to make an announcement, did you say?
GREG: Yes.
JENNY: Well, I hadn't thought of doing so today. I'd prefer to wait until we have the new forms printed up next month.
GREG: OK, well, let's leave that till next time, then.
JENNY: Sorry?
GREG: We can come back to it next time.
JENNY: OK, thanks.

5

LEO: The next thing is pretty serious – it's about IT security. Um, it sounds, from what our IT people are saying, that we've had a suspected attack by a hacker.
GREG: A hacker? Wow. That's pretty serious.
LEO: What they think happened is that someone got through to a secure database via the website, so the website and all our databases are now closed and out of use.
GREG: Sorry, I missed that. Does that mean that we can't use the system?
LEO: Not for the next two days.

6

ALISON: OK, I'm going to look at the spreadsheet on my laptop, which is plugged in over here. If I speak like this, can you all hear?
GREG: Yes.
LEO: Yes.

ALISON: Jenny, can you hear me too?
JENNY: What?
ALISON: Can you hear me?
JENNY: Not very well. Do I need to turn up the volume?
ALISON: Can you say that again?
GREG: Is it my volume that needs to go up?
ALISON: Probably.

SS 6.3

1 I just wondered if you sent an agenda.
   YOU:

   Did you send an agenda?
2 I might want to print a few documents. Do you mind?
   YOU:

   Can I print some documents?
3 Did you hear about the closure?
   YOU:

   Did you hear that they're closing the head offices?
4 Are you going to talk about performance reviews at the next meeting?
   YOU:

   Are you going to talk about performance reviews at the next meeting?
5 The intranet is shut down.
   YOU:

   We can't use the intranet. It's not working.
6 Can you hear me at the back of the room?
   YOU:

   I said, 'Can you hear me?'

SS 6.4

1 Now first of all I'd like to talk about the auditor's visit.
   YOU:
2 They'll need six days to do a complete audit.
   YOU:
3 We hope they'll be able to start on 22 March.
   YOU:
4 I'm going to let them work in the first floor conference room.
   YOU:
5 They're going to check all staff expenses again.
   YOU:
6 Last year they found £800 of fraudulent claims.
   YOU:

25.1

BOB: I wanted to make the point that we shouldn't launch in April – there are too many other things happening. I think we should delay until May. We can produce the brochure in January, samples in February or March, then be ready to ship in May. That gives us plenty of time. If we haven't prepared the launch properly and have to cancel, that would be far worse.

ANDREW: OK, thanks, Bob. That sounds sensible. All agreed? Right. Vanessa, anything you want to report on the financial side?

VANESSA: I wanted to talk about our investments in Zamrac. If we sell now, we may be at a disadvantage. I think we should continue to buy over the next few months and then sell in the autumn when we have a clearer picture. If we all agree, I can confirm with the brokers.

ANDREW: Right. Well, any comments?

26.1

1 My job involves writing software and training programmers. How about you? What does your job involve?
2 No one ever taught me to type properly. When did you learn to type?
3 My boss often wants me to buy presents for her family. What do you think about that? Is it OK for her to ask?
4 My boss is great. I can't imagine working for anyone else. Is there something you can't imagine doing at work?
5 On bad days I can't help thinking I'm in the wrong job. Do you ever get days like that? What job would you prefer to do?
6 You should keep quiet, even if you feel like complaining about your job to your boss. Do you ever feel like complaining about your job?
7 I never seem to get round to throwing out old papers and files. Do you have jobs like that, little things that you never seem to do? What do you avoid doing?
8 I often help my colleagues sort out their personal problems. What kinds of things do you help your colleagues do? Have you ever had to help a colleague in that way?

27.1

1 What's the biggest contract your company has taken on recently?
2 What kinds of things do you put off doing at work?
3 Has your company ever taken over another company?
4 Is your company going to set up a branch in another country?
5 Is it a good idea for businesses to cut back their training during a recession?
6 What do you think people should watch out for when buying an insurance policy?
7 Do you know anyone who has ever been laid off? Why and when did this happen?
8 Has demand for your products ever dropped off? If so, why?
9 Have you ever turned down the offer of a job? Why?
10 What kinds of things would put you off applying for a particular job?

28.1

With most of the companies I work for, I'll ask someone to think about this question: if you could put one message directly into the mind of a prospective customer, what would it be? After thinking for a moment, they'll mention something. Then I'll talk to a different person and I'll get a different answer. In fact, I get as many different answers as there are people working for the company! That's bad.

In general, the only messages that customers are interested in are short, powerful and repeated. So every single employee has to focus on what the company's message is, and then they have to take responsibility for sharing it – in conversation, on the company website, in writing and on the phone. Consistently.

This is called positioning. It means thinking about your customers, your competitors, and your goods or services while you look for the most powerful words to describe your business. It's worth it: good positioning may improve your marketing for years!

SS 7.1

Let's have a look at the objectives of an effective PR strategy. Firstly, PR adds to the good image and reputation of the organisation – organisations can use PR to send out positive messages about their activities and performance. Secondly, with good PR you attract and keep not only good customers, but also other parties such as employees, shareholders, etc. These other parties are the people that the organisation interacts with – I'll come back to that with an example in a minute. Thirdly, PR also deals with negative publicity, especially when something goes wrong, and can help overcome false ideas people might have about the organisation. Finally, you can also create good relations with the wider community.

SS 7.2

LUCY: Right. Let's start. First of all let's welcome Bryan Murphy from Dublin to our meeting. Now, there are several things we need to do. First and foremost, we must find out what Irish customers really want. That's the most important thing of all. As you know, there are two reasons for opening up in Ireland: A, it's got a good economy, and B, Dublin is a great city to work in.

JAMES: Before we go on, I just want to raise the concerns over the Ireland plan that we discussed at the last meeting. So, first there was the issue of health insurance, secondly public holidays in Ireland, thirdly Irish tax laws and lastly the exchange rate. We've looked at all four and now at last I think we've solved all the problems we raised in that meeting.

LUCY: That's good to hear. Now Bryan, at first we found it difficult to make contacts in the west of Ireland, but we've made lots of progress since you joined the team. Thank you for all your help. And I'd also like to thank Benny and Hilda for getting the Irish website ready so quickly, and last but not least, thanks to Joseph for doing the photographs. Thank you, everybody. Dublin, here we come!

29.1

1

CUSTOMER: What's on the menu today?
WAITER: Well sir, we have some lovely fresh Scottish salmon. I can also recommend the spicy tomato soup.
CUSTOMER: They sound good. I'll have the soup to start and then the salmon.

2

RECEPTIONIST: Good morning, how can I help you?
PAULA: Hello, it's Paula from Seymour Ltd. Can I just double-check our order, please?
RECEPTIONIST: Of course. You wanted fifty, black, personalised pens, didn't you?

3

SALES REP: Where's your office?
NEW CLIENT: It's on Lausanne Road, in that old, stone building – number 62.
SALES REP: Oh yes, I know it, next to the luxury sports car dealer.

4

PROPERTY DEVELOPER: So, if you look at this part of the diagram, you can see we've got a thousand square metres of storage space in the basement. Above that there's a huge shopping area and behind the shop we have the underground customer car park.
COLLEAGUE: Sounds good, doesn't it?
PD: Yeah, and don't forget the busy pedestrian area out front. Thousands of potential customers per hour!

30.1

DAVID: Lena, tell me a little bit about recent projects you've been working on.
LENA: Well, basically, we've created a system for monitoring attitudes, preferences and needs across Europe, which manufacturers of fast-moving consumer goods, such as cosmetics or paper products, can use. Hopefully, this will give them reliable information to support their products.
DAVID: But customer attitudes towards fast-moving consumer goods have probably been tested on a country-by-country basis in Europe many times before now, haven't they?
LENA: Yes, they have. But in the early days market researchers tried to identify the differences between one country and another. Nowadays, the fast moving-consumer goods sector is actually looking at the similarities with our friends across the rest of Europe. That's why, for example, we've seen pan-European and global marketing and advertising campaigns from the leading brands.
DAVID: Yes, there have certainly been changes in advertising policy. But is there an advantage in targeting a marketing campaign at just one country, perhaps?
LENA: Yes, maybe. But I think that what our research really shows is that we have to think very carefully. Obviously, we are now one trading community in Europe, but there are definitely still some important differences between the countries.

31.1

PERSONNEL MANAGER: So what do you think? I mean, they're both good but I think Gisela is the better candidate. Paola was not as impressive as Gisela.
SALES DIRECTOR: Um, I think they're about equal. For me, Paola was just as strong as Gisela.
PM: But Paola's not as old as Gisela and she's less experienced.
SD: True, but on the other hand Gisela's qualifications aren't as good as Paola's. Paola hasn't worked for as long as Gisela, but Gisela is less well-qualified than Paola.
PM: How about personality? I mean Gisela wasn't as shy and quiet as Paola.
SD: Well, Paola wasn't as talkative as Gisela, but I actually think Gisela was less confident. And Paola's test results were also as high as Gisela's. I'd like to offer her the position.

31.2

PM: So what do you think? I mean, they're both good but I think Gisela is the better candidate. Paola was not as impressive as Gisela.

YOU:

PM: But Paola's not as old as Gisela and she's less experienced.

YOU:

PM: How about personality? I mean Gisela wasn't as shy and as quiet Paola.

YOU:

31.3

YOU:

SD: Um, I think they're about equal. For me, Paola was just as strong as Gisela.

YOU:

SD: True, but on the other hand Gisela's qualifications aren't as good as Paola's. Paola hasn't worked for as long as Gisela, but Gisela is less well-qualified than Paola.

YOU:

SD: Well, Paola wasn't as talkative as Gisela, but I actually think Gisela was less confident. And Paola's test results were also as high as Gisela's. I'd like to offer her the position.

32.1

Welcome to European Business Today. Europe is one of the world's most attractive markets and many businesses from outside the EU have branches or manufacturing bases here. But where should a new business locate itself? Where are the best places to live? Let's consider the options.

Well, if you're looking for a country which will give you a big domestic market, then you're probably looking at Germany. Germany has the largest population in the EU, so lots of customers close to home. However, the downside is that labour costs are pretty high there, along with France and Austria. German, Austrian and French workforces are the most expensive in the EU25.

If your company makes products aimed at an older market, however, you might well think of setting up in Italy, because Italy has the oldest population in Europe and the second-oldest population in the world after Japan.

If you want a long life (and we all do!), then you should consider moving to France, because the French live the longest in the EU. French men live an average of 75.5 years and women 83, putting them well ahead of other European countries.

France and Italy are good places to go if you're wanting an early retirement as they have the lowest retirement ages in the EU.

In terms of lifestyle there are other factors to consider, such as the standard of living. In terms of per capita GDP, Luxembourg is the wealthiest country in the EU, so that is one option.

The happiest cities in the European Union are Copenhagen, Luxembourg and Tallinn, whereas the least satisfied citizens are to be found in Athens, Bucharest and London.

In terms of getting around the city, the public transportation systems run most efficiently in Munich, Helsinki, Hamburg and Vienna.

People in Denmark, Sweden and Finland said they felt most secure. So Scandinavia is a good place to live as these are some of the least corrupt countries in the world.

SS 8.1

1 I've failed one of my accountancy exams.
2 Three new electronics factories have opened just in that one small town this year!
3 Right. I'm setting off for Madrid now.
4 We're going to have to close some branches – we're losing money.
5 We've just heard we've won a design gold medal!
6 We won't be able to exhibit at Expoenergy this year. The dates don't fit.

SS 8.2

1 A: So, shall we say 4 pm on Wednesday 26th for our next conference call?
   B: That's great.
2 A: So I can contact you on 745 538, and that's a direct line?
   B: That's right.
3 A: Sales are up for the third quarter running.
   B: That's good news.
4 A: I'm afraid delivery is going to be delayed by a day.
   B: That's OK. It's not a problem.
5 A: Customer support is just as important as selling.
   B: That's true.
6 A: They're giving me a lovely big new office all to myself!
   B: That's great!
7 A: OK, so we'll have two more meetings before the launch date.
   B: That's fine.
8 A: So the current rate is $1.45 to the pound, yeah?
   B: That's correct.

33.1

ARIANNA: Would you like to share a bottle of mineral water?
BRONA: Yes, OK. Can I get a glass of orange juice, too?
ARIANNA: Sure. Now, I'd like to ask you for a piece of advice, actually. I've had a bit of luck on the stock market and I've made a bit of cash, and I want to start my own company.
BRONA: And you need a bit of help from me?
ARIANNA: Yeah. I've developed a piece of software that searches the web. I'd like you to help me do a bit of advertising. We could both make a bit of money on it and have a bit of fun, too.

34.1

1 A: It took ages to get the photocopier repaired.
   B: I know. We're trying to cut maintenance costs and that means delays.

2 A: Sorry I'm late. I had to finish the marketing report you asked for.

B: That's OK. I had loads of emails to deal with.

3 A: What's the best time to discuss your plans for tomorrow's presentation?

B: How about Tuesday at 3 o'clock?

4 A: I've just spoken to Parkers and $60 is the lowest price they'll give us.

B: Well, prices are going up everywhere. I can't say I'm surprised.

5 A: I need help with finding our delivery schedule. Where can I find it on the system?

B: Didn't you receive the information I emailed you yesterday?

35.1

SAM: OK, well, I see that we've got some time left, so do we have any other business? Or would you like to go and get some lunch?

CAROL: I have an item. David, can we have some feedback on the new catalogue?

DAVID: It's a bit early to say just yet. I haven't heard any negative comments at least. But, um, actually I've got some bad news. It looks as if one of our biggest customers, DDE, is going out of business. They're not paying any suppliers by the looks of things. They're generating profit but they've got no cash.

SAM: Do they owe us any money?

DAVID: Ten thousand. And, you know, there was no warning either. I mean we haven't had any problems with them in the past. But we're going to have to make some big changes to the budget forecast.

35.2

1 Do you have much foreign currency in your wallet?
2 Do you do much travelling in your job?
3 Have you had any training this year?
4 Do you usually have enough time to have lunch?

36.1

FA: Many investors prefer to make their own investment decisions, but if you would like some help with yours, then we can certainly provide that.

CLIENT: That's great.

FA: I can assure you that my company's financial advisors are among the best in the UK. We also work well as a team, always keeping each other informed of any financial opportunities that we find.

CLIENT: That's good. Well, I have made these decisions myself in the past, but with last week's news about the problems in the stock market, I've lost confidence.

FA: Yes, many people have had the same reaction, but I'm sure we can help. First, we need to look at your attitude to risk. Do you like to take risks, or do you prefer to be safe with your money? All investors should ask themselves, 'Do my investments reflect my feelings about risk?' We all want to maximise our income from investments, but we also want to feel comfortable with how much risk we're taking, don't we?

SS 9.1

1

CHRIS: So the summary plan, the one with the objectives and so on, is almost done?

LINDSAY: Yes. I just want to add a bit more on market positioning and so forth. Then I'll email it to everyone with all the forecast documents and what have you.

CHRIS: Good. So now we can concentrate on other issues like recruiting new staff and so on.

2

JO: Hi there. So, can we have a chat about next year's conferences and things?

SAM: Yeah. I've just got all the dates and costs and stuff.

JO: Then there's the budget for the website and things like that to look at.

SAM: Yeah. We need somebody to keep it up-to-date, change the photographs and that kind of thing.

37.1

INTERVIEWER: Welcome to the topic of today's discussion, which is 'Women in the workplace'. First, I would like to ask the panel what they believe are the significant issues at this time.

CHIE: I think that in many companies male and female employees can work without discrimination. However, sometimes both male and female employees resent family-friendly policies, such as maternity leave. They feel that they are unfair to people who don't have families. I remember one manager who said that women shouldn't have a job and a family.

LISA: For me, the biggest problem at the moment is that there are still many talented women who are not being paid as much as their male colleagues. Also, women often miss out on promotion. The fact that there are very few women at senior management level makes me believe there are still too many male managers whose attitudes have not changed. I feel that it is a great waste not to make full use of the strengths of female employees.

ALINE: The first thing that needs to be done is to publicise the issue. Then we need to start working on solutions. These solutions should not be vague ideas or initiatives. Instead, it is important to set specific targets which all employers can try to meet. Then you can create a system of rewards which are given to the best employers. We should congratulate employers whose record of employing women is good.

INTERVIEWER: Well, that's a very interesting start to the discussion. Perhaps we could pick up on your point about …

38.1

RICK: I used to be a successful high flyer, but the company for whom I was working went out of business and I was made redundant. Being unemployed for a long time really destroys your confidence and I was getting to the point where I thought that I'd never get another job. Eventually, a suitable job came up near to the place I was living at the time. I went to meet the technical manager, who I got on very well with, and she offered me the job immediately.

GRAHAM: When I first started, I loved my job on the factory floor and I became very good and fast at it. Unfortunately, this meant that I was disliked by the people I worked with because they weren't as efficient as me. But on a more positive note, I was promoted several times, until there came a time when I became a full-time manager of a small section of the factory. The funny thing is that when this happens you get to a point when you don't do any technical work any more and I found myself in a situation where I didn't really have enough to do!

39.1

Improving productivity is a constant battle in business. Working longer hours is a depressing option, though many of us choose it. How can we get the same results quicker: how can we work smarter?

My advice may not be very original, but it could be useful for business people who have no time to think about their lives and working styles. First, multi-tasking. Although many people say they are good at multi-tasking, trying to do lots of things at once is distracting. Try closing your office door, diverting calls to voice mail and doing some real work. Despite making you feel busy, multi-tasking often means switching from task to task rather than making real progress.

Email is a great invention. However, it is also a great distraction. Even though it may only take up an hour or two a day, it's a significant proportion of your working time. If you double the time you spend on activities which produce real results and stop doing the others, you will double your output, despite only working for the same length of time. Concentrate your time on the customers who really matter. You might think you are treating some of your customers badly, but don't forget that 80% of your profits come from 20% of your customers.

Delegation also improves results. When delegating a task, however, it doesn't mean you can sit back and relax; get on with another task.

Working faster, identifying 80/20 tasks and delegating will all improve your efficiency. They all benefit from careful planning, though. That's my final tip.

40.1

JOHN: Focus groups are not just groups of people who answer prepared questions, then?

CLARE: No. Seeing as you want the group just to talk freely about how they use a product, it's a good idea to ask them simple, general questions first and just let them talk, otherwise you run the risk of focusing too much on your own ideas. But in the second stage it's important to test out your own ideas. In that case, you'll probably use a questionnaire. Now, seeing that a lot of people find questionnaires difficult, and given that you want to get the best out of people, it's important to allow them plenty of time to fill them in properly.

JOHN: In which case, we always have to have two main goals in planning a focus group, is that what you're saying?

CLARE: Yes. You want to collect both spontaneous comments and answers to the questions that you've prepared in advance, or else you're only doing half the job you set out to do. That's very important.

SS 10.1

1 INTERVIEWER: How long does it take you to get to work in the morning?
   MANAGER: It takes ages. Well, just over an hour.
2 INTERVIEWER: How far is it?
   MANAGER: 60 or so kilometres. Yeah, 60 or thereabouts.
3 INTERVIEWER: What time do you start work?
   MANAGER: It depends, usually about 8:30 or just before.
4 INTERVIEWER: And when do you leave usually?
   MANAGER: I usually finish at about six.
5 INTERVIEWER: How much do you think you spend a month on commuting?
   MANAGER: Somewhere in the region of €200.
6 INTERVIEWER: How many hours a week do you work, roughly?
   MANAGER: Around about 45.
7 INTERVIEWER: How many people work in your company?
   MANAGER: Roughly 560.
8 INTERVIEWER: How often do you meet with your boss?
   MANAGER: A couple of times a day, but only for a few minutes.
9 INTERVIEWER: How many emails do you get a day, would you say?
   MANAGER: Approximately 30.
10 INTERVIEWER: How much time do you spend answering them?
   MANAGER: Loads! About an hour or so every day.

SS10.2

How long does it take you to get to work in the morning?
How far is it?
What time do you start work?
And when do you leave usually?
How much do you think you spend a month on commuting?
How many hours a week do you work, roughly?
How many people work in your company?
How often do you meet with your boss?
How many emails do you get a day, would you say?
How much time do you spend answering them?

Appendices

Appendix 1 Spelling

A Verbs

A1 Present simple verbs *he/she/it*

◀ See Units 1 and 3.

most verbs	+ -s	*work – works; come – comes*
verb ends -s, -ss, -sh, -ch, -x,-z	+ -es [adds a syllable]	*watch – watches; fix – fixes*
verb ends -o	+ -es	*go – goes*
verb ends consonant + y	y → i + -es	*study – studies*
verb ends vowel + y	+ -s	*employ – employs*

⚠ *Have* and *be* are irregular.

- *I/you/we/they* **have**   *he/she/it* **has**
- *I* **am**   *you/we/they* **are**   *he/she/it* **is**

A2 -ing form

◀ See Units 2, 5, 9, 11 and 26.

most verbs	+ -ing	*work – working*
verb ends -e	remove e + -ing	*come – coming* (**but** *be – being*)
verb ends -ee	+ -ing	*see – seeing*
verb ends vowel + b, g, m, n, p, t ⚠ except if final syllable is *not* stressed	double consonant + -ing	*get – getting* *visit – visiting*
verb ends -l ⚠ North American English has one l	double l + -ing	*travel – travelling* *traveling*
verb ends in -ie	ie → y + -ing	*lie – lying*

A3 Past simple

◀ See Units 5 and 6.

most verbs	+ -ed	*work – worked*
verb ends -e	+ -d	*like – liked*
verb ends consonant + y	y → i + -ed	*try – tried*
verb ends in vowel + y ⚠ except *pay, lay, say*	+ -ed y → i + -d	*employ – employed* *paid, laid, said*
verb ends vowel + consonant ⚠ except if final syllable is *not* stressed	double consonant + -ed	*chat – chatted* *visit – visited*
verb ends -l ⚠ North American English has one l	double l + -ed	*travel – travelled* *traveled*

B Adjectives and adverbs

B1 Adverbs ending in -ly

◄ See Unit 30.

most adjectives	+ -ly	direct – directly
adjective ends -l	+ -ly	careful – carefully
adjective ends -e	+ -ly	polite – politely
adjective ends -le	e → y	simple – simply
adjective ends consonant + y	y → i + -ly	busy – busily
adjective ends -ic	+ -ally	economic – economically

B2 Comparative and superlative adjectives and adverbs

◄ See Units 31 and 32.

most words	+ -er/-est	cheap cheaper cheapest fast faster fastest
word ends -e	+ -r/-st	nice nicer nicest
word ends consonant + y	y → i + -er/-est	early earlier earliest
word ends vowel + consonant	double consonant + -er/-est	big bigger biggest

C Nouns

C1 Regular noun plurals (countable nouns only)

◄ See Unit 33.

most nouns	+ -s	car – cars; phone – phones
noun ends -s, -ss, -sh, -ch, -x, -z	+ -es [adds a syllable]	watch – watches; tax – taxes
noun ends vowel + -o	+ -s	radio – radios
noun ends consonant + o	+ -es	tomato – tomatoes
noun ends consonant + y	y → i + -es	diary – diaries
noun ends vowel + y	+ -s	day – days

C2 Irregular noun plurals

man	men
woman	women
child	children
person	people
tooth	teeth
foot	feet
life	lives
knife	knives

Appendix 2 Common prefixes and suffixes

What are prefixes and suffixes?

Prefixes come at the beginning of a word, for example *dis-* in *disagree*. Sometimes prefixes change the meaning of a word. For example, *disagree* is the opposite of *agree*.

Sometimes words with a prefix do not have an equivalent without the prefix, for example *collaborate* (there is no word *laborate*). But knowing the prefix can help you with the meaning of the word.

Suffixes come at the end of a word, for example, *-ship* in *partnership*.

Suffixes tell you what type of word it is, for example a noun, a verb, an adjective or an adverb. Words ending in *-ment*, for example, are nouns: *government*, *agreement*.

Most prefixes and suffixes are part of the word. Some are joined to the word with a hyphen, for example *anti-* in *anti-virus*.

Here are some examples of the most frequent prefixes and suffixes in spoken business English.

A Prefixes

Prefix	Meaning	Examples
anti-	against	*anti-virus (software)*
co- *(col-, com-, con-)*	with	*cooperate, co-worker* (N Am Eng) *collaborate, combine, connect*
dis-	opposite	*disadvantage, disagree, disappear*
ex-	previously	*ex-student*
il-, im-, in-, ir-	not	*illegal, impossible, indirect, irrelevant*
in-	inside, in	*involve, income, including, input*
mis-	wrongly	*misunderstand*
re-	again	*restart (a computer), resell*
super-	bigger	*supermarket, supervisor*
un-	not	*unfortunate, unlikely, unnecessary*

There are also a number of particles that work like prefixes.

down	make less	*downsize, downgrade, downtime*
out	outside	*output, outline, outcome, outlet, outsource*
over	across more than	*overnight, overview, overseas, overhead,* *overdue, overtime, overload,*
up	make better	*update, upgrade*

B Suffixes

Suffix	Type of word	Examples
-able	adjective	available, profitable, unbelievable, comfortable
-ant	noun adjective	accountant, tenant, assistant important, brilliant, relevant, significant
-cy	noun	policy, contingency, consistency, agency
-ee	noun (person)	employee, interviewee, trainee
-ful	adjective	useful, awful, successful, careful, helpful, wonderful, powerful
-hood	noun	likelihood
-ic	adjective	specific, basic, fantastic, realistic
-(ic)al	adjective	technical, critical, electrical, physical, medical
-ify	verb	identify, justify, modify, clarify
-ism	noun	criticism, tourism, mechanism
-ist	noun (person) verb	specialist, chemist assist, insist
-ise	verb noun	advertise, exercise, realise*, revise, advise, organise*, apologise* exercise, enterprise
-ive	adjective	expensive, effective, massive, active
-less	adjective	stainless, wireless, pointless, useless
-ment	noun	management, environment, development, equipment, department
-ness	noun	business, fairness, illness, awareness
-ous	adjective	various, previous, obvious, ridiculous, serious, conscious, miscellaneous, dangerous
-ship	noun	relationship, membership, ownership, partnership, dealership, leadership

*These verbs are spelt -ize in North American English.

► See Appendix 3 (North American English).

◄ See Unit 29 (Adjectives).

Appendix 3 North American English

The English grammar used in North America is basically the same as British English grammar, but there are some small differences, mostly in how often some structures are used and differences in spelling. The main ones are listed below.

A Verbs ◄ See Units 1–12.

British English	North American English
People use both negative forms of: *he/she/it's not / you/we/they're not* and *he/she/isn't / you/we/they aren't*. The *'s not / 're not* forms are more common.	People mostly use the *'s not / 're not* negative forms of *be*. *Isn't* and *aren't* are not as common, especially after pronouns.
People use the present perfect, especially for recent events, with *yet*, *already* and in questions with *ever*. *Kellie has already left.* *Have you finished your report yet?* *Have you ever seen the sales training video?*	People use the past simple even for recent events, and it can be used with *yet*, *already* and in questions with *ever*. *Kellie left already.* *Did you finish your report yet?* *Did you ever see the sales training video?*
Have got is more common than *have*. *I've got a meeting with Rosie next Tuesday.*	*Have* is more common than *have got*. *I have a degree in information management.*
The past participle of *get* is *got*. *White-collar crime has got a lot worse.*	The past participle of *get* is *gotten*. *White-collar crime has gotten a lot worse.*
People use *going to* to talk about the future and their plans. *We're going to grow our online sales.*	People also use *going to* to give directions. *You're going to make a right on Broadway.*

B Modal verbs and expressions ◄ See Units 9, 13–16.

British English	North American English
People say *I have to* and *I've got to*. *I've got to / have to tell you something.*	*I have to* is more common that *have got to*. *I have to work at six tonight.*
Shall is more common. People use *shall* in suggestions *Shall we start, then?* or to talk about the future. *I shall need to know your decision soon.*	*Shall* is less common People use *shall* mostly in questions like these: *My boss is a little – how shall I say it / how shall we say – unpredictable?* *Shall I just wait for you to call me?*
Must is more common. People use *must* mostly for speculation but also for necessity. *We must never do this again.*	*Must* is less common People use *must* mostly for speculation and very rarely for necessity. *It must be difficult to keep costs down.*
People say *don't need to* or *needn't*. *You don't need to / needn't come early tomorrow.*	People say *don't need to* not *needn't*. *You don't need to come early tomorrow.*
May I …? is less common. People say *Can I …?* more. *Can I help you?*	*May I …?* is more common. *May I help you?*

C Tags ◄ See Unit 22.

British English	North American English
Question tags are more common, especially tags to confirm information. *You're a designer, **aren't you?***	The tag *right?* and the very informal tag *huh?* are more common than in Europe. *You worked in sales, **right?*** *He's a great guy to work with, **huh?***

D Nouns ◄ See Unit 33.

British English	North American English
Accommodation is uncountable. **Accommodation has** to be booked by May.	*Accommodation* is countable. *We get two nights' hotel **accommodations**.*
People use a singular or plural verb after some nouns such as *board, company, government, team.* *The board **is/are** meeting now.* ◄ See Unit 33.	People mostly use a singular verb after these nouns. A plural verb is not used in writing. *The company is relocating.* (**not** ~~are relocating~~)

E Prepositions ◄ See Unit 28.

British English	North American English
People say *for* after the present perfect to talk about duration. *I **haven't been** to Paris **for** a long time.*	People also say *in* after the present perfect negative to talk about duration. *I **haven't been** to Paris **in** a long time.*
People say: *The office is open Monday **to** Friday.* *It's (a) quarter **past** five.* *The office is **in** Argyle Street.*	People say: *The office is open Monday **through** Friday.* *It's (a) quarter **after** five.* *The office is **on** West 20th Street.*
People say: **at** the weekend / weekends different **from** / **to**	People say: **on** the weekend / weekends different **from** / **than**

F Adjectives and adverbs ◄ See Units 29, 30.

British English	North American English
People say: *It was **really** good/nice etc.*	People also say: *It was **real** good/nice etc.*
Likely is an adjective. *Inflation **is likely** to rise next year.*	*Likely* is also an adverb. *Inflation **will likely** rise next year.*

G Speaking strategies ◄ See Speaking strategies 3 (Emphasising and softening).

British English	North American English
Sort of is more common than *kind of* as a softener. *Jeremy is **sort of** the decision maker there.*	*Kind of* is more common than *sort of* as a softener. *I **kind of** agree with that.*
I think and *I suppose* are more common than *I guess*. ***I suppose** if you've got a ten-year contract, you're OK.*	*I guess* is more common than *I think* and *I suppose*. ***I guess** it's taken a long time to get this design right.*
People often show interest or that they are listening by saying *Do you? Did you?* etc. A: *I work in media relations.* B: ***Do you?** That's interesting.*	People also say *You do? You did?* etc., especially in informal conversations. A: *I worked all weekend.* B: ***You did?***

H Spelling

British English	North American English
-ise is more common with verbs like *advertise, organise, specialise.* *-yse* is used for some verbs, e.g. *analyse.*	Many verbs end in *-ize* (e.g. *organize, realize, specialize*) but *advertise, advise, promise, surprise.* *-yze* is used for some verbs, e.g. *analyze.*
The spelling of these nouns and verbs is different: noun: *practice, licence* verb: *practise, license* *Delaying payments is common **practice**.* *I need to **practise** my English more often.*	The spelling of these nouns and verbs is the same: noun and verb: *practice, license* *I don't have my driver's **license**.* *I'm **licensed** to **practice** law in Texas.*
Participles of verbs ending in *-l* have *-ll*: *cancel – cancelled, cancelling* *travel – travelled, travelling*	Most verbs have only one *-l*: *canceled, canceling* *traveled, traveling* Verbs stressed on the final syllable have *-ll*: *control – controlled, controlling* *instal – installed, installing*
The past tense and past participles of some verbs have two spellings. *dream – dreamed* or *dreamt* *learn – learnt* or *learned*	The past participles of these verbs have only one spelling (*-ed*). *dreamed* *learned*
These words end in *-our*: *colour, humour, neighbour*	These words end in *-or*: *color, humor, neighbor*
These words end in *-ogue*: *analogue, catalogue, dialogue*	These words end in *-og*: *analog, catalog, dialog*
These words end in *-re*: *centre, kilometre, theatre*	These words end in *-er*: *center, kilometer, theater*

I Dates

British English	North American English
Dates are written as day/month/year. *11/04/2010 = 11th of April*	Dates are written as month/day/year. *11/04/2010 = November 4th*

Appendix 4 Formal and informal English

A What do formal and informal English mean?

People change the way they speak or write depending on the situation they are in and the person they are communicating with.
Their English will be more formal or more informal.

⚠ There are not two different types of English called 'formal' and 'informal' but there are different levels or degrees of formality.

Written and spoken English can both be either formal or informal. Here are examples of very formal and very informal contexts of written and spoken English:

	formal	informal
spoken	Speech Presentation at a conference Board meeting	Lunchtime conversation with colleague Quick chat at the coffee machine
written	Contract letter Minutes of a meeting Annual report	Email to a colleague to arrange lunch Note to a colleague with a phone message

⚠ Most of the grammar in this book is 'neutral'. You can use it in almost all situations. There are notes to tell you if something is very informal or very formal.

There are no strict rules about when to use more formal or more informal English, but here are some general guidelines.

- Your English should be more formal when you are talking or writing to someone you do not know and in many work situations.
- In some organisations, you may need to communicate more formally with senior colleagues but you can be more informal with people at your level.
- Your English can be more informal when you are talking or writing to someone you know well and in social situations.
- You can communicate with the same person in both informal and more formal English depending on the situation. For example, you may speak to your boss formally in meetings at work but more informally at lunch. You might write a formal letter to a customer or supplier with a contract, but also write a more informal email to arrange to meet for dinner.

⚠ Informal English is not bad English. It can be just as polite as more formal English. Using it in the right situations can make you sound more friendly, fluent and natural.

B What types of grammar and vocabulary do people use in formal and informal situations?

B1 Contractions and full forms of verbs (◀ see Units 1–20) (*I'm / I am*; *don't / do not*; *haven't / have not*, etc.)
- You can use contractions in all speaking situations and in many types of writing (e.g. emails).
- People use full forms mostly in very formal letters, reports, contracts and some formal speaking situations such as speeches and presentations. But it is difficult to speak using only full forms and you could sound slightly strange.

	more formal	more informal
Contractions *I'm, don't, hasn't,* etc.	Fine to use *I'm, don't, hasn't,* etc. in speaking.	Fine to use *I'm, don't, hasn't,* etc. in speaking.
Full forms *I am, do not, has not,* etc.	Use mainly in writing, (e.g. letters, contracts, reports).	Do not use full forms too much in either speaking or writing.

B2 Verbs and tenses

- In formal written letters the simple forms of verbs often sound more formal than continuous forms.
- The passive is more common in formal written English than in spoken or informal English. ◄ See Unit 19 (The passive 1) and Unit 20 (The passive 2).
- Some modal verbs sound more formal , for example, in suggestions, requests and instructions. ◄ See Unit 14 (Modals 2) and Unit 15 (Modals 3).
- People often use the past tense in polite requests and questions. ◄ See Unit 5 (Past simple and continuous).

	more formal	more informal
simple or continuous	I **look** forward to meeting you. We **hope** to complete the project by May.	I'm **looking** forward to meeting you. We **are hoping** to complete the project by May.
passive	The contract **was signed**.	They **signed** the contract.
modal verbs	**Shall** we meet at 10? **Would/Could** you look at the figures? **May** I come in?	**How about** meeting at 10? **Will/Can** you look at the figures? **Can** I come in?
past tense	**Did** you **want** to talk to me now?	**Do** you **want** to talk to me now?

B3 Reported speech

- *Like* is very informal when it is used for reporting speech.
- The past continuous is not used in formal writing to report speech. ◄ See Unit 23 (Reported speech 1).

	more formal	more informal
like	He **said**, 'That's impossible!'	He's **like**, 'That's impossible!'
past continuous	The CFO **explained** the new tax rules.	The CFO **was telling** us about the new tax rules.

B4 'Simple grammar'

- People often use shorter, simpler grammar in informal communication. ◄ See Speaking strategies 4 (Simple spoken grammar).
- There are a number of very common structures in spoken English that some people think are incorrect or mistakes. They should not be used in writing. For example, *there is/was* + a plural noun, *less* + plural noun, *who* instead of *whom* ◄ See Unit 38 (Relative clauses 2).

	more formal	more informal
Simple grammar	**Are you leaving** now? **Do you want** a coffee?	**You leaving** now? **Want** a coffee?
Grammar 'mistakes'	We had **fewer requests** for samples this month. **There were a lot of people** at the shareholders' meeting.	We had **less requests** for samples this month. **There was a lot of people** at the shareholders' meeting.

Other

- Some phrasal verbs can be more informal, for example, *give up* (*stop*), *get out of* (*avoid*).
- People think of some uses of *get* as informal. *Have* is more formal than *have got*.
- *Stuff* is a very informal word; *things* sounds better in formal situations. ◄ See Speaking strategies 9 (Vague language 1).
- Some determiners and expressions such as *loads* (*of*) and *a bit* (*of*) are informal. ◄ See Speaking strategies 10 (Vague language 2) and Unit 31 (Comparisons 1) and Unit 35 (Quantifiers).
- People use *most* + adjective instead of *very* or *really* in formal situations.
- People use more nouns in very formal and especially written English, where they would use verbs in more informal and spoken English.
- Conjunctions such as *therefore*, *as a result*, and *consequently* and *in order to* are more common in formal business language, especially writing. ◄ See Unit 40 (Conjunctions and linking words 2).

	more formal	more informal
phrasal verbs	They won't **tolerate** another delay.	They won't **put up with** another delay.
get	I **received** your letter today. We **purchased/bought** our cars in Belgium. We **have** several problems.	I **got** your letter today. We **got** our cars in Belgium. We'**ve got** several problems.
thing/stuff	Are these your **things** here?	Is this your **stuff** here?
quantifiers	There are **a number of** MBAs on our staff.	There are **loads of** MBAs on our staff.
most	I would be **most** grateful for your advice.	I'd be **very/really** grateful for your advice.
nouns and verbs	What are your **recommendations**? **Completion** of the building work will be on time.	What do you **recommend**? We'll **finish** the building work on time.
conjunctions	Jen's performance has been excellent. **Therefore / As a result / Consequently** we recommend her promotion to senior analyst.	Jen's done a great job this year **so** I think we should promote her to senior analyst.
in order to / to…	Staff were laid off **in order to** make savings.	Staff were laid off **to** save money.

Appendix 5 Irregular verbs

These are the most frequent verbs with irregular forms which appear in the top 3,000 words in spoken business English.

Infinitive	Past simple	Past participle
be	was/were	been
beat	beat	beaten
become	became	become
begin	began	begun
blow	blew	blown
break	broke	broken
bring	brought	brought
broadcast	broadcast	broadcast
build	built	built
buy	bought	bought
catch	caught	caught
choose	chose	chosen
come	came	come
cost	cost	cost
cut	cut	cut
deal	dealt	dealt
do	did	done
draw	drew	drawn
drive	drove	driven
eat	ate	eaten
fall	fell	fallen
feed	fed	fed
feel	felt	felt
fly	flew	flown
find	found	found
forget	forgot	forgotten
get	got	got
give	gave	given
go	went	gone
grow	grew	grown
have	had	had
hear	heard	heard
hit	hit	hit
hold	held	held
keep	kept	kept
know	knew	known
lead	led	led
leave	left	left
lend	lent	lent

Infinitive	Past simple	Past participle
let	let	let
lose	lost	lost
make	made	made
mean	meant	meant
meet	met	met
pay	paid	paid
put	put	put
read	read	read
ring	rang	rung
rise	rose	risen
run	ran	run
say	said	said
see	saw	seen
sell	sold	sold
send	sent	sent
set	set	set
shake	shook	shaken
show	showed	shown/showed
shut	shut	shut
sit	sat	sat
speak	spoke	spoken
spend	spent	spent
split	split	split
stand	stood	stood
stick	stuck	stuck
take	took	taken
tell	told	told
think	thought	thought
throw	threw	thrown
understand	understood	understood
wear	wore	worn
win	won	won
write	wrote	written

Appendix 6 Verb patterns

A Verbs followed by *-ing*

A1 These verbs are followed by *-ing*.

admit	dread	justify
avoid	enjoy	love
can't help	fancy	like (enjoy)
consider	feel like	mention
delay	finish	mind
deny	hate	miss
detest	imagine	postpone
dislike	involve	risk

I **avoid / enjoy / can't help / don't mind working** late.

A2 Verbs with prepositions and most phrasal verbs are followed by *-ing*.

base on	get around to	look into
carry on	get into	put off
come up with	get on with	put up with
decide on	go on (continue)	rely on
depend on	give up	talk about
do away with	keep on	think about
end up	insist on	work on
forget about	look forward to	worry about

If we **carry on / get around to / get on with / insist on updating** the database, the information flow will be much better.

B Verbs followed by *to*-infinitive

These verbs are followed by *to*-infinitive.

afford	deserve	plan
agree	expect	prepare
appear	fail	pretend
aim	guarantee	promise
arrange	help (also with infinitive without *to*)	propose
ask	hesitate	refuse
attempt	hope	seem
choose	intend	tend
claim	learn	threaten
dare (affirmative only)	long	train
decide	manage	want
decline	neglect	wish
demand	offer	would like/love/hate/prefer

Can we **afford / promise / threaten to take** legal action?

C Verbs followed by *-ing* or *to*-infinitive

C1 These verbs can be followed by *-ing* or the *to*-infinitive with no change in meaning.

begin	hate
bother	intend
can't bear	like
can't stand	love
continue	prefer

Don't **bother to write / writing**. Just call me.

C2 These verbs can be followed by *-ing* or the *to*-infinitive with a change in meaning.

forget	*remember*
go on	*stop*
mean	*try*
need	*want*
regret	

I **remember meeting** you last year.   **Remember to call** me when you arrive.

D Verb + infinitive without *to*

These verbs are followed by the infinitive without *to*.
modal verbs (*can, could, may, might, must, ought to, should*)
help (also with *to*-infinitive)
had better
would rather

Can you **help sort out** *this problem? We*'**d better look** *at it together.*

E Verb + object + *to*-infinitive

These verbs are followed by an object and the *to*-infinitive.

advise	*forbid*	*recommend*
allow	*force*	*remind*
ask	*get* (persuade)	*request*
challenge	*help*	*teach*
command	*instruct*	*tell*
direct	*invite*	*urge*
enable	*mean* (intend)	*want*
encourage	*order*	*warn*
expect	*persuade*	*would like/love/prefer/hate*

My boss **encouraged/forced/invited/wanted me to go** *to the conference.*

F Verb + object + infinitive without *to*

These verbs are followed by an object and the infinitive without *to*.
help
let
make (= to tell or to force; use in active not passive form)
sense verbs (*feel, hear, notice, see, watch*)

We **help/make/let our staff find** *their own solutions to problems.*

G Difficult verbs: *suggest, recommend*

G1 *suggest*

I **suggest(ed) taking** *the M6 motorway.*
I **suggest (that) you take** *the M6 motorway.*

The most common way of using *suggest* in speaking is *what I (would) suggest is that …*
What I (would) suggest is that *we go to an advertising agency.*

G2 *recommend*

I don't **recommend you do** *that.*
We were **recommended to accept** *the most expensive proposal.*

The most common way of using *recommend* in speaking is *recommend* + noun/pronoun.
I don't **recommend that. / this system. / those computers.**

Appendix 7 Prepositions

A Prepositions of place or movement

Prepositions of place

above (in a higher position than something or someone else)
*Jessica works in the office **above** the accounts department. /*
*There are two people **above** me in my department – my manager and her boss.*

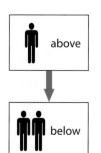

at (an exact location or particular place)
*I'm going to be **at** home / **at** a conference tomorrow.*

behind (at the back of)
*Paul's standing **behind** that tall man.*

below (in a lower position)
*HR are on the floor **below** the finance team. / The two staff **below** me deal directly with our corporate clients.*

between (in the space that separates two people, places or objects)
*Our city branch is **between** the supermarket and the post office.*

by (near, at the side of)
*I sit **by** the window.*

from (the place where something starts)
*You can drive **from** the airport to the city centre in 20 minutes.*

in (inside a container, place or area)
*Oh no! I left my wallet **in** New York / **in** the office / **in** the drawer.*

in front of

in front of (close to the front part of something)
*There's a visitor's car park **in front of** the factory.*

opposite

opposite (in a position on the other side; facing)
*Her office is **opposite** ours, on the other side of the road.*

near (not far away)
*Their HQ is **near** London – only 20km away.*

next to (two things that are close, with nothing between them)
*You left your glasses **next to** the book you were reading.*

over

on (in a position above something else, touching it)
*Can you hear me? I'm **on** the train. / The meeting room is near reception, **on** the right.*

over (above or higher than something else)
*The light **over** my desk isn't working.*

under (in a position lower or below something else)
*I keep a spare pair of shoes **under** my desk. / The restaurant is **under** new management.*

Prepositions of movement

across

across (from one side to the other, with clear limits, such as a road)
*The cycle courier can get **across** the city more quickly than a car.*

along (from one part to another)
*Walk **along** Station Road for about five minutes. We're on the left, by the gym.*

around/round (in a direction going along the edge of or from one part to another)
*We drove **around** the town for ages, but we still couldn't find your office.*

down (to a lower position from a higher one)

*If there's a fire, walk **down** the stairs to your nearest exit.*

into (towards an enclosed space, and about to be enclosed by it)

*I walked **into** the meeting room where everyone was waiting for me.*

out of (no longer in a certain position)

*Could you pass me the red folder? I need to take some documents **out of** it.*

over (like *across* – from one side to another)

*At rush hour the smog spreads **over** the city.*

past (to a position that is further than a particular point)

*Go **past** the industrial estate and turn left.*

through (from one end or side of something, to the other)

*The new tram goes **through** the city centre.*

to (in the direction of)

*I usually walk **to** work. / The FTSE fell **to** its lowest point for three months on Tuesday.*

towards (in the direction of someone or something; moving closer)

*The board is working **towards** an agreement with the unions.*

up (to a higher position)

*You have to drive **up** a steep hill to get there.*

B Prepositions of time

at

after (something else has happened)

*Hans arrived 10 minutes **after** lunch.*

at (use with clock times or particular time)

*We can meet **at** 10:00 or **at** lunchtime.*

before (at or during a time earlier)

*Don't phone **before** 11:00. I won't be at my desk.*

between (in the period of time that separates two different times or events)

*Next week, I'll only be in the office **between** Monday and Wednesday.*

by (not later than)

*Please complete the report **by** Friday.*

during (from the beginning to the end of a particular period)

*I'm sorry, I couldn't take your call **during** the meeting.*

for (an amount of time)

*I've worked here **for** 12 years.*

in (during part or all of a period of time)

*I'll see you **in** the morning / **in** May / **in** ten days.*

on (use with days of the week or dates)

*Will you be at the meeting **on** Monday / **on** 4th June?*

over (while doing something)

*The conference will take place **over** two days.*

since (from a particular time in the past until a later time, or until now)

*The company has been in business **since** 1935.*

until/till (up to the time that)

*We'll continue the research **until/till** next year.*

C Verbs and prepositions

C1 These are some of the most common verb and preposition combinations in business English.

afford to	*depend on*	*refer to*
apply for	*focus on*	*result from/in*
agree with*/to**/on**	*forget about*	*speak to*
ask about	*hear about**/from**	*specialise in*
belong to	*invest in*	*talk about*/to***
compare with	*know about*	*think about*
compete with/against	*lead to*	*wait for*
complain about**/to*	*learn about*	*worry about*
comply with	*listen to*	*work as*
consist of	*look for*	*work with*/for**
cooperate with	*pay for*	*work on ***
decide on	*qualify for*	*write to*/about***

* = someone ** = something

*We can't **afford to** buy this machine.*
*This report **consists of** 50 pages and an appendix.*

C2 *By* is most commonly used in passive structures.

*US stocks are setting record highs, **boosted by** very low interest rates.*
*The supermarket chain **is owned by** Tengelmann Group of Germany.*

C3 Common business-related verbs that don't take a preposition include *lack, (tele)phone, meet, discuss, emphasise* and *stress.*

*I think the first candidate **lacks** any ambition* (**not** ~~lacks of~~)
*Lets **discuss** this at our next meeting* (**not** ~~discuss about~~)

D Adjectives and prepositions

These are some of the most common adjective and preposition combinations in business English. Common negative prefixes are included in brackets.

careful about/with	*bad at*	*dependent on*
(un)clear about	*good for*	*responsible for*
concerned about	*bad for*	*responsible to*
excited about	*different from/to*	*answerable to*
(un)happy about	*(too) late for*	*similar to*
optimistic about	*famous for*	*used to*
pessimistic about	*(un)suitable for*	*concerned with*
serious about	*interested in*	*(in)compatible with*
worried about	*involved in*	*(in)consistent with*
good at	*rich in*	*(un)popular with*

*Honda is **famous for** its engine technology.*
*I'm **answerable to** my line manager, the marketing director.*

E Nouns and prepositions

These are some of the most common noun and preposition combinations in business English.

ability in
advice on
agreement with*/on**
alternative to
answer to
application for
benefit from**/of**
complaint about
concern about
competition with
cooperation with
cost of
dependence on
excitement about

experience in**/of**
help from*/with**
interest in
involvement in
knowledge about
lack of
means of
method of
optimism about
payment for
pessimism about
popularity with*/of**
price of
qualification for

reason for
reference to
reply to
responsibility for
result of
similarity to
solution to
success at
suitability for
tax on
trouble with
worry about

* = someone ** = something

*We have received a **complaint about** our service.*
*Have you got much **experience in** marketing?*

F Prepositional phrases

These are some of the most common prepositional expressions used in business English.

at a good/low/high price
at cost price
at a profit/loss
at short notice
at risk
at this stage/point
at your convenience
by mail/post/phone
by car/train/truck
by law
by mistake
for breakfast/lunch etc.
for a while
for/on sale

for years/ages
in advance
in cash
in charge (of)
in conversation
in credit/debt
in favour (of)
in general/particular
in a hurry
in person
in stock
in terms of
in touch with
in writing

on business
on the Internet (website)
on the market
on loan
on order
on the phone
out of order
out of stock
out of date
out of business
under discussion
up to date
with reference (to)

*Can you pay **in cash**?*
*I'm afraid the coffee machine is **out of order**.*

Appendix 8 Saying numbers, weights and measures

A Saying numbers

A1 Large numbers

Written*	Spoken
1,000,000,000	a billion
1,000,000	a million
100,000	a hundred thousand
10,000	ten thousand
1,000	a thousand
100	a hundred (**one** hundred sounds more formal than **a** hundred)

* Write numbers of 1,000 + with a comma (,) in front of every thousand.

When you say large numbers follow this pattern:
2,348,678, 987 = two **billion**, three **hundred** and forty-eight **million**, six **hundred** and seventy-eight **thousand**, nine **hundred** and eighty-seven.
In American English, *and* is not used after the hundred (987 = *nine hundred eighty seven*).

⚠ Do not make exact numbers plural: *ten million dollars* (**not** ~~ten millions dollars~~). You can use plurals when you are talking in a general way: *Millions of people bought this product.*

A2 The number 0

You can say 0 in three ways: *zero, oh* or *nought*.
In British English, people use *oh* in telephone numbers, reference or account numbers, and hotel room numbers.
*My phone number? It's **oh** two **oh** seven six one **oh** eight five.* (0207 61085)
*I'm in room nine **oh** three.* (903)

In British English, people use *nought* if it is the only number before a decimal (and *oh* after the point).
***Nought** point **oh** four* (0.04)

You can say *zero* in any situation.
*Call me on **zero** three **zero** one two eight **zero** one four.* (0301 28014)
*Room two **zero** one, please.* (201)
***Zero** point **zero** two* (0.02)

A3 Decimal numbers and money

In British English, people say each individual number after a decimal point. In American English, people use whole numbers.
2.754 = *two **point** seven five four* (UK); *two **point** seven hundred fifty four* (US)
You can say whole numbers after the point in British English when you are talking about money.
£6.45 = *six pounds **forty five*** or *six pounds **forty five** pence* (**not** ~~six pounds four five~~)

A4 Telephone numbers

People often say telephone numbers individually with a pause after two or three numbers to make it easier for people to understand.
703 2178 = *seven oh three, two one, seven eight*
(**not** ~~seven hundred and three, twenty one, seventy eight~~)
When two numbers are the same you can use *double;* when three numbers are the same you can use *triple* or *treble.*
566 21555 = *five double six, two one, treble/triple five*

A5 Dates

Written*	Spoken
1st May / May 1st / 1 May / May 1 2nd / 3rd / 4th May 1998 2010	*the first of May / May the first* (but *May first* in the US) *the second/third/fourth of May / May the second/third/fourth* *nineteen ninety eight* *two thousand and ten / twenty ten*

In British English people usually write day/month/year. Americans usually write the month first.

5/12/63 5/12/63	*the fifth of December nineteen sixty three* (UK) *May twelfth nineteen sixty three* (US)

A6 Other numbers

Written*	Spoken
25%	*twenty five per cent*
¼	*a quarter*
1¼	*one and a quarter*
½	*a half*
¾	*three-quarters*
2¾	*two and three-quarters*
25°	*twenty-five degrees*

A6 Pronunciation: *thirty* or *thirteen*?

When a number ends in *-ty*, you can stress the first part of the number to make it clearer to a listener.
When it ends in *-teen*, you can stress the end of the word to make it clearer.

thir*ty   thir*teen*   *for*ty   four*teen*   *fif*ty   fif*teen

B Saying weights and volumes

In the UK, people usually use the metric system for weights and measures in business, but many people still use imperial measurements in speaking. These are some commonly used expressions.

UK Imperial / US weights	Metric
1 oz / one ounce	28 grammes
1 lb / one pound (16 oz)	0.45 kg/kilogrammes
1 ton (UK)	1016 kg
1 ton (US)	907 kg

*This laptop weighs **three pounds six ounces**.*
*A Boeing 747 can lift about **a hundred tons**.*

UK Imperial / US volume	Metric
1 pint (US)	0.47 litres
1 pint (UK)	0.57 litres
1 gallon / 8 pints (US)	3.79 litres
1 gallon / 8 pints (UK)	4.55 litres

*Can I have **a pint** of milk?*
*I'd like **ten gallons** of petrol (UK) / gas (US).*

C Saying distances and areas

All road distances in the UK and the US are in miles.

UK/US	Metric
1 inch	25.4 mm (millimetres)
12 inches = 1 foot	30.48 cm (centimetres)
3 feet = 1 yard	0.914 m (metres)
1,760 yards = 1 mile	1.6 km (kilometres)

He's **six feet two** (**inches**) tall.
It's eight **yards** long.
It's a hundred **miles** to London.

1 sq (square) foot	929 cm^2 (square centimetres)
9 sq feet = 1 sq yard	0.84 m^2
4840 sq yards = 1 acre	0.4 hectare
640 acres = 1 sq mile	259 hectares

This office is about forty **square yards** in size.
I have eight hundred **acres** of farmland.
The factory site covers two **square miles**.

CD tracklist

Recording	Track	Recording	Track
1.1	2	25.1	40
2.1	3	26.1	41
3.1	4	27.1	42
4.1	5	28.1	43
SS 1.1	6	SS 7.1	44
SS 1.2	7	SS 7.2	45
5.1	8	29.1	46
6.1	9	30.1	47
7.1	10	31.1	48
8.1	11	31.2	49
SS 2.1	12	31.3	50
		32.1	51
9.1	13	SS 8.1	52
10.1	14	SS 8.2	53
11.1	15		
12.1	16	33.1	54
SS 3.1	17	34.1	55
SS 3.2	18	35.1	56
		35.2	57
13.1	19	36.1	58
14.1	20	SS 9.1	59
15.1	21		
16.1	22	37.1	60
SS 4.1	23	38.1	61
		39.1	62
17.1	24	40.1	63
18.1	25	SS 10.1	64
19.1	26	SS 10.2	65
20.1	27		
SS 5.1	28		
21.1	29		
22.1	30		
22.2	31		
22.3	32		
22.4	33		
23.1	34		
24.1	35		
SS 6.1	36		
SS 6.2	37		
SS 6.3	38		
SS 6.4	39		